The Vancouver Achievement

John Punter

The Vancouver Achievement:
Urban Planning and Design

UBCPress · Vancouver · Toronto

09 08 07 06 05 04 03   5 4 3 2 1

Printed in Canada on acid-free paper ∞

National Library of Canada Cataloguing in Publication Data

Punter, John Vincent, 1945-
   The Vancouver achievement : urban planning and design / John Punter.

   Includes bibliographical references and index.
   ISBN 0-7748-0971-X (bound); ISBN 0-7748-0972-8 (pbk.)

   1. City planning–British Columbia–Vancouver–History. I. Title.
HT169.C32V35 2003   307.1'216'0971133   C2003-910695-0

Canadä

UBC Press gratefully acknowledges the financial support for our publishing
program of the Government of Canada through the Book Publishing Industry
Development Program (BPIDP), and of the Canada Council for the Arts, and
the British Columbia Arts Council.

This book has been published with the help of a grant from the Canadian
Federation for the Humanities and Social Sciences, using funds provided by
the Social Sciences and Humanities Research Council of Canada.

UBC Press
The University of British Columbia
2029 West Mall
Vancouver, BC V6T 1Z2
604-822-5959 / Fax: 604-822-6083
www.ubcpress.ca

*This book is dedicated to the
planners and urban designers of Vancouver –
past, present, and future.*

Contents

Appendices:

Acknowledgments

It was never my intention to write a book on Vancouver. It remains an over-ambitious project for someone who lives on the other side of the world and who has a range of ongoing research commitments in the United Kingdom. The idea of researching Vancouver's design achievements was suggested to me in 1994 by Seattle's city planning commissioner, Marty Curry. At the time I was beginning a study of design policy and review practices in five west coast cities of the United States. Looking for best practice to inform my critiques of the British system and commencing my researches in Seattle, I was somewhat taken aback when Marty suggested that Vancouver was the real North American exemplar. At the time I felt I had missed a valuable research opportunity. My research on US west coast cities provided an overview of a number of best practice design guidelines and review practices (Punter 1999a). But there was not time to evaluate how these mechanisms were working in practice, nor what was being achieved on the ground. To do that would require a much more detailed study in a particular locality. In 1996, on a visit to Vancouver after a conference in Toronto sponsored by the American Colleges and Schools of Planning/Association of European Schools of Planning, I interviewed one of the co-directors of Vancouver's planning department. In ninety minutes Larry Beasley provided such a rich and positive description of the city's design and planning initiatives that I was hooked. I resolved that, when the US work was complete, I would look closely at what was happening in Vancouver.

In 1998 the Canadian High Commission funded a research proposal to compare urban design initiatives and practices in Toronto and Vancouver. At the time I thought I would be able to handle a "compare and contrast" study of practices of the last three decades, particularly since I had studied and taught in Toronto between 1967 and 1975 and continued to visit at regular intervals. I used the first of two grants from the Canadian High Commission to collect documents and undertake interviews in both cities, spending most of September 1998 in Vancouver and late November in Toronto. In both cities it was the same story. An extremely rich vein of city planning documents had received very little academic comment or synthesis of contemporary planning practice at large, and virtually no analysis of the design dimension. I was faced with the daunting prospect of having to abstract the last three decades of the design dimension of planning – my principal intention – as well as reconstruct the planning and development context, including an outline of the political economy of the city, without which the interpretation of design outcomes would be one-dimensional and hugely flawed. During 1999 I synthesized the data I had collected into separate accounts, first of Toronto and then of Vancouver. Armed with a second travel grant from the Canadian High Commission early in 2000, I began to focus solely on Vancouver with the intention of completing that study before returning to the Toronto research. In June 2000 I spent a further three weeks in Vancouver, adding another fourteen interviews to the twenty-two I had conducted in 1998 and completing my document collection. I spent the rest of 2000 and the early months of 2001 completing a final draft of the study, returning to Vancouver in midsummer to conduct a further dozen interviews and to tie up numerous loose ends.

The Vancouver research has been aided by three important factors. First, Vancouverites involved in design development and planning have been generous with their time and interest to talk about their practice within the city. Picking their brains, some of them on several occasions, has been a truly rewarding experience. It has been helped by the fact that so many of the informants have spent their working lives in the city, and thus are deep repositories of urban history and design, development, or planning experience. Second, the planning department has a library that provides a remarkably complete and well-organized archive of planning publications that stretches back into the 1960s. It also has its own newspaper clippings service organized by subject. The library's resources are backed by an up-to-date listing of all recent and extant planning documents that can be purchased – although most were given to me. These marvellous research resources are eloquent statements of the planning department's long-standing professionalism, and are legacies of planning innovations made in the early 1970s. Third, a contemporary illustration of Vancouver's continuing commitment to an open, accessible government and a highly professional planning service, the municipality's website provides very full documentation of current planning initiatives. From the perspective of this study, the website provides full minutes of all Development Permit Board and Urban Design Panel meetings since January 1997, and e-mail accessibility to all city officials, whose responsibilities and expertise are clearly defined. Collectively these resources have made this study possible from 8,000 kilometres away.

For the research that underpins this study, I have placed heaviest reliance on an exhaustive trawl through city planning documents, a much-neglected information source for planning research. Inevitably these documents present a planner's viewpoint and they have to be read in this light. Because they are required to rehearse the relevant arguments and to record the public consultations and council's views, these documents do on many occasions contain opposing views and criticisms of current policy initiatives. Three sets of documents have been subjected to particular scrutiny. The Annual Reviews of the planning department that were produced during Ray Spaxman's tenure as director from 1973 to 1989, and the monitoring reviews that accompanied them in the later 1980s are very useful records of internal views, pressures on resources, and tensions with other agencies and with council. The planning department's *Quarterly Review* is similarly useful because it contains a series of articles largely reflecting background research from policy making and implementation during the 1980s. These documents are heavily used to support Chapters 2 to 4. The third set of documents is minutes of the Development Permit Board and the Urban Design Panel, which provided the basis for the analysis in Chapter 9 and some of the detail for Chapters 4, 6, and 7. In some dozen instances, these have been supplemented by committee reports, which provide a complete record of application processes.

Finally, I conducted interviews with forty-three people, many more than once. To establish their perspective on events, I included past and present planning staff (23), architects (6), developers (4), current and former councillors (8), academics (2), and a design consultant. Most of these interviews were for information gathering and, while I asked some vital questions going to the heart of the issues in this book, only now would I be able to frame a truly penetrating set of questions. My ability to cross-examine my respondents and dig deeper was not as great as I would have wished, but I hope this book will encourage others to pursue this task with greater rigour.

On the subject of research resources, while I have criticized the lack of useful syntheses or even analyses of the city's planning practices, I wish to acknowledge the value of three bodies of work. The first is that of the human geographer David Ley, at the University of British Columbia, and generations of his graduate students. Ley has made Vancouver's social and physical landscape his major subject of inquiry, linking contemporary social, economic, political, and cultural theory that most urban designers ignore at their peril. The second is the 1993 architectural guidebook, *Exploring Vancouver: The*

Essential Architectural Guide, by Vancouver's architectural historians, Harold Kalman, Ron Phillips, and Robin Ward, and the regular columns by Robin Ward on architecture and heritage in the *Vancouver Sun*. The latter offers a consistently critical view on all planning and architecture matters, especially heritage, and the expert insider's perspective on the processes that have produced designs. The third valuable body of material is that of the political scientist Donald Gutstein, including his early work on the Vancouver development industry and his later works on Vancouver city politics. I have drawn heavily on all three bodies of work throughout this book.

An intention of this study is to evaluate the buildings, streets, parks and plazas, neighbourhoods, and natural areas that Vancouver's planning and design review processes have delivered. Reliance is placed on a range of local views derived from press commentaries; community consultation exercises; the published works of architectural critics, design commentators, geographers, and travel writers; and the recorded peer review of design professionals and lay advisors of projected schemes. In addition, the interviews sought the evaluations of many of the key local players – planners, architects, politicians, developers, conservationists, and other consultants. These evaluations can be reinforced in places by architectural and planning awards that are listed in Appendix 1 of this book. While the selection of evidence reflects my views as a close observer of Canadian, American, and European cities, the comparative evaluations in these researches have been used largely to illuminate plans, policies, and processes rather than as a systematic evaluation of design outcomes because of the difficulty (and time-consuming nature) of objective comparison.

I want to thank many people who have provided particular support to this project. Foremost among these is Larry Beasley, current co-director of city planning, who first whetted my appetite for the study, then offered local design and development contacts, subjected himself to several interviews, and meticulously reviewed the first draft of the study, pointing out numerous errors of fact and interpretation. Ann McAfee, the other co-director, also reviewed the draft with a similar eye for detail and numerous suggestions for improvement, as did an anonymous reviewer. Others who carefully read and commented on individual chapters include Ray Spaxman, Bob McGillvray, Rick Scobie, Randy Pecarski, and Ralph Segal. All staff in the Vancouver planning department were extremely receptive to my inquiries and helpful with the pursuit of documentation. I would particularly like to thank Vicky Biddle, the former planning librarian, for her help to find so much material for the 1970s and early 1980s, and Carol Hubbard who supplied numerous committee reports and minutes. The forty-three interviewees have my thanks for the assistance they provided and the interest they showed in my inquiries.

I hope all these respondents consider that this volume reflects their insights and repays some of their generosity.

At Cardiff University, Adri Stoffaneller has willingly typed interminable drafts of chapters over a three-year period. Her impeccable grammar and spelling have been indispensable. Isabel Sawyer also helped produce the final draft. Janice Edwards has redrawn some twenty figures for me and scanned all my slides. Dan Campbell in the graphics section of the Vancouver planning department has hunted out drawings and supplied me with quality originals. All of their efforts have been much appreciated.

I owe a particular debt to the Canadian High Commission in London for its financial support of study visits in 1998, 2000, and 2001. Strictly speaking, this work does not satisfy their publication requirements, which seek publications outside Canada, and I want to thank Vivien Hughes for her understanding of the particularities of this project.

At UBC Press, Randy Schmidt and Holly Keller-Brohman have proved to be very supportive editors, coaxing a shorter, more readable document from my original draft, while continuing to allow me so many illustrations. Susan Quirk played a major role in restructuring the book to make it less repetitive and more accessible to a lay audience. UBC Press has been clear, efficient, and particularly rigorous in all its editorial processes and this has been much welcomed. While I have spent many hours walking and photographing the streets of Vancouver, I have not developed the intimate familiarity with the city to which an urban design critic might aspire. Simultaneously poring over *Collier's* excellent property map and trawling through my extensive Vancouver slide collection has been some compensation, especially during wet Welsh winters that replicate, but regrettably extend, their Vancouver equivalent. I want to thank Richard and Sandra Peddie of New Westminster, soulmates for more than thirty years, for their hospitality, friendship, advice, and support while I was doing my fieldwork. They made it as easy to study in Vancouver as it would have been at home.

Introduction:
Urban Design as Public Policy
in North America

The researching of a city's design achievement is not an end in itself but a means toward a broader goal of seeking to improve the design dimension of planning generally. For a planner/urban designer interested in critically appraising the system in which he practises or researches there are few exercises as revealing and rewarding as an extended study of how a different system of planning and design regulation works. It is not simply the prospect of finding exemplary, innovative practices, or resolution of the persistent problems that beset all planning intervention, but rather the sharper more critical perspective with which the practitioner/researcher returns to interrogate his/her native system. Such research has special difficulties and pitfalls. The effort required to understand the full complexity of another planning system is prodigious, and then it is necessary to explore its outcomes and to come to grips with the particularities of local politics, development practices, public values, and urban traditions. Then there are the potential pitfalls of uncritical cross-comparative research, and the perils of failing to appreciate why particular policies and processes have emerged and how and why they have actually been successful.

Why Study Vancouver?

There are two particular reasons for studying Vancouver's contemporary planning and urban design practices. First it has an international reputation for achieving a generally high standard of design and for generally making the most of its superb natural setting. This reputation is founded upon a number of innovative practices, of which three are widely recognized. First, the Vancouver Urban Design Panel could be an exemplar for aesthetic advisory committees of the kind that are now being reformulated in the Netherlands and introduced in Belgium and Germany. Second, the citywide design strategy of CityPlan and its neighbourhood visioning has much to teach Britain and other countries about how urban intensification will have to be negotiated with local communities if it is to be successful. Third, Vancouver's megaproject planning process offers valuable lessons, for both the United Kingdom and the United States, on participatory master planning, building public/private development partnerships and community consensus, and developing more inclusive communities that can afford quality infrastructure. Numerous other facets of Vancouver's planning practices will be of interest to national and international audiences, from the development of neighbourhood design guidelines for single-family areas, to the ways of managing permitting methods to increase applicant support and decision-making efficiency; from how to execute view and skyline studies to how to bring engineering, planning, and urban design together to create a high-quality public realm. The technical ingenuity and imagination of much of this work is of particular interest, especially to someone whose national and local planning system is almost bereft of such innovation, and unable to grasp the nettle of such issues as design panels, development levies, or statutory master planning.

Second, Vancouver, more than any other city, bridges the gap between the two traditions of discretionary versus administrative planning systems, which is the essential divide between British and American/Continental European planning practice. Vancouver has a highly discretionary development control/permit processing system similar in some ways to that which operates in the United Kingdom. But that system is also based upon an elaborate zoning system that is characteristic of North American and European planning practice and their essentially administrative systems based on clear rules of decision making. Vancouver's system of discretionary zoning sounds like a contradiction in terms, but it can offer important insights into the practice of discretionary design review now common in North America, and clues as to how to make discretionary control more transparent, consistent, and equitable, as well as more design literate.

To more fully understand Vancouver's particular system and to assess its achievements, it is necessary to situate it in the context of North American urbanism and its evolution since 1960. In this Introduction a general account is provided of the emergence of urban design as public policy in American and Canadian cities. Four themes are given particular attention. The first is the shift from modernist to postmodernist planning and design principles, and the emergence of much more place- and history-sensitive urban design, albeit at the expense of modernism's more utopian and socially redistributive goals. The second is the shift away from direct public intervention to shape the urban landscape (urban renewal) toward public regulation of private development (design review) in a bid to achieve some of the same, and some different, community goals. Third is the development of a range of critiques of these regulatory practices and the emergence of substantive principles with which to both evaluate practices and to construct systems capable of developing better design outcomes. Finally there is a range of more socio-political critiques of planning and design practices that attempt to go behind the facades of the postmodern city to explore issues of social equity and the construction/destruction of community, and which question both the assumptions and outcomes of contemporary practice. Each of these perspectives can be usefully employed to frame a study of the design dimension of a particular North American city's planning practices.

So while the body of this book is concerned with Vancouver and its invention, construction, and implementation of a very sophisticated form of urban design as public policy, this Introduction situates the city within North American planning and urban design at large over the last four decades. Most importantly, it establishes an evaluative framework that can act as a structure for assessing Vancouver's practices and their outcomes, drawing on all the aforementioned themes, to develop a set of principles for progressive design review with which this study can be both launched and concluded.

Urban Design as Public Policy

So the Vancouver achievement can be situated within the context of design regulation and city planning at large, and the radical and rapid changes in the socioeconomic, physical, and cultural character that have taken place in urban areas in North America since the 1960s. Located close to the American border, arguably Vancouver has been more exposed to American practices than any other Canadian city, and it regularly exchanges ideas and experiences with the west coast American cities of Seattle, Portland, and San Francisco. The practice of "urban design as public policy" has been much debated in the United States but largely ignored in Canada. The phrase was coined by Jonathan Barnett in 1974 to describe his work in New York City in the late 1960s. For Barnett, it embraced new systems of design review, special district zoning and landmark protection, comprehensive design of the public realm, and participatory neighbourhood planning that built on the 1961 reform of New York's zoning ordinances. In that city and elsewhere, urban design as public policy grew out of the death throes of national urban renewal programs, and the shift in urban design practice away from large-scale public sector redevelopment projects. It was distinguished by a movement toward review processes and the safeguarding of the cities' interests in privately funded real estate development (Barnett 1974; 1982).

In San Francisco some of the last federal renewal funds allowed the city to retain leading planning and design consultants to undertake a series of as yet unsurpassed analyses of citywide design issues, and to develop the 1971

Urban Design Plan. This provided the basis for the rewriting of the city's zoning ordinances and codifying a set of design principles that could be readily absorbed into comprehensive plans and design guidelines (Punter 1999a: 106-11). Other cities developed sophisticated design guidelines and review practices, most notably Portland, Oregon, which created a proactive approach to urban design in its 1972 Downtown Plan, 1974 neighbourhood planning, and 1977 transportation and street planning (Abbott 2001). Twelve American cities had large-scale urban design plans by 1972 (Southworth and Southworth 1973) – by 1988, ten times that number were in existence (Southworth 1989). Over the 1960s, some one hundred design review boards had been established and, over the following two decades, 83 percent of US towns and cities had set up some form of design review (Scheer 1994: 1). In the United States, urban design as public policy had become more or less universal in its principal urban communities (Shirvani 1992; Habe 1989).

Public regulation of design was a recognition of the fact that the with-drawal of federal funding meant that cities could no longer directly reshape their form through publicly initiated downtown redevelopment, slum clearance, or highway schemes. Recasting a city's capital web of public infrastructure, as Boston had done in the 1960s, was also no longer an option because of budgetary constraints. Cities had to use such regulatory controls as zoning to achieve their public objectives (Lai 1988: 350-51).

From Modernist to Postmodernist Urban Design

The late 1960s and early 1970s saw a decisive break in the pattern of public and private investment in US cities that was intensified by the 1973 oil crisis and the subsequent economic recession that marked the end of the postwar economic boom. Use of federal urban renewal and highway funding had laid waste vast areas of inner cities and downtown cores, spreading "aggressive urban design and an impoverished version of modernist architecture" across the urban landscape and creating deeply unpopular "glass box derivations of Miesian exemplars, set in dreary Corbusian plans" (Larson 1993: 78-80). The citizen revolt against urban construction of freeways and expressways started at the end of the 1950s. Within the next few years, movements for neighbour-hood preservation and heritage or landmark conservation began, reinforced by damaging critiques of urban renewal (Gans 1962, 1968; Fried 1963). By 1967, urban renewal had dispossessed 400,000 households in US cities – the highways program alone displacing 330,000. The more ambitious the city's plans, the greater the social damage (Frieden and Sagalyn 1989: 29). The Watts, Los Angeles, riots of 1965 and subsequent insurrections, the accelerated flight of business out of northern cities to the American south and west, the Republicans' reversal of the Democrats' "great society" programs, and the withdrawal of federal funding from cities collectively deepened the urban crisis into the 1970s (Larson 1993: 80-82). Cities were turning into "a garrison state, ungovernable, out of control, unloved, unlivable, and frightening" (Frieden and Sagalyn 1989: 88).

Many cities went to the verge of bankruptcy in the property crash and oil crisis of 1973, deflationary economic policies, and drastic cuts in public expenditures by a neoconservative federal government. This forced municipalities to abandon many social programs and to concentrate on rebuilding their tax base by competing for commercial development and service jobs. A combination of "entrepreneurial cities and maverick developers" promoted major downtown redevelopment initiatives, frequently focused on reclaimed waterfronts with major "festival shopping" complexes or shopping malls (Frieden and Sagalyn 1989: 108-31). Generous federal depreciation allowances fed a massive office construction boom in the early 1980s and the development of new corporate centres. Hotels and convention centres pursued tourists, the attraction of which tended to justify the conservation and commodification of selected historic landmarks and districts. The privatization of public space became the norm, as developers created, furnished, and controlled the creation of urban amenities. James Rouse, the developer of Quincy Market in Boston and Harbor Place in Baltimore, spawned the "Rousification" of America, fusing historic conservation and Disneyland design and management, using public land and federal subsidies to create sites of spectacular consumption. Public/private partnerships and flagship projects were the first stage in attracting the surge of baby boomers and young urban professionals (yuppies) back to the city as a place of leisure and residence, in turn regenerating the historic and accessible neighbourhoods of the inner city, often through gentrification (Hall 1988: 347-51).

Often the vanguard of gentrification were artists, their pursuit of converting lofts for work and home providing the cue for developers and municipalities to promote gentrification (Zukin 1989; Smith 1996). Gentrification revived inner-city retailing and services, but transformed them into a sophisticated café and fashion culture. Urban design in the form of improvements of street and public space and conservation of the historic fabric led and followed the process, until the wholesale re-creation of "historic" districts or "urban villages" from scratch became a profitable activity, highly approved by city governments (e.g., Battery Park City in New York: Russell 1994). New urbanism had arrived and urban prosperity, at least in selected enclaves, was assured.

Postmodern Design Theory

The deep unpopularity of the debased modernism promulgated by urban renewal programs and corporate America found expression in postmodern theories of urban design. These theories emerged directly from critiques of downtown redevelopment and inner city renewal in the 1950s and 1960s. Jane Jacobs's *The Death and Life of Great American Cities* (1961), the most telling of these, emphasized the values of traditional urbanism, advocating mixed-use, high-density, easily surveyed streets, active ground-floor frontages, short city blocks, and "gradual rather than cataclysmic investment" (see also Berman 1982). The critiques were reinforced by the writings of Gans (1962, 1968) and Fried (1963), who stressed the potential for removing slums from many inner-city ethnic communities, as well as the value of advocacy and pluralistic planning to support community development.

Another seminal text, Kevin Lynch's *Image of the City* (1960), explored people's perceptions of places and their mental maps and way-finding techniques, which he described as legibility and "imageability." He reasserted the importance of strategic urban design, the historic character of the city, the identity of its diverse districts, and the need to deal sensitively with its assets. Throughout the 1970s and 1980s Lynch added design methodologies and theories of equal importance, embracing site planning and sensuous form (1971), conservation (1972), citywide and regional design (1976), and performance measures for urban design (e.g., access, control, efficiency, and justice, as well as vitality, sense, and fit) (1981). Lynch's special interest in the sensuous qualities and meanings of urban form was complemented by a work that had less direct impact on design practice in the United States than in Canada, but which most clearly articulated the picturesque approach to urban design. Gordon Cullen's *Townscape* (1961) was a very British approach to urban design, encompassing such concepts as a sense of place, serial vision, and the virtues of contextualism that were to define postmodern design internationally (see Norberg-Schulz 1979; Brolin 1980; Rowe and Koetter 1978). Resonances were found in Robert Venturi's contributions to postmodern design theory, in his advocacy of complexity and contradiction in architectural design, pursuit of meaningful forms, and celebration of popular taste in suburbia and the commercial strip (Venturi, 1966, 1972; see also Rudofsky 1964; Scully 1969). Other theorists more directly addressed the design of urban space and the public realm, notably Christopher Alexander (1977) in his pursuit of cross-cultural, timeless rules of thumb for urban design and architecture. William H. Whyte developed design principles for small urban spaces (1980), while others looked at city streets, especially their management and redesign (Anderson 1978; Gehl 1987).

Theories with an environmental orientation were much slower to develop, not coming to the fore until the late 1980s. McHarg's *Design with Nature* (1969) had been seminal in its day, but his ideas were not positively reinforced until sustainable development became a policy and political issue in the mid-1980s (Van der Ryn and Calthorpe 1986; Hough 1985). Meanwhile, the new urban, or neotraditional, design theory largely ignored the ecological dimension of sustainability, while espousing the ideas of pedestrian and transit orientation (Calthorpe 1993). It drew in part on neorationalist ideas and critiques of modernism developed in Europe (Rossi 1982; Krier 1978; Portoghesi 1983) and the celebration of indigenous vernaculars and pre-industrial settlement forms. The new urbanist design codes of Andres Duany and Elizabeth Plater-Zyberk regulated building forms and their relationships to the public realm, developing street and building typologies mainly, but not exclusively, for master planned upper-middle-income residential communities (Krieger and Lennertz 1991). The first Congress for New Urbanism in 1993 linked the movement internationally, although it thrives in affluent US suburbs created by private master plans (Katz 1994). New urbanism struggles to lose its *Truman Show* superficiality – and to achieve its sustainability credentials. But its policy relevance increases as it broadens its program to include urban intensification, urban villages, livable downtowns, and the retrofitting of suburbia. New urbanism, however, faces huge challenges from the realities of contemporary development practices and the processes that give priority to function, flexibility, affordability, marketability, and profit over any notions of urban or landscape design. Garreau codified some of these anti-planning impulses into "the laws of edge city," which constitute the forces of darkness for most urban designers, although they largely shape the new landscapes of suburban and ex-urban America (Garreau 1991). While the design problems of "the fractured city" were tackled by Jonathan Barnett (1995), Soja (1996) and others focused on the new urban areas of "exopolis" with their theme parks, new commercial spaces, and "hyperspace" (Winner 1992).

Critiques of Postmodern Urban Design

While postmodernism enjoyed a period of grace from the critics, save for those who still subscribed wholeheartedly to the modernist project and its minimalist aesthetic, it did become the subject of vilification. Critics who saw it as a device to obscure equity considerations, promote social exclusion, and stimulate consumption, while selective in their targets, were vitriolic in their scorn. Michael Sorkin, the New York architecture critic, argued that

> today, the profession of urban design is almost wholly preoccupied with repro-
> duction, with the creation of urban disguises. Whether in its master incarnation
> at the ersatz Main Street of Disneyland, in the phoney historic festivity of a
> Rouse marketplace, or the gentrified architecture of the "reborn" Lower East
> Side, this elaborate apparatus is at pains to assert its ties to the kind of city life
> it is in the process of obliterating ... The architecture of [New York] is almost

purely semiotic, playing the game of grafted signification, theme park building. Whether it represents generic historicity or generic modernity, such design is based on the same calculus as advertising, the idea of pure imageability, oblivious to the real needs and traditions of those who inhabit it. Welcome to Cyburbia. (1992: xiv)

Numerous design critics, journalists, and academics have identified other persistent negative themes of postmodern urban design. These include the privatization of public space (Loukaitou-Sideris and Banerjee 1998; Boyer 1994); dis-investment in the public realm (Sennett 1990; Pawley 1974); the social exclusion – even social apartheid – of gentrification (Smith and Williams 1986; Smith 1996); the preoccupation with the defence of property, citizen surveillance, and the creation of the fortress city (Davis 1990); the pastiche, facadism or "facodomy," and Frankenstein effects of postmodern stylings (Huxtable 1976; Boyer 1994); and the over-decoration, over-furnishing, and over-landscaping of public space punctuated by corporately commissioned public art of dubious quality (Relph 1988). David Harvey summarized it thus: "Fiction, fragmentation, collage and eclecticism, all suffused with a sense of ephemerality and chaos, are, perhaps, the themes that dominate in today's practices of architecture and urban design" (Harvey 1989: 98). Critics of postmodern design, however, generally ignore the positive benefits ensuing from the full range of planning and design initiatives, plans, policies, and review processes of the last three decades, which have been enjoyed by a large proportion of urban populations. Among them are:

- a concerted mending of the historic fabric of cities to restore a coherence to urban form
- a reclamation of city streets for pedestrian use, and the creation of new public spaces
- the reconnection of central cities to their waterfronts and their adjacent neighbourhoods – to create more possibilities for walking and cycling for community and leisure
- the restoration of historic districts and the protection and re-use of historic landmarks
- private development that is now more likely to respect the scale, grain, and character of the locality and to reinforce its positive rather than its negative qualities.

Some critics have tried to articulate "a postmodernism of resistance" against "a postmodernism of reaction" in a bid to reclaim the positive aspects of the movement as a basis for contemporary design practice (i.e., Frampton 1985).

They focus on resisting placelessness, reinforcing the public realm, and going beyond the purely visual preoccupations of design to reassert the values of community, multi-sensory stimulation, and sustainability.

Postmodern urban design theory was translated into new regulatory instruments and analytical methodologies as the focus of activity shifted from public sector urban design to the regulation of private development. Urban design plans became increasingly common, underpinned with image studies, view analyses, pedestrian surveys, public space inventories, and urban-form analyses (Southworth 1989). New plan policies and design guidelines were derived from syntheses of the urban design literature and refined through review experience, being extended from downtown to established residential districts. Zoning regulations were revised to accommodate urban design objectives, to respond to the diversity of urban forms in the city, and to replicate desired urban forms and architectural treatments (Wakeford 1990). Design guidelines were developed for public spaces, alongside streetscape and landscape manuals (Barnett 1982). The technical emphasis of these documents was variously matched by innovations in review bodies, procedures, expert and public involvement, policy evaluation, and the addition of design skills in the planning function (Shirvani 1981, 1992; Punter 1999a). The stage was set for thoroughgoing critiques of review processes and the development of clear principles to guide best practice. By the late 1980s such innovations were coming under strong scrutiny from academics (Lai 1988; Costonis 1989) and facing direct challenges from professional bodies and development interests, and more sophisticated and accountable approaches to design review were being sought (Scheer 1994).

Canadian Urbanism

These changes have shaped Canadian cities in similar, but also quite different, ways. Of course Canada had a much "kinder, gentler form" of urbanism than that of the United States (Garreau 1991: 471) and a much more even distribution of affluence, better social and community services, and a better public school system. Its cities and neighbourhoods are younger and have not been riven by racial tension and ghettoization, not least because urban ethnicity is more diverse, social minorities are smaller and more affluent, and there is less crime, especially of the violent sort. The public sphere has been less eroded by neoconservative politics (Lemon 1985: 12), although this is changing, particularly in Ontario and Alberta. So Canadian planning and urban design are working in a much less polarized society where the social welfare safety net is still largely in place, despite the progressive retreat of the federal and most provincial governments from funding social housing. Canadian cities shared the general postwar North American boosterist, business-led municipal politics of the 1950s and 1960s, and its drive to expand and modernize the city through infrastructure investment – especially downtown freeways – and large-scale commercial redevelopment.

Many had ambitious urban renewal plans, hatched in the 1950s, that sought extensive clearances of nineteenth-century housing, but these were comparatively slow to start. The edges of the downtown core had not been extensively cleared for commercial redevelopment or ravaged by freeways, nor had they been plagued by disinvestment and large-scale abandonment of housing. Indeed, in the late 1960s they were in the early stages of being recolonized by middle-class residents filling the new service jobs in the private sector downtown and in the public sector (government, health, education) on its margins. These young childless couples, highly educated and predominantly employed in the well-paid quaternary services, were joined by large numbers of older families and empty-nesters keen to enjoy living in diverse neighbourhoods, preferably with a heritage character, in close proximity to downtown or midtown, which retained a wide range of social, recreational, commercial, and cultural facilities (Ley 1996; Caulfield 1994).

Opposition to large-scale unsympathetic redevelopment of the downtown developed rapidly in the second half of the 1960s (Sewell 1993). Resistance to urban renewal came from low-income residents who would be displaced, but was strongly reinforced by middle-class support so that, by 1969, the federal government had abandoned its renewal funding and, more regrettably, its public housing programs. By 1972 it had initiated instead neighbourhood improvement and residential rehabilitation programs, along with support for non-profit and cooperative housing. David Ley characterizes this change as "a new urbanism of participatory places supplanting the conventional shaping of authoritarian spaces" (1996: 224). Middle-class opposition was particularly focused on high-rise apartment redevelopment, the market's response to the growing demand for housing downtown. High-rise apartment development directly threatened the better residential neighbourhoods and led to community demands to reduce density by rezoning (i.e., downzoning) to protect existing character and housing stock. Municipal councils found these pressures politically irresistible. Opposition intensified to any further downtown or cross-town freeways that would slice through such neighbourhoods, while the heritage lobby pressed for extensive designation of historic buildings or, better still, of historic districts.

By the end of the 1960s the ideology of preservation and neighbourhood planning, of the livable city and a socially mixed, compact, and diverse central area, had become a major plank of urban reform. This movement opposed business- and developer-led politicians from the old guard who had controlled cities in the postwar era and who advocated rapid development.

The introduction of reform politics into major Canadian cities in the early 1970s brought immediate changes in housing policy, planning policy, and zoning, and with it the rejection of modernist approaches to urban design and architecture, although it did not fundamentally affect the pursuit of commercial development (Sewell 1993; Hardwick 1994). The introduction of a much higher level of citizen participation in planning – as in many other areas of local governance – led to demands for heritage programs, carefully tailored zoning designations, design guidelines, neighbourhood improvement programs, new parks and greening initiatives, and traffic calming. Citizen participation transformed planning policies, processes, and procedures. Rapid gentrification of the poorer downtown neighbourhoods consolidated these initiatives but also began to reduce the social diversity and mix of neighbourhoods, even to the extent of preventing the insertion of sympathetically designed social housing units in some neighbourhoods. The conflict between neighbourhood livability and housing affordability became a major issue but by then, the reform movement was losing its commitment to social goals and its control over municipal governments (Ley 1996; Lewinberg 1985).

In the 1980s Canadian municipalities faced problems finding areas where major residential intensification could take place without incurring forceful citizen opposition. They did not need to embark on policy initiatives for gentrification as American cities did because it was already proceeding apace. The fringes of downtown and midtown offered important opportunities that were exploited, particularly in the late 1980s, when a deep recession led to the collapse of demand for new offices and commercial space. Older and declining but accessible industrial areas became the main target for high-density residential rezoning. Redevelopment of rail, port, and industrial lands was sought by entrepreneurial senior governments and municipal councils, in partnership with large-scale corporations and developers, to accommodate an affluent population. In Vancouver, Canada's selective immigration policy (in particular the creation of the "business" immigrant in 1984), insecurities in Hong Kong in the late 1980s, and citizen unrest in China in 1989 collectively stimulated in-migration and the high-rise condominium market in particular. Investment in housing accelerated the globalization of Canadian urban property markets, helping to defray the effects of a prolonged economic recession.

In the 1990s the gentrification of Canadian central cities continued apace despite significant economic difficulties. Office development almost dried up in central business districts in the 1990s, but redevelopment for high-rise residential condominiums and rentals proceeded on the margins of the rezoned rail, port, and industrial lands, colonizing areas formerly zoned commercial. Meanwhile, social housing production was severely depleted by withdrawal of senior governments' funding. The pursuit of affordable housing became a major planning concern – one difficult to achieve, given municipal budgets – and social exclusion intensified, resulting in a crisis in homelessness. Many commentators note that the critical politics that accompanied the reform movement and the planning programs of the early 1970s were supplanted by a much more individualized, consumerist orientation toward lifestyle, leisure, culture, and conviviality. Carefully linking politics, society, and landscape, David Ley notes: "The erosion of the redistributive arm of the state leaves an unmediated aestheticism paired with vigorous entrepreneurialism. The outcome of this liaison is the release of a forceful culture of consumption, the unleashing of the pleasure principle" (Ley 1996: 333). Affordable housing sites remained undeveloped, and the new neighbourhoods were socially exclusive, lacking the land-use diversity, varied activities, services, and incubating businesses that create a truly urbane environment. More positively, there was a heavy public investment in new parks, waterfronts, cycling and walking paths, greenways, and public art, which was matched by private investment in fitness clubs, cafés and bars, clubs, restaurants, art galleries, and boutique or festival shopping to create more convivial cities. For the critics, the contemporary urban preoccupations are consumption rather than community. Urbanity has taken on a particular aesthetic dimension through popular architecture, urban design, arts festivals, sports or cultural events, and local tourism (Ley 1996: 298-339; Berelowitz 1997, 1998).

Urban design policy and review processes have reached new levels of sophistication and achieved some striking and widely admired new streetscapes and largely private amenities. But doubt and disquiet remain about the kind of city that is being created. Participatory citywide planning efforts have attempted to negotiate an acceptance of nodes of denser service and residential uses and the intensification of development on arterial roads in the central city residential neighbourhoods, but many residents groups, representing mostly single families, remain resistant. Sustainability concerns, focused on air pollution, environmental health, water quality, and the retention and extension of natural areas within the urban environment have been incorporated into plans, but more radical policies to restrain traffic or promote energy-efficient building have been dropped or deferred. The Canadian new urbanist design agenda includes the drive for more compact suburbs and neotraditional settlements, but it is significantly different from its American counterpart in being focused primarily on inner-city and downtown, medium- to high-density residential development, rather than suburban master planning. The latter does exist, for instance, in the Greater Toronto area. The new urbanist agenda delivers the attractive living environments that existing homeowners want, but not the affordable environments that new households need.

The Pursuit of Better Design Review Practices

These broader, more profound critiques of urban planning, urban design, and its resultant landscapes did not have a direct impact on urban design as public policy in North America at large. Some politicians and planners were aware of the dangers of the aestheticizing city planning, but most recognized their limited powers to influence the strong economic and social processes that were shaping urban form. The criticisms of design policies and review with which they had to deal were promulgated not by radical academics and architectural critics, or even aggrieved members of the public, but primarily by the development industry and frustrated architects. Developers and their designers objected to the delay and design costs incurred in review, the reviewers' lack of skills, and the susceptibility of the process to political and bureaucratic manipulation. There were objections to the interference of lay people in the design process and the dominance of personal rather than public interest in their protests. American architects saw design review as a violation of the First Amendment regarding freedom of speech and noted the tendency of review to encourage mediocrity, pastiche, mimicry, and facadism. They objected to the lack of clear principles and pre-established criteria for review and the lack of due process in review processes (Scheer and Preiser 1994: 3-9). Some architects considered design review to be a "good concept, but with serious flaws" (Gordon, quoted in Scheer 1994: 1), and others noted that it could be effective, substantially improving many projects but also raising costs (Schuster 1990).

The academic critique emerged in the later 1980s. Researchers systematically outlined the failings of design review and tried to reconstruct a set of processes that would not only be fair and efficient for applicants and effective for municipalities, but obviate the criticisms made of so much postmodern urban design (Lai 1988; Blaesser 1994; Scheer 1994). Richard Lai, drawing on detailed studies of New York City and San Francisco in the 1970s and 1980s, recommended a set of principles as a basis on which future practices could be established. The more recent concerns of other researchers elaborate and extend these principles. Figure 1 sets out twelve principles that ought to guide the establishment of urban design as public policy. They have been recast here into four groups of concerns and require a minimum of elaboration.

Under community vision, good practice would seek to establish a comprehensive and coordinated approach to the many facets of design quality and environmental beauty as defined by a broad public. This might be expressed in some kind of design plan that had both public and development industry support and was regularly reviewed. For the design dimension of planning and zoning, good practice would establish a multi-faceted approach to design quality going beyond mere review to create incentives for good design

Figure 1   Principles for progressive urban design review

Community Vision

1 Committing to a comprehensive and coordinated vision of environmental beauty and design (Brennan's Law) (Lai 1988: 426).

2 Developing and monitoring an urban design plan with community and development industry support and periodic review (Lai 1988: 429).

Design, Planning, and Zoning

3 Harnessing the broadest range of actors and instruments (i.e., tax, subsidy, land acquisition) to promote better design (Lai 1988: 430-31).

4 Mitigating the exclusionary effects of control strategies and urban design regulation (Lai 1988: 430).

5 Integrating zoning into planning and addressing the limitations of zoning (Lai 1988: 431-32).

Broad, Substantive Design Principles

6 Maintaining a commitment to urban design that goes well beyond elevations and aesthetics to embrace amenity, accessibility, community, vitality, and sustainability (Scheer 1994: 9).

7 Basing guidelines on generic design principles and contextual analysis, and articulating desired and mandatory outcomes (Blaesser 1994: 50).

8 Accommodating organic spontaneity, vitality, innovation, and pluralism, and not attempting to control all aspects of community design (Lai 1988: 428; Blaesser 1994: 50).

Due Process

9 Identifying clear a priori roles for urban design intervention (Lai 1988: 425; Scheer 1994: 6-7).

10 Establishing proper administrative procedures with written opinions to manage administrative discretion, and with appropriate appeal mechanisms (Lai 1988: 427; Scheer 1994: 3-4).

11 Implementing an efficient, constructive, and effective permitting process (Scheer 1994: 5-6, 7).

12 Providing appropriate design skills and expertise to support the review process (Scheer 1994: 4-5; Lai 1988: 431).

or heritage or environmental conservation, by means of fiscal devices, public investments, and land acquisitions. Zoning would be carefully integrated with planning objectives to improve design quality and accommodate the necessary changes of form and use. Ameliorative measures would be taken to mitigate the tendency for urban design initiatives to gentrify areas or to exclude the less affluent. In terms of design principles and policies, good practice would not be preoccupied just with the external appearance of development and the control of elevations but would take a deeper view of environmental quality, embracing such concepts as safety, sustainability, and residents' amenity. Design policies and guidelines would be based on widely accepted generic design principles, but would be tailored to the locality through contextual analysis, and would clearly establish what was required as against what was advised. Such policies and guidelines would not be over-prescriptive and would allow design imagination, innovation, and pluralism to flourish. Finally, good practice would be based on due process with clear rules for intervention, proper administrative procedures to manage discretion, clear records of decisions, and appeal mechanisms. The permitting system would be efficient and positive, conducted by personnel with appropriate design skills and expertise.

Overall it is the exclusionary tendency of design review and postmodern design practice that deserves the most attention and that has most exercised such radical critics as Harvey (1989), Sorkin (1992), Davis (1990), and Lai (1988: 178). These best practice principles, based on widely researched critiques of American practice, provide a corrective to much existing practice, and a framework for the examination and evaluation of Vancouver's planning system and its design achievements that follows.

Using the Book

This book is a study of Vancouver's planning and design review regimes: how they were invented; how they work; the new buildings, projects, streets, and spaces they have produced; and the broader changes they have induced in the urban landscape. It is a study of development pressures and political responses, of planning policies and the response of designers and their clients. It is a study in part of the roles, relationships, and interactions between politicians and bureaucrats; planning, engineering, and park staff; planners, architects, and developers; and journalists, design critics, and the Vancouver public. In short, this book presents an exemplar of urban design as public policy over the last three decades of the twentieth century, seeking in Vancouver's achievement lessons for Anglo-American planning practice and urban design at large.

This book is intended primarily for planners and urban designers who are interested in new ways to regulate urban form and urban design to create better cities, and are always on the look out for new exemplars. It may also be of interest to Canadian urbanists who to date have no comprehensive study of contemporary planning and urban design and its impact on the contemporary cityscape of a major city. They also have very little popular or academic literature on their urban design practices, despite the sophisticated controls that operate in numerous cities. Vancouverites at large, particularly members of residents associations and other urban activist organizations, may find the evolution and critique of the city's review processes of interest, and enjoy comparing their evaluations of contemporary developments with those of the author. Likewise, the city's development and professional design communities can compare their personal experience of working within the system with the broader assessment of the city's discretionary processes and their achievements offered in these chapters. Certainly local planning, development, and architecture students should find the comprehensive overview of city planning practices and the incorporation of urban design and architecture perspectives useful and a departure point for their own researches and projects.

Following the first chapter, which introduces Vancouver, the book is structured in three parts, examining the emergence and refinement of the city's planning and design practices over the period from 1970 to 2000. Part 1 presents pivotal reforms of planning in Vancouver that occurred in the 1970s. Part 2 explores four essential aspects of Vancouver's achievement: the conservation of single-family residential neighbourhoods; citizen participation in the creation of a citywide, then neighbourhood, vision; megaproject developments on False Creek and Burrard Inlet waterfronts; and strategies for a livable downtown. Part 3 presents an evaluation of permit process and development reforms and a detailed analysis of the operation of design review. The book concludes with a four-part evaluation of Vancouver's urban design and planning achievement.

Chapter 1 sets Vancouver's physical, socioeconomic, environmental, and political contexts in relation to urban planning and design.

Chapter 2 describes the changes in Vancouver politics in the early 1970s that ushered in the vision of a "livable city" and associated reforms by a new local party. It explains how discretionary zoning and permit processing were reinvented, alongside a range of policy and practice innovations that laid the foundations for the Vancouver achievement. The development of False Creek South as a model residential community is examined in some detail as the embodiment of the ethos of the "livable city."

Chapter 3 explains the completely discretionary 1975 downtown plan for renewing the central business district and its design controls. It illustrates federal and municipal initiatives in neighbourhood planning, with ensuing conflicts between the goals of livability and affordability in rapidly gentrifying neighbourhoods and tensions between public participation and council decision making. The rise of residents associations in neighbourhoods on the margins of downtown coincided with the availability of federal funding for neighbourhood improvement.

Chapter 4 shifts the focus onto Vancouver's single-family neighbourhoods and the invention of new forms of zoning demanded by residents to protect neighbourhood character. The fierce defence of residents' sense of place and heritage resulted in a privatization of public planning to create neighbourhood-determined zoning. This clearly exclusive initiative threatens the city's ability to intensify residential neighbourhoods in a rational manner and creates a time-consuming permitting process that cannot be maintained. However, it proved to be effective in improving the design quality of new housing.

Chapter 5 describes preparations in the early 1990s for Vancouver's first city-wide plan, with an emphasis on thoroughgoing public participation and community visioning. This process teased out a consensus vision of a city of neighbourhood centres and integrated a range of policy initiatives supporting focused intensification. The initial stages of the implementation of neighbourhood-by-neighbourhood visioning and management are discussed and their tensions highlighted.

Chapter 6 focuses on the largest of Vancouver's residential megaproject developments on the north and east shores of False Creek and on the south shore of Burrard Inlet downtown. Several key planning innovations emerged through these megaprojects, including a system of high-quality public facility benefits, a park and seawall path network that now encircles the downtown peninsula, and the tower and townhouse urban form. In these projects, the cooperative planning model was invented, in which a developer and design team works in partnership with a city corporate team (planning, housing, engineering, and park staff) in an integrated process that includes extensive citizen participation and detailed design review.

Chapter 7 returns to downtown and its margins to examine the aftermath of the 1991 Central Area plan. It looks at the high-density residential intensification of Triangle West and Downtown South upslope of the waterfront megaprojects, and the revitalization of adjacent neighbourhoods. The challenges in the Downtown Eastside dramatically illustrate the processes of social exclusion operating despite policies to protect low-cost housing in this part of the city. A pernicious concentration of health, welfare, and public safety issues obstructs regeneration initiatives. In the downtown core, conflicting visions for the public realm pose challenges for city planners as much as for developers and their designers.

Chapter 8 is a detailed account of the pressures to reform permit processing, and the department's response, over the last twenty years. How the city administration developed a fair and efficient system of permitting through a sequence of reviews is discussed, including the current review of development and building regulation. Parallel concerns over the financing of infrastructure and the extension of development levies and community-amenity contributions to pay for a range of basic services and quality neighbourhood facilities and amenities are discussed. These are two areas where new processes are being invented to sustain the "livable city."

Chapter 9 explains the current operation of the Development Permit Board and the Urban Design Panel and their inputs into improving the design of development. It reveals the checks and balances that have been introduced into the discretionary processes and illustrates how the various experts and specialists involved collectively work to achieve high design standards. It considers the verdicts of the Urban Design Panel on potential design outcomes in some depth.

Chapter 10 offers a synthesis of how Vancouver has accomplished its urban renaissance and urban design achievements. A set of principles of good practice for urban design policy (see Figure 1) is used to evaluate the city's current processes and practices. The book concludes with a look at the planning and design challenges ahead.

Most chapters in the book have a specific geographical focus, as development and planning activity shift toward particular neighbourhoods. But most also explore a specific set of themes that relates to the preceding discussion about good design policy practices, the evolution of particular built forms, and the variables that explain policy and development outcomes. Issues within and between each chapter are explored in a broadly chronological account. To assist the reader, a chronology of key planning initiatives, policy documents, major developments, and local and senior governments' politics can be found in Appendix 2. Organization charts of the planning department, identifying key individuals and departmental roles, can be found in Appendix 3.

The Vancouver Achievement

1
Introducing Vancouver

In the 1990s, Vancouver established a reputation as one of the best-planned cities in North America, a city where the design quality of development achieves a consistently high standard. It has become a place of pilgrimage for American planners and developers (Blore and Sutherland 1999: 41), even from cities with such distinguished planning and design traditions as Seattle, Portland (Oregon), and San Francisco. It has consistently come close to the top of the rankings in quality of life studies of major cities. In 2000 it was placed top equal with Zurich, Switzerland, for livability for business people in the Mercer Ratings and in 2002 top again equal with Melbourne, Australia, in *The Economist* Intelligence Unit Ratings. The city's spectacular natural setting; its attractive residential vernacular and well-treed streets; its relatively smooth transition from railhead and resource-exporting port to provincial corporate centre and now to high-amenity Pacific Rim metropolis (Hutton 1994); and its sustained postwar prosperity all have provided a platform for the development of an environmentally conscious planning regime since 1970. This regime has stopped freeway intrusions, promoted neighbourhood conservation, replaced redundant industrial and port lands with new high-density residential neighbourhoods, reclaimed the waterfront for public use, and reinforced the diversity, vitality, and attractiveness of its downtown and inner neighbourhoods. Vancouver has achieved an urban renaissance more comprehensively than any other city in North America. Of particular interest are the city's achievements in the sphere of urban design, secured through its unique discretionary zoning system, cooperative planning model for megaprojects, discretionary control of major developments, development levies, management of neighbourhood change, and strategic citywide approach to building intensification.

A Setting in Search of a City?

Much of the lure of Vancouver relates to its setting and to the particular juxtaposition of its high rise-dominated downtown peninsula and dark forests of Stanley Park against a backdrop of the heavily rain-forested and often snow-capped Coast Range (see Plate 1). The mountains rise sharply to 1,200 metres on the north shore of Burrard Inlet, which, like False Creek to the south, brings the ocean right into the heart of the city. Together, mountains and ocean provide the raw material for the "cult of the view" (Berelowitz 1997) which has driven high-rise residential development in the central area over the last fifty years. Vancouver's location at the "edge of wilderness" (Boddy 1994a) is an essential part of its attraction, ethos, and lifestyles, fostering a higher level of environmental awareness – as evidenced by the founding of Greenpeace in Vancouver in 1969 – and a higher proclivity for outdoor recreation among its citizens than most other world cities. Dubbed locally as a "setting in search of a city" in typical Canadian self-effacement, Vancouver has acquired an urbanity and environmental quality to live up to its fabulous setting. Nonetheless, on cloudy days when the mountains are invisible and Vancouver must rest solely on its human-made qualities, there is a massive sense of loss and the city seems much more humdrum.

However, some of the city's eastern and southern neighbourhoods are indistinguishable from many other North American cities, and merge imperceptibly with extensive tracts of inter- and postwar suburbia in the municipalities to the east. With the weakness of the Canadian dollar this has helped to ensure its emergence as "Hollywood North," becoming the backdrop for hundreds of American movies and TV series, most notably *The X-Files,* where the forest settings can reinforce primeval fears of the natural, supernatural, and extraterrestrial worlds (Miller 1994). The writer Douglas Coupland neatly expresses one of the city's enduring contradictions – "Vancouver's unique: you can morph it into any North American city or greenspace with little effort and even less expense" (Coupland 1997: 81). So there is a paradox in the "edge of wilderness" character of Vancouver and in the dichotomy between its heritage early-twentieth-century Craftsman homes on the West Side and more standard, domestic, and commercial architecture on the Eastside. An east-west divide encapsulates differences in housing affordability, environmental quality, levels of traffic, ethnic diversity, and politics.

The temperate climate of Vancouver is also significant, best described as wet and warm, particularly in comparison with other major Canadian cities that have a continental climate. The midwinter mean lows are about 4°C, while the midsummer mean highs are 29°C. While there is rain on 40 percent of days and 94 centimetres of rainfall overall, there are over 2,100 hours of sunshine annually. Foggy days are not unknown (17), but snowy days rare

(5), so the city has not needed to create underground or skywalk pedestrian systems downtown, though it has had to give attention to rain protection (Vancouver 1998g: 48). An important by-product of this climate is that vegetation grows lushly and matures rapidly, helping to ensure that Vancouver is a very green city, and making gardening, walking, cycling and other forms of outdoor recreation extremely popular year-round activities. These environmental advantages are tempered by the threat of major seismic activity.

Much play is made of Vancouver as the "terminal city," its prosperity being inextricably linked to it becoming the terminus of the Canadian Pacific Railway, which built its line to Burrard Inlet in 1886 (Boddy 1994a). Huge land concessions were granted to CP Rail in order to get the company to extend its transcontinental railway to the Granville Townsite, just east of contemporary downtown. These tracts of land provided CP Rail with the opportunity to shape much of the large-scale development as the town became a city, a process that continues today through CP's property arm, Marathon. This sense of being at the end of the line and at the edge of the continent is pervasive in Vancouver. "Canada stops at the Rockies" continues to be a widely held belief, particularly as Vancouver looks more and more to the south for its trade, commerce, and tourism and, with Seattle and Portland, contemplates the emergence of the Cascadia urban region (Pivo 1996). This isolation is reflected in the relatively weak high-level retail catchment of the city, and the impression of the downtown core being under-shopped. More positively, it is reflected in the stability and longevity of service of the planners in its planning department and the strong sense of community among design professionals. Robert Kaplan makes reference to a "unified elite of investors and urban planners" (Kaplan 1998: 54), not an entirely accurate description but one which conveys the sense of a close-knit development, design, and planning community in agreement about the need for a considered approach to urban development.

A Twentieth-Century Grid City

Founded in 1886, Vancouver had only 2,700 people by 1900. Vancouver is very much a twentieth-century city. By 1931 it had increased its population tenfold and, by the early 1990s, twenty-fold to surpass the half-million mark. By 1890, the town had established an electric street-railway that developed an inter-urban system of links and provided the mechanism for what was then suburban growth. The streetcars established the grid of commercial arterial roads whose fine grain of commercial enterprises is one of the endearing and enduring qualities of the city today (see Figure 2). Most domestic building was of timber frame construction, but Edwardian, Stick, Craftsman, and West Coast bungalow styles – especially the latter two – proliferated from

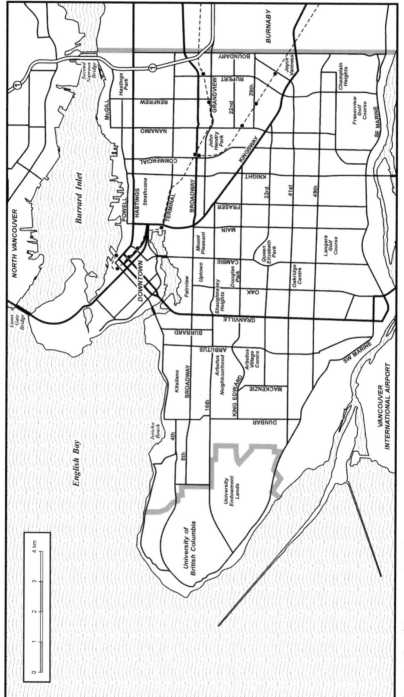

Figure 2 City of Vancouver: principal streets (*Source:* Cartography by Jan Edwards)

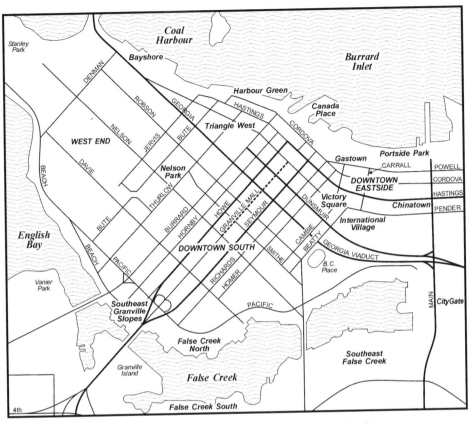

Figure 3 Downtown Vancouver: principal streets (*Source:* Cartography by Jan Edwards)

1890 to 1930 to give many of the city's older neighbourhoods, especially those on the Westside, a particularly high-quality housing environment. There was virtually no rowhousing. These neighbourhoods were enhanced by boulevard tree planting and heavy investment in landscaping by the new residents. The housing is highly adaptable and easy to demolish and rebuild but is also prone to rot in the west coast climate. Some of it is nearing the end of its natural life and is being replaced, but the defence of single-family character and early-twentieth-century vernacular housing and streetscapes against conversion, replacement, or intensification is a major feature of contemporary planning practice.

Vancouver's port origins meant that much of its waterfront was devoted initially to shipping and then to storage and manufacturing. Most of the Burrard Inlet and False Creek waterfronts were extended into the ocean to provide railway yards and industrial sites, particularly sawmills. Stanley Park, established in 1888, preserves the shoreline and a remnant of the original forest on on the third of the peninsula that projects into the Strait of Georgia (see Figure 3). In the same year the independent Vancouver Park Board was established and this has continued to play a very important role in city planning in its broadest sense. The subdivision of the West End created parklands on English Bay and Sunset Beach, as did subsequent subdivision across much of the south side of English Bay, providing public access to the ocean and a chain of public beaches, walkways, and cycling paths. Elsewhere the downtown core was blocked from the water by the railways, warehouses, sawmills, and other industries. Reclaiming the waterfront for public use became a major planning policy from the late 1960s onward, as industry moved to cheaper land to the east and these sites became ripe for high-density commercial and residential uses. Spectacular views across the city to the nearby mountains and the blue expanses of the Strait of Georgia would be obtained from tower blocks. The potential attractions of the waterfront meant that people might readily move back into the downtown peninsula if quality neighbourhood design could be achieved.

In the postwar era, Vancouver experienced an economic boom driven initially by the resource economy of British Columbia, port activities, industrial consolidation, and immigration. While the downtown core benefited from the development of office buildings to house major companies' headquarters, its fringes experienced considerable industrial out-migration, leaving large areas derelict and ripe for redevelopment. Conventional industry contracted back to the flatlands east of False Creek and on Burrard Inlet east of Main Street, progressively priced out by commercial and residential developments. Today heavy industry has almost disappeared from the city and Vancouver attracts only 10 to 15 percent of the new industrial development in the region.

The city's planning department responded to economic and demographic growth by encouraging large scale redevelopment in the downtown area through rezoning, and allowing apartment development in other residential areas. Major downtown redevelopment was promoted jointly by developers, financial institutions, and the city in the late 1960s – the latter proposing to support that growth with a new system of freeways and road bridges that would further encourage large-scale redevelopment. While manufacturing employment declined in the city from the 1950s, service jobs enjoyed a sharp rise and, as early as the mid-1980s, there was much discussion of Vancouver as a post-industrial city. The city has benefited particularly from rapid growth in higher-order service jobs – professional, managerial, financial, and business tourism services – which have all increased dramatically over the last four decades (Hutton 1994: 224). This has created a new professional-managerial class with distinctive politics, tastes, and locational preferences that has resulted in the gentrification of large tracts of the city (Ley 1980; 1993).

Social Geography

The City of Vancouver, with its population of just less than half a million people, is the historic core of one of the fastest-growing regions in North America (see Figure 4). It now has less than a third of the population of the regional district and, by 2021, this figure is projected to be less than a fifth, as the municipalities to the east and southeast grow at rates of 20 to 30 percent a decade. While the region grew rapidly, primarily through immigration, the City of Vancouver showed steady growth – about 1-2 percent per annum – until the 1970s when the population started to decline. By the mid-1980s, the city had returned to steady growth of 2 percent per annum, driven by increasing Asian immigration that has exceeded inter-provincial migration over the last two decades. The Anglo-Canadian population of Vancouver is now just less than half of the total; more than a quarter of the total populace speak Chinese as their first language. The Asian influx, coming from high-density urban settings, was popularly believed to have helped the increased demand for high-rise apartment living. But recent Asian immigrants have moved mainly into the low-density neighbourhoods of southern Vancouver, such as Kerrisdale and Sunset (see Figure 5). One of the distinguishing characteristics of the Asian immigrants has been their affluence. Most are "business" immigrants arriving since 1984, who had to have substantial personal wealth to invest in Canada in order to gain entry, and whose arrival has helped promote a significant increase in real estate investment.

Major changes are underway in family structure and household size, with single-parent families expected to increase to 17 percent and non-family households expected to reach 37 percent by 2006. Average household size is declining steadily from 3.4 in 1961 to an anticipated 2.4 persons by 2021. Mention must also be made of changing gender relationships and identities. Divorce rates have quadrupled since the 1960s and the city houses a disproportionate share of these divorcees and of unmarried women within the region (Ley et al. 1992: 236-42). The West End of Vancouver has become the home to a sizable male gay community that has grown substantially since the decriminalization of homosexual acts in 1969. The population is also ageing, with average age to reach 41 years by 2016 (CMA data in Tomalty 1998: 34).

The social geography of Vancouver reveals a clear east-west split, broadly along Clark Drive, with the West End and westside neighbourhoods being the most expensive and most sought-after. The westside neighbourhoods of Vancouver benefit from markedly lower levels of traffic and collectively remain a privileged enclave, resisting the introduction of rapid transit that would densify its eastern margins. Some of the most contested residential intensification battles since 1980 have occurred in the central neighbourhoods from Fairview through Shaughnessy to Kerrisdale and Oakridge. Eastside neighbourhoods

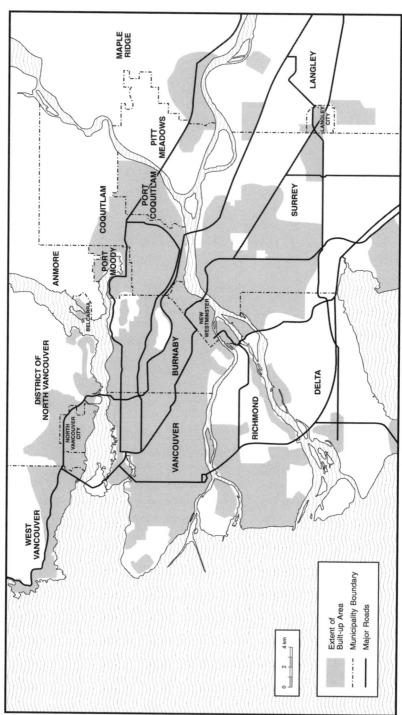

Figure 4 Greater Vancouver: the City of Vancouver and adjacent municipalities (*Source:* Cartography by Jan Edwards)

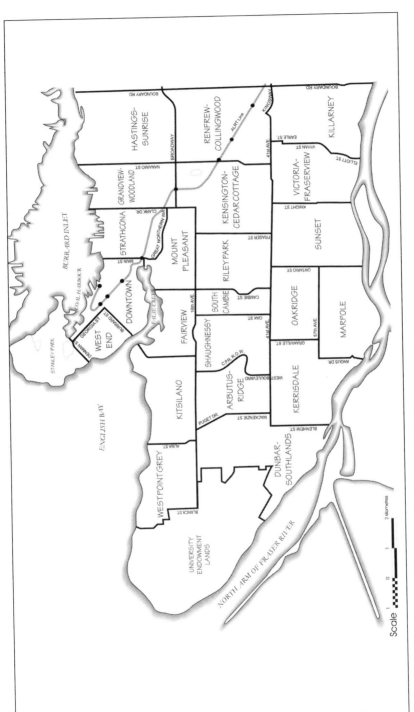

Figure 5 City of Vancouver: neighbourhoods (*Source:* Vancouver City Graphics)

have always been markedly poorer, particularly the Downtown Eastside and Strathcona and the blue-collar neighbourhoods of Hastings–Sunrise and Grandview–Woodland (see Figure 5). While the areas west of Granville Street have remained staunchly Anglo-Canadian, the areas to the east have become much more diverse, with a large Asian population – more than 20 percent through most of the area. This is particularly concentrated in Strathcona, where Chinatown is located, and in Kensington–Cedar Cottage and southern Sunset (Ley et al. 1992: 249-56).

As a result of population increases, Vancouver has been experiencing very strong intensification. Gross densities have risen by 21 percent over the period 1976 to 1999 but, as the supply of derelict industrial land diminishes or is protected for future employment growth, these intensification pressures are directed much more forcefully into existing residential areas (Vancouver 1999w). This is a very evident theme in Vancouver's recent planning history, particularly the search for a citywide strategy to accommodate projected demographic changes and to build the new forms of housing that older people and smaller householders will need and can afford. While the city accommodated an additional 47,000 people between 1971 and 1991, this is only 9 percent of regional growth over the period, indicative of the potential pressures from growth that lie ahead.

The Demand for Development

Affluent immigration, internal population growth, and steadily reducing household size have created a vigorous and largely uninterrupted demand for housing development throughout the city in the postwar era. Property has been in high demand, development has been profitable, and competition between developers has helped the city to establish a demanding regulatory system in terms of the provision of infrastructure and amenities, and the achievement of design quality, the latter now enshrined in higher market standards. The same demands for property have driven Vancouver's urban regeneration initiatives and the creation of a series of high-density residential neighbourhoods around False Creek, on Burrard Inlet, and on the very margins of the downtown core. When office development collapsed at the end of the 1980s, high-rise residential development was already taking its place and pressures for residential rezoning were already evident. Thus, the planning objectives of repopulating the central area and creating a "livable downtown," set in the early 1970s, have been realized much more quickly than anyone anticipated.

If a persistent demand for new development has been a boon to urban regeneration and the repopulation of the central area, it has only exacerbated housing affordability. High rates of development have probably protected many moderate-rent apartments throughout the city from upgrades and rede-velopment, but housing affordability has become a major issue in the city. Vancouver and Victoria have the most expensive housing in Canada, with only a fifth of renters able to afford a starter home in 1998 (Canada Mortgage and Housing Corporation 1998), but the proportion of rental apartments re-mains at 55 percent of the stock (Vancouver 1999w). Housing affordability problems have been accompanied by rises in welfare and poverty levels in the city and the region, with nearly 20 percent of all Vancouver families being classed as low income by 1991, nearly double the rate for other Canadian metropolitan areas. Steady growth, then, is a mixed blessing.

Vancouver Politics and Planning

Vancouver's unique discretionary planning system has evolved against a particu-lar political background of a small council, elected citywide and given consider-able independence from the province, with a high level of delegation given to planning officers alongside a high level of discretion in day-to-day deci-sion making. In 1936 the electoral system in Vancouver was changed from a ward system to a citywide system. This change created a small council and contributed to the emergence of a small business oriented, pro-development political elite. From 1937 to 1972, the city was run by the Non-Partisan Asso-ciation, established in 1936, which had been formed explicitly "to oppose the introduction of party politics into Vancouver's civic administration" (Gutstein 1983a: 196). The Non-Partisan leaders, drawn from the city's social and busi-ness elite, favoured business leadership, efficient and lean government, and generally discouraged public participation. The West End and westside neigh-bourhoods – especially south of Broadway – supported the Non-Partisan Association to near monopoly power between 1937 and 1968, and from 1990 to 2002. The main characteristics of the municipal government were typical of the American reform tradition: a weak mayor, a small number of council-lors elected citywide – and therefore owing no allegiance or accountability to specific segments of the citizenry – and a dominant city manager (Hardwick 1994: 341). This slim-line government has its critics, particularly of the lack of ward representation and the small proportion of the electorate that actually votes for the majority party (Tennant and West 1998). It does, however, help to maintain political non-interference in local development politics and to reduce not-in-my-backyard (NIMBY) political responses to necessary development.

Also contributing to Vancouver's distinctive politics was the Vancouver Charter. Granted by the province in 1953, the Charter gave the city much greater powers of self-government than other British Columbian or Canadian cities, which remain subservient to provincial municipal acts. The city could amend its Charter by means of private bills submitted to the BC legislature, and this has allowed council and the director of planning very significant scope for policy innovation and direct response to local circumstance. In Vancouver, council shapes policy and approves all plans, rezonings, and design guidelines but generally does not interfere in day-to-day planning practices; most notably, council delegates all decisions on development permissions to the director of planning.

At the end of the 1960s, two reform parties were established in Vancouver politics to oppose the pro-business Non-Partisan Association. One, calling itself The Electors Action Movement (TEAM), assumed control of the council in 1972. It had a more considered and sensitive approach to development, advocated more participatory planning practices, and a more inclusive vision for the future of the city, which appealed to the younger, better educated, more urbane and environmentally conscious electorate. For a while TEAM councillors were ably supported by the Confederation of Progressive Electors (COPE), a more left-wing group with organized labour affiliations. The reformers' hold on power was relatively short-lived and, by 1986, a Non-Partisan council was returned to office and the city returned to being virtually a one-party council throughout the 1990s. COPE returned two councillors in 1999 but, to the surprise of most, took control for the first time in 2002. Many commentators conclude that most city councillors since 1970, certainly those who have most influenced planning practices, have shared a common approach to planning and development. There have been differences of emphasis, for example, some pursuing affordable housing initiatives, and others more concerned to protect existing neighbourhoods. But broadly speaking, since 1986 Non-Partisan politicians have implemented the vision of the "livable city" first articulated by the TEAM council in 1970.

The political twists of municipal and provincial politics and their implications for planning practice form an important strand in the narrative of this book (see Appendix 2). So too, in this relatively small political, administrative, and professional circle, do the contributions of individual politicians and senior planning officers who have helped shape the concept of the livable city through the city's unique discretionary planning system (see Appendix 3). Thus far local practices have survived global economic forces, and Vancouver's planning and design review practices have resisted the deregulatory forces that have emasculated planning in so many equivalent cities in Anglo-America.

Part 1
Setting a New Planning Agenda

2
TEAM and the Reform of Planning, 1972-80

The first part of this book consists of two chapters, the first of which explores how, in the early 1970s, the new council reformed planning practices in Vancouver through the establishment of a new planning regime that included changes to development review, new official development plans, and the creation of a model inner-city neighbourhood. The second chapter explores how a new downtown plan was established and implemented, and how the redevelopment of the central area was planned during the 1980s. New zonings, design guidelines, and development levies were established to manage the emergence of new high-density residential and mixed-use neighbourhoods on the edge of the commercial core, as the city faced new development pressures and the impetus of reform weakened. These reforms were to set the framework for planning and urban design through to the present.

Council had first taken advantage of its Charter-based independence and scope for innovation in the planning sphere in 1956, by introducing discretionary zoning and an element of design review. But it was the innovations of the new reform council between 1972 and 1975, especially refinements to discretionary zoning and official development plans, that largely produced its contemporary design-sensitive planning system. Key innovations were the requirement for discussion of concept proposals at the beginning of the control process, the streamlining of the Development Permit Board, and the addition of an advisory panel to that board to give more transparency and public input into the discretionary process. The defining characteristics of the Vancouver approach to urban design review – inclusive and transparent processes, clear delegation of decision making, political non-interference, clear design obligations and incentives, and peer review – were established. These remain the cornerstone of positive, enlightened regulation of design in city development. Major steps were taken in this period to solicit community support for design policies and guidelines, and to establish due process for decision making, so that Vancouver had a firm foundation for design-led planning, following many of the principles outlined in Figure 1.

Delegated and Discretionary Planning Powers

From 1937 to 1972, Vancouver's council was run by the Non-Partisan Association, which promoted business interests, downtown commercial development, and efficient decision making. Under its regime, a planning department had been established in 1952 with a council-appointed planning commission, which was an advisory body only. The Board of Variance was created in 1959 to hear appeals against development permit refusals. Composed of a chairperson, two city councillors, and two lieutenant-governor appointees, the board was usually packed with Non-Partisan sympathizers and pro-development lobbyists (Gutstein: 1975b). A technical planning board (forerunner of the Development Permit Board) composed of officials handling the physical development functions was more influential than the Vancouver Planning Commission, while a board of administration – composed of the mayor and two commissioners – effectively ran the council and conducted its business.

One of these commissioners, formerly the planning director, was Gerald Sutton Brown, an engineer from England. Considered "the most powerful person at City Hall, his power verging on the absolute" (Gutstein 1983b: 199), Sutton Brown was the first port of call for potential developers. It was Sutton Brown who, from 1959 onward, proposed Vancouver's freeway system and associated major redevelopment. Sutton Brown also controlled Bill Graham, the planning director, and managed the planning process so that very little was made public. Sutton Brown and Graham took full advantage of the city's relative independence from the province, the high level of delegation of powers to bureaucrats, and the opportunities for the exercise of discretion in development decisions – characteristics rooted in the Vancouver Charter.

In 1956 a new zoning and development bylaw (#3575) was passed for the West End and Kitsilano that permitted uses "as of right" in particular zones, but also allowed other uses as long as their "negative impacts ... could be mitigated ['conditional approvals' or 'discretionary zoning']" (Vancouver 1994k: 2). Under this bylaw, the planning department gained the power to relax certain zoning regulations and to create such incentives as underground car parking and larger sites for development.

The 1956 bylaw was driven particularly by downtown businesses concerned both to foster retail expansion and to provide housing for the increasing number of white-collar workers in downtown offices. An immediate result was a wave of demolitions of the existing 3-storey housing, accompanied by the construction of many tall towers. By the mid-1970s, the population of the West End had virtually doubled from its 1951 total (Gutstein 1975b: 98-102)

(Plate 1). Street closures and one-way systems to reduce traffic did significantly improve living conditions and had the additional positive effects of controlling curb crawling for prostitutes and creating space for street trees and seating. Redevelopment continued to the point that, in 1963 and 1972, city planners requested new regulations to reduce density in the West End, but both times the council controlled by the Non-Partisan Association rejected them.

In addition to residential development in the West End, the key planning concerns for Vancouver throughout the 1960s and early 1970s were urban renewal, commercial development downtown, and proposals for freeway development and associated area clearances. The ways in which officials responded to each issue exemplified the potential scope for planning – and revealed the failure to develop policies and operate discretionary controls to be open, accountable, and sensitive to specific areas of the city.

The West End

Between 1941 and 1981, the population of the West End almost doubled; between 1951 and 1981, however, the number of dwelling units quadrupled as lower-income families were replaced by single-person households. Residents lived in taller buildings and had much more floor space per person than before – a trend that has continued, as many condominium units increase in size, and average household sizes shrink. Developers' architects took advantage of a later bylaw change that provided for larger balconies to provide more external space for apartment dwellers. In the mid-1970s there were those, such as Alderman Walter Hardwick, who celebrated the new West End as a place to live and who recognized that density could provide "security, colour, excitement, interaction, privacy" (Hardwick 1974: 203). Eyeing the shores of False Creek as potential sites for new communities, Hardwick argued that the key to securing these advantages without the associated disadvantages lay in good planning. Nonetheless, the West End continued to provide a salutary lesson in the dangers of over-generous zoning to increase density, uncontrolled building height, and simplistic development incentives. Many residential neighbourhoods heeded these lessons when their rezonings were proposed.

A forest of high rises sprang up rapidly in the West End. The towers, set against Stanley Park and the shoreline, gave Vancouver the distinctive and dramatic skyline that remains its dominant marketing image (see Plate 1). The initial commercial developments downtown were modest, the first office towers being completed in 1956. Two built in the international style – the Burrard Building designed by Van Norman & Associates in 1956 and the BC Hydro Building designed by Thompson, Berwick & Pratt in 1955-57 – were both distinguished. Described as a "beacon to modernism" (Kalman et al. 1993:

Plate 1 West End towers and English Bay from Kitsilano Pool. This view northward to the West End captures the essence of Vancouver: high amenity waterfront, sea views, and apartment towers set against a backdrop of spectacular Coast Range mountains. Beach Towers is on the right.

133), the BC Hydro Building became the first postwar building to be given a heritage designation. These buildings closed out the initial commercial office boom, with little new floor space being added until the late 1960s.

Few of the new towers from the next wave of construction, however, had any architectural merit, as Kalman, Phillips, and Ward have argued. Some of the late 1960s poured-concrete towers designed by Erickson/Massey were well received at the time they were built. Among the best were the four cruciform-plan Beach Towers on English Bay (on the right in Plate 1), de-signed by Van Norman & Associates, well site-planned, and evoking Corbusian precedents (Kalman et al. 1993: 121). While architectural critics applauded some of the other new towers, the few slab blocks were widely reviled. Those attracting the most criticism were the 30-storey Imperial Apartments – then the tallest building in western Canada – designed by Peter Kaffka for Non-Partisan Mayor Tom Campbell in 1963, and the considerably more elegant 18-storey Ocean Towers designed by Rix Reinecke in 1957-58, the first tall building on English Bay. Both projects revealed the need to control the floor plan of such developments, as well as the positioning of tall buildings in relation to public views of the water and mountains. These controls did not emerge until 1989. The 1956 zoning bylaw had introduced an element of design review into development decisions, as the Technical Planning Board could then refer any development proposal to an Architectural Advisory Panel appointed by council in 1956 (Leung 1984: 7). Design did not become a significant preoccupation in development review, however, until the 1970s.

Public Reaction to Downtown Redevelopment

Public reaction to the quality of new development in downtown Vancouver became increasingly hostile. The push for large-scale redevelopment began in the early 1960s, responding to the growth of white-collar jobs and driven by the closely interlocking relationship between the business elite, the banks, the development industry, aldermen, and bureaucrats. (See Gutstein 1975b for a close analysis of these connections.) In 1960 a redevelopment advisory board had been established by the Downtown Business Association, and the city was engaged to help assemble significant land holdings for commercial redevelopment. A 1963 consultants' study suggested six possible sites down-town for major redevelopment, of which the block formed by Hamilton, Dunsmuir, Seymour, and Hastings streets was selected. Subsequently, Eaton's department store changed the city's mind so that the block bounded by Howe, Georgia, Granville, and Dunsmuir streets was selected instead for the first phase of the Pacific Centre project (Gutstein 1975b: 69-71). This incident provides clear evidence of the way in which private capital could direct public resources.

By the mid-1960s numerous major commercial developments were under-way, the largest of which was the triple-towered Bentall Centre designed by Musson & Cattell, part of an eventual five-tower complex. This development was of particular interest because it greatly exceeded the zoning provisions, the second tower being twice the regulation height. Appeals to the Board of Variance achieved this circumvention. The board agreed to increase the height of the first tower by 10 metres (33 feet) and the second by a staggering 67 metres (220 feet). The scheme created a minimal amount of public space on Burrard Street, with a plaza and "Picasso-style" sculpture and fountain (Kalman et al. 1993: 90). Although the black towers of the Bentall Centre were relieved by concrete framing on the building corners, columns, and uppermost storeys, these architectural additions had the effect of making the towers seem even more banal. Major commercial buildings of more architectural distinction included the Miesian Guinness Tower designed by Charles Paine and the MacMillan Bloedel headquarters designed by Erickson/Massey. The latter's massive concrete frame tapered dramatically as it rose to 27 storeys, its deeply recessed windows providing a strong relief and shadowing in the elevations (Kalman et al. 1993: 90). Each created some additional pedestrian space but little real public amenity.

The completed first phase of Pacific Centre aroused great public antipathy. The whole complex had an austerity that endeared it to few people, while the underground shopping mall simultaneously undermined Granville Street as a retail artery. Planned by Victor Gruen & Associates and designed by Cesar Pelli with McCarter Nairne & Partners, the city assisted in the land assembly and then gave large parts of the site to the developer. Pacific Centre became the largest downtown redevelopment when building began in 1969: it occupied two blocks on the west side of Granville at Georgia. Linked by an underground shopping mall, it was anchored at the south end by the block-wide Eaton's Department Store. The latter was designed as a huge blank box faced in white reconstituted stone cut away on the northeast corner to provide an entrance to a corner plaza. On the west side of the plaza, the Toronto-Dominion Bank built a 30-storey sleek black curtain-walled tower and to the north was the 19-storey IBM Building and a 20-storey hotel tower (see Plate 2). Vancouverites expressed their antipathy toward the complex, coining such epithets as "the black towers" and "the towers of darkness" – later borrowed to describe other downtown office blocks. The mayor responded by personally intervening to require that a subsequent fourth tower for the Vancouver stock exchange be clad in lighter-coloured materials (Kalman 1974: 65). The blank walls of Eaton's department store were the final insult to the public streets and the civic spaces at this pivotal point of the downtown retail core.

The developer of the Bentall Centre, the Pacific Centre, and other projects was able to manipulate planning and zoning controls, and to strike highly advantageous land deals with civic officials. A series of major development proposals that followed began to arouse public opposition and to erode support for the Non-Partisan Association. As early as 1961, the Coal Harbour proposals for the waterfront areas between downtown and Stanley Park provoked the opposition of West Enders and people wanting to protect the park. William Zeckendorf, who had designed Place Ville-Marie in Montreal, proposed

Plate 2 Pacific Centre, Toronto Dominion, IBM, and Stock Exchange towers, looking across the Granville Street Transit Mall towards the Pacific Centre "towers of darkness." Most of the pedestrian movement is sucked into the underground shopping concourse. The sleek IBM Tower (centre) and the Stock Exchange Tower (behind it) were later additions.

twelve high-rise towers for Coal Harbour. By 1965 fifteen towers had been approved on the site, although the project did not proceed. In addition, public opposition was galvanized by the 1967 urban renewal proposal for large-scale clearance and redevelopment in Strathcona–Chinatown, east of downtown. They formed the Strathcona Property Owners and Tenants Association that successfully halted demolitions in 1968 and initiated a housing rehabilitation program supported by the federal government – a forerunner of the Neighbourhood Improvement Program (discussed later). The huge Arbutus Village Regional Shopping Centre proposals on the westside of the city – promoted by Canadian Pacific – prompted a five-year struggle to reduce the scale of the development and its impact on the surrounding single-family neighbourhood.

This latter controversy damaged electoral support for the Non-Partisan Association in its heartlands (Gutstein 1974-75: 14). What lost the NPA most support among business leaders, thereby sealing its political fate, was a land deal made by Mayor Tom Campbell in a secret council session. This deal aborted plans for expropriation of land owned by businessman Peter Birks to create a park in the West End and instead allowed Birks to retain most of his property for high-rise office development. Four days later Birks was elected president of the NPA, but the association did not recover from the bad publicity and subsequently lost control of the council in the 1972 election.

The Freeway and Burrard Tunnel Proposals

The development industry, downtown business interests, growth-oriented civic officials and aldermen, and Commissioner Sutton Brown all agreed that further development of downtown depended on new freeway access. However, as Gutstein demonstrates, the planning of the freeways proceeded on the basis of who could be made to pay for them rather than on strategic thinking about desirable patterns of new development. (For a detailed discussion see Gutstein 1975b: 151-56, 162-66.) A tunnel under Burrard Inlet from Coal Harbour was discussed on the basis that a crossing of a federal waterway might be paid for by the federal government. An east-west freeway would be feasible because Canadian Pacific would grant rights-of-way in order to access its own extensive redevelopment sites in the area. An east-west freeway was planned through Chinatown on the southern edge of the proposed Strathcona urban renewal project, again with the possibility of attracting federal funds. This would link with a north-south freeway on Main Street that would run around the northern edge of downtown, along the waterfront to Coal Harbour and the proposed Burrard Inlet tunnel.

When these clandestine plans were presented in June 1967 to council as "the Vancouver transportation study," angry citizens convened public meetings citywide. Business owners in Chinatown–Strathcona – those most adversely affected by the proposals – were most vociferous against the multi-lane freeway cutting through their neighbourhood (Hasson and Ley 1994: 117-21). When it became clear that the proposals were being steered by such powerful landholders as the National Harbours Board, Canadian Pacific, and BC Hydro – all enhancing their own development interests – even development supporters such as the Downtown Business Association and the Vancouver Board of Trade began to question city planning and development practices. In the end, only the Vancouver Planning Commission supported the freeway proposals. The commission chair resigned in November 1967 after a second public meeting brought mass opposition to the proposed freeways.

Attempts to scale down the freeway proposals to try to reduce public opposition were made in 1968 and 1971. The freeway around downtown was then proposed to follow the north side of False Creek and Drake Street before turning northeast and tunnelling under Thurlow Street to link with the proposed Burrard Inlet third crossing. A major push in 1971 by the mayor for council approval and funds for the Burrard Inlet tunnel failed, and protesters campaigned for a plebiscite on the third crossing. Forced to hold a public meeting that was bound to attract citizens opposing the project, Mayor Tom Campbell made his notorious comment that the project was being sabotaged by "Maoists, Communists, pinkies, left wingers, and hamburgers [his term for people without a university degree]" (Gutstein 1975b: 164-66). The meeting confirmed almost unanimous opposition. Council scrapped the route through Chinatown but did approve the viaducts extending Georgia and Dunsmuir streets, which were completed in 1971. These viaducts continue to blight redevelopment prospects in the area and are constant reminders of the severe urban design problems that the completed freeway system could have posed (see Gutstein 1975b: 154-56).

By 1972, even the Downtown Business Association was favouring investment instead in rapid transit. The city had failed to lobby the federal government, which had agreed to fund a large part of the Burrard tunnel project but shelved its plans prior to the impending election. In the election, the Conservatives, who favoured funding for the tunnel project, were almost obliterated in British Columbia when the Trudeau government swept to power. By then both provincial and city governments were favouring transit. Thus, Vancouver avoided being ravaged by freeways, a critical factor in the quality of its environment and subsequent pursuit of a livable, sustainable city.

The proposed freeway through the northern edge of downtown was to have serviced a huge downtown waterfront redevelopment complex, Project 200, between the Marine Building and Woodward's department store in Gastown. This scheme proposed a pedestrian deck over the CP tracks on which were to be built fourteen high-rise mainly office slab blocks. Promoted by a consortium – of Marathon Realty (part of Canadian Pacific), Grosvenor-Laing (a British development-construction company), and two department stores – this ambitious project was held up by public protest over its potential impact on Gastown and the potential impacts of the freeways on the Downtown Eastside (Ley 1996: 235-37). Only a parking garage for Woodward's, a telecommunications centre, and a major office building were completed from the project in the 1970s. The latter, the 32-storey concrete-framed Granville Square designed by Francis Donaldson, was built over the railway tracks (see Plate 41). It included a bleak plaza enlivened only by a piece of public art that seems to satirize totemic high-rise redevelopment (Kalman et al. 1993: 85). But it did provide for a rapid transit stop, indicating city planners' turn to transit rather than freeways as the means of promoting and accessing downtown development (Gutstein 1975b: 162-63). The citizen campaigns against the freeways in Vancouver were a pointed expression of the changing political climate in the late 1960s and a testament to growing opposition to the kind of development favoured by the Non-Partisan Association and civic administrators.

TEAM's Planning Vision

The late 1960s saw a major public reaction against the scale, form, and quality of development downtown and in some of the suburban shopping centres. Public unease over the extensive freeway proposals was compounded by the demolition of historic buildings and questionable ethics in some develop-ment deals. In 1968, two political organizations formed to challenge the Non-Partisan Association. TEAM, The Electors Action Movement, had strong professional management and academic representation. The other opposi-tion group, calling itself the Confederation of Progressive Electors (COPE), was dominated by union officials and teachers with more socialist leanings. In the 1968 civic election, both challengers made inroads into the Non-Partisan majority. By the 1972 election, support for the Non-Partisan Association had waned sufficiently that all its candidates were defeated.

Between 1970 and 1972, TEAM Alderman Walter Hardwick and COPE Al-derman Harry Rankin became strong anti-development voices on council and helped pave the way for the Non-Partisan Association's defeat. In the August 1972 provincial election, a stunning New Democrat upset victory over the Social Credit signalled a major change in west coast politics. Vancouver vot-ers in the 1972 civic election opted for the moderate TEAM intellectuals and professionals rather than the COPE socialists to replace the Non-Partisan in-cumbents. Eight TEAM aldermen and a TEAM mayor were elected, ending thirty-seven years of Non-Partisan control. This victory has been largely cred-ited to the loss of faith in the Non-Partisan Association by downtown devel-opment interests and Westside middle-class voters, who were looking for a more considered and ordered approach to growth and redevelopment of their city.

A New Planning Regime

TEAM made significant changes to the way Vancouver was managed, strength-ening the mayor's role, and giving council committees more influence – though not control – over their departments. Among the most significant immediate changes were the dismissal of Gerald Sutton Brown (as city manager) and Bill Graham (as planning director); a transfer of powers away from the Board of Administration to the mayor, committee chairs, city manager, and depart-ment heads; and an opening up of city hall meetings to the general public and citizen delegations. Alderman Walter Hardwick, a University of British Columbia geography professor first elected in 1970, noted that TEAM was "committed to see political leadership wrest direction of civic affairs away from the bureaucracy and leave it to its rightful function of managing pro-gram implementation" (Hardwick 1994: 342). One of Hardwick's major plat-forms was the promotion of a livable city through good planning practice; toward this goal, he recommended the reorganization of city planning prac-tices and the appointment of a new planning director to implement them. His choice was Ray Spaxman, whose watchword for development in Toronto had been neighbourliness. Each man has put his particular stamp on the city's reformed planning system and its cityscape. But both were also creatures of the mid-seventies conjunction of Vancouver politics, community aspirations, and design thinking.

One early TEAM project was the turning of Granville Street into a mall, an attempt to revitalize a street badly affected by conflicts between heavy pedestrian and vehicular traffic, as well as drug dealing, prostitution, and petty crime. Businesses on Granville had campaigned for tougher police action on the street reputed as Canada's "roughest main drag." Under the Non-Partisan administration, the social planning department had been given responsibility for action on the social issues and, in 1972, a special joint committee was established to study the feasibility of a mall to revive business. At the same time approvals were given for underground links below Granville Street between the Vancouver and Pacific shopping centres and the completion of Eaton's and the Pacific Centre, thereby draining the street of its retail interests. The TEAM council committed itself to turn Granville into a transit mall, using the Nicollet Mall in Minneapolis as a model. Sidewalks were widened to create a two-way bus lane but merchants were reluctant to have public benches or bus shelters included, as these might encourage loitering and anti-social behaviour. Despite this opposition, they were installed in 1976. Police patrols were doubled and controls on massage parlours, street vendors, and window displays were simultaneously tightened (Gutstein 1974-75: 24). The Granville Mall was not, however, a success, despite initial improvements in business and the greater efficiency of transit – the mall could accommodate 100 bus movements an hour. The removal of retail businesses underground, and the arrival of single-room occupancy hotels being ousted from areas such as Gastown as they were refurbished, meant that transient inner-city residents mingled with shoppers and theatre-goers (Vancouver 1985b). For the next thirty years Granville continued to be the street where marginalized and mainstream Vancouver residents met. No beautification project or other manipulation of the public realm could obviate the inevitable tensions that gave the street its edge, and much of its appeal, especially to the young (see Figure 50).

TEAM's planning agenda was broad and diverse, embracing neighbourhood planning, affordable housing, heritage protection, transit provision, and enhancement of the built environment. But initially it was primarily focused on the improved control and better design of major development downtown. This required reform of the permitting process, new plans and guidelines for downtown, an effective urban design policy, and heritage conservation initiatives. (Other major concerns are the subject of Chapter 3).

Initial reforms tackled visual blight in the downtown and commercial areas. The first target was sign ordinances, removing the worst abuses, and developing more appropriate regulations for individual neighbourhoods. Alderman Hardwick began to formulate an urban design policy through a series of discussion papers (Vancouver 1973) and meetings with the general public and special interest groups. Emerging general themes included the need for more comfort, amenities, and space at street level; the elimination of street-level parking; and an end to the rules preventing residential development downtown. Design consultants were retained to develop these ideas, and The Environmental Analysis Group led by Gerald Davis was also asked to produce bylaws through which the city might control the design of development and beautify the downtown area. These consultants dissected the existing planning powers, seeing the potential for overlapping a set of discretionary controls for improving design quality with the traditional land-use and building-dimension regulations of the zoning bylaw. They recognized that 1966 amendments to the downtown zoning (CM-2 for commercial development) – which permitted design review of developments that maximized the floor-space ratio – could lead to the more sophisticated system of guidelines and discretionary design control sought by the TEAM councillors (Vancouver 1974a).

Reforms to permit processing began with an interim bylaw to bring all development permits and licences under the control of the director of planning. Another bylaw turned the Architectural Advisory Panel into the Urban Design Panel, strengthening its advisory role to city council and the director of planning. The revamped Technical Planning Board was to decide on major applications, and planning groups from areas affected by proposed developments were invited to comment early in the application process. These positive but incomplete reforms contributed to debates about the procedures and composition of advisory and decision-making bodies, which continued until the end of 1974; at that time, new proposals were put forward and largely accepted by city council (Vancouver 1974c). By then, Ray Spaxman had become the new director of planning responsible for shaping reformed structures and processes.

A New Director of Planning

Ray Spaxman brought to Vancouver his extensive experience of neighbourhood planning and public participation in Toronto, and valuable architect-planner experience in England. Aware of the increasing significance of design, he was committed to working with people and neighbourhoods. And he was determined to create a strong planning department with adequate resources that could distance itself from developers' interests, establish independence within the city bureaucracy, and provide clear advice to the city council.

Gutstein described him as a "strong, politically aware, ambitious planner" (1974-75: 146).

Spaxman was quick to focus, redirect, and restructure the City of Vancouver planning department and to appreciate the work undertaken by TEAM-directed consultants. Through 1974 and 1975 there were numerous initiatives, reports, and policy statements that started to define a new permitting system for development control, as well as different processes for generating plans, guidelines, and neighbourhood initiatives. The Vancouver Charter provided for municipal preparation of official development plans, but this provision had not been used until Spaxman's arrival. The preparation of official development plans for False Creek South (1974) and downtown (1975) was backed by new zoning ordinances and, in the case of downtown, innovative design guidelines. The planning department's analysis explained that: "The objective of the new zoning can be summed up in the word 'neighbourliness.' Sunlight preservation, view protection, privacy, topographic adaptation, tree preservation, social and recreational amenities, safe parking garages – all these things are deemed to be part of this neighbourliness" (Vancouver 1981b: 2). Spaxman, using the Roman architect Vitruvius's concepts, noted that the "commodity and firmness" were left to the regulations while the "delight" was pursued through the guidelines and careful design negotiations (interview).

Beyond the development of citywide planning goals and policies, other major planning initiatives under Spaxman and the TEAM council included taking up the new federal programs for neighbourhood improvement and rehabilitation; the introduction of annual goal statements and work programs, and published reviews and evaluations of the department's work. Through the 1970s and early 1980s, discretionary zoning was progressively introduced in downtown, False Creek South, uptown on both sides of Broadway, in the neighbourhoods west and south of Broadway, and parts of Grandview–Woodland. The clamour for similar controls in the more affluent residential areas was about to begin. But the initial focus of the planning department's work was on downtown development planning and controls and, in April 1974, council funded the department to begin an intensive new planning program.

A New Planning Approach Downtown

Work began immediately through the downtown study team, headed by the planning director, to prepare an official development plan with a new set of development controls. Also involved was Gerald Davis's consulting company, which had been seeking ways to improve planning and design bylaws. By July they had made astonishing progress, developing policies, design guidelines, and controls that were a model of clear thinking. The results formed the basis not only for the 1975 downtown plan but for the whole approach to planning until the end of the century (Vancouver 1974a). The downtown study team was careful to identify the planning values that Vancouver had established implicitly and explicitly through more recent consultations with the public on downtown. The study sought to articulate these values as a set of planning principles or ways of working. Criteria by which their achievement of these goals and principles could be measured would be established through guidelines – some mandatory, some optional – but all backed by floor-space incentives. The expression of these outcomes in the new downtown plan and their implementation is discussed in the next chapter.

A supplementary report released in September by the downtown study team proposed a working committee to manage permit processing and consultations and negotiations on development applications, recommending "a mandatory preliminary dialogue at the concept proposal stage" (Vancouver 1974c: 14). The working committee could submit recommendations on each application to a proposed independent urban development board to be composed of senior civic officials not in the planning department for decision. The study team report carefully rehearsed arguments for and against regulatory versus discretionary controls. The report noted that regulatory control tended to produce uniformity and monotony, and to encourage developers to meet only the minimum requirements. Discretionary controls had the potential to encourage higher standards of design, although they could, the study team acknowledged, produce unpredictable outcomes, follow personal prejudices, and increase administrative costs and resources. Through the report's recommendations – to retain the legally defined standards and quantities in zoning but to add explicit guidelines against which planners, design experts, and the general public could evaluate proposals during review (Vancouver 1974e) – the key aspect of Vancouver's unique discretionary system was defined.

Reforms to Development Review Process

At the end of 1974, Vancouver council approved the abolition of the Technical Planning Board and the establishment of a new three-person Development Permit Board chaired by the planning director and including the city engineer, the medical officer of health, and the director of permits and licences (Figure 6). The board would meet in public and keep minutes of its proceedings, an innovation that could provide transparency to its decisions. To work with this board, council also added an advisory panel made up of two representatives each from the development industry, the design professions, and the general public as an important move to create a more open and participatory process and to balance the views of the administration. The

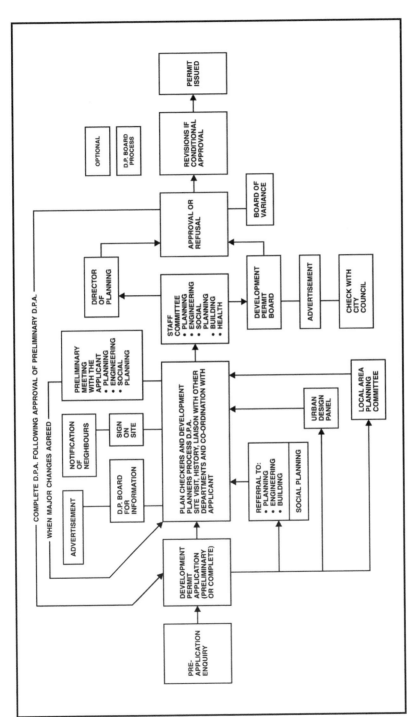

Figure 6 The development permit process, 1975–80 (*Source:* Redrawn from Vancouver [1981b])

advisory panel was to be polled for its opinions but decision making was left to the board. The board was not empowered to delay a development project if it met the provisions of the zoning bylaw, the official development plan, and design guidelines – nor to approve a development if it failed to meet these regulations. Conditions imposed by the board on development to control aspects of design and other planning matters became an important feature of the permitting process. The board itself was to handle only a small proportion of applications – the largest and most controversial – while about 95 percent would be managed solely by the planning director and staff. The Development Permit Board was empowered to consider applications in downtown, the West End, Downtown East, the central waterfront, False Creek, and Central Broadway (uptown) – the latter added when these proposals were approved as bylaw 4876 in June 1975. Applications outside these areas – and those which would not have a significant effect on the environment, traffic, surroundings, heritage buildings, or public amenities – were delegated to the planning director to resolve. The TEAM council thus brought into being a design-sensitive permitting system that could be efficient and free from day-to-day political interference.

The new boards first met in October 1975. By 1980, the jurisdiction of the Development Permit Board was extended to major applications citywide. Decisions of the board could be appealed to the Board of Variance, which provided the all-important check on the exercise of discretionary controls in the review process. Applications of particular significance or with a difference of expert opinions could be referred to council for further advice. Council specified that "controversial matters on design" not be referred to it, however, preferring that the board make a decision after receiving guidance from the Urban Design Panel (Vancouver 1979d).

Injecting Urban Design into Planning Policy

The Urban Design Panel was created in 1973 by broadening the mandate of the Architectural Advisory Panel established in 1956 to give "impartial, professional advice to the Director of Planning, Development Permit Board or city council on any proposal or policy affecting the community's physical environment" (Vancouver 1996y). In particular, the advice sought included evaluations of development permit and rezoning applications, civic works, and the formulation of design policy. The panel's focus on urban design was defined to include "the design and interrelationship of all physical components of the city" (Vancouver 1996y). Council appointed thirteen experts, each for two years, eight of whom constituted a quorum for each meeting of the panel. Six of the appointees were members of the Architectural Institute of British Columbia, while two others were drawn from each of the provincial bodies for professional engineers and for landscape architects. Other appointees represented the Vancouver Planning Commission, the planning director, and the director of permits and licences (Vaughan 1984: 7). The Urban Design Panel provided high-quality, authoritative, and independent design expertise to council on some two hundred applications annually, operating at the cost of about one junior planner's salary. Through the panel, the planning department built bridges with other design professionals, gaining wider understanding and respect for their policies and procedures within the design community. Neither the planning director nor council was required to accept the panel's recommendations; should they consistently ignore the expertise they had solicited, however, the professionals involved could express their criticisms in public, thereby undermining the legitimacy of civic planning decisions.

An urban designer was appointed in 1974 to work alongside a planner on the downtown plan. This designer supported the independent Urban Design Panel and took on such specific beautification projects as the sign guidelines for Gastown and Chinatown and the development of the city's heritage program. By 1976, the urban design complement of the planning department – increased to three – contributed to design guidelines for family housing and an ill-fated competition for small lot design-and-build housing. The urban design group was to have delivered an overall design policy framework for the city; however, lack of staff resources and increasing day-to-day work pressures meant that, by 1978, only the first three reports of a city patterns study were completed (Vancouver 1979e). These papers were much preoccupied with the overall image of the city and distilled four urban design values: clarity and understandability (derived from the work of Kevin Lynch 1960); comfort, safety, and usability; uniqueness; and diversity with order and vice versa (French 1977). Although Vancouver's planning department clearly had ambitions to produce a range of design studies similar to those undertaken in San Francisco in the late 1960s (see Punter 1999a), it did not have the necessary resources and was forced to be much more pragmatic (see Appendix 3).

TEAM's vision for a contemporary planning system for Vancouver was implemented through reforms to permit processing; refinement of discretionary zoning; and the introduction of new design goals, guidelines, and expertise. The fourth major contribution by TEAM was the activation of official development plans to guide major redevelopment. The Vancouver Charter enabled the city to create its own system of official development plans for the whole metropolis, particular areas, or large redevelopment projects. The first of Vancouver's nine existing official development plans were prepared for False Creek South (1974) and downtown (1975). They introduced a sophisticated set of planning controls, including both mandatory and interpretive requirements. Council had to enact a bylaw to adopt an official development plan or to revise it, but the powers that such plans afforded were largely unlimited. They included the authority to acquire land necessary to carry them out and the responsibility to ensure that any development was "not contrary to or at variance with" an approved plan. In the case of False Creek South the plan included design principles. In the downtown plan, a set of "character area" design guidelines were adopted to accompany the plan (see Chapter 3).

False Creek South: TEAM's Planning Exemplar

The False Creek South redevelopment project was the brainchild of TEAM Alderman Walter Hardwick. With fellow University of British Columbia Professor Wolfgang Gerson (architecture), Hardwick had used the site for a major student project in 1965. The results showed how False Creek could be transformed from an obsolete industrial area around a largely polluted inlet to a high-quality, mixed-use area, and this became part of TEAM's plans. A special committee for this development, chaired by Hardwick, had been formed under the Non-Partisan council early in 1972 and, when TEAM took power later that year, this committee pushed ahead with plans for the south side of False Creek. (The north side was owned by Marathon, the land and property division of Canadian Pacific, which had very ambitious high-density redevelopment plans for that area [Gutstein 1975b: 49], as discussed in Chapter 5.) By 1974 an official development plan with a set of design guidelines had been prepared. To obtain much of the land, the city negotiated with the provincial government to undertake necessary land swaps. Land on Burnaby Mountain – which the province desired for its development of Simon Fraser University – was exchanged so that the city gained title to the land between the Granville and Cambie bridges. Thompson, Berwick, Pratt & Partners were appointed to prepare a preliminary scheme, and development began in 1975 (Kalman et al. 1993: 129).

Various public-private partnerships were considered for the False Creek redevelopment by the city. The final decision was that the city required returns only to cover its land assembly and servicing costs, so it could use its market disposals to subsidize sites for non-market federally sponsored housing. The city also decided not to sell development sites but to dispose of them on sixty-year leases, retaining ownership over the entire project. Leaseholders understood that they could renew their leases or purchase their property at market value. Council made the further decision not to entrust this development scheme to their fully engaged planning and property departments; instead, a project development manager, E. Douglas Sutcliffe, was appointed, with the False Creek special committee acting as a board of directors. Hardwick notes that this resulted in "strong political leadership ... combined with sub-stantial managerial experience" (1994: 352). Together, they managed the im-plementation of the project.

The Design Philosophy and Its Implementation

False Creek South included public amenities such as parks and the seawall, and several cooperative and private housing schemes. The three main design principles for the project were a social mix to reflect the diversity of incomes in the greater Vancouver region, enclaves of clustered housing to promote social contact, and a hierarchy of open space – from private yards to semi-private open areas – linked by paths to a large public park (Figure 7). High-rise living – like that which had engulfed the West End – was specifically rejected and priority was given to family housing. The official development plan for the central section of the site was drawn up first (Vancouver 1974c). This early phase included two areas of development: the low-rise family-housing Spruce neighbourhood to the west and the medium-rise mixed life-style Heather neighbourhood to the east, each subdivided into three or four distinct enclaves (Plate 3).

The design guidelines for False Creek's south shore – largely prepared by consultants Richard Mann – have been described as "a quite deliberate and unusually direct transfer of prevalent social science theses concerning the

Plate 3 False Creek Housing Cooperatives, Fairview Slopes, and uptown. On the south side of False Creek, the cluster developments of the first phase of False Creek South nestle into Charleson Park, with the Fairview Slopes townhouses behind. Vancouver General Hospital looms behind, with the Broadway Office Centre, an early brutalist insertion, and the moderne City Hall (upper left).

Figure 7 False Creek South Plan: design guidelines, 1974
(abbreviated and paraphrased extract)

Neighbourhood enclaves

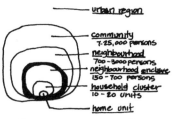

- form separate enclaves of residential use, perhaps no more than 500 feet (166 metres) across
- shape round neighbourhoods with length never more than twice the width
- establish a community forum within each enclave
- ensure adaptability, i.e., unbuilt spaces for future use
- allow communities to flow over traffic arteries
- create pedestrian activity focus
- place a natural pedestrian thoroughfare through public places
- shape development to provide vistas of natural amenities or other urban reference points
- ensure social mix by combining various household types in adjacent enclaves
- use level streets to ensure "browsing"
- make streets subtly convex to create usable spaces
- raise pedestrians above cars, and houses above the street to create privacy
- create usable, visually accessible courtyards with private areas
- build public outdoor rooms

Residential design guidelines

- build townhouses, garden apartments, and multi-storey building types
- build studio to 3+ bedroom units
- avoid bridge shadows and ensure development is of adequate scale in adjacent areas
- build residential clusters focused on open space
- avoid overshadowing, and ensure taller buildings have visually interesting and apparently receding upper floors
- ensure flat roofs are accessible and landscaped
- ensure each dwelling has an intimate "natural" view, a neighbourhood glimpse of community life, and a distant view of the sea or the mountains
- ensure the most frequently used habitable rooms receive sunlight
- make habitable outdoor spaces (including balconies) at least 6 feet (2 metres) square
- where high-rise buildings face each other, ensure deep balconies
- above grade, provide "earth balconies" to allow gardening
- ensure every unit has an identifiable front entrance
- give each doorway and entrance an appropriate transition

Source: Redrawn from Vancouver (1974c)

built environment" (Cybriwsky et al. 1986: 112). They were fully endorsed by the academics on the TEAM council. The design sought to encourage social mix and community interaction through the creation of small residential enclaves, drawing directly on *Cells for Subcultures*, Christopher Alexander's forerunner to *A Pattern Language* (1977). Each enclave was to be small – parcels with a maximum diameter of 153 metres (500 feet) – to foster opportunities for social contact and a sense of belonging. Focused on communal spaces, they were to be separated from one another by parks, schools, or pedestrian paths (see Figure 8). The guidelines also subsumed ideas from Gans (1962, 1968), Jacobs (1961), McHarg (1969), Lynch (1960), and Cullen (1961) to reflect the progressive – almost utopian – urban design approaches that Hardwick and Gerson had advocated in their 1965 student project (Hardwick 1994).

The Spruce and Heather neighbourhoods were separated by a large park occupying most of the waterfront and extending into each of the residential enclaves and along the public seawall. On the seawall Henriquez & Todd designed a scheme of mono-pitch tiled roof townhouses and an award-winning elementary school (Kalman et al. 1993: 132). The Spruce neighbourhood to the west of the park included three sets of linked townhouses clustered around internal streets, and play and sitting out areas. As elsewhere in the project, the landscaping was generous and lush, so much so that the interior spaces now require some thinning to let in more sunlight. Other enclaves used similarly complex forms executed with contrasting materials, with balconies and small enclosed gardens, and car parking underneath. One set of units used timber siding and brown-tiled roofs, the other concrete and stucco and red-profiled metal roofs.

In the Heather neighbourhood to the east of the park, much more use was made of exposed concrete. A 3-storey complex of condominiums – designed by Rhone & Iredale 1975-77 with strong planar features, high-tech detailing, and fully glazed upper storeys – broke away from the original design conceptions but still provided a very urbane frontage to the shoreline. Around the marina to the east, the project architects developed a much denser scheme at Leg-in-Boot Square as the commercial centre of the project (see Plate 4). There, 5 storeys of apartments were located above ground-level retail units lining the walkways, offering a European feel and focus to the project, though its architecture and use of concrete was less distinguished. On the western edge of the Heather enclave a well landscaped cream stucco 3-storey townhouse complex was developed, designed by Thompson, Berwick, Pratt & Partners 1975-77, with decks and balconies and "a village-like intimacy" (Kalman et al. 1993: 132) (see Plate 5).

The first phase of False Creek South is remarkable for its low-rise nature and generosity of open space. Only 40 percent of the site was taken for

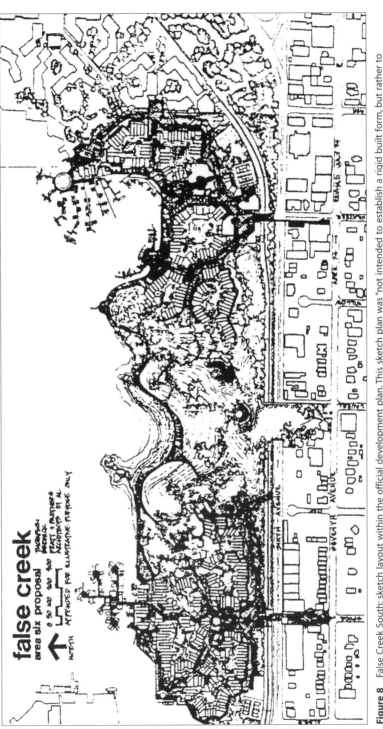

Figure 8 False Creek South: sketch layout within the official development plan. This sketch plan was "not intended to establish a rigid built form, but rather to communicate the development character" and a continuous public walkway at the water's edge. It had already been amended to replace housing with parkland at Heather Point (centre right). (*Source:* Vancouver (1974a))

development, while 47 percent was allocated to two large parks. Net densities were kept high (although they were not to exceed 100 units per hectare [40 units per acre] but gross densities were very low for an inner-city site. It was a classic demonstration of cluster development maximizing public space and waterfront access while creating intimate courtyards and play and sitting areas within housing enclaves to serve local residents.

Plate 4 Leg-in-Boot Square and Millbank, False Creek South. The denser, more urbane character of the later phase of this development is evident as it wraps around the marina and provides a small retail focus for the community.

Plate 5 Sawcut Street, False Creek South. The design of the western end of the second phase had much in common with the first. These intricate and animated townhouses look out over Charleson Park and are richly landscaped front and back (another Thompson, Berwick, Pratt & Partners design).

Evaluation of False Creek South's Early Phase

The essentially democratic, public amenity-oriented design principles, with strong social engineering and community planning components, were the subject of professional and political debate at the time. The federal government commissioned a post-occupancy evaluation of this early phase before it was completed: it revealed that the project was achieving the desired social mix but not always providing adequate visual and aural privacy. The study showed that semi-private spaces, which were the focus for the enclaves, were differentially but generally under-used, while the park and seawall were very well used and widely enjoyed. The evaluation concluded that the close-grained social mix did not enhance residents' experience of environmental quality; that residents might prefer "less personal, more anonymous, possibly higher density site plan[s]" than that provided by the enclaves; and that privacy was as important as community in the design of gradations of public space (Vischer 1983: 121). These important conclusions provided a justification for much higher density housing development on the north side of False Creek in the 1990s.

A comparison of redevelopment in False Creek South and in the St. Lawrence neighbourhood of Toronto shows particularly striking similarities and differences (Hulchanski 1984). St. Lawrence was the Toronto reformers' showpiece project, twice the size of False Creek South (3,750 homes). Driven by the housing department as the first project in its new moderate- and low-cost housing program, St. Lawrence was an equally interesting collaboration between local planners, design consultants, and ten architectural practices that were each given commissions for individual blocks. The planning process was even more open and democratic than that of False Creek South. Both communities had a mix of public and private development, densities, income, lifestyle, and aspirations for use. But in Toronto the historic context of the location – just to the east of the original townsite – was paramount, alongside the reassertion of the social importance of the street as a driving force for the design. The architectural sameness, unrelieved red-orange brick finishes, and European *grande allée* open space of St. Lawrence have been criticized. But the development provided many precedents for subsequent non-market housing initiatives that were both urbane and sensitive to city neighbourhoods in their design. It certainly set the high-water mark for social inclusion with 55 percent non-market, non-profit housing – similar to False Creek South. Densities for St. Lawrence – more than twice those in False Creek South – were much more useful as prototypes. In design terms, False Creek South is more of an escapist (sub)urban village, an engineered community epitomizing TEAM's strong commitment to parkland and the provision of public amenities on the waterfront. Conversely, its social-mix targets have proven to be lasting legacies capable of being imposed on private developers even if its net and gross densities had to be trebled in subsequent projects (see Figure 45 and Chapter 7).

Subsequent phases of False Creek South were developed under sub-area official plans using the same design guidelines. The area immediately west of the Spruce neighbourhood and the area to the south of Burrard Bridge were both added to the plan in 1976, with the area in between planned in 1981 and the area east of the Heather neighbourhood in 1982. Much less design intervention and social engineering was planned for all four areas, and there was significantly less emphasis on public amenities; net densities remained similar (35 to 65 dwelling units per hectare). All four areas feel significantly denser, however, because parkland had to be more constrained.

All later phases of False Creek redevelopment were more market driven and less utopian than the early phases. They lack the architectural distinction and the intricate site planning of the Heather and Spruce neighbourhoods, and they provide a neutral backdrop to the seawall and the park behind Granville Island. Collectively, they complete one of Vancouver's major public amenities: a park network with a system of well-landscaped bike and pedestrian paths across the south side of False Creek, linking to Vanier Park on the west and the Cambie Bridge on the east (see Plates 4 and 5).

Granville Island

To many visitors the crowning glory of False Creek South is the federal government's Granville Island project, the sensitive redevelopment of an old industrial area underneath the dramatic southern viaduct and pier of the Granville Bridge. One of the early conceptions for the island was for a park resembling Tivoli Gardens in Copenhagen, but the federal government opted for a commercial, arts, and entertainment area. The Central (now Canada) Mortgage and Housing Corporation (CMHC) commissioned the site planners of the False Creek development to prepare a concept plan and strategy (Figure 9). The plan recommended that a board of trustees oversee the development under the federal body.

CMHC bought out most of the industrial leases, retaining the most noxious but most visually interesting, the Canada Cement plant. Under the board's direction, the overall concept plan was developed with Norman Hotson Architects undertaking the urban design, the rehabilitation of the existing buildings and the creation of public space. Hotson's formative concepts were urbanity; space for creative artists, artisans, performers, and entrepreneurs; and active art and recreation (Seelig and Seelig 1990: 79-80). A careful selection of tenants ensured interest and vitality. The proposals retained as much of the reusable industrial elements as possible, including the rail lines in the

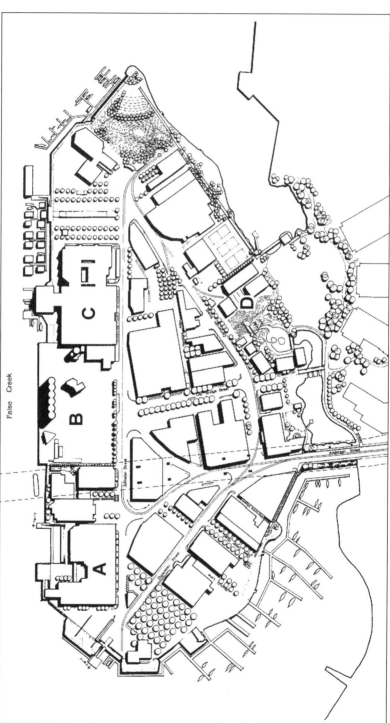

Figure 9 Granville Island. The public market (A) is the main attraction, adjacent to the retained cement works and its silos (B) which generates significant truck traffic. Emily Carr Institute of Art and Design (C) brings students into the area during the week, and a children's play area (D) is a major draw for families. The rest is a mix of festival shopping, artists studios, and eating and drinking establishments. (*Source:* Canada Mortgage and Housing Corporation)

streets. Deciding not to build sidewalks, the designer sought to encourage a complete mix of car and pedestrian access so that traffic moved very slowly. Public waterfront access was maximized. New buildings were in a robust industrial style with widespread use of corrugated metal sheeting and strong colours. And robust street furniture was built using heavy timber poles to reinforce the industrial character (Gourley 1988: 72-73) (see Plate 6).

The focus of the complex was a large public farmer's market with an indoor-outdoor all-season flexibility that allows it to spill out on to the streets and parking areas in warmer weather. As the project's generator, the market is housed in six early-twentieth-century single-storey warehouses that were retro-fitted and unified with canopies and awnings on cedar poles consistent with the street furniture. Other successful industrial conversions were architecturally distinguished. The Emily Carr Institute of Art and Design, by Howard/Yano, brought student life into the project daily. And the Granville Island Brewery designed by Boak Alexander took over and extended a building in the moderne style that is attached to one of the viaduct's massive concrete piers.

Visiting tourists, as well as urbanists, are inclined to cite Granville Island as their most memorable place in Vancouver. Part of this is a product of its dramatic setting at the narrowest point of False Creek beneath the sweeping

Plate 6 Granville Island from Granville Street Bridge. The public market (centre) is the generator of Granville Island and epitomizes the very functional and low-key recycling of the industrial buildings. The spectacular site has views down False Creek to the Burrard Bridge and English Bay. The public realm has an unsegregated, undifferentiated treatment.

viaduct of the Granville Bridge, with a backdrop of yacht clubs and architecturally spectacular apartment buildings on the Granville Slopes opposite (see Plate 22). But two factors make it a particular success. First, the design deliberately limited beautification, maintaining the small-scale industrial feel and unselfconscious atmosphere. Second, a tremendous vitality was achieved by combining artistic and cultural institutions with catering, festival, and market shopping, as well as mixing vehicular and pedestrian traffic to add to the bustle and activity. It well fulfills Norman Hotson's ambitions to create an atmosphere of "randomness, curiosity, delight, and surprise" (Kalman 1996: 859-60). For an outlay of a relatively modest $25 million, $11 million of which was spent buying out leases, the federal government had delivered a unique amenity for Vancouver. The Granville Island festival shopping complex managed – through urban design and proactive management – to avoid the theme park overstimulation or heritage quaintness to which similar projects in other cities have been prone.

David Ley's more profound reading of Granville Island emphasizes the transformation of a private industrial production site into a place of conspicuous public consumption and play:

> The island is carefully themed to convey the message of historic continuity. But it is the stability of still life that is on display, for what has occurred is an aestheticization, a taming of a once wild and vigorous industrial landscape. The visual environment now reveals contradiction, complexity and not a little parody, for beneath rough industrial shells are cultured postindustrial interiors. The only major problem of the island is its own success, the crowds and congestion drawn to share this experience. Granville Island is a quintessential public space in the postmodern city. (1996: 7)

Ley also notes that the island generates an excellent economic return for the various enterprises and for the federal government, the market itself performing twice as well as the most profitable shopping centre supermarket and attracting a large proportion of high-income consumers (1996: 304). For many visiting urbanists, Granville Island remains singular: it has an authenticity that other festival markets lack, Pike Place Market in Seattle being one of its few equals.

Fairview Slopes

False Creek South was a bold, publicly led and successful project, but the Vancouver planners faced much more familiar challenges from developers in the neighbourhoods upslope that overlooked False Creek. In the 1960s the Fairview Slopes between Broadway and 6th Avenue was a counterculture rooming-house district of decaying frame houses. Red-lined by mortgage companies, it was ripe for redevelopment, especially once the False Creek South plans were unveiled: they guaranteed an accessible, clean waterfront and large park as the foreground to splendid views across the downtown to the mountains. Fairview Slopes was rezoned in 1972 – not to high-density residential, as developers had requested, but to a medium-density mix of residential and commercial uses with building forms that would respect the contours of the site and maximize views. The Fairview Residents Association and Community Action Society (FRACAS) campaigned for a freeze on development, a downzoning to preserve the existing housing stock, and for federal funds to improve their neighbourhood. But the TEAM council ignored these aspirations, perhaps, as Gutstein points out, because three leading TEAM members were property owners in the area (1975a: 19). Instead, zoning bonuses were added in 1976 to encourage good design and the creation of semi-public landscaped space within each low-rise project and the provision of corridors northward to enhance residents' views of the mountains. These provided the incentives for larger-scale renewal and gentrification (Mills 1988: 173). A local planning committee was established to provide a measure of neighbourhood participation in the design of the area, which was attracting many young professionals.

One architectural critic has noted:

> Using a set of guidelines untested before implementation is always risky, and one is reminded that the success of discretionary zoning depends a lot on the discretion of those exercising it. In this case the basic density allowed was probably either too low or too high, with the result that a rather expensive form of development occurred, at the cost of many of the original buildings intended for preservation. (Gruft 1983: 320)

The area did attract a number of developers who retained young architects to produce high-quality schemes, several during the late 1970s and early 1980s winning architectural awards for imaginative responses to the steeply sloping sites. Among the most celebrated was James Cheng's townhouse complex on West 7th Avenue (see Plate 7). The architect has indicated that the flexibility of planning controls not yet in existence elsewhere in the city and the value of dialogue with residents contributed to the design: "What we learned was to try to create an urban streetscape that is beneficial to the community as a whole. Since then it has become an automatic consideration" (quoted in Vancouver 1981a). A second project by the same architect on the same street also won an award. Like the previous scheme it involved three groups of townhouses facing onto interior courtyards set at right angles to the street

Plate 7 730 West 7th Avenue, Fairview Slopes. James Cheng's townhouses, which won a Governor-General's award, look out on a semi-private courtyard running at right angles to the street.

with public walkways up the slopes. Each was built in brick but had different elevations, all more industrial in character than the earlier scheme. Another award winner was a warehouse conversion by Roger Hughes Architects, with contrasting postmodern additions on an internal street with landscape and courtyards and broad steps (Kalman et al. 1993: 143). Not all the developments were so successful and the area attracted a wide range of eclectic styles to match the new urban lifestyles (Ley 1987; Mills 1988).

In 1976 city planners generated urban design guidelines for Central Broadway immediately south of Fairview Slopes. This area was developing uptown characteristics, attracting significant office development with about 12 percent of the office space available downtown in 1974. A rezoning to mixed commercial (up to 3.0 floor-space ratio) with residential uses and special concerns about adjacent residential neighbourhoods was accompanied by guidelines developed by Norman Hotson to amplify general and citywide guidelines. Seven sub-areas were defined for uses, access and servicing, spaces, views, microclimate, and weather protection. Unfortunately, the guidelines have not done much to civilize Broadway as a street for shopping and services. They have failed to encourage either the mix of small-scale retail and catering, or the fine grain and human scale that makes other arterials such interesting streets (see Plate 8). More recent redevelopment has not

Plate 8 West Broadway at Oak Street, looking west along Broadway. It is clear that zoning (C-3A) and design guidelines have failed to deliver quality urban design and an attractive, vital public realm. The street's future depends on the transit investments that will be made on or under the street.

compensated for the drive-in plazas, boxy high rises, and drab architecture built before 1976.

Redevelopment of inner-city neighbourhoods elsewhere in Vancouver was less radical. With Ray Spaxman's commitment to neighbourhoods, planning programs were begun in several such areas before tensions arose between planners and politicians over the level of involvement by local residents. The head of the West End planning group quit in frustration over perceived political subversion of neighbourhood ambitions, and the Kitsilano residents organization was told that its desires for a zoning change to reduce density must await completion of the city's neighbourhood plan. What was described as a "well-publicized showdown" between TEAM politicians and the planning director resulted in something of a reprimand and a cutback in local area planning. In mid-1974, the TEAM council reduced its commitment to citizen participation in planning; many commentators, such as Gutstein (1974-75), argue that these events set the limits of devolved planning and urban reform in Vancouver.

Planning for Neighbourhood Improvement

In 1974 neighbourhood planning in Vancouver was given impetus by two major federal programs: the twelve-year Residential Rehabilitation Assistance and eight-year Neighbourhood Improvement Programs (RRAP and NIP). Federal funds provided for greatly expanded council staff resources in the planning department to administer these programs. By 1981 6,000 housing units had been rehabilitated in the poorer areas east and southeast of downtown under these programs. Kitsilano took nearly one-third of the grants, and more moderate income areas such as Riley Park and Mount Pleasant benefited disproportionately. Kensington, Grandview–Woodland, and Cedar Cottage also benefited. The $6 million of federal funds levered in as much again in provincial and city moneys, with significant capital funds from the city, the park board, and other agencies to add another $5 million to neighbourhood improvement. Council effectively adapted its local area planning to include neighbourhood rehabilitation that met federal program criteria, even though the objectives differed. Resulting tensions between ratepayers groups, who preferred better streets, parks, and community facilities and were generally opposed to non-market housing, and tenants groups, who sought low-income housing and daycare, were played out in project selection with the former generally prevailing (Gutstein 1975a: 19).

Area planning was well-established in the West End and Kitsilano by 1974 and programs were just commencing in Fairview and Mount Pleasant. Three areas also under active consideration were in the east of the city: the Downtown Eastside, Grandview–Woodland, and Cedar Cottage. Kitsilano proved to be a flashpoint. A West Broadway Citizens Committee was founded to oppose plans to revitalize the commercial strip of West Broadway and to create a regional shopping centre. This was the starting point of a concerted local campaign to prevent wholesale neighbourhood change and gentrification. In 1974, the city agreed to a significant rezoning to low-rise development. A concept plan was approved and a very successful federal residential rehabilitation program set up. Although public participation was a major plank of the federal program, the local citizens group withdrew from the process soon after it had begun, complaining of manipulation by city officials (Hasson and Ley 1994: 248). The group engaged in high-profile opposition to several development proposals.

The formation of a further residents group, Renters United for Secure Housing, to oppose redevelopment projects was followed quickly by establishment of the Kitsilano Housing Society to develop cooperative rather than private housing. Its first project at First and Maple, outbidding a condominium developer, was completed in 1976. One of the housing society's key advocates, Jacques Khouri, went on to found the Inner City Housing Society and to incorporate 25 co-ops delivering 1,200 units in Kitsilano and other parts of the city.

The West Broadway Citizens Committee pursued its campaign for more devolution of planning control to neighbourhood co-ops but was subverted in part by the council's unwillingness to delegate such decision making (Gutstein 1983a: 208). A change in the provincial government back to Social Credit robbed the group of its funding to pursue housing initiatives. Meanwhile the city's Kitsilano Neighbourhood Plan featured various improvements to be funded by a federal program, including community facilities, streets, and open spaces. There were also bonus provisions to encourage lower-cost housing units, an active rehabilitation program, and a scaling down of commercial development proposals. But the plan's approval by council effectively marked the end of an era for citizen activism and devolved planning controls in Kitsilano.

Evaluations in 1983 of the federal Neighbourhood Improvement Program in Vancouver revealed a diverse set of impacts and planning issues. Major improvements were seen in social services and school facilities in Grandview, the creation of state-of-the-art recreational and sports facilities in Kensington, the curbing of streets in Mount Pleasant, and all aspects of area appearance in Kitsilano. The experience of committees representing these neighbourhoods broadly echoed that described above in Kitsilano, with widespread dissatisfaction with the purely advisory role accorded to local communities. In all neighbourhoods, however, higher levels of awareness and better organization among residents resulted from the programs and from city planning initiatives, especially where planners had encouraged resident participation. Several area councils were set up to manage change – although few survived into the mid-1980s.

Multi-Family Housing

Many resident protests were provoked by the demolition of Craftsman houses and small frame houses and bungalows to make way for denser forms of housing. Typically, the new housing in Kitsilano and similar areas consisted of 3-storey flat-roofed apartments with balconies. Multi-family zoning (RM-3) applied across much of the area and the incentives to follow the design guidelines were significant. A floor-space ratio of 1.0 could be achieved as of right, but a ratio of 1.9 could be achieved by following the discretionary regulations. In a 1981 report on the successes of discretionary control (Vancouver 1981b), the planning department celebrated the particularly well massed and landscaped design of a twenty-unit apartment complex on Balsam in the Victorian Kitsilano style (see Plate 9). Local residents were similarly enthusiastic. Later schemes achieving architectural distinction included a group of eighteen 4-storey apartments completed in 1990 on West 2nd Avenue (see

Plate 9 1620 Balsam Street, Kitsilano. An early success for discretionary zoning, where the achievement of a floor-space ratio of 1.45 was conditional on good design. Setbacks and height limits were relaxed during the design negotiations to achieve this density on the steeply sloping site. The building relates very well to its three road frontages and demonstrates that significant intensification can be achieved without destroying the character of the locality.

Plate 10). Designed by Hughes Baldwin, this complex provided an exemplar in a modern idiom with curved roofs and balconies and full height windows (Kalman et al. 1993: 168). Most designs adapted vernacular elements for standard 3- to 4-storey walk-ups to retain a semblance of neighbourhood character and a traditional relationship to the street.

Within the inner suburbs north of 16th Avenue and west of Nanaimo, the remaining residential areas were zoned for residential multiple-housing units (RM). Where the general intent was to develop family housing compatible with the existing streetscape and amenities, and to include some mixed uses, the designation was RM-5. The most common zoning applied to the eastern part of Kitsilano north of Broadway and to the inner areas of Mount Pleasant and Grandview–Woodland was an RM-4 designation, which permitted medium density and a variety of multiple-dwelling types with noise mitigation required on specific streets. In much of Fairview north of Broadway, RM-3 zoning allowed medium density, with high-rise apartments permitted through incentives to improve parking, open space, and sunlight access – even though they rather disrupted residential streetscapes. A wide range of building types evolved to take advantage of these new zoning entitlements, and they provided increased numbers of units to meet the needs of smaller households, while still delivering the benefits of living in street-oriented, well-landscaped,

Plate 10 Seascapes, 2405 West 2nd Avenue, Kitsilano. This Hughes Baldwin award-winning design is one of the most imaginative apartment blocks in the area, choosing to treat the site as level and landscaping its boundaries with great care. Exploitation of the views and the distinctive floating roofs are key design elements.

medium-density neighbourhoods. City planners continually monitored evolving built forms and amenities, and the range of market responses to zoning changes to ensure livability (Vancouver 1983b, 1995k, and 1997m).

Vancouver's medium-density condominium units demonstrated a wide range of creative responses to neighbourhood character and the postmodern stylistic preferences of new householders. But, looking ahead, many medium-rise condos completed in the 1983-88 boom, particularly those that were timber-framed and stucco-clad, proved to leak rainwater. Neither traditionally built single-family houses nor high-rise concrete-framed structures experienced these problems. "Leaky condos," as they were termed, had inadequate screening against wind, water, and vapour, which was exacerbated by poor-quality materials, shoddy construction, and poorly designed detailing. While not confined to Vancouver, there was a sufficiently heavy concentration in the city to prompt federal and provincial government studies in the late 1990s. A provincial commission of inquiry reported the average cost per unit of repairs at $23,300 (1998 dollars), suggesting a total repair bill province-wide of between $650 million and $1 billion (British Columbia 1998), and described by one condominium manager as a "world-class disaster in a world-class city." The commission linked the problem firmly to issues related to cost-cutting in construction to maintain profit margins, priorities given to external styling over building performance, and the commodification of housing – marketing rather than workmanship. The reality was that all parties had forgotten the design constraints imposed by the mild weather and significant rainfall in Vancouver, which constitute a powerful argument for following traditional designs in a thoroughgoing rather than a superficial way. The leaky-condo phenomenon offered essential lessons for designers, developers, consumers, and regulators, especially in the links between design guidelines and building code provisions for multi-unit wood-frame housing.

Heritage Policy in Gastown and Chinatown

Heritage concerns were an integral part of TEAM's planning agenda and they loomed large in the planning of two particular neighbourhoods. But in their reforms of planning, there were many verbal commitments to more protection for the city's fast-disappearing historic buildings but little concerted action, perhaps because the authority to designate buildings and areas as historic was held by the province until 1974. During the protests against proposals to turn Carrall Street into a freeway through Chinatown–Strathcona and Gastown, protection of the heritage of these areas was an important issue. To intensify interest in heritage conservation, the Community Arts Council ran walking tours that celebrated Gastown's considerable architectural history, and an association that later became the powerful Downtown Eastside Residents Association was formed to save two low-cost single-room occupancy hotels. Similar activism in Chinatown was focused against federal urban renewal plans. The protests, led by the Strathcona Property Owners and Tenants Association, were particularly vociferous.

A certain amount of upgrading and restoration had begun in Gastown, the result of individual efforts and a council beautification initiative in 1968. In 1972, on the basis of recommendations in a consultants' report, the council requested the province designate 236 properties – largely on Water, Carrall, and Pender streets – as historic (Birmingham and Wood 1972). The designation of this district as historic has proven to be a mixed blessing because the informal regeneration by a diverse range of property owners, entrepreneurs, artists, and architects was supplanted by a formal large-scale beautification operation. This encouraged private investment but in the view of Robin Ward (Ward 1998e: 13) divorced the historic district "from mainstream city life ... [and] promoted a tourist image that has erased most of its authentic urban character."

Several recommendations in the consultants' restoration report were implemented, such as the concept of a series of public squares along Carrall Street. Maple Tree Square – at the junction of Water, Alexander, and Powell streets – was refurnished and repaved. The junction was graced with a statue

Plate 11 Water Street at Carrall Street, Gastown. The 1970s beautification of Water Street with its red paviors and Victorian street furniture was uncontroversial at the time, but is now the object of considerable criticism, not least because so many other heritage districts elsewhere have followed suit. The maturing of the trees has made it difficult to appreciate the heritage quality of the buildings.

of Gassy Jack, the keeper of the original saloon on the site in 1867. The beautification of Water Street included heritage paving, cast-iron bollards and chains, Victorianesque globe street lamps festooned with flower baskets, the planting of trees, and the removal of overhead wires. The final addition of a faux-Victorian steam clock completed what Ward has described as a "theme park revival" (1998e) (see Plate 11). In 1974, the city provided discretionary controls over signage as well as development. It imposed a 22.5 metre height limit on new buildings, a flawed idea, given the area's sawtooth skyline and very varied building heights (see Plate 53 and further discussion in Chapter 7).

In 1974 the province recognized "the need to put conservation into a more urban context" (Vancouver 1997j) and amended the Vancouver Charter to allow the city to designate historic buildings and to pass regulations governing their alteration. A second bylaw in 1974 established the Vancouver Heritage Advisory Committee to advise council on designations, alterations, and demolitions, and to advise the planning director on development and alteration permits. An inventory of historic buildings was initiated. Twenty buildings were designated in December 1974, and a further thirty in 1976 (Vancouver 1997j). Initially, designation required negotiation with owners, consultation with the public, recommendations from the planning director, formal notification in a public advertisement, and a hearing. But owners lobbied successfully to require that they be compensated if there was a loss in market value at the time of designation. This clause in the bylaw has shaped conservation practice in Vancouver, because it created what Kalman (interview) describes as the "quid pro quo process" whereby conservation, retention, or sensitive alteration of the original structure would be compensated by development bonuses and incentives to balance the costs incurred. Almost inevitably, conserved historic buildings are compromised by overdevelopment on the site or in the immediate locality. Ward has described the system as "all carrot and no stick," given council's unwillingness to designate heritage buildings without the owners' consent because of fears of compensation claims emanating from a clause in the 1977 provincial heritage legislation. This helps to explain why designations have been limited – only 103 buildings or sites by 1997 (Ward 1998e).

By contrast with Gastown, the imposition of heritage designation and design guidelines in adjacent Strathcona–Chinatown provoked controversy among property owners and merchants, and revealed some fundamental contradictions in design regulation. The initial response within the community on learning that their area had been designated historic was that the community was being subjected to an additional level of bureaucratic control. Plans for beautification of the area drawn up by city planners caused considerable mirth because they were so contrived (Hasson and Ley 1994: 128). Early in 1973, businesses in the area had formed the Chinatown Property Owners and Merchants Association, which was more interested in parking than beautification. The local design proposal – to build free-standing canopies to provide shelter for pedestrians along three blocks of Pender Street – was not well received by the planners. A compromise to create additional parking sites in return for a joint beautification scheme failed because the local association would not commit funds to the project. Rezoning, historic area designation, accompanying design guidelines, and the establishment of a Chinese Historic Area Planning Committee all tried to reinforce the conservation ethic and apparent "Chinese" character of the area (see Plate 12). Local merchants, however, were reluctant to "conform to copies of tourist photos of temples in Asia" and "museumized" versions of Chinese facades (quoted in Hasson and Ley 1994: 130).

The city had to scale down its streetscaping plans, but by 1975 the Chinatown planning committee had campaigned to get seventy-five Pender Street merchants to contribute a total of $300,000 to "orientalize" their area with special street furniture, lantern lighting, tree planting, curbing, new sidewalks, and crosswalks. This was completed in 1980. In a parallel venture, a Chinese

Plate 12   23-59 East Pender Street, Chinatown. Typical heritage-listed commercial buildings in Chinatown with their recessed and highly glazed frontages and balconies. They provide small, inexpensive office and shop premises that allow enterprises to incubate, and their protection featured strongly in the Chinatown design guidelines.

Cultural Centre and an adjacent classical Chinese garden were proposed, which could not be implemented until the federal government committed funds in 1977. The design for the cultural centre by James Cheng and Romses, Kwan & Associates disappointed the area planner because of the lack of Chinese architectural features on the facade. The planner's suggestions to increase the "Chinese" content – a recessed entrance balcony, bright colours, stepped gable walls, signage – were incorporated into revised designs. A traditional Chinese-made gate from Expo '86 was incorporated into the design to provide a screen on Pender Street. Next door, a full-scale classical Chinese garden of the Ming Period was built as a public park (Kalman et al. 1993: 36).

The irony of foisting traditional Chinese architectural features on reluctant merchants of Chinese and other Asian ancestries seems to have been lost on planners and government officials who saw the conservation of Chinatown as part of a cultural preservation project (Anderson 1988: 44). The irony intensified in the mid-1980s when contemporary Chinese aesthetics and *feng shui* began to be applied in Vancouver's more affluent suburbs – provoking existing residents to request new forms of discretionary zoning to protect their heritage (see Chapter 4).

By the early 1980s, city planners were recognizing that neighbourhood protection and enhancement measures were, if anything, intensifying gentrification by making inner areas even more attractive for high-income households. Some planners were concerned that rehabilitation, increased amenities, and enhanced design were being achieved at the expense of affordability and efficiency (McAfee 1983). A review of neighbourhood planning efforts since 1974 was initiated but became overtaken by events. By 1986 an unmistakable shift occurred in area planning away from mixed inner-city neighbourhoods toward single-family housing and the threats posed by unneighbourly houses that maximized their zoning entitlement (Vancouver city planning department annual report 1987: 11). By then, the Non-Partisan Association had returned to power and the phenomenon of the "monster" house was disturbing the affluent west- and southside neighbourhoods, the Non-Partisan electoral heartlands. Planning initiatives to address this issue then became a political priority (see Chapter 4).

TEAM's Planning Accomplishments, 1972-78

The election victory for the reformers of TEAM did not mark a profound break with the politics of development of the postwar era, but it did signal a desire to much more carefully and consciously manage redevelopment and the reshaping of the city. TEAM councillors, notably Walter Hardwick, were determined to create a much more professional and politically accountable planning process to deliver urban design objectives. The appointment of Ray Spaxman was an inspired decision, as he provided strong leadership for the planning department, encouraging it to develop effective control processes and an ambitious neighbourhood planning program. Within three years of assuming power, TEAM had transformed planning practices and laid the basis for the discretionary control process that has served Vancouver so well since.

While the TEAM council was determined to wrest the direction of policy away from the old bureaucracy - particularly the degree of control wielded by the city manager – it did not wish to interfere in the management of planning programs or the everyday tasks of development control. So once council had defined the direction of policy, it delegated decision-making powers to the planning director, subject to a system of checks and balances and due process. In this way, other departments, members of the development industry, the general public, and design professionals could contribute to decisions and monitor deliberations. Although these processes and practices have been hotly contested, particularly through the 1980s (as discussed in Chapter 8), they have been progressively refined and improved. Council has not intervened in actual decisions, allowing the regulations and guidelines to set out the requirements and enabling planners to exercise their skills. In this way, TEAM significantly increased the predictability and professionalism of the process.

The TEAM planning regime put in place a development control process that was transparent and clearly based on policy and guidelines. Instituting review of major permit applications by the Urban Design Panel not only enhanced the quality of design, but helped build a closer-knit community of architects and planners. The benefits of discretionary review were clear to many neighbourhood groups, to staff planners, and to some designers and developers. It was beginning to show major successes, not only with downtown commercial development but with new award-winning residential projects in areas such as Fairview Slopes and even small-scale commercial schemes (Vancouver 1981b). Council showed little reluctance to extend such controls throughout the city, expanding the area of operation of the Development Permit Board. But prominent development interests, certain councillors, and city managers contested the process at almost every turn, climaxing in a mini-crisis in 1983 and 1984, when the success rate of appeals exceeded 50 percent (see Chapter 8). TEAM also backtracked on its commitment to return Vancouver to a ward electoral system, in which each councillor represents a particular area of the city.

The general picture painted of planning in Vancouver in the 1970s is of major reforms changing the direction of planning practice and steadily improving the quality of development in the city, with notable successes like False Creek South and Granville Island, and mixed outcomes in the inner residential neighbourhood. However, there is another dimension, revealed in the planning director's annual reviews, 1974-78, of constant struggles to resource major planning initiatives, and of a rearguard action against those looking for a return to the unfettered development regime of the past. The next chapter describes the evolution of the downtown official development plan and how design control was applied downtown, using both plan and guidelines. It looks at conservation concerns in and around town, and how city planning generally was affected by TEAM's reduced majority in 1974, and changes in the political nature of council thereafter.

3
Creating a Livable Central Area, 1975-91

The late 1970s and the 1980s were a volatile period in Vancouver's planning and development history, as the city enjoyed an economic and property development boom from 1978 to 1981, a bust from 1982 to 1985, then a second boom in 1989. In 1975 council approved a downtown official development plan that was very optimistic in its commercial development projections but remarkably flexible in its ability to adapt to different economic circumstances. However, the extent of commercial zoning proved problematic as residential rather than commercial property investment led the market. In the middle of the 1980s Vancouver became drawn into the global property market, as Asian immigration and investment impacted on the city's commercial and residential condominium markets.

As development pressure intensified and property inflated in value, the loss of affordable housing and the under-provision of social housing became sensitive political issues. City politics changed sharply as the Non-Partisan Association re-established its control and the reform movement weakened. In the downtown peninsula the planners struggled to respond to a new scale and speed of development as the focus shifted from the downtown core to its margins, from commercial office development to high-density residential, and they began to invent a series of new approaches to managing neighbourhood redevelopment. By the end of the decade a new mayor and a new planning hierarchy were rethinking the planning agendas and preparing for a dramatically different scale of development and planning. They sought to create a much more diverse pattern of land uses and neighbourhood character in the downtown peninsula. They had assessed a range of high-density residential forms, developed a system of street treatments to enhance the public realm, and established development levies to pay for infrastructure like replacement housing, community centres, and parks. They had taken the discretionary system of control and reinforced it with new housing forms and new systems of delivering quality streets and neighbourhood amenities that was to reach its apotheosis in the waterfront megaprojects in the late 1990s.

City Politics, 1975-90

While the establishment of the new planning regime was proceeding steadily, significant political changes were afoot in Vancouver. TEAM's lack of experience, organization, and political cohesion meant that its hold on power was precarious. In 1974, TEAM lost three seats to a rejuvenated Non-Partisan Association and it lost interest in reforming the ward system or promoting public housing (Gutstein 1983a: 209). By 1976, TEAM had lost its majority and was at odds with the mayor, who ran with a Non-Partisan endorsement in 1978 when a Non-Partisan majority took over the council. The Non-Partisan re-ascendancy was short-lived and its dominance of Vancouver politics was not fully restored until 1986. In 1980, Mike Harcourt, a former TEAM alderman, ran for mayor as an independent with backing from the New Democratic Party and in partnership with the Confederation of Progressive Electors (COPE), leaving TEAM holding two seats and the balance of power. The 1981-82 council was more polarized and bitterly divided than any of its predecessors, but the TEAM councillors tended to vote with the Non-Partisan councillors to defeat COPE reform measures and to confirm their conservative, pro-development instincts. The TEAM councillors Mae Brown and Marguerite Ford were given key committee posts in finance and planning, respectively. Often described as "red Tories," they were consistent supporters of good planning and of strong controls on downtown development, and played an important role in resisting its retrenchment, even if they consistently opposed the initiatives emanating from the Downtown Eastside Residents Association, and more radical initiatives like demolition control and increased social housing provision (Gutstein 1983b).

As the development stakes became higher the Non-Partisan Association gradually re-established control. In 1986, Mayor Harcourt moved to provincial politics, COPE fielded an adversarial candidate for mayor, and the middle third of the electorate voted for the Non-Partisan candidates who, as a consequence, won nine of the eleven council seats and the mayoralty (Gutstein 1986-87). Their victory was considered to be the outcome of a well-organized and extremely well-funded Non-Partisan campaign with strong media support and backing from the provincial Social Credit party. Gordon Campbell, the new mayor – now (2002) provincial premier – was young, positive, and forward-looking. His strong pro-developer voting record on council had attracted major campaign contributions from the development industry. Campbell had been an employee in the planning department in the 1970s and had become executive assistant to TEAM Mayor, Art Phillips. When Phillips did not run for mayor in 1976, Campbell went to work as a project officer for Marathon, from which position he was actively lobbying councillors on behalf of the developers. Moving on, he founded his own development company and in 1984 he was elected as a Non-Partisan alderman at the first attempt, an unprecedented achievement for a new candidate (Gutstein 1986-87). By 1986 he was mayor. To many Gordon Campbell's mayoralty signalled a much more pro-developer attitude in city hall and a shift in the planning regime to make it much less restrictive, but within the planning department the change of policy was seen as much less radical and more subtle.

In the 1988 election, the biggest issue was central area development, with the opposition positing the "livable city" against the "executive city" that they saw the Non-Partisan Association promoting (Reid 1988). The lack of affordable housing was a major concern. In 1990 the Non-Partisan Association was almost defeated when COPE took five of the ten council seats, and the mayor's huge majority was eroded by mayoralty candidate Jim Green, from the Downtown Eastside Residents Association, with his socialist agenda (Reid 1991). However, the Non-Partisan Association clung on to power by means of the mayor's vote and, by 1993, had reasserted its grip on council, winning nine of the ten seats, leaving COPE with a single councillor (Reid 1993). Throughout the 1990s, the Non-Partisan Association consolidated that position, so that Vancouver became almost a single-party city until two COPE councillors were elected in 1999.

But this was not the pre-1970 Non-Partisan council dominated by developers, real estate industry, and business people, but a much more politically centrist group. Lacking ideology and manifesto, the association deliberately selected its candidates to represent a wide range of different communities and interests – gender, ethnicity, sexual orientation, neighbourhoods, environment, business – to keep its control of power. It maintained a careful balance between representing both the interests of business and the development industry, and the aspirations of the residents of the affluent westside neighbourhoods of the city, which have always been its electoral heartland. Close elections in 1988, and particularly in 1990, emphasized the importance of commanding the middle ground, of maintaining strong control of development, and of continuing the planning programs established by the urban reformers in the early 1970s.

Market Conditions

The key property market change in the late 1970s and the 1980s was the boom and then collapse of office development and its replacement by residential condominium development. The first half of the 1980s saw 100,000 square metres (a million square feet) of office space being completed annually. Thirty-six new office towers – largely undistinguished in design – were added to the downtown skyline, as a response to an economic boom that had peaked in 1981. Declining from 12 percent in 1977, office vacancies fell to only 1 percent in 1981; by 1986 they had risen to 18 percent to reflect the downturn in the economy. The same pattern was repeated later in the decade and in the next, with vacancy levels reaching a low of 8 percent in 1989 and 1996 and a high of 16 percent in 1992. By 1991, the downtown office stock had reached 2 million square metres (21.5 million square feet). Over the next decade, it did not rise much above this level because few new buildings were completed, and there were significant demolitions of older office buildings and conversions of others into residential space. Other market indicators were mixed. Retail sales increased 100 percent in real dollars between 1980 and 1995, and the number of cruise-ship passengers increased five-fold over the same period. Convention trade was more erratic, with good years in 1986 and 1989-91; hotel occupancy mirrored this pattern, reaching 75 percent in 1989-90 (Vancouver 1999w). Landowners, property owners, and investors were forced to look at other sectors of the market to maintain their anticipated returns: high-density residential development was the obvious alternative.

Continued growth of employment downtown in the first half of the 1980s and the increasing number of one- and two-person households with a preference for an urban lifestyle created a strong demand for high-density residential development downtown. Difficulties with commuting fed demand despite the completion of the rapid transit link to New Westminster in 1986. But what increased residential property investment dramatically in the second half of the 1980s was Asian investment. Expo '86 was widely credited with putting the city on the international investment map, but events in Tiananmen Square in June 1989, and the projected return of Hong Kong to the Chinese in 1997 heightened the interest of Asian investors. In 1984, the federal government had initiated a policy to encourage business migration. Vancouver, with a large Asian community and good capital appreciation prospects from condominium investment, was a particular target for Asians and was rapidly absorbed into the global property market. Up to 600 high-rise condominium units were built annually between 1986 and 1990. Meanwhile, the median price of condominiums rose 44 percent in real terms over the period 1986 to 1996 (Vancouver 1999w). As redevelopment proceeded the stock of low-cost rental housing dissipated year by year – so much that, between 1984 and 1986, there were no net housing gains in the central area. The overall result was a step change in development pressures that fully tested city planners' ability to operate their discretionary control processes, to evolve new patterns of zoning, and to establish new ways of paying for public amenities and infrastructure and protecting low-cost housing.

The Downtown Plan, 1975

The Electors Action Movement (TEAM) came to power with a commitment to change the pattern of development in the central area of Vancouver and to institute a system of planning that would create a much more livable city. A major focus of its planning efforts was the establishment of an official development plan for downtown. Whereas the False Creek South plan, TEAM's showpiece, was virtually a master plan, at least for the first two phases, the downtown plan was a different beast. A simple workable plan that was easy to understand and easy to amend, its most important feature was that its provisions were purely discretionary with no outright allowances on any site (Vancouver 1975b). Its retail and office space provisions were overly optimistic and its public realm provisions weak, but the accompanying character area guidelines provided contextual design principles with which redevelopment could be negotiated. The 1975 Downtown Official Development Plan was a flexible instrument that provided a very basic set of controls. Amended fifty times between 1975 and 1998, the plan has continued to provide a framework for development control up to the present. In 1985 it won a Canadian Institute of Planners award, a testament to its innovation, impact, and longevity.

In 1973 a Downtown Study Team had been set up and in 1974 a Downtown Guidance Panel was established by the Vancouver Planning Commission to represent a wide range of interests and professional perspectives. The panel, used as a sounding board by the study team and by senior officials and councillors, developed a mixture of goals, objectives, and principles for development and management processes to underpin downtown planning. The study team was heavily engaged in monitoring conditional permit applications and developing new development control procedures, but it also prepared a major report on development policies, implementation, a draft bylaw, and general and specific guidelines (Vancouver 1974c). Twenty design topics were covered in the policy section, including microclimate, views, conservation, and public realm. However, the official development plan covered only five topics: land use (see Figure 10), density, building height, parking, and amenities, but only building height was originally mapped (Vancouver 1975b; see Figure 11). Only the most basic provisions were introduced initially to control the design of development, and a clear distinction was drawn between regulations (i.e., maximum floor-space ratio, maximum parking, and minimum requirements for loading) and interpretive requirements (i.e., building height, social and recreational amenities, and facilities).

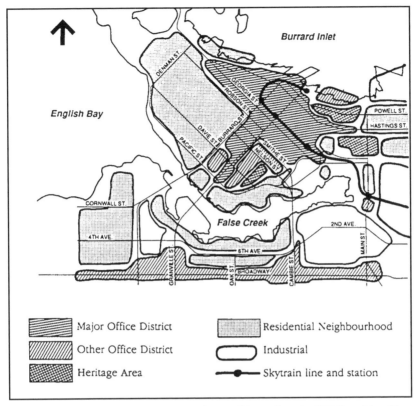

↑

Burrard Inlet

English Bay

False Creek

	Major Office District		Residential Neighbourhood
	Other Office District		Industrial
	Heritage Area		Skytrain line and station

Figure 10 Downtown zoning in the 1970s and 1980s. This map from the 1991 Central Area Plan illustrates the policy that operated in the 1970s and 1980s. The most noticeable feature is the size of the designated office district (compare with Figure 48). (*Source:* Vancouver [1991c])

In contrast with the False Creek South plan, design policies and guidelines were put in a separate document outside the plan (Vancouver 1996m). The plan stated the commitment to downtown as a living, working, shopping, and visiting area and encouraged mixed-use development but, in a departure from previous policy, it "both permitted and encouraged well-designed residential development throughout downtown" (Vancouver 1975b: 8). It discouraged car use for journeys to work and accepted the objectives of the Greater Vancouver Regional District to decentralize some office development. The plan stated the intention that all new development should "meet the highest standards of design and amenity for the benefit of all users of the downtown" but also provided for "flexibility and creativity" in the preparation of proposals. Particular stress was placed on "retail use continuity" to maintain active uses at the street level – "required" on much of Granville, Robson, and Hastings and encouraged on much of Burrard and Georgia.

Density provisions set a maximum of seven or nine times site coverage in the principal downtown areas and five times coverage over the area to the east of this. Elsewhere, floor-space allocations ranged from four times coverage in Downtown South to six to seven times coverage upslope of Coal Harbour, requiring a residential component to achieve this density. A number of zones had residential bonuses of 1.0 or 2.0 floor-space ratio to encourage residential development, and some provided for additional commercial bonuses of the same order. There were potential exclusions from floor-space calculations for the provision of recreational and community facilities and bonuses for the provision of "public, social, or recreational facilities." Building height limits were specified of up to 135 metres in the downtown core and 90 metres on its margins. Lower heights (51 metres) were set for Granville and Robson streets outside the downtown itself (Figure 11). Provision for view corridors and area-specific public spaces was added much later. But the plan did not provide any outright allowances for development and all of its allocations and provisions had to be negotiated with planning staff.

Character area descriptions that provide the downtown design guidelines to back up the plan were adopted by council in December 1975 and these too are in use today (Vancouver 1996k). In 1975, eight downtown areas were defined, which were not coterminous with the zonings, and periodic revisions and additions were made to the areas and the criteria as circumstances changed (Figure 12). The main thrust of character areas was to recognize the physical diversity of downtown, to encourage the development of distinct character in particular streets, and to reinforce the sense of place in areas where there was some design quality. The guidelines provided criteria to underpin discretionary control.

Each original character area statement was brief – no more than a page and a half. It explained some aspects of the area's existing physical character and social use, and stated the area's assigned role and general physical planning objectives. Thus, the objectives for the Financial District included: "The existing character should be strengthened and any new development should harmonize in terms of use and scale with the existing environment. As the waterfront is redeveloped, links between it and the financial district should be created so that it becomes a transition zone between other character areas and the waterfront" (Vancouver 1996k: 3). Each character statement then presented a set of individual recommendations in relation to the mix of uses encouraged, especially the desired ground-floor uses; essential requirements for public space and pedestrian networks; the buildings' relationships to the street; and some basic aspects of building frontage and architectural treatment, for example, "respect the scale and architectural rhythms of existing structures." Again this approach proved to be quite robust, being amended

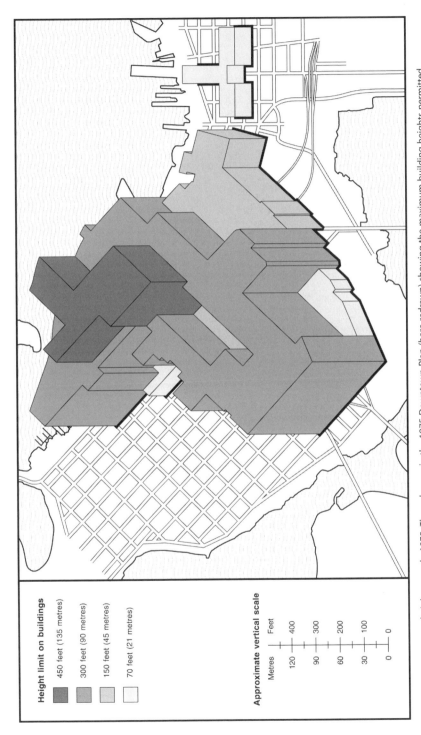

Height limit on buildings

- 450 feet (135 metres)
- 300 feet (90 metres)
- 150 feet (45 metres)
- 70 feet (21 metres)

Approximate vertical scale

Metres	Feet
120	400
90	300
60	200
30	100
0	0

Figure 11 Downtown height controls, 1975. The only map in the 1975 Downtown Plan (here redrawn) showing the maximum building heights permitted. All allowances in the plan were discretionary, but Yaletown, Granville Street, and Robson Street were all protected by a 21-metre height limit. (*Source:* Jan Edwards, redrawn from Vancouver (1975b))

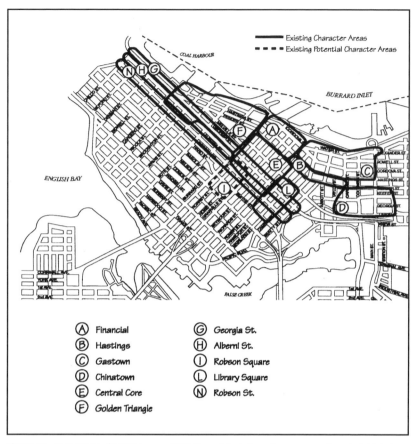

Figure 12 Downtown character areas, 1993. The original character areas numbered eight, but both plan and character areas were regularly modified to keep up with changing circumstances. Many of these areas had block-by-block guidelines. *(Source:* Vancouver [1993g])

seven times over the succeeding decades, the statements becoming increasingly sophisticated, and a further three character areas being added.

Redevelopment of the Law Courts: Robson Square

An early test of the new city council and its downtown urban design aspirations – and certainly the most important single piece of urban design of the period – was the redevelopment of the city's law courts. It began in 1973 as an unseemly disagreement between the province and the city. The province wanted to consolidate its legal offices and law courts and expand them in a single 55-storey tower, Vancouver's tallest, demolishing the city's 1909 neo-classical stone-built courthouse in the process. The city objected strenuously to the proposals, and the newly elected NDP provincial administration bowed to public opinion, commissioning Arthur Erickson to undertake design studies for the site while retaining the courthouse for public use. The city's character guidelines for Robson Square were rather sketchy and were never developed in conjunction with the province as promised. They assumed that the law courts would generate intense pedestrian activity, as well as further development, which proved to be very wide of the mark.

Arthur Erickson's proposals for the two and a half city blocks were ambitious, and they promised to give the city a series of dramatic new public spaces. He retained the neoclassical provincial courthouse, converting it to become the Vancouver Art Gallery. But he ignored all three porticos as potential entrances, building instead a three-sided flight of concrete steps and a terrace to enter the building from the rear. In this way, he created a very sheltered southwest-facing gathering area above a plaza on the southeast corner of Robson and Howe streets (see Plate 13), but denied any vitality to the larger green space to the north. The plazas created on both sides of Robson Street were compromised by large openings into a subterranean concourse, which regrettably does not provide a link to the Pacific Centre shopping mall. Nevertheless, Erickson's approach to the design of the law courts was to prioritize the provision of public space at the heart of the city. He developed the space to the south of Robson Street as a microcosm of provincial landscapes, ramping it up over the courtyard accommodation in a series of spectacular waterfalls, reflecting pools, and flights of steps relieved by groups and lines of conifers (see Plate 14). Erickson intended the huge atrium to the law courts to be a major civic space to bring the public into contact with the legal system, but few people without business in the courts find their way there. He made clever use of the rising ground to bring the atrium entrance almost to street level at the southwest corner of the project but, on this elevation, the megastructure's brutalism is all too evident, only slightly relieved by planting, which softens the box-like structure.

The architectural critic John Pastier noted that the law courts resemble a convention centre or a transportation terminal rather than court buildings, and suggested it might have been better to have left the courts in the original building. He argued that

> it is a splendid civic gesture, an excellent example of landscape design, a good piece of adaptive use, and a better than average working environment. But it is also problematic as urban design, variable in architectural quality, disappointingly underused as a pedestrian axis, unclear as a symbol, and definitely not to be held up as a good example of waterproofing. Yet whatever its inconsistencies of execution, this work embodies a generosity and boldness that one rarely finds in a government facility. (1989:65)

Plate 13 Robson Square, Vancouver Art Gallery, and the Hotel Vancouver. The concourse underneath Robson Street has a circular dance floor that doubles as an ice rink in winter. Sadly, the concept severely limits the space at street level – at this critical juncture of the city's retail *passeggiata*. The spaces around the art gallery are much more successful, but many feel that the mature landscape (left) needs rethinking.

But the key failure of the project lies in the way it dissipates pedestrian movement, kills the side streets, and fails to create space where it is most needed – adjacent to the ebb and flow of Robson Street. Ways need to be found to make the spaces Erickson created over the offices more heavily used. Ideas for remodelling the spaces were contemplated in 1999 as part of a major retail proposal, but Vancouver's principal civic spaces await some carefully considered, imaginative urban redesign, as discussed in Chapter 7.

Downtown Design Control

The impacts of city design guidelines and controls on the law courts scheme were negligible but, elsewhere, planners were beginning to use the provisions of the downtown plan and the character area guidelines to good effect. Three particular successes were celebrated (Vancouver 1981b). The Daon Building was the first scheme designed under the new system by Musson Cattell Mackey Partnership, who had completed a scheme to meet their clients' needs without pre-application negotiations; the planners recommended a refusal, as it did not meet city guidelines. The first design was a wedge-shaped high-rise brick structure with reflective glazing commanding the

Plate 14   Robson Square and the Law Courts, looking in the opposite direction to that in Plate 13. This view illustrates Arthur Erickson's ambition for Robson Square as a great civic space, and his concept of a microcosm of provincial landscapes wrapped over the car park and office buildings. Regrettably very few pedestrians make it as far as the spectacular atrium of the law courts.

Burrard-Hastings corner. The planners wanted to preserve more of the view down Burrard Street and open up views of the Art Deco Marine Building, while minimizing shadow on spaces on the waterfront. A new design was produced over a weekend as a result of a last minute meeting with architects, developers, and planning staff. Permission was granted by the Development Permit Board on the following Monday. The approved project is an elegant tower block that floats above its landscaped base, refracts the Marine Building elevations, and handles the complexities of its corner site with great aplomb (see Plate 15).

Two projects fronting on Bute Street allowed the planners to fulfill their ambitions to improve the views north to Burrard Inlet and the mountains and create a more pedestrian-friendly environment in the street. At 1176 West Georgia Street, the planners sought more of an "event" at a gateway to the downtown, but they also wanted the building set back on its western side to accommodate northward views and a double row of street trees. So the architects exaggerated the colonnade, creating a 6-storey "urban room" on the corner underneath the concrete-latticed tower (see Plate 16). On the corner site to the south (1185 Alberni), the developer had actually commenced

Plate 15 Daon Building and Vancouver Club, 999 West Hastings Street. Another celebrated success of the discretionary process on this key corner of Burrard Street, this building reflects and refracts the art deco Marine Building to create an always engaging exterior. It has a small plaza at its base with excellent views across Burrard Inlet, and handles the relationship with the Georgian Vancouver Club with aplomb.

construction on an office project when planners pushed for a corner plaza as part of their drive for pedestrian amenities; in return, they allowed the developer to add 5 storeys to the tower (Vancouver 1981b).

To counter criticisms of both the poor public consultation and high levels of discretion inherent in the control process, planners researched and published these three examples of discretionary control. But close comparison between the character area guidelines and the design issues that determined redesign of the developments reveals that the guidelines did not provide a clear basis for designers to anticipate planning requirements. A large measure

Plate 16 1176 West Georgia (centre) and 1185 Alberni streets, looking north on Bute Street. These are two projects where planners intervened to good effect at the end of the 1970s, improving the view corridor and creating a public urban room under the tower, and a green corner plaza at Bute and Alberni on the right.

of discretion was being exercised in site-by-site negotiations; with generous bonuses, developers were persuaded to meet at least some of the planners' urban design requirements. In their monitoring report the planners emphasized the need for policies and guidelines that had political and public support and were in tune with contemporary needs. They argued that architects, developers, and planning staff had to be both skilled and motivated to achieve positive results, noting that

> the maintenance and enforcement of high standards is very important under
> discretionary zoning. There is a danger of letting the difficulties of dealing with
> bad projects "wear down" the resistance of the city. The execution of the project
> after approval is often not under the architects' control, and many compromises
> are made then to the design that was negotiated. City enforcement at this stage
> tends to be lax. Architects emphasized that any drop in standards makes it
> harder to convince clients that good design is necessary for city approval. (Van-
> couver 1981b: 14)

This is a widespread problem with both design review and development control. The planners subsequently resolved some of the difficulties by developing standard planning conditions to append to each permit, but it was rarely easy to deal with violations of these. The planning department's 1981-82

annual review noted a number of very time-consuming enforcement problems, while the subsequent year's review noted the value of "creative careful
negotiation with a myriad of prospective public and private developers" and
the "difficult task negotiating ... a workable balance of public and private
goals" (Vancouver Annual Review 1982-83: 8). It argued that the few occasions when these negotiations broke down were "not representative of the
bulk of successfully negotiated development."

Throughout the late 1970s, Vancouver's planning department was under
strong political and development industry pressure to keep the permitting
process efficient, quick, and not unduly onerous for householders and developers (discussed more fully in Chapter 8). Control performance was carefully
monitored and the system was clearly on trial, being comprehensively reviewed and re-endorsed by council in 1976 and again in 1978-79. The department resolved to speed up permit processing and improve the clarity of
some of the guidelines (Vancouver Annual Review 1979-80: 5-7). In 1979 it
appointed two architect-planners as development planners to handle the
negotiations on major schemes and they quickly became the key players in
the discretionary process. The council, for its part, reaffirmed its commitment
to the discretionary process by extending it across the whole city.

The efficiency of processing, however, deteriorated. Heavy development
pressure in 1980 and 1981, coupled with a three-month civic strike in 1981,
meant that a backlog of applications was created; this was resolved with a
decrease in applications in 1982. The economic downturn led to a reap-
praisal of the level of office space proposed for downtown, including major
federal government proposals. The withdrawal of the Marathon proposals for
office development on the north shore of False Creek (see Chapter 6) provided evidence of a stand-off between planners and developers that was also
likely to become a major political issue. The Board of Variance was overturn-
ing many planning decisions on appeal. The percentage of appeals allowed
rose from 26 percent in 1981 to 59 percent in 1983 and 1984. The exercise of
discretionary powers by the planning director and the Development Permit
Board was under attack and, clearly, development interests were being given
more support by the political appointees on the Board of Variance. These
increasing tensions were to be a hallmark of planning debates in the 1980s as
development pressures intensified and development interests once again
became more strongly represented in City Hall. Planning practices were forced
to respond to new economic and political realities.

Some important comparisons in relation to central area plans, design guidelines, and discretionary controls might be drawn with Toronto, where an
urban reform council with similar aspirations for more sensitive development
downtown had commissioned state-of-the-art design guidelines that were

much more analytical than those developed in Vancouver (Toronto 1974). But the consultants' implementation recommendations contained in the guidelines were not heeded as the preparation of the Toronto central area plan became increasingly contested between residents and business groups. The size of the central business district was much larger, and the development pressures were very much more intense, in Toronto. The benefits of a rule-bound regulatory system as opposed to a discretionary review approach were debated – the Ontario Municipal Board would almost certainly have objected to a discretionary system; but Toronto did not enshrine key design performance criteria in the zoning, as the consultants had recommended. Instead, they set out seven principles for design control in the plan, promising – but not delivering until the mid-1990s – a set of design guidelines as a design handbook to support them. Although a 1981 review claimed that the "qualitative objectives" of the plan were being achieved, the evidence was very mixed and, in reality, no clear definition of what the city wanted in terms of urban design was offered (City of Toronto 1990). Fifteen years later, the planners reflected ruefully on the lack of guidance that had prevented proposals being "evaluated in a consistent and thorough way" (City of Toronto Planning Department 1991b) and which had paved the way for the highly politicized let's-make-a-deal planning that characterized downtown Toronto in the 1980s. Vancouver, by contrast, had both the guidelines, albeit rather general, and more importantly the discretionary powers to implement them.

The Livable Central Area

During the 1980s architects and planners progressively refined the substantive design principles that were to be employed in creating new high-density residential neighbourhoods on the margins of downtown. Principal public objectives were to re-create lively, safe, and attractive streets; architecturally diverse, denser building forms; and "livable" residential complexes with plenty of private (view, privacy, landscaped space, recreation space) and public (trees, sitting spaces, and parks) amenities. Commercial investment and redevelopment pressure in the downtown core rapidly diminished after the 1981 boom, allowing more scope for heritage conservation and greater intervention into the design of major office buildings and the creation of public space. Residential investment and development on the fringes of downtown became a much more attractive real estate proposition.

Investors purchased the best sites with residential redevelopment potential on the edges of the West End. Attention then began to shift eastward to the Southeast Granville Slopes (across False Creek from Granville Island) and then into Downtown South, the area east of Burrard Street and south of Robson Street. Pressures for residential condominium development were intense, and a sequence of urban design studies was commissioned to examine ways of improving the public realm and accommodating high-density residential development. So a set of interlocking planning and design challenges emerged that were only partly resolved during the 1980s: appropriate densities and urban forms, private versus public amenities, replacement and affordable housing, park provision, livable streets, and heritage conservation.

Urban Design Studies for Downtown and Adjacent Neighbourhoods

The city's successes with design control downtown at the beginning of the 1980s did not disguise the need for a more proactive approach to design. Late in 1981, three urban design studies were commissioned, two in the downtown area and one on the southern margins of downtown, to consider appropriate urban forms and public realms where pressure for redevelopment was significant. Both downtown studies were awarded to Toronto consultants, which sparked local professional protests (Gruft 1984: 24). A study of the Georgia-Robson corridor by Baird/Sampson developed urban design principles and character area guidelines for these two streets. Entitled "Greening Downtown" (Vancouver 1982g), the proposal focused largely on planting trees along both streets to create strong boulevards bisecting the city. Georgia Street would have a double row of trees on both sides, and Robson Street a single row on both sides. Georgia Street was to accommodate major redevelopment at high densities, but developers were to provide formal green spaces in each block animated by some adjacent public use that would support pedestrian activity. While the consultants recognized that retail uses could not be encouraged on this street, they failed to appreciate that there were not enough public uses to make many such spaces a viable proposition. Revisions to the character area descriptions for downtown picked up a number of the consultants' ideas but did not strongly enforce the recommended pattern of tree planting. They did include the provision of "significant green spaces in all major developments" on Georgia to be located close to street level, visually prominent and profusely planted, that would accommodate "a variety of small-scale 'people' activities" (Figure 13). Several of these green spaces materialized in the 1990s (see Plates 18 and 19). However, most are private spaces that can be accessed by the public only visually (see Chapter 7 and Plate 46). The consultants' proposals for Robson Street were added to the character guidelines, creating six different sub-areas to respond to its transition from West End residential through neighbourhood centre, to major retail and mixed commercial around BC Place Stadium. More amendments were made in 1986 and 1990 (Vancouver 1996k). But while it is possible to see the positive impacts of the character guidelines on Georgia Street, it is less easy to detect them on Robson Street, aside from tree planting (see Plate 67).

Figure 13 Character area guidelines: West Georgia Street, 1982. The Georgia Street guidelines emanated from the "Greening Downtown" study (1982). This extract from the nine pages of guidelines emphasizes the ceremonial character of the street. Later sections detailed the tree planting.

1.2   Development Objectives
The purpose of the following development objectives is to provide guidance and directions for the development of the character area. However, there is an emphasis on the opportunity for architects and developers to be flexible and creative. The development objectives are applicable to the whole of the Georgia Street character area. However, they should be considered in conjunction with any specific supplementary development objectives identified in each of the five Georgia Street sub-areas, and depending upon location, the West End and RM-6 District Schedules; applicable planning policies and design guidelines or the downtown district official development plan bylaw; and the downtown planning policies and design guidelines. In addition, consideration should be given to the central area pedestrian weather protection planning policies and design guidelines.
   The West End Georgia/Alberni guidelines provide more detailed direction between Cardero and Chilco and should take precedence.

1.2.1 Image and Character
These development objectives are to reinforce the dominant prestigious, ceremonial image and character of Georgia Street. It is a wide, tree-lined street with major buildings. New developments should contribute to and enhance this image of the street. It is important to maintain a human scale relationship by ensuring that the street does not generally exceed the present 99-foot width. In addition, the street should maintain the existing two-way traffic function to reinforce and enhance its west-east and east-west relationships.
   (a) Reinforce the existing dominant processional and formal character of the whole of Georgia Street;
   (b) Maintain two-way traffic on Georgia Street.

1.2.2 Views
The significant views obtainable from much of Georgia Street are an important component of the image of downtown. The views include Stanley Park, Lost Lagoon, Burrard Inlet, and the North Shore mountains. It is important, both for now and as a future legacy, to preserve and enhance all existing views from the street ends, ensuring that physical elements do not protrude into the view cones.
   A balance should also be achieved between respecting views from existing residential developments and creating views from any new residential developments.
   (a) Preserve the existing street and views of the North Shore, North Shore mountains, Burrard Inlet, and Stanley Park;

▶

◄ *Figure 13*

(b) Seek a reasonable balance between respecting existing residential views and providing views for new developments.

(c) Create a coherent high-quality environment within the public realm. Ensure that all new developments contribute to creating this high-quality street environment by providing elements such as street trees, decorative lighting, appropriate incandescent and colour-corrected lighting, banners, displays, decorative paving materials, and a variety of street furniture.

Source: Vancouver (1993g)

The second major urban design study, for Downtown South, was undertaken by Cunningham du Toit. The area was a backwater in the 1970s but by the early 1980s it was the subject of some nineteen major commercial/ residential development proposals, of which eight were being constructed. Increasingly evident was an imbalance between the amount of land zoned for office development and that for residential development in the core area. Here was a key opportunity to create a mixed-use, high-density, but strongly residential neighbourhood downtown that could reduce the growth in commuter traffic. The area was close to the central business district, had the prospect of excellent views southeast across the city but lacked open space and other amenities, and was plagued by heavy traffic and illicit sex and drugs trading. The consultants predicted that, by 1996, the area could accommodate some 2,000 new residential units, as well as 230,000 square metres (2.5 million square feet) of office space, and half that again in retail. Their key task was to recommend appropriate forms of development and to reconcile the competing issues of land values, appropriate densities, public and private views, amenities, street enclosure, and microclimate. At the heart of the report were floor-space allocations (mainly 5.0) and massing studies to consider how this floor space might be disposed on full and half blocks (see Figure 14). Floor-space ratios of 4.0 produced 5-storey street-wall apartments with two 25- to 26-storey apartments on opposite corners, and 7- to 15-storey blocks on smaller lots. Such a disposition left a rectangular courtyard as private open space protected from noise and with good natural light, opening onto back lanes that bisected each block and provided rear servicing. These issues were not resolved until the late 1980s, by which time development pressures were irresistible.

The third urban design study was of the area south of the Granville Bridge, called the Burrard Slopes. It was to assess the desirability of office and residential development in this predominantly industrial zone, and the consultants proposed rezoning most of the area residential but expanding the commercial area south of Broadway with mixed commercial and residential

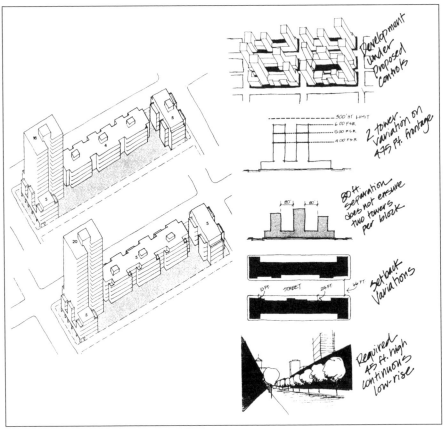

Figure 14 Downtown South: consultants' views of possible block development, 1982-89. These drawings illustrate the evolution of the ideas for twin towers and street enclosure on the blocks of Downtown South. The two drawings on the left, taken from Cunningham du Toit's 1982 study, indicate possible building forms at floor-space ratios of 3.0 and 4.0. By the late 1980s, floor-space ratios of 5.0 to 6.0 were being discussed and Aitken Wreglesworth Associates illustrated various possibilities for tower heights and separation, street setbacks, and enclosure. A key idea was to prescribe minimum lot sizes for the towers to ensure only two per block. (*Sources*: Vancouver [1982c, 1989])

areas on Burrard Street and 1st Avenue (Vancouver 1983c). Planners and council preferred to retain the light industrial uses in the area and to balance commercial and residential growth at that time, although they softened their view in 1990.

Heritage Conservation

Major urban design studies provided ideas for shaping the new neighbour-hoods, but to better protect the character of the downtown peninsula more concerted heritage conservation was required. The Heritage Advisory Committee had been lobbying council and, in 1983, the city instituted a Heritage

Conservation Program. This was to provide an inventory of heritage resources, establish a register of sites, and develop a management plan with a range of incentives and protective measures. An awards and historic plaque program was to be introduced as part of a public information drive. The preparation of the heritage inventory involved a comprehensive architectural survey of the city and an objective evaluation of each building, embracing architectural and historical value, historic context, and degree of alteration to the building. Three grades of heritage significance were recognized with A as primary, B as individual examples of some significance, and C as of heritage character, but the actual protection afforded to buildings on the inventory was minimal. Before they could be altered or demolished a permit was required, and this gave the city the opportunity to negotiate with owners or developers. Interiors were not protected until 1996 and then only rarely. Among the positive incentives provided to promote the conservation of heritage buildings were a range of bylaw relaxations, density bonuses, transfers of development rights, and the promise of speedy permit processing. Four planners were subsequently appointed to administer the program but the occasions when they were all in post were rare and the program suffered accordingly.

The Vancouver Heritage Register, as it is now called, was adopted by council in late 1986 and included 2,200 properties of which, at that time, only 60 were actually listed by the municipality and 230 by the province. At that time 40 heritage buildings were being demolished annually but, by 1988, this had fallen to 20 and has rarely risen above that level subsequently (Vancouver 1999w). However, in 1988, in the single strongest anti-conservation gesture since the program was initiated, Mayor Gordon Campbell removed buildings in the C category (i.e., of heritage character) from protection because they were considered to encumber too many potential redevelopment sites. Council used the heritage district designation in 1982 to help protect the elite suburb of Shaughnessy Heights from intensification (see Chapter 4), but did not designate more historic districts in the central area. Instead, to conserve the railway warehouse area of Yaletown, the city used Historic Area District zoning on Hamilton and Mainland streets to encourage the renovation of the turn-of-the-nineteenth-century buildings and their conversion into a rich mix of commercial, industrial, retail, catering, and residential uses (see Plate 66). Design guidelines introduced in 1982 emphasized that new development, extensions, and conversions should follow the proportions, rhythm, and details of the original buildings.

Critical conservationists consider that they have won only four development battles in the central area – the Courthouse Art Gallery (1973), the Orpheum Theatre (1976), the Sinclair Centre (1983), and the Roundhouse (1985: see Chapter 6). The Sinclair Centre was probably the city's biggest heritage success and is certainly the best example of intelligent conservation and adaptive re-use. An example of Richard Henriquez's remarkable architectural talent, the project renovates an entire city block occupied by four distinguished heritage buildings – a 1910 baroque postal station, its 1936

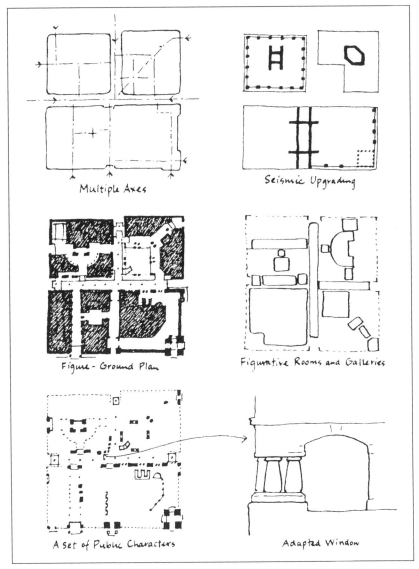

Figure 15 Sinclair Centre: concept plans. Richard Henriquez's concept sketches and plans reveal the ingenuity and imagination applied to the design and the creation of a highly permeable structure, with each internal space taking its character from the historic interiors and side/back elevations. (*Source:* Schack [1987])

neoclassical art deco extension, a 1908 renaissance palazzo, and a similarly styled but brick-faced 1910 Customs House. Given that each had to be gutted to allow seismic upgrading, the quality of restoration is admirable. But the creation of new interior public routes and spaces is its particular achievement. Henriquez covered the alleyways between the buildings and linked them with new passageways to the entrances to create a new atrium space at the centre of the block that provides a fine fusion of new and old (see Figure 15). Retaining the existing rear facades, he allowed each building to lend its character to each passageway and internal space (Schack 1987). Certainly the Sinclair Centre reflects what one critic has called "the authentic work of restoration [that] must be an act of personal interpretation" – and is about as good as it gets in terms of a sympathetic and creative response (Perez-Gomez 1994: 55). The work contrasts sharply with the anonymity of most similar complexes. The success of the Sinclair Centre poses the question of why other blocks with similar heritage characteristics have not been similarly conserved, but consolidated land holdings and client altruism and patience are rare.

Other projects of the period, such as the Tudor Manor condominium tower in the West End and the Palms Hotel on Granville, had to settle for facadist solutions. Most notable was the Hudson's Bay Insurance Company at Hastings and Burrard, which was completely demolished but had just its facade rebuilt around the corner on Burrard Street where it merely relieves a blank wall (Hlavach 1985). A very successful though facadist scheme was the conversion and extension of two stone-built Edwardian schools known as City Square, by Paul Merrick Architects. The facades of the schools were used to front a new pedestrian boulevard running parallel with 12th Avenue to create, with James Cheng's Cambridge Gardens, a very attractive pedestrian route between City Hall and the hospital (see Plate 21). The remaining facades of the school are contained within a large shopping atrium and food court with a new 6-storey stepped office building on the 12th Avenue frontage. The massing of the new building is excellent, as is its use of materials, with grey stone at pedestrian, sill, and lintel levels and green steel tying old and new together. The whole is beautifully landscaped – by Phillips Farevaag Smallenberg – and very unobtrusively serviced and accessed with an underground car park. A significant achievement of design negotiations (Vancouver 1999v: 22-23), it is an exemplary neighbourhood shopping centre.

Commercial Redevelopment and Postmodern Design

In the first half of the 1980s, thirty-six new office buildings completed in downtown Vancouver added some 650,000 square metres (7 million square feet) of floor space, driving vacancies up to 16 percent by 1985. Ten buildings accounted for more than half the space between them and most of them showed very little sign of responding to their contexts or any other design improvements (Crickmore and Holm 1986). Some were the later phases of such early 1970s megaprojects as the Bentall Centre (Musson & Associates) and the sleek Stock Exchange Tower (McCarter Nairne & Partners) completing the Pacific Centre scheme (see Plate 2). Few of the others had any redeeming features or architectural distinction, and only Park Place (discussed below) and the "science fiction space station" of the Price Waterhouse Centre (Tudor & Walters) warrant a mention in the city's architectural guide (Kalman et al. 1993: 71). Most were exercises in maximizing the floor-space ratio and contributed neither distinction to the city skyline nor amenities to the street; a number did contain a residential or hotel component. There was little evidence of the city's new permitting system positively influencing their design, a conclusion that is at odds with the carefully selected evidence presented by the planners in their 1981 report (Vancouver 1981b). However, by the mid-1980s more contextual approaches to design and experimentation with postmodern styles were being attempted, and there were more positive responses both to the new character area guidelines and conservation constraints.

Three postmodern office towers are worth close examination. The Hongkong Bank of Canada on Georgia Street, facing Courthouse Square, was the first of the city's postmodern towers. Approved in 1984 and completed in 1986, it anchored the important northeast corner of Georgia and Hornby streets, with the "muscular massing" of its deep-plan 25-storey tower (Kalman et al. 1993: 93). The tower was set back from Georgia Street and placed above a massive 7-storey atrium that provided a sunny, climate-controlled public space complete with public art, notably Alan Storey's pendulum. Designed by Webb Zerafa Menkes Housden Group, the building was finished in polished pink granite, at its best when viewed over the trees of Courthouse Square (see Plate 17). It is the least assertive of the three triangular-topped towers that enclose this corner of the Square. The new character area guidelines for Georgia, then probably in draft form, had required a strong sense of enclosure and definition of the street at this key intersection and the reinforcement of the "diversity and integrity" of pedestrian activity. The massive atrium performed both functions ably enough, and the development included boulevard planting with a single line of red maples as specified in the West Georgia Street Tree and Sidewalk Guidelines (Vancouver 1993g).

On the next block of Georgia to the west, opposite the chateau-style Hotel Vancouver, were two important heritage buildings. Christ Church Cathedral had been the second building designated under the heritage bylaw in 1974. Being the oldest surviving church in the city, which had become the Anglican

Plate 17   Cathedral Place (centre) and Hongkong Bank (right) of Canada from Courthouse Square. These two postmodern office towers on West Georgia Street provide an interesting backdrop to Courthouse Square, a space which lacks vitality because the art gallery (left) does not open out onto it. The Cathedral Square development responds well to the Hotel Vancouver (see also Plate 13). The granite-clad Hongkong Bank of Canada has an attractive atrium and public art.

Cathedral in 1929, had not prevented it from becoming a target for demolition and commercial redevelopment in 1973, a proposal that council rejected. The introduction of the heritage program had provided the cathedral with the opportunity to transfer its development rights to the Park Place office development at 666 Burrard (Musson Cattell Mackey Partnership, 1984). This rather bulky 31-storey tower, which tapers only above the twentieth floor, does have the benefit of a complex modelling, consisting of three sets of half bays on each corner. Combined with cladding of pale pink granite and flush fitting windows, this provides an always interesting reflective surface that transforms the colours of neighbouring towers at different times of the day (Kalman et al. 1993: 92). More important to most Vancouverites is the plaza – Park Place – that has been created between the cathedral and the tower along the length of the block of Burrard Street (see Plate 18). A sequence of spaces has been created from a generous easement, including a verdant grove of trees that provides shade and creates an outdoor room beyond the porch to the office building. This is one of Vancouver's most successful outdoor spaces, offering a variety of well-planted environments that catch the afternoon sun particularly effectively.

Plate 18 Park Place Plaza, 600-block Burrard Street. A sequence of spaces has been created behind the Anglican cathedral and alongside Burrard Street. To the right the sunken plaza is graced with a waterfall (not visible) on the retaining wall for Cathedral Square, helping to suppress traffic noise, while the grove of trees and manicured lawn provide relief from the street. Regrettably the lobby of the office tower is now less public than before and has been enclosed to eliminate drug dealing.

Although the cathedral was saved, the Georgia Medical/Dental Building was vulnerable to redevelopment. Built in 1929 this was a massive square 15-storey, brown-brick building decorated with richly ornamental terra cotta at ground level and on its roofline, as well as figures of nurses in terra cotta on each corner of the tenth storey. Above this, the building was set back to reduce its bulk. Inexplicably it was not included in the heritage inventory. The campaign to save the historic building, led by the Community Arts Council, which commissioned Peter Busby to produce an alternative scheme, was one of the most vociferous in the city's history. Busby showed how it was possible to retain the building and add an office tower behind it (Rossiter 1988). There were suggestions that Paul Merrick, the scheme's architect, was sympathetic to the building's retention, but the developer wanted a larger uninterrupted floor plate and extensive glazing to maximize views and rents. So the building was demolished. In its place, the architect designed a 22-storey tower, Cathedral Place, similarly massed to the building it replaced but taller. Its green-painted metal roof is skeletal at the ridge and eaves as a gesture of deference to Canadian Pacific's château-styled Hotel Vancouver opposite (see Plate 17). In fact, elements of the original building's terra cotta

Plate 19 Canadian Craft Museum, Cathedral Place. This intimate public courtyard behind Cathedral Place provides a green oasis in the manner suggested by George Baird's (1982) design study, while the building itself plays with several styles from Canadian Pacific château to art deco with its incomplete pitched roof and salvaged terra cotta friezes from the Georgia Medical/Dental Building.

friezes, coronas, and nurse statues have been reproduced and relocated on the new building because they were much-loved features of the original. Other reproduction decorative elements have been copied from the Hotel Vancouver – gargoyles, satyrs, and railings – to decorate the facade and complete the building's fit with its context.

Behind the office building, which fronts Georgia Street, there is a grassed courtyard raised above the side street, over an underground car park, reached from a walkway off Georgia Street between the new offices and the diminutive Christ Church Cathedral. On the north side of the courtyard, terra cotta panels from the original tower have been mounted above the generous windows of the Canadian Craft Museum to animate the facade and the space (see Plate 19). The courtyard is enclosed on Hornby Street by an arcade that reads as an extension of the museum, while on the west side a pergola provides a seating area above the waterfalls in Park Place. Looking back to the principles of the character area guidelines, it can be seen that the tower strongly reinforces and encloses Courthouse Square to the south by commanding this highly visible corner (Plate 17). It also adopts Baird/Sampson's concepts providing an oasis of green as a public space fronting an important public cultural building, although in this case it is not open to the street.

This project is one of the most urbane developments in the city, a refined design and a good example of a well-considered relationship to its context, but it has its critics. Lance Berelowitz (1993: 19) argues that "the inclusion of a museum devoted to the unique artefacts of Canadian crafts in a project that blithely appropriates so many pre-existing craft elements as appliqué is presumably an intended irony." The tensions in such evaluations – between lay and professional judgments, between what was there before and what is there now, between superficial and deep readings of the architecture and design – pose important questions for the practice of a sophisticated design control. But here were three interesting towers and two fine public spaces with an overall quality of urban design that has not been surpassed anywhere else in downtown Vancouver.

Condominium Developments and Postmodern Design

By the mid-1980s, downtown commercial redevelopment had stalled but the Vancouver property market began to be driven by a massive wave of Asian investment from Taiwan, Singapore, Japan, and, principally, Hong Kong. Overseas purchases were initially small scale in the office sector because existing investors were not keen to sell buildings for short-term gains. An exception was the spectacular purchase of the newly completed Hongkong Bank previously described. Most had to content themselves with smaller secondary office buildings, dozens of which were purchased in downtown throughout the mid- to late 1980s. One such purchase was the Burrard Building, a 1950s modernist landmark, which was immediately re-clad in "stylish reflective blue glass" (Gutstein 1990: 131) and then internally partitioned, much to the dismay of conservationists who considered that the building had been "literally stripped of its identity and integrity" (Kalman et al. 1993: 91). Retail purchases were more significant, concentrated on the prime stretch of Robson Street between Burrard and Bute streets (see Plate 67), and led to the development of "another trendy postmodern fashion mall" at Robson and Bute (Gutstein 1990: 124). Asian investment had the biggest impact on the West End apartment/condominium market, until the purchase of the entire False Creek North site in 1988.

Key buildings in the West End had been purchased by such investors as Robert Lee and Li Ka-shing ever since the 1960s. However, the development of the 26-storey Alberni Place, four blocks west of downtown, with huge suites of 235 square metres (2,500 square feet) each, was the first investment/development. It was slow to sell and local agents considered that the public was not ready to pay around $400,000 for such living space. But the same developers proceeded to build a second tower down the street, this time modelled on New York's Trump Tower and, in late 1988, they sold all these units, most of them to Hong Kong residents. "Condo-mania" hit Vancouver in 1988-89, with dozens of West End apartment buildings being bought by Asian investors, particularly in Hong Kong where they were marketed first. The Regatta Condominium, a low-rise condominium in False Creek South close to the Cambie Bridge was pre-sold in its entirety in Hong Kong in three hours (Mitchell 1993: 263), and achieved instant notoriety, but at least thirty Vancouver developments had previously been largely sold in the same way (Gutstein 1990: 157). Not only did the properties find a ready market that they would never have found in Vancouver; they also commanded an "Asian premium" calculated at something between 15 to 25 percent over Vancouver prices.

Residential Towers and Postmodern Design

Several architecturally significant condominium projects were developed by Asian investors. Five in particular are worthy of comment: four in the West End, close to the frenetic development activity on the north side of False Creek between the Burrard and Granville bridges, the fifth uptown across from City Hall. In 1987, the Tudor-style Huntington, a 3-storey, low-rent apartment block on Beach Avenue facing out to English Bay, was purchased and immediately resold to Hong Kong developers. They decided on a luxurious condominium project and commissioned Richard Henriquez to produce Eugenia Place, a 17-storey tower that was an instant postmodern architectural classic. The key design feature of Eugenia Place was its all-glazed facade to provide full panoramic views to the west and east (see Plate 20). Much has been made by architecture critics of Henriquez's witty iconography – in this case the height of the tower replicates the height of the original forest. This reference is reinforced by the tree that sits atop the saucer-shaped roof deck and the petrified tree stump sculptures in the front lawn at the base of the tower. Other architectural critics read the central glazed column and its tapered base as a giant pencil inscribing the site, a direct reference to the act of design (Boddy 1994b: 41). But, as so often, non-aesthetic readings of the building reveal quite different and more socially relevant interpretations. These might emphasize the site's appropriation of a view by seventeen wealthy owners justified as an "inevitable intensification," or the eviction of numerous larger but lower-income households, and an absolute reduction in population density but large increase in floor space.

Henriquez's two other celebrated projects in the West End are equally interesting socially and aesthetically. The Sylvia Hotel Extension, on the opposite side of the heritage hotel to Eugenia Place, was a similar project with

Plate 20 Eugenia Place and the Sylvia Hotel Extension, Beach Avenue. These slim, highly glazed towers overlooking English Bay are two of Richard Henriquez's masterpieces. His architecture admits many interpretations, none more so than the Eugenia (centre) which is a stimulating puzzle with its allusions to the height of the primeval forest and the act of design (i.e., pencils and screws). On the Sylvia Hotel Extension, behind the heritage-listed building, the architect's Edwardian pastiche dissolves into a glazed tower (Kalman et al. 1993: 120).

a single unit per floor and view-maximizing objectives (see Plate 20). The project involved the demolition of another 3-storey apartment block, but the site was much more constricted, with Ocean Towers, a slab block of the late 1950s, close alongside. So Henriquez's tower reads almost as a continuation of the slab, its balconies and square bay topped with gable and turret at an oblique angle to the apartment block to maximize the views west over English Bay (Kalman et al. 1993: 120). The third apartment building by Henriquez

– The Presidio – overlooks Stanley Park. Here the architect constructed a European townhouse at the base, a virtual facsimile of Adolf Loos's Villa Karma, recreating anew a historic context. The 19-storey tower reads as two towers superimposed on each other, the bedrooms expressed with recessed windows, the living rooms with full height windows within a dark steel grid frame decorated with two sets of external oval balconies that disrupt both facades and act as logos (Berelowitz 1992).

A fourth project in the same mould, although more derivative, was Paul Merrick's retention of the mock Tudor facade of Tudor Manor. Local residents were keen to keep the distinctive row of 3-storey apartments generously set back from Beach Avenue overlooking the mouth of False Creek. The complex was not designated as a heritage site but the developers asked for a 45 percent increase in density and a relaxation of the West End height guidelines in order to justify the retention of the facade and the landscaped setback. A 22-storey tower was built behind the retained facade. Kalman, Phillips, and Ward are sharply negative, bemoaning particularly the use of mock Tudor facades on the very top floors of the tower. They complain that "its style, bogus in 1928, has been used to ornament the otherwise elegant 1988 tower that shoots up behind in 20 storeys of crenellated pseudo-medievalism" (Kalman et al. 1993: 125).

The Henriquez projects deservedly captured the architectural plaudits, keeping the cognoscenti amused and providing a rich source of ideas for those designing towers elsewhere in Downtown South or the Southeast Granville Slopes. Contemporary with these projects, adjacent to Paul Merrick's City Square shopping complex, was Cambridge Gardens (see Plate 21). Much more prosaic in its design but ultimately much more influential as a prototype, Cambridge Gardens was one of the first high-rise projects to incorporate townhouses with its towers and create an internal private green courtyard for the residents' use. Architect James Cheng has stated that it was an attempt to introduce single-family living back into a high-density neighbourhood with semi-private gardens that create peace and sociability (Blore and Sutherland 1999: 54). All of its units were pre-sold in Hong Kong in two hours in 1988. The project was significant in another way, because the developer client was Victor Li, son of Li Ka-shing who was then engaged in purchasing the False Creek North (former Expo) site to provide his son with a megaproject with which he could continue his development ambitions (discussed in Chapter 6). Thus began a partnership that was to be instrumental in developing a particular form of high-density residential design that was distinctive to Vancouver in the 1990s.

Not all these postmodern pieces were popular. In the 1980s, the smallest piece of postmodern design caused the greatest architectural controversy.

Plate 21 Cambridge Gardens, uptown. The townhouses and towers of Cambridge Gardens front the walkway opposite City Square, Paul Merrick's radical but sensitive conversion of two Edwardian schools into a shopping centre, creating one of the most pleasant walkways and spaces in Vancouver. This was the prototype for the townhouse and tower model that James Cheng perfected at 888 Beach Avenue (see Plate 23).

The Terry Fox Memorial, placed at the eastern end of Robson Street in front of BC Place, was the result of a design competition held in March 1983 to commemorate Fox's battle against cancer and his courageous but fatal fund-raising run across Canada. The winning design by architect Franklin Allan was a modest triumphal arch executed in a postmodern form, although its full impact was impaired by cost cutting that robbed it of numerous features (Cepka 1984). The design provoked an astonishing debate in both public and professional circles. Some architects speculated that the modernist jury had deliberately selected it to discredit the postmodern. Many critics could not understand the apparent lack of reference to Fox himself and demanded additions to the monument; commemorative etched steel plates were subsequently inserted within the arch (Boddy 1994b: 29). The intensity of the debate was equalled only by that regarding the new library competition a decade later (see Chapter 7), which again touched the raw nerve that was the acceptability of postmodern pastiche in Vancouver.

Southeast Granville Slopes

Architects Richard Henriquez and James Cheng also played an important part in development and design controversies in the area of "hottest (development) action" (Gutstein 1990) in the 1980s – Southeast Granville Slopes between the northern piers of the Burrard and Granville bridges. The area north of Pacific Street was covered by the official development plan for downtown, but the area to the south was not. By 1984 the city had produced the Southeast Granville Slopes official development plan to cover 2.8 acres purchased by the province, which were not required for Expo '86 (discussed in Chapter 6). It was a prime site for development, with fine views over False Creek and Granville Island and a warm, sunny aspect for high rise condominium developments (see Plate 22).

The Southeast Granville Slopes official development plan encouraged high-density residential development in the area with active commercial frontages on lower floors and on the waterfront (Vancouver 1984d). There, an attractive walkway and park system were required, with building heights of no more than 30 metres stepped back from a maximum height of 19 metres at the back of the sidewalk. Both Hornby and Howe streets were to be continued to the water's edge to protect views and create pedestrian foci. Six development sites were identified with constrained building envelopes: buildings up to 12 metres high under the Granville Bridge, 30 metres high elsewhere on the waterfront and on the northernmost block, and an opportunity for two towers of up to 65 metres in height toward Beach Avenue.

Planning for this area was rather a case of locking the barn door after the horse had bolted, as two sites that had been the subject of prolonged negotiations were excluded from the plan. Discussions began in 1982 about the waterfront site at the foot of Burrard Street, alongside the abutments of the Burrard Bridge and, by 1984, the planning director went to council to ask for some directions as to maximum densities, tower positions and heights, and open-space provision on the site. Richard Henriquez's scheme for the site was taken to the planning and development committee because it vastly exceeded council's limits: 50 percent more density, two towers rather than one, and the height limit exceeded by 50 percent. Henriquez's proposals were typically bold, justifying the twin towers as a gateway marking the end of Burrard Street before it cranks westward onto the Burrard Bridge. Henriquez was able to show how the massing allowed excellent solar access to the plaza facing the water. But there were major concerns that the towers blocked lateral views out to English Bay and were too tall to be so close to the water. Henriquez reduced the tower heights closer to 60 metres (200 feet) but council would not approve the scheme despite the planners' positive advice.

A revised scheme with a single tower was designed by Rick Hulbert (of Hulbert Group), keeping broadly the same site plan with its seawall walk and sunny plaza with café above, and the two wings of apartments stepping down the slope to rest on pilotis over the seawall walkway (see Plate 22).

Plate 22   The Southeast Granville Slopes from Granville Island. The slopes provide a thrilling backdrop to the market on Granville Island. Despite the difficulties, city planners managed to create a series of sunny spaces and lightly trafficked streets, all fronted by buildings of an appropriate scale. The elegant 888 Beach Towers (centre) is further civilized by townhouses at street level, but the 5.94 floor-space ratio is obvious from this view (see also Plate 23). The tower third from the left was the Rick Hulbert-designed scheme inherited from Richard Henriquez. The False Creek Yacht Club (Bing Thom; on the far right) is a nautical response to Granville Island's industrial aesthetic.

The tower, with its five apartments per floor, brought together several different architectural treatments responding to the views from Burrard Street and Beach Avenue, as well as maximizing the views of False Creek and English Bay. Hulbert readily conceded that there was "too much going on" in the project (interviews), a view taken by the city's architecture critics who describe it as an "extremely mannered, postmodern high- and low-rise project, whose regurgitated constructivism, touches of Le Corbusier, and docklands vernacular are overlaid with a veneer of glitzy pretension" (Kalman et al. 1993: 105). But even the critics concede that the project fits well into the area and creates good spaces, preserves views, and provides a fine backdrop to Granville Island – even if the porte-cochere, featuring a swimming-pool with a transparent floor, provides one of the tackier entrances to a city apartment tower.

The second site, 888 Beach Avenue, was the key central block bounded by Howe, Beach, Hornby, and Pacific streets, just off the seawall. There, Expo chairman Jim Pattison wanted a major hotel to be developed to service Expo '86, arguing unconvincingly that, without the hotel, Expo would not go ahead.

Council, led by Mayor Harcourt, was persuaded to give the site 30 percent more floor space than any other in the city, despite the opposition of the planning department. Fortunately the project did not proceed, and the site was subsequently sold three times before Japanese developers bought it and proposed apartment towers on the site, acquiring all of the land in the block to improve their development prospects. The initial negotiations centred on allowable density and height. The development planner suggested a floor-space ratio of 6.0, much less than the projected hotel would have been allowed but still 30 percent more than adjacent sites. A key concession was to allow the project additional height to give the developer a better financial return on the two projected apartment towers. These rose to 77 and 87 metres, well above the planning director's preferred limit of 45 metres.

In the skilled hands of James Cheng, the project became one of the city's modern landmarks. Lance Berelowitz lauds it as "an exemplary response to the area specific ... urban design master plan and ... an important harbinger of high density urban housing in downtown Vancouver. It provided many lessons for maintaining livability and making a positive contribution to the public streetscape in the face of increased density" (Vancouver 1999v: 7). Here was a prototype that could be used on deeper city blocks without back lanes – unfortunately not that common – in the central area. It was an urban design solution that accommodated a floor-space ratio of almost 6.0, mainly in two elegant curved-facade tower blocks linked by townhouses and apartments to create a perimeter block enclosing a beautifully landscaped and well-sunlit private garden. The development, composed largely of townhouses, created attractive streets with a domestic scale, and these were elegantly landscaped (see Plate 23) and demonstrated how carefully detailed townhouses could be used to create streets with a human scale and an inhabited feel, even with adjacent apartment towers of over 75 metres. Subsequently, townhouses have become a popular housing form in the central city, and developers no longer have to be persuaded of their value.

As the rush for rezoning applications continued north of Beach Avenue, planning director Ray Spaxman consistently argued against buildings over 45 metres because they would block important views from the bridges and from the south side of False Creek, but he was clearly losing the argument to the development industry and the more pro-development council of the day. Gutstein records that in the 1980s the "city's planners fought a valiant rearguard action and were able to resist some of the more blatant development demands" between the bridgeheads, but he argues that they had in fact lost control (Gutstein 1990: 169). The planners considered they were still in command of the situation (interviews)and retained consultants Civitas to complete

Plate 23   888 Beach Avenue. One of the most important pieces of urban design in postwar Vancouver, James Cheng's tower and townhouse prototype handles very high density with consummate ease. The towers are staggered to maximize views and minimize apparent volume, while townhouses and apartments give the street a domestic but urbane atmosphere. There are rooftop and ground floor gardens, walkways, and a communal lawn as well as the reflecting pool (below) all designed by Phillips Farevaag Smallenberg.

a study of the North Slopes in 1989 which sought to establish the tower and townhouse/street-wall apartment form around a new park on Beach Avenue (Vancouver 1989e). Fortunately Henriquez, Merrick, and Cheng, as well as other architects and their practices, provided a particular burst of architectural creativity in the mid- to late 1980s, and the Vancouver cityscape benefited significantly from their interventions, particularly as lesser architects absorbed some of their ideas and innovations. But equal creativity and no less skill on much more tightly constrained budgets were being exercised by architects working on social housing projects in the same areas on the margins of downtown.

Social Housing Alternatives

Although Vancouver had created a municipal non-profit housing corporation in 1975 to develop low-cost housing, this did not actually get off the ground. The city failed to establish a municipal department to administer the program, as Toronto did so successfully. Instead, special short-term development groups were established to deliver specific housing projects such as False Creek South, and city staff worked to expedite projects initiated by non-profit and cooperative housing groups. In the downtown peninsula, social housing production totalled only about 1,000 units between 1975 and 1986, while 2,500 or so were built close to downtown in Strathcona–Downtown Eastside. Crucially, production failed to keep up with the rate of demolition of low-cost lodging units, which ran at some 400 units a year in the central area over the first half of the 1980s. Modernist urban renewal projects (e.g., McLean Park in Strathcona) had been halted in the 1960s, though more sensitive high-density but low-rise inner-city housing programs were revived under the TEAM administration and maintained through the 1980s under the Harcourt regime, the mayor being a particular advocate of affordable housing.

The city's main role was to lease land at below market prices to ensure that these groups would meet federally defined cost limits (Carter and McAfee 1990: 236). As of 1981, 90 percent of non-market housing had been built on city-owned land. In that year the city set up an affordable housing fund to receive developer contributions and capital allocations, aiding some thirty-two projects over the next two decades and, in 1988, it required that 20 percent of all mega-project housing units be affordable (see Chapter 6). But by the late 1980s and early 1990s, with declining federal commitment to affordable housing, social housing production in the city showed a steady decline, halving between 1989 and 1996. By that time, only just over 400 single housing units – all apartments – were being built annually in the city. While the housing cooperative movement became very successful in Vancouver, principally because of annual subsidies of about $8,000 per unit (1981 level), increasingly, these housed middle- rather than lower-income households, the Downtown Eastside Residents Association Cooperative being the honourable exception.

City planners for their part had undertaken an extensive study of how to house families at high densities (Vancouver 1992e) funded by the federal government to provide clear criteria with which to judge the livability of proposals. Housing planner Ann McAfee had written the study, which achieved national prominence and was subsequently translated into Japanese. She developed twelve basic principles for family housing in terms of access to recreation, project size (i.e., concentration of children), contextual design, clear definitions of private and semi-private space, privacy, multi-function pedestrian routes, active open space, specified play areas, safety and supervision, community identity, unit size, and interior layout (McAfee 1978). The best social housing projects in Vancouver certainly exemplified many of these principles. In the West End, two mid-1980s projects achieved particularly high design quality. The Barclay Square Heritage Park (Downs/Archambault and Iredale Partnership) was a joint initiative of the city and Heritage Canada that restored nine Edwardian homes for social and sheltered housing, in turn creating a neighbourhood backyard park in the heart of the West End. The Pacific Heights Housing Cooperative (Roger Hughes Architects) also retained a series of Edwardian balconied villas on Pacific Street. But behind and above them was built a 5- to 7-storey brick and profiled steel-clad block that creates a semi-private street courtyard at the rear of the Edwardian properties. A steel-braced elevator tower acts as a focal point to the entry to the scheme (see Plate 24).

A distinguishing feature of most of the social housing projects was their use of brick, whereas most private low-rise projects of the period used timber frame and stucco, often with disastrous weatherproofing results. Lance Berelowitz has argued that the much more expensive brick finish was a deliberate statement about the projects' permanence and a harking back to the Vancouver tradition of fine brick-built apartment houses (Berelowitz 1988). Not all the projects were as successful as Barclay Square and Pacific Heights. Berelowitz (1988: 37) cites Grandview Housing Cooperative, with fine views over False Creek and the downtown peninsula, as "a case of trying too much with too little" because of poor detailing and materials. A number of the schemes seemed to put more of their effort into the exterior of the dwellings and into imaginative street-making than interior amenities. Overall, however, these schemes revealed an urban sensibility rarely matched by the private sector. They offered more socially engaged urbane alternatives to the apartment tower as the means of increasing residential densities.

Plate 24 The Pacific Heights Housing Cooperative, 1035 Pacific Street. The much more innovative site planning, ground-oriented housing, and conservation instincts of social housing contrast with the standard speculative apartment blocks of the West End. The internal street between the new and the old creates a valuable social space, cleverly using the changing levels to gain access to apartments on the second floor of the Edwardian houses and to accommodate underground car parking. Another brilliant Roger Hughes Architects design.

The Downtown Eastside Residents Association

The achievements of the Downtown Eastside Residents Association (DERA) in the field of social housing during the 1980s were executed in Vancouver's skid row, the most deprived area of the city where a third its city's violent crimes and two-thirds of its incidents of public drunkenness occurred. In 1988, the average resident of the Downtown Eastside had lived there for ten years, was a white 51-year-old male welfare recipient with a 47 percent chance of being disabled (Gerecke 1991b: 12). So the population to be housed was particularly disadvantaged. Formed in 1973, the association was led by Bruce Eriksen, a former steelworker turned community activist, and Peter Davies, a social planner and community worker. They coordinated a small cadre of charismatic activists with a penchant for organizing and publicizing social causes that by 1989 had attracted a membership of 4,900, a third of whom were Canadians of Chinese ancestry. The association addressed a wide range of causes, campaigning for closure of the local liquor store, for better polic-ing of the streets, for a waterfront park, for better control of bars and beer parlours, for a vital well-staffed community centre, and against Expo '86 and its effects on affordable housing and cheap hotel rooms (discussed later in Chapter 6). At the heart of the association's campaigns were concerns to

build a community that could empower itself, despite its poverty and deprivations, to campaign for environmental, social, and housing improvements.
The issue of decent affordable housing being paramount, the organizers of
the residents association began a campaign to ensure that the housing codes
were enforced, particularly as regards fire standards, sanitation, and the quality of single-room occupancy hotels. Their well-publicized "crummy cock-
roach haven" contest was typical of their ironic and uncompromising approach.
In twenty-three low-rent hotels, they identified 10,000 code violations and
campaigned to get better enforcement to protect the vulnerable residents; the
fines were, of course, puny and rent increases invariably followed any improvements. A second initiative was to maximize the use of funds from the
federal Residential Rehabilitation Assistance Program while it was in place:
over the decade 1976 to 1986 1,200 units were upgraded, an especial achievement given the economic status of the residents.

The third dimension of their housing policy was the provision of various
forms of new housing. The main provider of social housing in the area was
the United Housing Foundation, which acquired three hotels and built three
lodges in the 1970s. The Downtown Eastside Residents Association began its
activities by compiling waiting lists for housing. After several false starts and
funding rejections it was not until 1983 that its first cooperative project was
initiated on city-owned land with federal funding. By this time two leaders of
the residents association had been elected to council and the majority on
council was more moderate. The co-op's second project was completed in
1987, a family project with mixed services that was essentially a warehouse
conversion with an innovative extension; it was also a design award winner
(Kalman et al. 1993: 22; see also Plate 25). The same architects (Davidson &
Yuen) designed two more innovative projects for the residents association,
completed in 1990 and 1991. The Pendera was built to a neo-Edwardian
warehouse design on West Pender, followed by a more architecturally exciting Cubist building on Alexander Street (Kalman et al. 1993: 60 and 48). By
1992 DERA had become one of the city's biggest east end landlords with 640
units in its control, and it was actively pursuing a range of other projects in a
management as well as a development capacity.

By common agreement, the achievements of the Downtown Eastside Residents Association were the most impressive of any resident association in
Canada. Kent Gerecke has argued that DERA took "the most neglected area
of the city, making the largest gain in community improvement of anywhere
in the country" (Gerecke 1991b: 11). In the 1970s and 1980s, they also became "a principal base of an oppositional socialist politics in the city" (Hasson
and Ley 1994: 204), in the process undermining the moderate reformist program of TEAM and becoming, to use Hasson and Ley's phrase, something of

Plate 25 Four Sisters Cooperative, 133 Powell Street. The second social housing project by the Downtown Eastside Residents Association encloses a safe, private garden to the rear where the warehouses have been extended to provide family accommodation. The elderly have the benefit of looking out onto the street.

a "Trojan Horse" in city hall. They certainly hastened TEAM's demise at the hands of the Non-Partisan Association, who were strongly opposed to any concessions to the residents association's social and political program. The consequences of this antipathy led to persistent council neglect of the Downtown Eastside and a major social crisis in the area by the mid-1990s, as discussed in Chapter 7.

Downtown South: Pressures for Rezoning

For the planning department the biggest challenge of the second half of the 1980s was resolving the future of the area immediately south of downtown. Developers' progressive abandonment of commercial zoning on the edge of the commercial core in favour of residential schemes at equivalent density led to approvals of over 300 apartments annually post-1984. These rezoning applications (using CD-1 comprehensive redevelopment provisions) were welcomed by city planners, but they recognized that such developments would pose important questions about neighbourhood services, public amenities, and livability, and about the provision of affordable housing, especially in view of the displacement of low-rent housing – about 1,100 units per annum downtown in the mid-1980s. In the 1975 downtown plan, the area to the south had been designated "major" (large commercial buildings) west of Granville Street and "other office districts" to the east in anticipation of a massive office expansion that did not materialize. By mid-1987 council had endorsed the principle of rezoning for high-density residential development, specifically noting the beneficial effects it would have on the commercial viability of Granville Street, and the fact that it would provide very accessible housing for downtown workers. In February 1988, rezoning proposals were put out for public comment and, in May, council approved a maximum floor-space ratio of 6.0, to be subjected to full public discussion on the range of possibilities, not least because the planning director had always recommended a maximum of 5.0. Council also suggested an overall height limit of 90 metres but noted that view preservation policies would be adopted shortly. Before proceeding with the rezoning, they also sought further studies on Granville Street and on built-form controls, view corridors, and other matters related to facilities and amenities. The latter was a specific reference to the possibility that community-amenity contributions might be imposed on developers applying for major rezoning, to provide social amenities in the neighbourhood. The city proceeded to seek these powers from the province under the Vancouver Charter.

City planners were particularly concerned about livability issues in Downtown South and had developed urban design criteria to parallel the emerging high-density residential design guidelines (Vancouver 1992e). A progress report noted that "up to four slim point towers per block, on a street-wall base, would provide the optimum form of development to ensure livability in terms of building separation, minimum project size to support maximum on-site services and limited overall crowding. The key concerns were visual and audial [sic] privacy, views, light and air penetration, security and open space" (Vancouver 1989b: 6). Another consultant's study examined potential dimensional regulations for floor-space ratios of 6.0 (Vancouver 1989l: Figure 14) and controls on minimum site sizes, setbacks, and tower floor plates.

By mid-1989, two major rezoning applications for a hotel/residential and a retail/office/residential development had been approved at high floor-space ratios and two more hotel/residential schemes had preliminary approval. Six other mixed-use applications were in the pipeline, three of which were seeking a floor-space ratio of 6.0. The city planning department was struggling to keep control, reluctant to rezone the area closest to downtown as residential because of probable long-term commercial demand, but keen to protect Granville Street and to devise a revitalization regime that retained the heritage buildings, particularly the theatres. In December 1989 council authorized the preparation of a community plan to resolve the area's future as a socially diverse, high-density neighbourhood.

Meanwhile, planners were trying to complete downtown view studies and to put policies in place to regulate building heights on a site-by-site basis.

The architectural consultants, headed by Busby Bridger, were charged with identifying residents' attitudes toward views and view protection, as well as listing and evaluating such views, developing protection mechanisms, and considering their implementation. Their five-volume report confirmed widespread resident support for view protection and identified twenty-seven views of significance, of which nine required some protection in terms of view cones with defined height limits (Vancouver 1989p). Three of these impacted on Downtown South but, responding to the interim report, the public sought the imposition of further view corridors from the south side of False Creek, so four narrow view corridors across Downtown South and the False Creek North sites were subsequently added (Vancouver 1989o: Figure 16). Collectively these view corridors did not preclude a zoning of 6.0 because apartment towers in each block could be located to avoid them. But considerable public opposition was expressed at five meetings that followed the council's decision to test a floor-space ratio of 6.0. The planning director advised council either to proceed with a public hearing and consider all objections to the area planning program or defer the rezoning until the planning issues, especially the matter of development-cost levies, could be resolved. Council opted for the latter.

Downtown South Design Guidelines

A year later, early in 1991, a brief community plan for Downtown South was approved by council. The plan established the concept of six distinct subareas with different densities, land-use mixes, and streetscapes (Vancouver 1991g) (see Figure 17). The rezoning resisted the widespread developer calls for a 6.0 floor-space ratio and set a maximum of 5.0, with only 3.5 on Granville Street, following the planning department's long-standing views. New design guidelines were developed and adopted by council in July 1991 and subsequently amended. In 1993 separate guidelines for Granville Street (Vancouver 1991k) and consultants' recommendations for particular streetscape designs were adopted (see Figure 18). It was acknowledged that neighbourhood identity had to be created anew in Downtown South, and the general design guidelines argued that the focus should be on the provision of parkland, the design quality of the shopping streets of Davie and Granville, and the re-creation of strongly enclosed streets that would be "safe, active, and attractive [and heavily] ... greened" (Vancouver 1987d). The preferred building form was medium-rise development to a minimum height of 9 metres (3-storey townhouses) at the back of the sidewalk with a maximum of four widely spaced towers per block, leaving the centre of the block as an "inner sanctum" of green spaces. The towers were to have a maximum height of 90 metres, subject to view and shadowing constraints; to achieve slimmer and

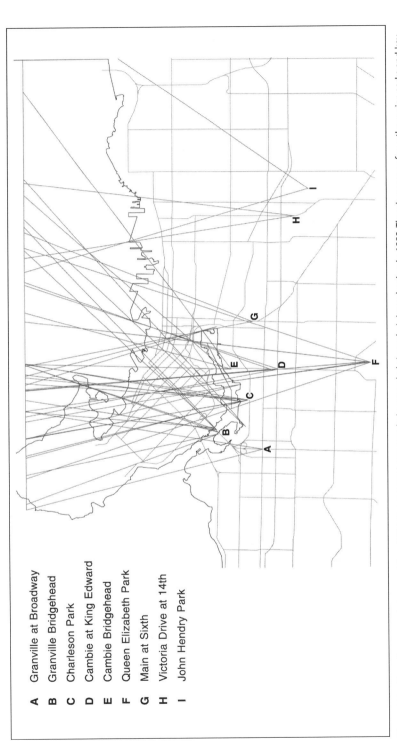

A Granville at Broadway
B Granville Bridgehead
C Charleson Park
D Cambie at King Edward
E Cambie Bridgehead
F Queen Elizabeth Park
G Main at Sixth
H Victoria Drive at 14th
I John Hendry Park

Figure 16 Council-approved view corridors, 2000. These have been regularly amended since their introduction in 1989. The view cones from the major parks and key vantage points on the arterials were suggested by the planners, but the public pressed for protection of additional view corridors from False Creek South. Within each cone, maximum building heights are delineated (not shown). (*Source:* Vancouver City Graphics [redrawn])

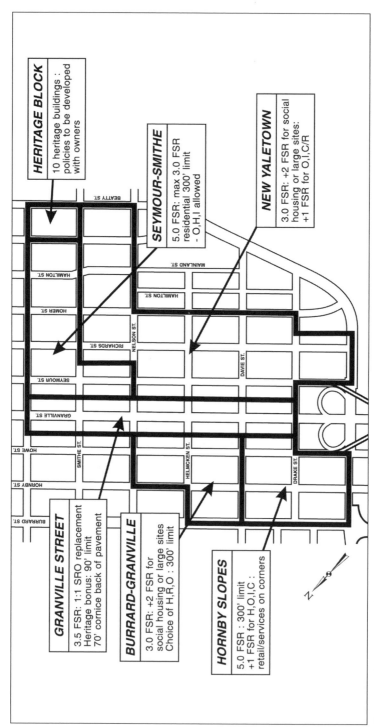

HERITAGE BLOCK

10 heritage buildings : policies to be developed with owners

SEYMOUR-SMITHE

5.0 FSR: max 3.0 FSR residential 300' limit - O,H,I allowed

NEW YALETOWN

3.0 FSR: +2 FSR for social housing or large sites: +1 FSR for O,I,C/R

GRANVILLE STREET

3.5 FSR: 1:1 SRO replacement Heritage bonus: 90' limit 70' cornice back of pavement

BURRARD-GRANVILLE

3.0 FSR: +2 FSR for social housing or large sites Choice of H,R,O : 300' limit

HORNBY SLOPES

5.0 FSR : 300' limit +1 FSR for H,O,I,C : retail/services on corners

BEATTY ST.
HAMILTON ST.
HOMER ST.
RICHARDS ST.
SEYMOUR ST.
GRANVILLE ST.
HOWE ST.
HORNBY ST.
BURRARD ST.
SMITHE ST.
MAINLAND ST.
HAMILTON ST.
NELSON ST.
DAVIE ST.
HELMCKEN ST.
DRAKE ST.

N

Figure 17 Downtown South rezoning, 1991. Developers pressed for floor-space ratios of 6.0 in Downtown South, and council put this to public consultation, settling on 5.0, which was the figure the planners suggested. The mix of land uses (office, industrial, commercial, and residential) varied subtly to create a series of differentiated neighbourhoods, with New Yaletown primarily residential and the Granville corridor protected by a lower floor-space ratio and height limits. (*Source:* Redrawn from Vancouver [1991g])

more compact towers, maximum and optimum widths, as well as maximum and minimum front setbacks were also related to height. Varied architectural expression would be permitted, incorporating sculpted towers, distinctive roof treatments, integrated roof plant, integral balconies, quality finishes to the lower floors, and townhouses on the majority of the street frontages. Active uses were encouraged on the ground floors, particularly at intersections.

In the detailed design guidelines particular attention was paid to private views, requiring that development be massed as compactly as possible and the towers configured so that views from future buildings on adjoining sites would be affected as little as possible. Shadow studies were required of all tall buildings to protect parks and public spaces. Noise considerations were included to influence the orientation of residential units and their construction, materials, and ventilation. There was a general adoption of "defensible space" strategies. All service access had to be from back lanes so as not to disturb the pedestrian emphasis on the streets, and there was a range of suggestions as to how the back lanes might be appropriately treated. Overall these design guidelines and livability controls were seen as essential to public enjoyment of the area but also "to ensuring that new development is economically viable and marketable" (Vancouver 1991f: 1). As for the streets, the general approach was to increase setbacks to provide more generous areas for pedestrians and more opportunities for private landscaping and tree planting(Vancouver 1991f). Horticultural design motifs were suggested for street furnishings, sidewalk finishes, and public art. The idea was to create a clear distinction between the busier retail streets and the much greener and quieter residential streets to improve legibility for pedestrians and drivers. Council adopted a streetscape manual for the area (Vancouver 1994n) with six distinct sub-area treatments (Figure 18)to be paid for by the developers. These have begun to ensure that Downtown South has a quality public realm.

Financing Social Housing and Amenities

In July 1990, the city achieved the authority, through a provincial amendment of the Vancouver Charter, to impose development-cost levies. As such, the city was merely catching up with suburban authorities who had for some time been levying charges on all new housing subdivision lots to pay for necessary infrastructure. Nonetheless, it was a significant move for the Non-Partisan council and its pro-development mayor to take, and a response to the election campaign of 1988 where the livability and the affordability of developments were criticized, along with the lack of protection of low-cost housing. Developers were already expected to pay for sewerage, water, drainage, and highways but the levy covered parks (45 percent of the levy), replacement housing (42 percent), and daycare facilities (7 percent) (see Chapter 8),

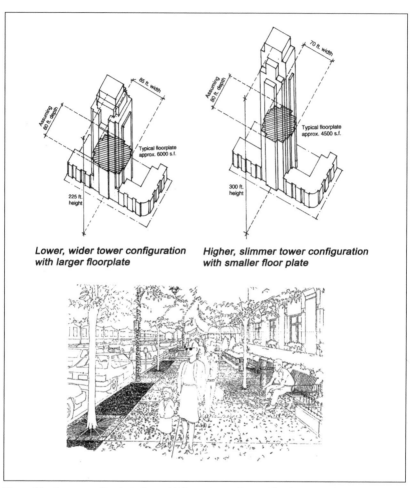

Lower, wider tower configuration with larger floorplate

Higher, slimmer tower configuration with smaller floor plate

Figure 18 Downtown South design guidelines, 1991 and 1994. The design guidelines developed for Downtown South were very detailed, but concentrated particularly upon "an animated and interesting street edge definition to create safe, active, attractive streets." The guidelines also insisted that the taller buildings were slimmer, and they encouraged distinctive architectural expressions and sculpted tops. Subsequently a streetscape manual was adopted to provide subtly different street treatments for each sub-area, executed by the city engineers, but paid for by developers. (*Sources:* Vancouver [1987d, 1994n])

the three particular infrastructure concerns of Vancouver. The public commitment to a high standard of park provision was long-standing. Replacement housing was an urban reform commitment that was strengthened with the council adoption of an affordable housing policy in 1989, specifically mentioning downtown lodging house residents (Vancouver 1989j). And daycare facilities allowed women to work, affirming an important component of gender equality.

To apply a development-cost levy, a bylaw had to be passed for each selected area. It was imposed as a condition on a building permit, with payment possible in instalments up to the occupation of the building. In theory, all the money collected had to be spent within the area concerned. Small developments of fewer than four self-contained residential units, social housing, and alterations (i.e., not extensions) of existing buildings were all exempted. Bylaws for development-cost levies were passed for two key central areas – Downtown South and Triangle West – but other areas undergoing intensification were also designated. The rates varied by land use and by area, but were set between $62 and $94 per square metre for residential, commercial, or industrial development in Downtown South and Triangle West, down to only $19 in the Dundas/Wall area (see Figure 19).

While development-cost levies were introduced to cover basic infrastructure costs, community-amenity contributions were introduced in 1989 to pay for amenities in areas undergoing significant intensification through private rezonings. This decision did not require provincial approval. The city regarded it simply as a discretionary levy, and entirely appropriate since they were significantly raising the developers' land values while the ensuing developments generated a need for more neighbourhood facilities and amenities. These amenities included parks, community centres, and social housing. These contributions were to be collected prior to the enactment of residential rezonings, and their rate was established on a case-by-case basis, dependent on predicted community requirements in the area concerned. The rates varied between $63 and $74 per square metre of floor space in the mid-1990s, with $40 per square metre being the norm. By 1998, this norm had risen to $55, a figure that does not include amenities and facilities provided on site. The contributions were mainly levied on rezonings in the central area but the tool has remained a very flexible way of ensuring that new public facilities are provided in areas of major private residential intensification (see Chapter 6).

The Planning Achievements of the 1980s

During the late 1970s and the 1980s architects and planners progressively refined the substantive design principles that were to be employed in creating the new downtown core and its frame of high-density residential neighbourhoods. Much effort went initially into ensuring that downtown development responded carefully to the character of different streets and spaces. Then, as the focus of redevelopment shifted to the margins of downtown, much thought went into ensuring that development delivered a diversity of mixed-use and high-density residential areas in the downtown peninsula. The objective was to re-create lively, safe, and attractive streets that could be "inhabited" by residents and business people. The tower and townhouse/apartment model

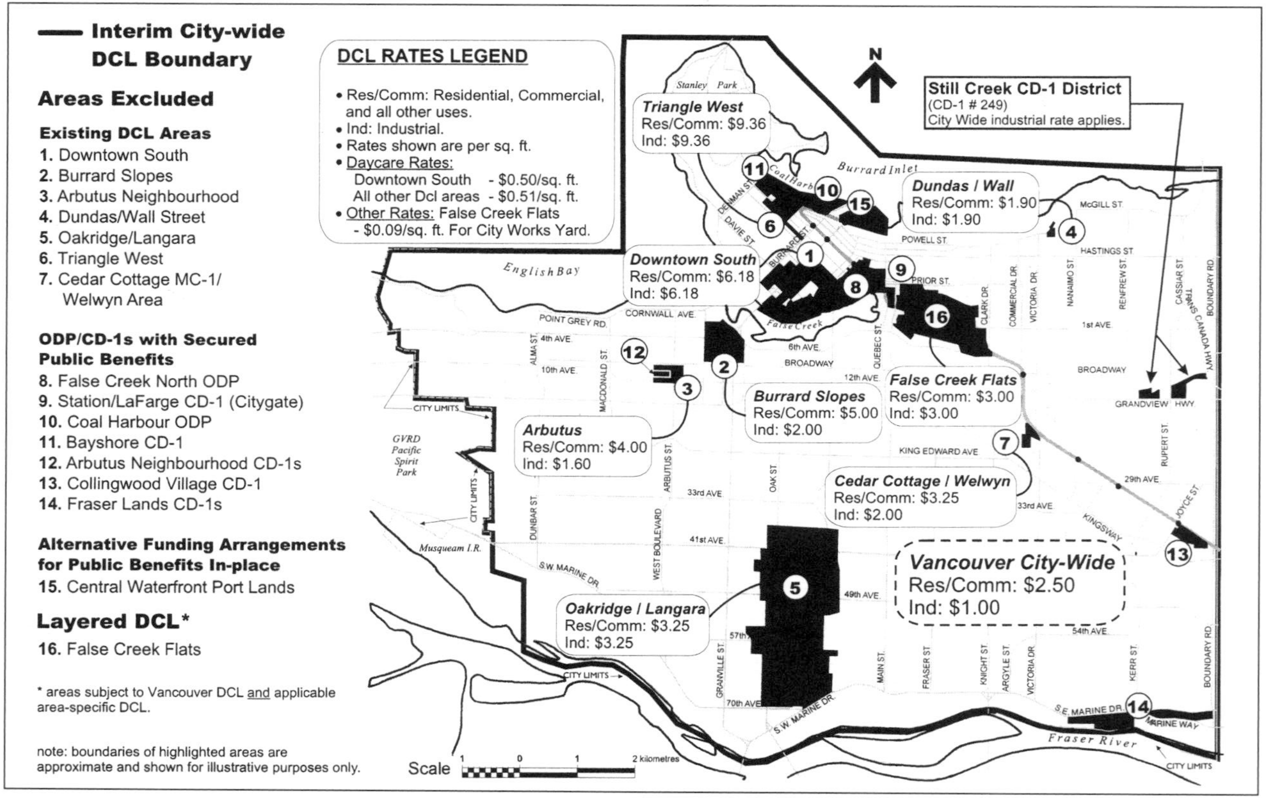
Interim City-wide DCL Boundary
Areas Excluded
Existing DCL Areas
1. Downtown South
2. Burrard Slopes
3. Arbutus Neighbourhood
4. Dundas/Wall Street
5. Oakridge/Langara
6. Triangle West
7. Cedar Cottage MC-1/ Welwyn Area
ODP/CD-1s with Secured Public Benefits
8. False Creek North ODP
9. Station/LaFarge CD-1 (Citygate)
10. Coal Harbour ODP
11. Bayshore CD-1
12. Arbutus Neighbourhood CD-1s
13. Collingwood Village CD-1
14. Fraser Lands CD-1s
Alternative Funding Arrangements for Public Benefits In-place
15. Central Waterfront Port Lands
Layered DCL*
16. False Creek Flats
* areas subject to Vancouver DCL and applicable area-specific DCL.
note: boundaries of highlighted areas are approximate and shown for illustrative purposes only.
DCL RATES LEGEND
• Res/Comm: Residential, Commercial, and all other uses.
• Ind: Industrial.
• Rates shown are per sq. ft.
• Daycare Rates:
Downtown South - $0.50/sq. ft.
All other Dcl areas - $0.51/sq. ft.
• Other Rates: False Creek Flats - $0.09/sq. ft. For City Works Yard.
Still Creek CD-1 District
(CD-1 # 249)
City Wide industrial rate applies.
Triangle West Res/Comm: $9.36 Ind: $9.36
Downtown South Res/Comm: $6.18 Ind: $6.18
Dundas / Wall Res/Comm: $1.90 Ind: $1.90
Burrard Slopes Res/Comm: $5.00 Ind: $2.00
False Creek Flats Res/Comm: $3.00 Ind: $3.00
Arbutus Res/Comm: $4.00 Ind: $1.60
Cedar Cottage / Welwyn Res/Comm: $3.25 Ind: $2.00
Oakridge / Langara Res/Comm: $3.25 Ind: $3.25
Vancouver City-Wide Res/Comm: $2.50 Ind: $1.00
N
Stanley Park
Burrard Inlet
Coal Harb
English Bay
False Creek
Fraser River
GVRD Pacific Spirit Park
Musqueam I.R.
CITY LIMITS
Scale
1 0 1 2 kilometres

Figure 19 Development-cost levies and area of application, 2001. This map shows the areas that were designated for development-cost levy (DCL) collection or subjected to public amenity requirements after 1990. Also shown is the levy by type of floor space and its significant variations by location and type of use. (*Source:* Vancouver City Graphics)

was evolved to enclose and provide "eyes on the street," but also to accommodate high-density living. The livability of apartments and townhouse complexes was as important as the generation of an attractive urbane form. Architectural diversity was encouraged within these forms with opportunities for architectural innovation and expression. The Heritage program was restructured and given some tools to encourage building retention and conversion as neighbourhoods were redeveloped and intensified. But a major contribution of the period to best practice design policy was the invention and development of cost levies and community amenity contributions to ensure that each redeveloped neighbourhood had quality public amenities and facilities, and replacement housing to prevent wholesale (but not widespread) gentrification.

Developers, architects, design consultants, and planners all participated in the search for new forms of development that could accommodate up to a five or even six floor-space ratio and still provide a quality living environment. While Henriquez, Merrick, and others articulated new towers with complex modelling and diverse architectural treatments to maximize the best views (therefore values) for each apartment on each floor, James Cheng designed a series of prototypes in the tower and townhouse mould. The city planners focused upon the qualities of the street and the neighbourhood, drawing on Jane Jacobs's (1961) concerns with "eyes on the street" and active small-scale ground-floor uses, Christopher Alexander's (1977) articulation of the importance of domestic thresholds and the necessarily subtle transitions from public to private space, Herman Hertzberger's (1991) notions of active facades with bays, balconies, and porches, and William Whyte's (1980) treatises on social spaces. These became components of the design approach to higher-density neighbourhood design. The design concerns synthesized in the medium-density context of the False Creek South plan were rethought at higher densities, but the fundamentals of underground car parking (an original TEAM principle), sunny streets, rear servicing, street trees and sitting spaces, and active public space became the substantive design principles to underpin high-density inner-city living.

In the design of the projects themselves the key concerns were visual privacy and quiet; unobstructed views and aspects; quality communal amenity space; and a positive relationship to the street providing animation, surveillance, and a domestic scale. These had to be achieved without intruding upon the defined public view cones or overshadowing sidewalks and open spaces. From a neighbourhood perspective it demanded adequate parks, accessible retail and commercial services, a well-designed public realm, and childcare and community facilities. Consultants and planners worked hard on the design of the public realm, seeking to differentiate the streets with various landscape treatments, species selections, furnishings, and forms of weather protection. The city planning department, park board, and engineering department began to develop a corporate approach to street design, requiring developers to pay the engineering department to implement a new set of treatments. The introduction of development-cost levies in Downtown South and Triangle West, and the addition of community-amenity contributions for major rezoning, began to address the question of how to fund improvements in public amenities in order to increase residential livability in these areas. But this had no impact until after 1992. All these principles and practices were to underpin the megaproject planning that began in earnest in 1987 (fully discussed in Chapter 6).

Vancouver's design preoccupations contrasted sharply with those of Toronto. Toronto built 30,000 new housing units, some 19,000 net additions, in the margins of downtown in the decade after approving its 1976 Central Area Plan, but it specifically eschewed floor-space ratio controls in favour of controls on unit or dwelling per hectare. This delivered taller, fatter buildings often awkwardly angled to the street so as to ensure prime views of the downtown skylines and the lake beyond, creating significant microclimate problems and discomfort for the pedestrian. There were similar difficulties with the control of downtown development, partly because of the lack of zoning requirements and design guidelines, and partly because politicians repeatedly became involved in giving density bonuses in return for amenities, heritage conservation, or social housing. This approach was the antithesis of Vancouver's, and contributed to the demise of Toronto's pro-development council in 1988. Consultants commented that Toronto had palpably failed to define publicly acceptable forms of development (Toronto 1990). This was where Vancouver succeeded.

However, in Vancouver, looming over all concerns about design was the issue of the loss of affordable housing in the core and the familiar pattern of wholesale gentrification that tends to accompany redevelopment. The achievement of livability at the expense of affordability was always a pointed political issue in downtown and the inner suburbs, especially in the 1988 election. It helps explain the council's affordable housing policy statements in 1989 and 1991. However, progressive withdrawal of the federal government from the funding of social housing, and the declining influence of reformers on city politics, meant that any response to the issue was likely to be modest. Although a number of excellently designed social housing projects in the city offered valuable design alternatives to market approaches, increasingly the cooperative movement was housing middle- rather than lower-income households. While the influential Downtown Eastside Residents Association achieved a great deal with its social housing program in its heartland, its efforts in

Downtown South came to nothing. Nearly half the development-cost levies in Downtown South would be devoted to replacing low-income housing, but council policy was only to provide one-for-one replacement for the 1,400 single-room occupancy units in the area. The nub of the affordability problem was that social housing was not increased despite the proposed addition of some 6,000 new residential units in the area by 2016.

Politics and Planning Changes at the End of the 1980s

In the late 1980s, the rapid globalization of the city's real estate market, the influx of affluent Asian immigrants and investors, the increasing pace and scale of development, the difficulties of financing high-quality construction and infrastructure, and the increasing resistance of residential neighbourhoods to change impacted on city politics and set new planning agenda and policy initiatives. The new Non-Partisan Association Mayor Gordon Campbell, elected in 1986, was only too aware of these tensions, given his early professional career and his backing by the development industry. Campbell had a strong liberal orientation and a deep interest in planning and development issues, and he was undoubtedly the most policy-oriented mayor in the city's recent history. He had a strong tendency to intervene in the management of the bureaucracy, and an interest and considerable ability in policy formulation and development. These attributes, and the need to respond positively to a dramatically different scale of development, drew him into inevitable conflict with the planning director, Ray Spaxman, who had always fiercely defended the high level of delegation accorded to planning since 1972. Close observers have remarked on how similar the planning ideals of these two men were, despite their clashes. Campbell's relationship with the planning director was of long standing but, over the first two years of his mayoralty, it became very strained; early in 1989 the director resigned.

Simultaneous with Spaxman's departure were budget cuts that brought an end to the *Quarterly Review*, as well as the exemplary system of Annual Reviews. However, although Campbell was strongly backed by the development industry, he was not about to unravel the planning practices that had been established over the previous fourteen years. Campbell's label as the developers' friend worked to his advantage, and with all the opposition coming from the political left he was able to finesse right-wing interests and convince developers that they had to accept development levies, selective changes to zoning, master planning of major redevelopment, and elaborate participatory planning processes in return for large-scale projects and development certainty. The property market worked to Campbell's advantage because there was both a strong and sustained interest in residential development and strong competition for permits from a wide range of developers.

The resignation of Ray Spaxman brought to an end a remarkable fifteen-year career during which the city had transformed its planning practices and established a completely different and very demanding planning agenda. Ray Spaxman's personal contribution to Vancouver's achievements was immense. In 1993, he was inducted as a Fellow of the Canadian Institute of Planners, in recognition of his outstanding contribution to Canadian planning. The valediction noted his innovations in participative planning, local-area planning processes, creating livable communities, restoring integrity to inner-city neighbourhoods, and establishing the discretionary system for managing development. While Ray Spaxman always acknowledged his particular debts to Councillor Walter Hardwick and Gerald Davis of The Environmental Analysis Group, he remains proof that individual planners can make a difference, notwithstanding the local and global economic and political forces that shape cities.

While the planning department lost its leader, it did not lose its momentum, as senior planners who had been groomed under Spaxman emerged as innovators of policy and practice in the 1990s. The new planning director, Tom Fletcher, had a brief and uncomfortable career following in Spaxman's footsteps. Then, for several years, the director's post remained unfilled. However, a generation of senior planners who had worked their way through the ranks gradually assumed the key position of power. By 1990 Larry Beasley was the associate director of central-area planning and was playing a major role in megaprojects, Ann McAfee was associate director of overall planning in charge of general policy and taking responsibility for citywide planning, and Ron Youngberg was associate director of neighbourhood planning (see Appendix 3). Youngberg was succeeded by Jacquie Forbes-Roberts who took over the reorganized Community Planning Division, while Rick Scobie became associate director of the department that managed development applications. Referred to as the "four amigos" by developers and architects, these planners established a tradition of coordinated and joint management of the planning function that rather bemused those accustomed to dealing with a single director.

When the expanded Community Services Group was established in 1994 to deliver a more corporate approach, as part of the *Better City Government* initiative, Jacquie Forbes-Roberts took the post of general manager, and Larry Beasley and Ann McAfee became co-directors of planning. Rick Scobie remained in charge of development services and, from 1998, chaired the Development Permit Board. Their respective roles, responsibilities, and personalities are important to the development of planning practice since 1990, but their well-defined, positive relationships and complementary skills and interests have made their collaboration a hallmark of Vancouver's planning system and a key to its achievements. Collectively, these individuals, ably abetted by a generation of experienced planners, many of whom had come through the ranks of the department, refocused the planning agenda of the 1990s. They were still council-directed, and the city manager's department kept a very close eye on resources, budgets, and efficiency of decision making, but there was significant scope for innovation and initiative. The department maintained a strong 1960s urban reform ethos in its collective intellectual commitment to participative neighbourhood planning, to the functional and affordability aspects of livability (McAfee) and its aesthetic dimensions (Beasley), and to sustainability through the compact city, vehicle restraint, and the walkable city. This ethos was shared by a number of prominent Non-Partisan councillors, notably Gordon Price, and by Mayor Gordon Campbell before he stepped down. This was the planning team and the ethos that steered the city through the 1990s, as the attention shifted away from downtown to the waterfront, to the single-family neighbourhoods, and to the construction of a citywide vision and strategy to develop a city of neighbourhoods.

Part 2
Designing Neighbourhoods

4
Single-Family Neighbourhoods, 1980-2000

Having established the nature of the reforms made to planning and design practices in the 1970s, and the development of neighbourhood planning of various kinds, our focus now shifts to specific neighbourhoods. Four chapters, each with a different geographical focus, explore the range of planning approaches developed during the 1980s and the 1990s. Chapter 4 examines the single-family neighbourhoods that still occupy about half of the city, and the pressures for the retention of their character. Chapter 5 looks citywide at the new Cityplan approved in 1995 which sought to achieve a city of neighbourhood centres. Chapter 6 assesses the waterfront megaprojects, their master planning and urban design, while Chapter 7 returns to the downtown area to re-examine a range of planning issues, including the particular social and economic problems posed by the Downtown Eastside, which represent the downside of an otherwise very successful urban renaissance. In each case the evolution of current planning and design approaches is carefully explored and a broad evaluation conducted of the success of policies, guidelines, and control processes, measured against the best practice design review criteria defined in the Introduction (Figure 1).

Thus far in the book almost nothing has been said about the fate of the single-family neighbourhoods that are one of Vancouver's enduring attractions. During the postwar period through to the late 1970s, most of these neighbourhoods remained stable and subject to only modest pressures for change. But as postwar baby boom families matured, so turnover rates increased. New householders moved in with different needs and values, and the housing stock began to change. House prices began to rise in real terms in the late 1970s, and especially in the late 1980s, as population growth impacted on a limited stock. Householders sought ways to manage housing affordability by creating secondary suites, many not legalized, while small-scale developers and builders began to see the potential in maximizing generous zoning entitlements through the redevelopment of individual lots. When the full potential of the zoning was exploited, the result was often a very "unneighbourly" house that overlooked and overshadowed adjacent properties and was architecturally out of scale and out of character. There were campaigns waged by neighbourhood groups against boxy "Vancouver Specials" in the 1980s and highly eclectic "monster houses" in the 1990s. The most affluent neighbourhoods were quick to devise their own solutions to the problem, but the zoning and design guidelines granted to them were soon demanded by adjacent neighbourhoods. The city found itself drawn into complex and resource-intensive review processes that it could neither sustain in resource terms nor support in strategic planning terms.

In successive chapters it will be demonstrated that most of the City's innovations in urban design and public policy conform to a set of principles regarded as best practice by international critics (see Figure 1). In this chapter, by contrast, there is evidence of zoning, guidelines, and processes achieving significant improvements in design quality, at least in terms of the way that new houses fitted into existing neighbourhoods, but failing on several other dimensions by preventing necessary adaptation of the housing stock to meet the needs of smaller households, exacerbating housing affordability, restricting innovation and pluralism in design, and intensifying social exclusion.

Single-Family Neighbourhoods

In 1986, 70 percent of Vancouver south of 16th Avenue and east of Nanaimo Street was zoned for single-family housing. Introduced in the 1930s, it had been only sporadically eroded by commercial zoning along arterial roads. Virtually all the city's low-density neighbourhoods were governed by a single-family zoning that was prescriptive in terms of height, setbacks, maximum floor area, and front and backyard dimensions (i.e., RS-1 zoning). The majority of development permits were approved outright and variations could be granted only by the Board of Variance. The 1930 zoning, with its generous height and setback provisions, had begun to erode the turn-of-the-nineteenth-century building forms and street enclosures (Pettit 1992: 65-66) (see Figure 20). Further changes in 1938 introduced a floor-space ratio of 0.45, which was raised in 1974 to 0.6, including basements, to increase floor area. Site coverage was set at 45 percent, however, decreasing the buildable floor space by nearly one quarter, a significant reduction. Overall the potential building envelope was still nearly twice that of the average pre-war house, but property owners and builders were seeking other ways to increase housing density.

Secondary Suites and Vancouver Specials

Early pressures to intensify single-family neighbourhoods came in the form of the creation of secondary suites, self-contained rental units frequently in basements. In 1940, this had been encouraged to relieve wartime shortages. In 1954 some areas had been rezoned on a conditional basis to accommodate conversions to multiple and two-family dwellings (i.e., an RT zoning), as discussed later. By 1956 secondary suites were discouraged in order to protect

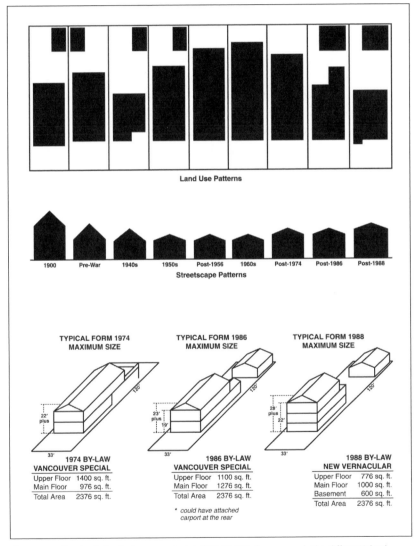

Figure 20 The single-family house on its lot, 1900-90. This figure reveals the differential volume and site plans of single-family housing through the twentieth century, as shaped by zoning controls since 1930. Impacts on the Vancouver Specials from bylaws in 1974, 1986, and 1988 are illustrated in some detail, showing how by 1988 the Special was effectively forbidden by the backyard provisions in the bylaw. (*Source*: Redrawn from Pettit [1992])

neighbourhood character. Council debated but postponed taking action to close secondary suites in areas zoned RS-1, not implementing enforcement until 1959 – and granting major exemptions in 1961 and 1963, and temporarily halting the policy in 1967. Surveys by the planning department in 1974 revealed that two-thirds of homeowners did not want secondary suites in their area, but plebiscites in 1975 led to significant rezoning to accommodate them as a conditional use. The issue continued to fester and council continued to vacillate through the early 1980s. Estimates in 1986 suggested that, in areas zoned for single-family dwellings, as many as 21,000 suites existed, many accommodating university students. In neighbourhoods closer to midtown, such as South Kitsilano or Riley Park, more than half the houses had at least one suite and they met a significant housing need.

In the late 1980s, council asked planning staff to develop a strategy to control secondary suites. In 1987, RS-1 zoning was amended to prevent the construction of second kitchens – and thereby the creation of secondary suites; in the eastern half of the city and in small portions of the west where residents supported it, RS-1S zoning allowing secondary suites was progressively introduced, reinforcing the social distinction between the affordable Eastside and the expensive Westside of the city.

Secondary suites were particularly common in newer houses that maximized the allowable building envelope and left the ground floor unfinished, so that, subsequently, this could be converted into a rental apartment to help pay the mortgage or accommodate relatives. It was not so much the preponderance of secondary suites in these newer houses – the so-called Vancouver Specials – that provoked a reaction from neighbours as their sheer size and ugliness. The full potential of the zoning entitlements had rarely been exploited until the late 1960s. But, almost immediately, residents in some areas began complaining about the extent of the lot covered by these new buildings, the way they overlooked and overshadowed adjacent lots, and their lack of architectural complexity and fine detail. The latter had so distinguished the pre-war Craftsman houses and revivalist styles that had prevailed in much of the city (see Plate 26).

In the 1970s, Vancouver Specials were distinguished by their "boring flat fronts, boxy shapes, and low roofs" (Kalman et al. 1993: 202) (see Plate 27). They were direct products of limits introduced in 1974 in areas zoned RS-1 that allowed coverage of 45 percent of the lot and the creation of 238 square metres of floor space on two floors, with each side yard 1.2 metres wide and rear sundecks 3 metres wide. (At the time, a standard city lot was 10 × 36 metres, or 33 × 120 feet.) Typically, Specials provided about 140 square metres of living space upstairs and 100 square metres on the ground floor. Initially, they were constructed by small-scale house builders on cheaper lots

Plate 26   Craftsman houses, 2100-block Macdonald Street, Kitsilano. These fine 1911 examples of the Craftsman tradition pick up on earlier West End precedents while incorporating the "wider proportions, broader verandahs, and wood brackets" derived from California bungalows of the time (Kalman et al. 1993: 168).

Plate 27   Vancouver Specials. These 1970s examples in Sunset exemplify the very basic, value-for-money design that attracted considerable criticism whenever they were inserted into established neighbourhoods. They could be personalized in a wide range of ways, but the open plan lawns, rear decks, and carports emphasize their functionality.

in the eastside of the city for German, Italian, and Greek immigrants; then, some buyers began to demand such larger houses constructed with better materials. It was recognized that, in terms of the housing market, they were "an unparalleled bargain," providing "the most house for the least space" (Anne Buchan, quoted in Vancouver League 1988: 5). But a 1981 planning survey recorded that 58 percent of respondents disliked the bulk, uniformity, and external appearance of the Specials, and more than 85 percent considered that the city should do more to regulate house design generally (Pettit 1992: 88). The Specials were essentially an eastside phenomenon, but as the demand for single-family houses increased, Specials began to appear in the more affluent Westside – where their designs rapidly attracted opposition (Pettit 1992).

A Protective Plan and Design Guidelines for First Shaughnessy

Perhaps unsurprisingly, the first neighbourhood to lobby for more controls over lot subdivision and housing design was Vancouver's most prestigious. First Shaughnessy was developed as an elite residential district by CP Rail at the turn of the nineteenth century. Lot sizes were huge – 4,000 square metres on average – and the favoured house style was mock Tudor, apparently because of its "English ancestry and picturesque appearance" (Keenan, quoted in Ley 1995: 87). The area had long received special protection against subdivisions and conversions through provincial legislation, individual restrictive covenants, and the activities of the Shaughnessy Heights Property Owners Association, established in 1938. Eventually First Shaughnessy was declared a historic district, in the first and last time that this designation was used for a residential area in Vancouver.

In 1970, the city assumed responsibility for the zoning in the area, establishing large minimum lot sizes – 950 square metres with a 26-metre frontage. But, given that these were respectively one-quarter and half the dimensions of a typical Shaughnessy lot, there were still opportunities for subdivision (Duncan 1994: 43-45). The city was persuaded to allow the property owners association to prosecute violators, but even these powers did not satisfy them; the association retained consultants to prepare their own plan for the area to retain its Anglophile character. City planners, presented with this plan in 1978, established a working committee composed of ten members of the property owners association, three rooming-house owners, two tenants, a member of the Vancouver Heritage Advisory Committee, and a planner to draw up an official development plan to protect neighbourhood character.

Although the Shaughnessy Heights Property Owners Association recognized the pressure from the housing market for lot subdivision and property conversion, they were determined to keep the English country-house ambience of their neighbourhood. They were politically astute and anxious that their plans to de-convert rooming houses and exclude low-cost housing from their area should not inflame opposition from the minority Confederation of Progressive Electors (COPE) councillors. When council finally approved the plan in 1982, the only dissent came from property owners who wanted to resist all conversions and housing infill (Hasson and Ley 1994: 80-83). Council's approval emphasized the goals of protecting the city's architectural heritage – rather than property values – stating the intent "to encourage the conservation and restoration of old meritorious houses, preserve the traditional character of First Shaughnessy, increase the development potential of eligible large sites, and discourage further subdivision in the area" (Vancouver 1982f). The plan went on to set out a series of built-form, siting, landscaping, and streetscape issues and servicing criteria for new development that would closely conserve the character of the area. The zoning was highly restrictive, with large minimum lot sizes (929 square metres) and an overall maximum floor-space ratio of 0.45. Nonetheless, there was allowance for the "possibility of innovative design and more flexible siting ... provided the proposed development respects the estate-like appearance of large properties" (Vancouver 1982f: 3).

Design guidelines added to the Shaughnessy official development plan in 1982 were the first for single-family housing in the city. An analysis of the character of the area, which had established a set of design principles in the official development plan, was converted into design guidelines to preserve "the strong home/garden/street relationship that distinguishes this area within Vancouver" and to promote "neighbourly" design (see Figure 21). The guidelines ventured into the use of materials, looking for "a sense of timelessness," "substantive structural qualities," "aesthetic appearance," "qualities of workmanship and craft," and "qualities of appropriateness and compatibility" (Vancouver 1994t). They also considered architectural detailing that had to "reinforce the traditional residential character of the area" with prominent roofs, windows, and doorways, projecting or recessing volumes, and traditional window treatments. Separate advice was provided for principal and secondary buildings. Landscape design principles were also defined – enclosure, screening, layering, filigree, filtering, revealing, and skyline – to be "implemented to a degree conforming to the archetypal Shaughnessy residence" (Vancouver 1994t: 26). There was similarly detailed advice for the streetscape. Car parking had to be well screened. The guidelines sought to replicate the late-nineteenth-century architectural and landscape traditions of Shaughnessy Heights; as one member of the property owners association expressed it, without a hint of irony: "we are striving for tasteful seclusion, privacy, trees, [and] setbacks. We hate tacky bungalows with their open lots. They look functional, like they are for living and nothing else. We love old Tudors, Victorians, things which are authentic" (quoted in Duncan 1994: 47). A sympathetic councillor mused that the association wanted "design guidelines to make people imitate a 1920 imitation Tudor" (quoted in Hasson and Ley 1994: 75).

Principal Buildings

1. Siting

Siting of principal buildings should vary from the required minimum setback regulations. A tradition of neighbourliness in siting should be respected such that there is a balanced relationship between the principal building, street, secondary buildings and neighbouring structures and outdoor areas. The siting of new development must address the following guidelines:

a) the siting of various buildings must create designed in-between places with a purpose and character;

b) front yard setbacks should respond to the rhythm of principal buildings along the street and vary from the minimum front yard regulations;

c) new development must be carefully sited on the property to retain as many mature trees and existing vegetation as possible;

d) new development must be carefully sited on the property in order to respect adjacent private outdoor areas such as patios, swimming pools, etc.;

e) new development must be prominently sited with consideration to its street presence.

many estates provide numerous options for sensitive development.

2. Massing

Principal buildings must be comparable in scale and massing to other existing buildings on the street. New development must be relatively in

proportion to its neighbour, be enriched with interesting detail, texture and colour, and be partially screened from direct view from the street in a manner that is characteristic of the area. The massing of the principal building should not overwhelm the site.

The archetypal Shaughnessy composition: base, 'piano nobile', & roof.

3. Height

The minimum height of principal buildings must be at least two storeys in order to preserve the traditional architectural scale in First Shaughnessy. Consideration must also be given to the relationship with adjacent buildings, roofscape modulations, volumetric limitations, etc.

Figure 21 First Shaughnessy design guidelines, 1982. This excerpt from the guidelines accompanying the official development plan outlines the design principles that were to govern new buildings in First Shaughnessy. Other guidelines embraced secondary buildings and landscape design. Also included were terms of reference for the Advisory Design Panel to advise council and the planning director. (*Source:* Vancouver [1982e])

As a further concession to the Shaughnessy Heights Property Owners Association, a thirteen-person design panel was established to advise the planning director and Development Permit Board; the majority of its members were drawn from the association, but design heritage and real estate professionals were also included. Professional designers who have served on the panel are not complimentary about its design judgment and are very critical of its deep conservatism. But the panel has been very effective in ensuring that new housing and extensions and alterations to existing houses have been "in character."

David Ley has pointed out the deep contradictions of Shaughnessy residents' objections to market forces as they sought to protect their area against intensification and maintain the "tradition" of the mock Tudor house designs (Ley 1993b). These were mostly the people who had owned and developed the city's industry and commerce and who were benefitting most from the redevelopment progressively sweeping away so much of historic Vancouver. In sanctioning the property owners' escapism by creating a heritage area under the guise of a public good to be enjoyed by all Vancouverites, the city had created a private advantage that greatly enhanced wealthy residents' interests and property values. The Shaughnessy Heights Property Owners Association was but one – albeit extreme – expression of a general sentiment emerging across the Westside, as neighbourhoods sought to defend their character and amenities in the face of increasing house conversions, demolitions, and new construction that maximized zoning allowances.

Heritage Concerns and Two-Family Housing

One positive alternative to the maintenance of neighbourhood character would have been to allow conversions to two-family dwellings (RT zoning). Where building conservation was a major planning objective, in areas with quality housing stock constructed before the First World War, zoning for twin dwellings had been invented. Many residences, converted to rooming houses in the 1950s and 1960s, were already in multiple occupation, although there was a trend to convert the rooms into larger self-contained units. The change to RT zoning offered an incentive for development of a second dwelling unit, provided "that development occurs in a manner that retains the physical character of buildings having 'character merit,' or enhances the physical character of architecturally undistinguished buildings, and ensures that development is compatible with the surrounding street and neighbourhood" (Vancouver 1997e). The guidelines common to all RT zoning designations required applications to "match," "incorporate," "respect," or "maintain" the specific architectural characteristics of the street or adjacent buildings. These characteristics included such architectural elements as roofs, windows, entrances, porches, details, materials, and colours, as well as landscaping and setbacks (see Figure 22). The general principle was "to have development blend with (but not necessarily mimic) the existing context"; designers were encouraged to work with "a fairly disciplined street rhythm using primarily traditional

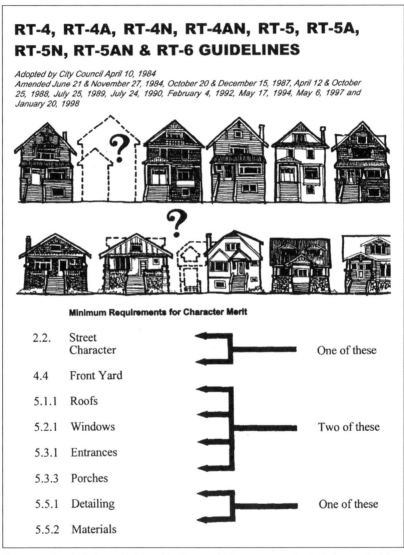

RT-4, RT-4A, RT-4N, RT-4AN, RT-5, RT-5A, RT-5N, RT-5AN & RT-6 GUIDELINES

Adopted by City Council April 10, 1984
Amended June 21 & November 27, 1984, October 20 & December 15, 1987, April 12 & October 25, 1988, July 25, 1989, July 24, 1990, February 4, 1992, May 17, 1994, May 6, 1997 and January 20, 1998

Minimum Requirements for Character Merit

2.2.	Street Character	One of these
4.4	Front Yard	
5.1.1	Roofs	
5.2.1	Windows	Two of these
5.3.1	Entrances	
5.3.3	Porches	
5.5.1	Detailing	One of these
5.5.2	Materials	

Figure 22 RT-4/6 design guidelines, 1984. These guidelines set out a simple design methodology whereby new houses had to pick up on some four of eight characteristics of the detailed design of adjacent housing frontages. While their main purpose was to retain buildings of character merit, and ensure compatible designs of new housing, there was extensive advice on how to maintain the protection of neighbours' livability and the retention of the backyard when new buildings were added on the back lane. (*Source:* Vancouver [1997r])

architectural forms," except "where new ground should be broken in architectural style" (Vancouver 1998dd).

To the east of City Hall, the area of west Mount Pleasant was regarded as one of "particular character merit." Mount Pleasant was built between 1890 and 1913 in a variety of styles and was, at the time, the first "suburb" of Vancouver. As the locus of some meticulous restoration by the Davis family and others in the late 1970s and 1980s (Kalman et al. 1993: 138), it was given a zoning designation (RT-6). This allowed careful control of additions and alterations to existing character buildings, as well as "in character" redevelopment of sites where buildings did not meet the overall "character standards" of the neighbourhood. The guidelines stated that there was no requirement to copy the styles of an existing property exactly, only to follow the "general components" of those styles (see Figure 21). Conversion into multiple units was permitted to retain an existing building; however, if a building was on the heritage register or had character merit, its overall architectural character and important exterior features had to be kept. In areas with such a zoning designation, all permit applications had to have written and pictorial analysis of the design in its context, and had to identify the historic source of any architectural design feature that varied from the original or from the block character. A number of architects adopted inventive design solutions similar to those developed in the Vancouver Specials competition, described later. The most celebrated example is the Mayor's House project on West 15th Avenue, which used this zoning to add three new buildings to a lot only 15.25 metres (50 feet) wide. It uses the 0.75 floor-space ratio bonus to restore the heritage house and to build a compatible near-reproduction house alongside, tucking in two smaller units and garages on the rear lane (Vancouver 1999e: 28-29) (see Figure 23). While this near-facsimile approach helps to retain much of the heritage charm of the neighbourhood, it is not favoured by many conservationists, who consider that it devalues the original, nor by many architects, who consider that it constrains design solutions unnecessarily. Such solutions are popular with residents.

Heritage Revitalization Agreements
To retain the city's best pre-1920 housing, alongside the introduction of new residential designations for zoning, the city's heritage policies and guidelines were reorganized. A set of specific development permit guidelines and a separate approval process were adopted by council in 1986. The policy clarified the status of buildings on the heritage inventory and reaffirmed council's intention to use designation that was voluntary (i.e., with owner consent). It also began to establish bonuses and incentives for protection of heritage buildings, and restoration and compensation packages for designating buildings

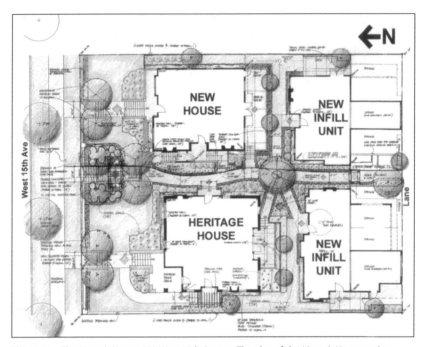

Figure 23 The Mayor's House, 320 West 15th Avenue. The plan of the Mayor's House project shows the three new housing units created, and the intricate site planning to create private entries and sitting out areas. James Hancock Architects did the house designs, with Wendy Grandin Ltd contributing delightful landscaping. Six parking places are provided on the lot. (*Source:* Wendy Grandin Ltd)

of extraordinary merit. Prior to demolition of buildings of the most heritage merit (i.e., category A), council required an independent consultant's report on the proposal; with proposed alteration of a building, council required that the treatment of adjacent public lands was to be considered. The planning director was allowed to increase floor-space ratios as long as the cost of the heritage conservation, the impacts on livability and environment quality, and the "appropriateness of requiring heritage designation as a condition of approval" were considered (Vancouver 1995e: 2). Any increase in floor space over 10 percent of that allowed in the zoning had to be approved by council. The amount of a bonus was to be calculated on the difference in the value of the land encumbered and unencumbered by the heritage structure, yielding an amount of floor space of similar market value. A premium bonus could be given for restoration projects, and any bonus could be used on- or off-site with the agreement of city planners and the developer. Development standards could also be relaxed.

Formalizing these negotiations and agreements, the province amended the Vancouver Charter in 1994 to create the heritage revitalization agreement to be used to vary or supplement zoning, subdivision, heritage, or development-cost bylaws or development or heritage-alteration permits. This agreement was a "powerful and flexible tool specifically written to suit unique properties and situations" (Vancouver 1997j: 1), requiring a public hearing only if land uses or density were varied from zoning. Its use has actually encouraged owners to get their buildings added to the register because of the greater scope it provides for development negotiations and access to additional development rights. Examples of agreements in action include the restoration and rear infill of a Parr & Fee House at 410 West 12th Avenue, which won a Heritage Award (Kalman et al. 1993: 139), and the restoration and extension of the Thomas A. Fee House on the corner of Pendrell and Broughton streets in the West End (Kalman et al. 1993: 122). The latter example, where the new is clearly distinguished from the old, is strongly favoured by Robin Ward, the city's conservation conscience and architecture critic. He has argued vociferously against facsimile buildings, facadism, and pastiche infill in architectural conservation. His fundamental principle is for change to "respect and keep what's original but use contemporary design for additions or alterations ... [I]t offers hope that the past can have a place in the postmodern city without being trivialized" (Ward 1998e: 21). To many, this is at the heart of the argument against zoning that is considered to discourage contemporary design and insist on pastiche and facsimile (e.g., RT-6 and RS-5, respectively). Those who take a less fundamentalist view of heritage conservation would argue that the real achievement of RT-6 zoning is being seen on the back lanes of Mount Pleasant. There, a new generation of small houses and integral garages in Craftsman style is allowing significant intensification and the development of much more diverse housing units and, in the process, reordering and urbanizing the utilitarian spaces of the back lanes (see Plate 28).

The Search for Acceptable Forms of New Housing

Westside single-family neighbourhoods were not inclined to consider any form of intensification, particularly not in the most affluent areas around Shaughnessy. The Shaughnessy Heights Property Owners Association, for example, not content with its success in First Shaughnessy, set about extending its preservationist controls over a much wider area to the south. In 1984, the association commissioned a consultant's report that noted the threat to the wider area from "oversize" houses. Local agents, speculators, and small-scale developers had recognized the development potential of many of the lots with smaller houses in the south and west of the city and had begun to purchase them. They demolished the houses and in their place built variants of the Specials that maximized the floor space allowed by the zoning. These houses invariably looked out of scale in the neighbourhood and, by the mid-1980s,

Plate 28 Back lane/end-of-street infill, 300-block West 15th Avenue. An example of the infill possibilities with RT-6 zoning, on an end lot creating a new frontage to a side street. A well-detailed building makes a positive response to its context.

were being dubbed "monster" houses. Kathryn Mitchell has summarized the general characteristics of a monster house in this way:

> A rectangular, usually symmetrical shape occupying the maximum allowed lot surface coverage and height and built to the maximum allowed square footage in size; a large entranceway with double doors and 2-storey entrance hall; large symmetrical unshuttered windows with occasional glass brick detailing; and external finishes that are often composed of brick or stone on the first storey and stucco, vinyl, or cedar siding on the second. The interiors are spacious and plain, with an average of five to seven bedrooms and an equivalent number of bathrooms. The landscaping is often bounded by a stylized hedge or a fence (both of which are uncommon in Vancouver) and tends to be more formal and minimalist in the use of shrubbery and trees than traditional Vancouver yards are. Occasionally the entire yard is paved. (1997: 190)

The "plague" of monster houses became the major planning issue in single-family residential neighbourhoods in the 1980s and 1990s (see Plate 29).

Civilizing Vancouver Specials

The first attempts to define rules for more "neighbourly" and more "in character" larger houses came at the beginning of the 1980s. From surveys of

Plate 29 Westside monster house. An example drawn almost at random from Arbutus Flats epitomizes some of the characteristics of the monster house – bulky, boxy, low-pitched roofs, strongly emphasized double front doors, and very large windows. The landscaping emphasizes the "see and be seen" nature of modern suburbia – and perhaps elements of *feng shui*, another contrast with the Vancouver vernacular.

eastside working-class districts, city planners were already aware of the problem of the much larger Vancouver Specials replacing older, smaller houses (Pettit 1992: 83-89). But the same survey revealed discriminatory practices by the planning department. Applications to build Specials on slightly smaller lots required relaxations that the city granted automatically in areas east of Cambie Street but denied in the more affluent Westside. Instead, many of the latter applications were reviewed by the Urban Design Group to improve their fit into the neighbourhood. This uneven practice, revealed in the surveys, led to clusters of slightly better designed Specials in the west of the city, but far higher numbers of standard Specials in the east (Vancouver 1981a). City planners did not report this phenomenon to the public but undertook to treat east and west in the same manner in the future.

Vancouver's architects were the first to make constructive suggestions as to how to improve the design of large single-family houses. A competition to find an acceptable replacement form for the Vancouver Special was promoted by the Vancouver League for Studies in Architecture and the Environment. In doing so, the league recognized the hypocrisy and obsolescence of RS-1 zoning, given prevailing economic, demographic, and lifestyle trends and the demand for densification and two-family living. But the league also emphasized the need to respect the existing architectural context and to create "friendly yards" (Catherine Alkenbrack, quoted in Vancouver League,

1988: 4). The competition sought design flexibility to accommodate contemporary households, as well as neighbourliness, economy, and usable interior and exterior spaces. In the entries, one of the most common design solutions was the creation of an accessory building to the rear of the house – a coach house opening onto a back lane – frequently treated in a vernacular form to promote neighbourliness. Other potential design solutions included the intensification and diversification of the space within a typical single-family home: the semi-excavation of basements, the addition of accessory apartments, the incorporation of "unfinished space" to allow future expansion, and the enhancement of livability through improving aspect, light, and privacy. These were the sorts of issues that revisions to the RS-1 zoning needed to address. The prize-winning design, by Californian architect Stuart Howard, was built at 4360 West 11th Avenue in 1985 (see Figure 24). But the prototype was not adopted as the zoning was not changed to accommodate it (Kalman et al. 1993: 172). However, the idea of the coach house was taken up by many developers and architects, and it became a feature of many two-family dwelling areas zoned RT-2.

Planning director Ray Spaxman, one of the jurors in the competition, noted that none of the proposals was an obvious replacement to the Specials. He worried about the unneighbourly nature of the long side walls that were

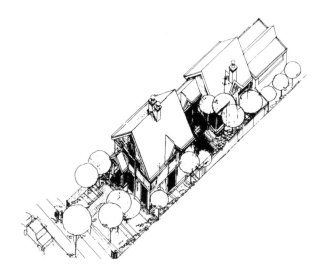

Figure 24 The Vancouver Special competition winner, 1984. The competition-winning design by Stuart Howard established a second housing unit (or extension) to the rear of the main property, attached to a double garage at the rear. Planners were not enamoured with the long unbroken frontages presented to neighbouring houses, particularly on the side not shown, and the replacement of the backyard with a small enclosed garden. (*Source:* Vancouver League for Studies in Architecture and Environment [1988])

features of many solutions, one reason why the zoning was not changed. He placed more reliance on "the resources, values, and tastes of the community" to improve design than on zoning bylaws or design guides (quoted in Vancouver League 1988: 11). However, the Vancouver architect who took third prize in the competition wrote to the director with a set of ideas for reformulating the RS-1 zoning – allowing coach houses, reducing setbacks, shortening the building envelope, and creating more usable space (Rob Grant, quoted in Vancouver League 1988: 36) – and some of these were accepted in changes to the zoning over the subsequent four years.

Preventing Vancouver Specials

The pressure to redevelop leftover plots and small houses, and to put in their place buildings that maximized floor space, increased steadily in the mid-1980s – along with residents' protests. During 1986 and 1987, city council and the planning department received 1,500 to 2,000 unsolicited letters from distressed householders whose livability had been affected by the invasion of large houses overlooking and overshadowing their lots, blocking their views, and disrupting their streetscapes. The problem was greatest in the east because of the preponderance of 10-metre-wide lots, which exacerbated these impacts. In the west, aesthetic issues loomed larger, as evident in 164 letters to councillors and the city manager written by Westside residents, particularly from South Shaughnessy and Kerrisdale (Ley 1995: 194-95). Studies were undertaken of the form of very large monster houses and the characteristics and aspirations of their owners. These were fed into proposed revisions of the RS-1 zoning early in 1986 – a top-down quick fix with no public participation, for which council accepted responsibility (Pettit 1992: 113). The key changes made were to reduce building heights to 9 metres (from 10.5), to limit gables and dormers protruding above a roof plan, to increase rear yard sizes to 45 percent of the lot (from 35), to reinstate front yard setback averaging, and to prevent attached garages. (The latter was regarded as a major improvement: see Figure 20.) The changes prevented a few very large houses, but they meant a reversal of the disposition of space in the Special, with the upper floor, the main living area, being restricted in depth and becoming too small for many prospective purchasers. Otherwise they failed to address the negative features of the Special.

The city monitored new construction activity to assess the impact of the new regulations and immediately discovered that the height restrictions were eliminating gables and dormers, and producing higher site coverages and longer side walls. Meanwhile, reduced upper floors led to the construction of first-storey decks at the rear, exacerbating overlooking issues. The 1986 changes had made problems worse. A second review began early in 1987 to evaluate construction activity. Five architectural firms were hired to examine various facets of the problem in consultation with the public and builders (Vancouver 1987c). Valuable suggestions from members of the Vancouver Neighbourhood Association recommended a return of dimensions akin to the 1938 system. The study results agreed, concluding that careful control of house volume and more neighbourly massing were required, and that a return to traditional patterns of development and the 1930s controls was the best approach. In 1988, council implemented another set of changes, raising eaves heights but not overall height limits, standardizing front yard depth (20 percent of the lot) and rear setback (45 percent), and adding a formula for above grade floor-space calculation. These changes helped to restore the concept of a rear yard between the house and the detached garage, and resolved most of the overlooking and view-blocking issues (see Figure 20). But there was still some division of opinion between those wanting more controls and reduced house sizes, and those seeking larger houses and fewer constraints (Pettit 1992).

The 1986 changes had discouraged the Special but the 1988 changes made it virtually impossible to build. The construction of Vancouver Specials fell dramatically from 55 percent of the larger houses built in 1986 to only 8 percent in 1988, but the new monster house – squarer, symmetrical, and more stylistically pretentious – increased from 18 to 75 percent (Pettit 1997) (see Plate 29). One poor form was substituted for another, as the new designs merely maximized the new building envelope as the Specials had done.

Barbara Pettit has carefully analyzed the changes in Vancouver house plans and volumes over the period 1930 to 1990, and she has argued that a gradual return to pre-war building patterns was taking place (Pettit 1992) (see Figure 20). The shape of the 1988 house was different from that of the 1930s, with higher eaves but a much shallower roof pitch. But Pettit's analyses show that the zoning changes in 1988 still did not allow the 3 storeys and the steeply pitched roofs that were characteristic of the earlier dwellings in the city. Criticisms of the new zoning persisted. In 1990, in something of a panic reaction, city politicians made more zoning changes, following inadequate public consultation and a muddled response from a directorless planning department. The planners' proposals suggested two possible zoning changes, including a relaxation of the 10.5-metre maximum height, which would have enabled a return to two-and-a-half-storey houses. Instead, council voted for the lower height and for a setback on the upper floor, which resulted in massing that resembled a wedding cake or, even worse, a one-sided version that was particularly ungainly. Ill-considered intentions to control cladding materials and prevent Tudor-revival copies were rejected by council. The broader issues of the appearance of the housing and landscaping remained unresolved, although westside neighbourhoods continued to agitate for more controls and guidelines. Monster houses made press headlines and dominated planning debates as they appeared in greater numbers in the affluent area of South Shaughnessy adjacent to Shaughnessy Heights, intensifying calls for new zoning codes.

The Monster House Invasion

The issue of very large new houses that maximized lot coverage became increasingly controversial as it acquired racial overtones. The major purchasers of these homes tended to be wealthy Hong Kong immigrants. Vancouver's housing market had experienced a sharp recession in 1982, and a recovery at the end of 1986, but particularly sharp price increases (up to 60 percent) were recorded through to 1989 on the Westside and were frequently associated with the impact of Expo '86 on the city's image and economy. Realtors, however, noted that the major inflation in prices began in 1988, and became spectacular in 1989 when they rose 30 percent in a single year (Sutherland 1998: 68) as a direct result of Asian investment. Immigration from Hong Kong to Vancouver trebled in 1987 and doubled again in 1990 in the wake of the Tiananmen Square massacre in China, and the impending political turnover of the colony from Britain to China in 1997. These business immigrants were easily able to afford large houses in better neighbourhoods.

Local agents noted that, at the end of the 1980s, 10 percent of all detached housing and 90 percent of all new homes were being purchased by people with Asian names. Many of these new houses were one-off constructions on empty lots, but in such areas as Arbutus Flats just south of Kitsilano, the transformation was particularly dramatic. Here builders demolished numerous smaller 1920s and 1930s bungalows and replaced them with monster houses that maximized the allowable floor space (see Plate 29). Agents and builders began to cater specifically for Asian tastes, which were perceived to be quite distinctive in terms of architecture and landscaping. Especially sought after were larger homes with numerous bedrooms and bathrooms, which suited the immigrants' large, often extended families. David Ley explained how Asian architectural and landscape tastes embraced but also subtly altered these forms:

> They have bought into a new landscape aesthetic that accompanies their economic vigour. This group favours new, large houses on a cleared lot, usually more than 4,000 square feet in area. The newness of the house, access to light through large windows unimpeded by vegetation, the alignment of doors, and other details of urban design, are inspired in part by the traditional metaphysics of *feng shui* ... But traditional design elements arguably make only a minority

contribution to the iconography of the home. Wealthy residents of Hong Kong or Taiwan sustain interest in traditional cultural forms like *feng shui*, and, far more actively, the centrality of the family unit, but they also eagerly embrace the modern world and the capitalist urge for creative destruction. In identity formation, traditional culture is often subordinated to modernity's fascination for the new ... The home is an important opportunity to demonstrate one's appropriation of progress, one's purchase upon modernity. (1995: 191-92)

Too much could be made of the distinctive nature of Asian architecture and landscape preferences. Barbara Pettit's research reveals that these purchasers were not particularly enamoured with the architectural styles that builders provided for them. She reported that only 39 percent liked the look of the new houses they were buying, with an equal percentage liking some features but not others, and the remainder thinking that the houses were ugly (Pettit 1992: 134).

Character Zoning to Prevent Monster Houses

While the city was making general changes to the single-family residential zoning RS-1 in 1986, 1988, and 1990, pressures were intensifying to create zoning codes to respond to the character of individual neighbourhoods. It was obvious to many architects and neighbourhood activists that a single RS-1 zoning could never be adequate for citywide application. Equally, some staff in the planning department did not want to become embroiled in design regulation of single-family houses because of the staff resource implications of preparing and administering a proliferation of specific bylaws, particularly as applications for individual houses, alterations, and extensions constituted the bulk of the permit-processing workload. More perceptively, some planners considered that such zoning would further entrench single-family house forms in a city that needed to develop new forms of multi-household living in its most accessible neighbourhoods.

The matter came to a head in Second Shaughnessy where planners had discussed the possibility of creating "neighbourhood character areas" under a provision contained in revisions to the 1988 zoning bylaw. City planners worked closely with the Shaughnessy Heights Property Owners Association and the Kerrisdale/Granville Homeowners Association, formed in 1988, to devise zoning bylaws and design guidelines for a measure of design control that could satisfy the majority of the long-term Anglo-Canadian residents. But in Second Shaughnessy, the Shaughnessy Heights Property Owners Association ran out of patience with the city's efforts. To prepare a zoning bylaw to the specifications of the association, a local homeowner, John Pitts, commissioned architects Neill Cumberbirch and Paul Ohannesian, who had already undertaken studies for the city on the failings of RS-1 zoning. They photographed all houses in the neighbourhood and studied their site planning to reveal ways in which the new zoning permitted inappropriate new forms in the area. They proposed the creation of a heritage preservation district to embrace architectural and landscaping controls as well as revised dimensional controls. Sufficiently impressed with the idea, council required the planning department to work with the architects to refine their suggested controls. When the revised proposals went to a public hearing in June 1990, there was no opposition to them (Ohannesian 1990). The area was zoned RS-3A, allowing the same maximum size of house as RS-1 as long as it adhered to contextual guidelines, which are discussed later.

In the words of Non-Partisan Association Alderman Gordon Price, city planning had been effectively privatized and a wealthy neighbourhood had been allowed to devise its own zoning and design controls without regard to broader city needs for new forms of housing and more affordable units. But Mayor Gordon Campbell had stated his belief in neighbourhood self-determination and protectionism, and his views were shared by a majority of councillors who recognized the political sensitivity of the proliferation of monster houses in the Non-Partisan electoral heartlands (Pettit 1992: 158-59). It was evident that other neighbourhoods would now demand their own tailor-made zoning bylaws.

Discretionary Zoning for Residential Neighbourhoods

Hard on the heels of the invention of the RS-3A zoning, city planners experimented with different levels of zoning and tested these against neighbourhood preferences. Council presented three alternatives to the residents in South Shaughnessy, Kerrisdale, and West Oakridge, reducing permissible house sizes by 40, 25, or 10 percent. A postal survey revealed that the 25-percent reduction was the most favoured option. But there was a differential response across the three neighbourhoods: the favoured level of reduction varied in inverse relationship to the proportion of monster houses but in direct relationship to the level of mock Tudor picturesqueness in the affected area. So the less "spoilt" an area, and the stronger its mock Tudor character, the more residents were prepared to restrict the size of new houses and vice versa. However, an upturn in demolitions in areas adjacent to South Shaughnessy and a petition to council resulted in a hastily convened public hearing to discuss two rezoning options for that area. The hearing lasted six nights, heard 97 submissions, and attracted an audience of up to 500 people and television cameras. The lobby by the Shaughnessy Heights Property Owners Association and others for heritage protection, neighbourly design, and natural landscaping was strongly challenged by the South Shaughnessy

Property Owners' Rights Committee, which represented mostly Asian house-holders and some Anglo-Canadians. This committee presented over 60 per-cent of the briefs to convince council that a more generous rezoning was more appropriate than the one espoused by the Shaughnessy Heights Prop-erty Owners Association. So, in July 1993, council rezoned most of the South Shaughnessy area down to 41st Avenue as RS-5, leaving the area to the south and east of Granville as RS-1. The area to the west of Granville was zoned RS-3 and RS-6. The pattern of zoning was carefully tailored to the sentiments expressed by each neighbourhood in the 1992 survey (Ley 1995) (see Figure 66 for each neighbourhood's zoning).

The differences between the zoning designations are complex and subtle, but significant. RS-1 was the standard single-family residential zoning with basic dimensional controls on site planning but few controls on house de-sign, giving maximum freedom to householders (and least certainty to neigh-bours). The RS-3 zone allowed the same area of floor space above basement as RS-1, but only if the new house complied with RS-5 guidelines (Figure 25) to ensure it was compatible with its neighbours. Planners respected the de-sires of residents in these areas to have a simpler, more comprehensive, system and less contextual guidelines. The RS-5 zoning offered an increase in above-basement floor area (over RS-1 or RS-3) to encourage the use of RS-5 design guidelines. Those who did not wish to follow this approach could build a smaller house by conforming to a set of maximum dimensions and having it approved without any guideline review. RS-5 was preferred by those areas that had the least intrusions of monster houses and the most coherent architectural character.

Finally, in RS-6 zoning, a set of landscape design guidelines was included, and if these were followed an increase in floor space was allowed (above RS-1 levels) on the third floor of a dwelling. Those who did not wish to comply (to date all have) could build a smaller house (smaller than RS-1) to a specified dimension. RS-6 zoning also included a number of specific regulations relat-ing to external design details, roof form, windows, porches, materials, and colours. It was a simpler system applied to areas where much new develop-ment had already occurred. It made significantly less demands upon those processing permits (Vancouver 1997s). Discretionary zoning was now firmly enshrined in Vancouver's single-family areas.

Contextual Design with RS-5 Guidelines
The rezoning and guidelines (RS-5) first adopted in South Shaughnessy be-came the favoured model for resolving neighbourhood desires for design controls. They ensured a high level of control over replacement and infill housing or large extensions. If applicants conformed to the guidelines, they

could take advantage of an increased floor area (0.7 floor-space ratio compared to 0.6 floor-space ratio permitted under RS-1 or RS-3). Owners who did not want to conform to the guidelines could build a smaller house without any guideline review. The guidelines were driven by the desire for design compatibility with the character of the immediate streetscape. While the adjacent houses and gardens would provide the basis for the selection of architectural and landscape elements, the choice of materials and design details would be derived from overall neighbourhood characteristics (see Figure 25).

Applicants seeking the extra floor-space incentive had to provide a design rationale based on a streetscape analysis of adjacent buildings (primary and secondary elements); the composition of facades, door and window patterns, materials and detailing; and landscape design in depth. As well as the design rationale, applicants had to provide plan analyses, photo-montaged views of the streetscape, samples of materials and colours, detailed drawings, and a landscape plan (1:100 minimum) as part of the permit submission. To assist permit applicants, the planning department prepared a workbook (Vancouver 1996v) which suggested how to use the process to ensure compatible design. This workbook provided a list of tasks in sequence to deliver each of the design requirements (Figure 25). While not intended to be comprehensive, nor to dictate a particular design solution, the workbook suggested a contextual design approach that "implies that the designer's creative process includes careful consideration of the site's context ... and responds to the existing contextual character while pursuing the site owner's specific requirements" (Vancouver 1996v). While the workbook examples display a high level of design conformity and a lack of architectural innovation, elsewhere the workbook tries to illustrate examples of good quality design, and how a variety of stylistic responses, from traditional to contemporary, are possible. City planners subsequently found it necessary to emphasize that applicants should not undertake streetscape analysis or prepare "preliminary sketch concept drawings" of both architectural and landscape treatments prior to their first discussion with planners.

By the time the rezoning in South Shaughnessy and Granville was complete in June 1996, many more of the city's single-family residential neighbourhoods were clamouring for similar rezoning. City planners argued against offering them the incentive-based guidelines of RS-5 zoning, preferring the simpler regulations of the RS-6 zoning, which were less staff intensive. But council directed them to offer residents the choice. This was to be an interim measure until a citywide planning process (discussed in Chapter 8) addressed the long-term planning of each neighbourhood. Again there were reservations among some planners at the further carving in stone of the single-family character of the city's more attractive residential neighbourhoods. A two-stage

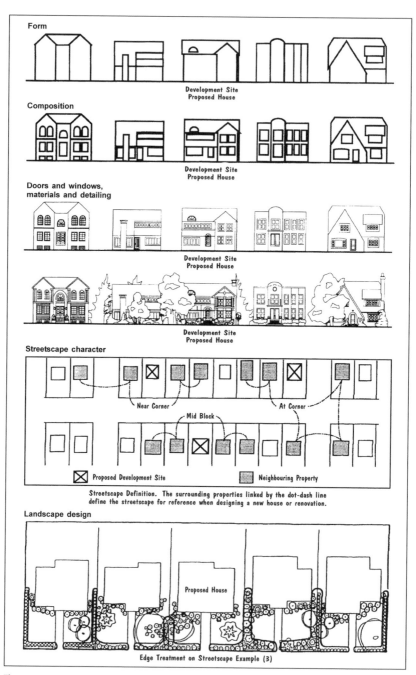

Figure 25 RS-5 Design Workbook, 1994. These excerpted diagrams from the RS-5 Design Workbook interpreted the design guidelines for applicants and showed them from which buildings they might derive the form, composition, or details for a new house. Landscape also had to reflect the norms of the street. The guidelines included a typology of historic styles at period streetscapes and a detailed work sequence and description of a contextual design approach. (*Source:* Vancouver [1997o])

referendum-style consultation process with residents and property owners ran citywide. Sixteen neighbourhoods went through the process and, by 1998, ten were rezoned RS-5 and one RS-6. This program prompted residents and property owners in areas zoned RS-1A and RS-2 to ask for the same rezoning, and staff undertook this consultation in five areas in 1999. Successive surveys explored the regulations most in need of revision, and staff concluded that they could create a single new zone (RS-7S) with supporting design guidelines to cover these areas. The building-envelope regulations for RS-7 were similar to those adopted in RS-5 but the minimum standards for exterior design were similar to RS-6. A floor-space incentive was included to encourage better landscaping. Although the design regulations might modestly increase the cost of dwellings in some cases, residents and property owners still supported them. The RS-7S design regulations that accompany the zoning have been kept deliberately brief and simple, to focus on architectural components. There is no intention to prescribe a particular style of development, only to ensure a certain level of quality of finishes and details. Equal importance is placed upon good landscaping, particularly planting in the front yard (Vancouver 2000f). The proposals were adopted in Douglas Park (South Cambie) and Sunset–Riley Park in November 2000.

Monitoring Impacts of the New Zonings

Many academics studying the output of housing design review processes in the United States criticize the lack of monitoring of design review practices. Their empirical studies of single-family housing have concluded that design review practices generally do not result in significant improvements in design quality, particularly in the eyes of the general public (Stamps and Nasar 1997; Nasar and Grannis 1999). Vancouver's planners both monitored the processes and were able to record public acknowledgement of improved outcomes.

The planning department monitored the effectiveness of both RS-5 and RS-6 zoning and indicated that the results were generally very positive (Vancouver 1999l). Designs based on the RS-5 guidelines were better received by neighbours, receiving 80 percent support. (Compare designs in Plate 30.) Designs under the RS-6 regulations received 60 percent support from neighbours. In both cases the major negative comment – from 23 percent of neighbours – concerned building bulk and site coverage, but the significant reduction in the level of unsolicited complaints about the larger buildings suggests that the design guidelines were having a positive effect. Residents associations were generally satisfied with the design of recent houses in all the areas, though in Dunbar, residents suggested that market conditions might have been responsible, as houses built under RS-5 guidelines were not appreciably better

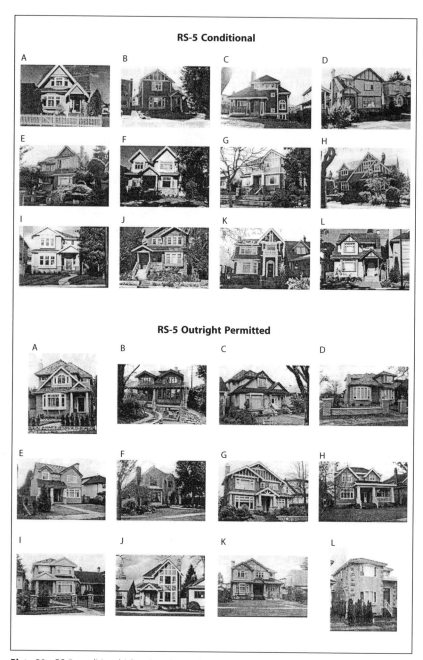

Plate 30 RS-5 conditional (above) and outright permitted (below) houses. These photographs are part of a 1999 inventory collected by planners monitoring the impacts of RS-5 zoning. The builders of the larger houses (conditional) went through the discretionary process, while the builders of the smaller houses stayed within the zoning regulations to earn outright approval.

designed than those in RS-1 areas. About 80 percent of owners in areas zoned RS-6 believed that they could build the house they preferred, as against 65 percent in areas zoned RS-5.

Architects and designers were generally content with the regulation-based process in areas zoned RS-6, which was comparatively simple and quick. Some regulations, such as those establishing roof dimensions and thereby reducing the potential for loft conversions and other design options, were considered problematic. They gave a more mixed response to the RS-5 guidelines, noting that the approval process was too time consuming. They also argued that less emphasis should be placed on the context of the adjacent four or five houses (see Figure 25) and more on basic design principles and area characteristics. Some architects complained that the new rules were so prescriptive that they were "copying copies," with the result that neo-Tudor and historicist styles proliferated. It was acknowledged that the latter was a general market preference and not necessarily a product of the guidelines (Vancouver 1999l: 5). Architects also complained that they were unable to design contemporary, modern houses, although planners always argued that such solutions were possible within the compatibility principles. The good news for architects was the dramatic increase in their commissions, with 50 to 75 percent of the new homes being architect-designed, compared with only 10 percent in 1993. This was regarded as firm evidence that a much higher level of care was being taken over design by builders and developers (Vancouver 1999l: 4). But the design controversies were also easing because the demand for larger houses was decreasing.

The monitoring study revealed that, in South Shaughnessy between 1993 and 1997, 70 to 75 percent of all permits used the discretionary guideline process. Significantly, no applicant opted for the design review route because of its uncertainties. The proportion of outright applications was increasing, partly because of market conditions and the speedier process. Builders had devised customized designs that conformed with the zoning to go through the outright process (see Plate 30). When examined collectively, photographs of the house designs do reveal a very strong sense of contextual design, as well as a high level of individuality. Most could fit unobtrusively into neighbourhoods zoned for RS-5 and RS-6, even if few display much innovation, and there are a handful of ill-conceived designs. A particular success was achieved with the RS-6 landscape guidelines, with all developers electing to conform to these in return for third-storey attic space. These two zoning and guideline changes (RS-5 and RS-6) had solved the problem of how to ensure that new houses respected their neighbourhood context. However, RS-5 in particular had dramatically increased the staff time required to process a single-family permit, as well as the costs of a permit, and both zonings had conceded that single-family neighbourhoods could be preserved more or less as they were. RS-5 became known colloquially among planners and developers as the "Mercedes Benz" of zoning.

From a citywide planning perspective, rezoning for multiple-family dwellings (RT designations) would seem to have offered a much more positive route to residential intensification. It would have allowed nearly twice as many households to take advantage of the high-quality services and amenities in these neighbourhoods, and to live in the ground-floor housing that is their preferred choice (as discussed in Chapter 5). It would have promoted more social inclusion, been more sustainable in terms of urban form and of service provision, and had a relatively low impact environmentally and socially. But, of course, the preservation of single-family character was the most important, though often unacknowledged, neighbourhood goal underpinning these new forms of zoning.

Landscape Controls

Although the scale and design of new houses was the principal concern of residents in single-family areas between 1986 and 1996, the removal of trees from properties often evoked as much angst. The felling of two 25-metre (80-foot) giant sequoia trees by a Chinese property owner on his Kerrisdale lot in 1990 became a particularly poignant expression of the clash between Anglo- and Asian-Canadian values in some Vancouver neighbourhoods. Not only did this spark extensive neighbourhood protests and physical attempts to prevent the felling – including private offers to buy the property at greatly inflated prices – it made headline news in Vancouver and Hong Kong simultaneously (Ley 1995). It also provided a major impetus for changes to the tree bylaw to protect mature specimens.

While the new residential design guidelines addressed matters of landscaping and encouraged extensive tree and shrub planting, further controls on tree removal were considered necessary. Tree retention and replacement provisions had been included in revisions made to the bylaw enacted in 1991. But in 1994, a Private Property Tree Bylaw was passed requiring that all property owners obtain a permit to remove any tree with a trunk diameter of 20 centimetres or more. Exceptions also provided that an owner could remove one such tree per twelve-month period as long as it was replaced, as well as trees that were diseased, dying, interfering with foundations or roofs, or within the curtilage of a proposed building. Lists of approved species, fines for non-compliance, and regulations for protection, siting, and replacement were included in the bylaw. Design guidelines emphasized environmental sustainability, noting the role of trees in ameliorating the microclimate, absorbing carbon dioxide and particulates, attracting wildlife, and enhancing the beauty and value of the property (Vancouver 1997l). The guidelines also included advice on preparing permit applications, planting, transplanting, and pruning. Some planners considered that these elaborate provisions were unnecessary and that it would have been more effective to require the planting of a certain number of new trees, especially since so many of the mature trees were nearing the end of their lives (interviews). In May 2000, a further landscape innovation – primarily directed at reducing rain runoff – set a limit of 60 percent site coverage by impermeable materials. Originally introduced in RS-5 and RS-6 in 1995, it was subsequently added to all single-family zones to reinforce landscape and sustainability considerations.

The Failures of Single-Family Zoning

Vancouver has been a leading exponent of sophisticated single-family zoning, and it has developed new codes to protect neighbourhood livability and aesthetics. It has been largely successful in retaining the character of its mature neighbourhoods, in protecting their architectural diversity, lush landscaping and trees, and in improving the design of individual houses. It has successfully resisted the invasion of oversized and fairly featureless box forms of replacement housing. However, the zoning innovations fail on several counts when measured against the principles for progressive urban design policy (see Figure 1). First, the new zoning failed to respond to the need to cater to a wide range of smaller households who are now seeking ground-oriented housing in attractive, well-serviced neighbourhoods. Second, the zoning has been very sensitive to aesthetic and livability issues – and particularly sensitive to landscaping – but it has only just begun to embrace specific issues of sustainability and has not addressed issues of community. Third, the guidelines are strongly contextual and, while they provide a methodology with design choices, they are considered too prescriptive and destructive of architectural innovation. This point is contested by city planners who note how the guidelines have dramatically increased architectural patronage, and are flexible enough to allow a range of creative responses, albeit through using selected contextual cues. Finally, there are severe doubts about the efficiency of the permitting process, about the time taken to get a permit and the negotiations required, but more importantly whether planning can afford to devote substantial resources to such minor applications. In this sense alone, the RS-5 rezoning and guidelines are particularly unsustainable.

It is easy to see why residents wanted to keep the architectural and landscape qualities of their mature neighbourhoods, and why designing in context was so important to them. The challenge to planners was to prevent such policies and guidelines from being used to freeze neighbourhood social character. The planning department was put in a no-win situation, caught between the aesthetic zealotry of long-established residents and the pressing housing needs of the smaller and newer households; between neighbourhoods accusing planners of being design-insensitive and obstructive, and architects' complaints of over-prescriptive, context-obsessed guidelines. Much worse, of course, were the accusations made by Asian property owners that city planners exhibited systemic discrimination against them.

Not surprisingly, these innovations in single-family zoning were not supported by the development industry. Developers were keen to reduce the unpredictability and cost of the system and wanted a one-stop plan-checking process, but they accepted the need for the community to play a role in both guideline preparation and permitting. They made their own proposals through the Development Permit Process Liaison Committee in 1992-93 (as discussed in Chapter 8), suggesting simplified district schedules that concentrated on maximum building envelopes and "unambiguous and attainable" design guidelines. They also advocated the idea of neighbourhood design panels composed of design professionals and chaired by a planner to support plan-checkers (Vancouver 1994k: Appendix C).

The Potential for Reform

By 1997, the impacts and implications of discretionary zoning operating across many residential neighbourhoods were evident to city planning staff. The department commissioned a broader follow-up to the 1990 study, extending it to include thirteen American cities to establish practice elsewhere (Pettit 1997). By mid-1998, the director of community planning services, Jacqui Forbes-Roberts, had produced a detailed "RS Rethink Issues Paper" that explored the performance of the discretionary controls, and reactions from the public, developers, and architect/designers (Vancouver 1998bb). This paper considered

- the processes of communication and conflict resolution, especially with city residents
- comprehensibility of the regulations and guidelines
- intensification and its broader sustainability implications
- social dimensions, both actual and potential, of the system.

The paper provided an excellent synthesis of these issues, noting the failures, as well as the successes, of the discretionary system (see Figure 26). It argued that many conflicts needed resolution if the process was to remain manageable and ensure quality outcomes and that "the expansion of discretionary zones and the complexities they bring is not sustainable within the present system of city processes, tools, and administration" (Vancouver 1998bb: 4).

Figure 26   Key shortcomings of discretionary zoning in single-family areas. Planners prepared this comprehensive list of the inadequacies of discretionary zoning in their pursuit of a simple and more efficient system.

Quality and compatibility in design
- Adherence to a narrowly defined "context" can often produce a less than desirable result.
- The intent is not to prescribe particular styles, but "context" principles exclude many options.
- Designers want flexibility and freedom but builders often want certainty and clarity.
- Two-dimensional controls, e.g., floor-space ratio, are not a good means to control three-dimensional form.
- A number of controls undermine sound construction and simple, timeless forms (e.g., bays, overhangs, height limits, building envelope controls).
- Building bulk remains a key concern in terms of overshadowing gardens, reducing views and privacy, and incompatibility with adjacent buildings.

Administration, interpretation, and discretion
- Inconsistencies between neighbourhoods and zones reflect dates in which new controls were introduced.
- Expansion of discretionary zones and processes is not sustainable.
- Complex processes take longer, demand more staff, frustrate applicants, and cost more money.
- "Precedents" are becoming increasingly important; desire for consistency conflicts with treating applications "on their merits."
- Guidelines become regulations and "rules of thumb" are created as standard responses.

Enforcement
- It is too complex and time consuming.
- Some elements in the bylaw contravene the city's Charter and are unenforceable (e.g., grade alterations).
- The more complex the regulations and exclusions, the greater the abuse and need for enforcement.
- Many infringements are enforced on complaint but this produces inconsistencies (e.g., fence heights).
- Maximum envelopes are often exceeded by the use of ecology-efficient materials and higher ceilings.
- Infractions for illegal suites cannot be enforced.
- Standard orders are written in confrontational language that encourages non-compliance.

Neighbourhood participation
- Neighbours are generally notified after receipt of an application and are excluded from pre-application discussions.
- Guidelines do not embrace all neighbourhood concerns (e.g., view protection).
- Neighbours often object to all "relaxations" or increases in floor space.
- Neighbours resent permits being granted if they have objected to them.
- Planning staff have to mediate between developers and neighbours and are blamed by both sides.
- There is no forum for mediation except the Board of Variance, which is unsuited to the task.

▶

◀ Figure 26

Clarity of documentation
- Multiple documents create confusion.
- Some requirements, departmental positions, and guidelines contradict one another.
- The legal language is obscure.
- There is a lack of explanatory graphics.
- "Interpretive notes" to guide planners are not made public.

Source: Vancouver (1998bb)

The achievement of livability at the expense of efficiency, predicted in 1983 by Ann McAfee, had become a reality.

City planners were also concerned about two other key factors – those of environmental and social sustainability. The former comprised encouraging building retention rather than demolition, control over the amount of impermeable surface on the lot through restrictions on such materials as paving, and alteration of the grade of the lot. Social sustainability related to the supply of affordable housing and the continued provision of secondary suites. There were clear planning department desires to facilitate secondary suite provision throughout the city, to increase the level of legalization, and to allow for home-working businesses, all of which were intended to promote housing diversity and flexibility as well as affordability. The solutions to some of the problems with the control process were seen to lie in a public-consultation process that would enable the community to influence design at an early stage. The report argued that an appropriate forum needed to be provided for the resolution of conflicts between developers and the community, and that developers must be accountable to community goals. The planners identified a need for a simple, separate, and easily understood bylaw with an illustrated guide.

In June 1999 the planners submitted a proposal for an eighteen-month program to rethink the RS zoning issues. It would endeavour to balance neighbourhood, applicant, and city aspirations within a process that was administratively sustainable. An advisory group, with representatives from the community and from the design and development industries, would consider how conflicts might be resolved, how regulations might better accommodate change over time, and how the regulations might be made more comprehensible. The report noted the importance of this rethink because neighbourhood visioning processes were "showing that willingness to accommodate growth within neighbourhoods is dependent on the retention of ... the look and feel of the neighbourhood" (Vancouver 1999n). The program would examine how neighbourhood notification procedures and comments might contribute to decisions, and how mediation and conflict processes might be incorporated. It would also investigate the actual intent of the regulations, their over-prescriptive nature, and the multiplication and mutation of different zoning designations; how to achieve better illustrated and written documents; and the coordination of planning, building, and other relevant codes. At the time of writing, this program was on hold.

Design Quality versus Social Inclusion

A decisive moment in Vancouver's planning history occurred when the Non-Partisan Association mayor and council decided that existing residents and property owners in neighbourhoods should be allowed to choose their own forms of zoning and design guidelines. At that moment, politicians committed their planners to providing a neighbourhood protection service to the affluent, a service that was always likely to be a major drain on staff resources and, worse still, likely to prevent smaller, less affluent households from gaining access to ground-floor housing in these well-serviced neighbourhoods. Mayor Gordon Campbell was prepared to exact appropriate levies from the development industry, but he was not prepared to attack the positional goods of the affluent neighbourhoods who contributed to his party's electoral base. And so single-family zoning was retained across almost half of the city, and reinforced with elaborate design guidelines, making these neighbourhoods much more resistant to change in the future. At the end of the 1980s, academics, architects, and councillors all commented on the lack of planning vision and the failure to plan for growth and change in the city (Pettit 1994: 187). These zoning changes only further entrenched protectionism and allowed aesthetic concerns to obscure wider social needs, including the future housing needs of the existing residents themselves. Finding a way out of the impasse will not be easy, because it will mean reversing recent political and economic gains made by the most affluent.

A 1996-97 consultants' study of single-family zoning regulations in other Canadian and US cities revealed that Vancouver continued to lead the trend toward more complex regulations and increasing use of discretionary design guidelines (Pettit 1997) as it had for a decade (Pettit 1992). Alternative regulatory frameworks were identified – the "modest building envelope," which provides outright permits, in Calgary; contextual guidelines on cladding materials and colour to achieve neighbourhood harmonization in Pointe-Claire, Montreal; and the sophisticated combination of sustainable and affordable concerns in Portland, Oregon. The latter is particularly relevant to Vancouver because it adds such useful sustainability criteria as solar access and street surveillance and directly addresses affordability by allowing large floor-space ratios generally and by employing "affordable housing overlays" to encourage the provision of revenue-producing secondary rental suites. The Portland model also offers the possibility of transition areas between single- and multi-family zones; adds a neighbourhood advisory process; and provides for an alternative to discretionary review through supplemental compatibility standards that are specific and inflexible design constraints (Pettit 1997: 6, 7, 74). But even Portland has not been successful in persuading all single-family neighbourhoods to accept secondary suites.

A major conclusion of the comparative study was that a quite simple combination of minimal site coverage controls and ample height limits might encourage "graceful" and "neighbourly" new houses that would minimize local complaints and staff resources (Pettit 1997). A return to simpler controls would avoid the dangers of subverting architectural creativity, committing too many staff resources to regulation, and slowing down decision making. This would conform to a widely held view that administrative systems are greatly preferable to discretionary systems when it comes to matters of design detail and the regulation of architectural style (Nasar and Grannis 1999; Varrki George and Campbell 2000). The two new zoning designations, RS-6 and RS-7, have taken this point on board to some extent.

Ultimately, the task must be to produce affordable, sustainable housing, and efficient permit processing to create less exclusionary neighbourhoods. By the early 1990s, the city was fully embarked on a single-family rezoning program that seemed likely to exacerbate its housing affordability problems and reduce its ability to deliver a more diverse housing stock to meet demographic and lifestyle changes. The negative reaction of single-family neighbourhoods toward even modest intensification had significant impacts on housing choice, availability, and affordability. Some affordable housing was offered through the late 1980s and the 1990s by the production of apartments on the edges of the West End, in Downtown South, and later in False Creek North to maintain the city's rental market at around 55 percent of available stock. City planners developed a housing opportunity strategy to provide more housing sites and to protect the supply of industrial/employment land in the city, but they were forced to retreat because council feared that the neighbourhoods would be fiercely opposed to the idea. These policy dilemmas pointed to the need for major strategic decisions about how and where to accommodate growth. They emphasized the need for a citywide plan that the public and politicians could support, and that would direct growth and provide a framework for neighbourhood and sub-area planning.

5
CityPlan, 1992-2000

By 1990 the absence of an agreed citywide planning strategy for Vancouver had become a political issue, with all parties complaining about a lack of appropriate policy for urban growth and patterns of intensification. Council recognized that it had to tackle development capacity, affordability, provision of amenities, and neighbourhood protection, as well as the environmental concerns evident in the 1990 *Clouds of Change* report (Vancouver 1990a). The approach adopted was to get neighbourhood groups and development interests to participate in the preparation of a citywide planning strategy for future growth that would retain the city's environmental and social quality. The result was CityPlan, which originated in council debates in the late 1980s. The elaborate consultation process for CityPlan, involving all community interests, exemplifies a deep commitment to community "visioning," which is one of Richard Lai's founding principles for progressive design review (see Figure 1). But the question remains as to whether the plan's strategy, and its subsequent neighbourhood visioning exercises, are capable of resolving the key issues of housing choice, affordability, and neighbourhood quality that preoccupy Vancouverites.

Preparing for Citywide Planning

Until the late 1980s Vancouver's council showed little inclination to develop a comprehensive citywide plan, being content to prepare sub-area official development plans for neighbourhoods undergoing large-scale redevelopment, and a goals and policy statement for downtown. In 1928 Harland Bartholomew and Associates of St. Louis, Missouri, had prepared a citywide plan for Vancouver, but it was not formally adopted by council. Nonetheless, much of Bartholomew's vision had come to fruition by 1970: a great seaport city on Burrard Inlet; a widely spread, lower-density downtown, with apartment concentrations in the West End; and the retention of the single-family neighbourhoods. Within that vision, however, only fragments of the master plan were realized, notably the city's grid pattern and sections of boulevards on Cambie Street and King Edward Avenue. Bartholomew updated the Vancouver master plan in 1948, but council did not revise or adopt it. By the 1970s, the emphasis was on neighbourhood planning, and it was not until the late 1980s that the relationship between regional planning issues and neighbourhood impacts became a major focus of policy (Oberlander 1997: 248).

There was very little mention of a citywide plan in the planning department's annual reviews between 1974 and 1989. The Vancouver Planning Commission was charged with the task of preparing a goals statement for Vancouver in 1977; despite being given some provincial funding and extra staffing to achieve this, their resources were clearly inadequate and their report never surfaced. In 1978 the Plan Review Committee, which had been set up to develop an overall corporate view of the future of the city, was dissolved (Vancouver annual review 1979: 5), but council did at least debate the need for a new plan. A small plan group was established in 1981 to focus on the central area, and its report was endorsed by council in 1984 (Vancouver 1984e). Retitled "The Vancouver Plan," it included a ten-point action plan that focused on the core but had fundamental implications for the whole city. None of these plan initiatives embodied any significant public consultation.

At the regional level, a planning board for the Lower Mainland was established in 1949 to coordinate approaches to regional development issues; its plan was approved in 1966. However, the provincial government split the board into four separate regions in 1968, creating the much smaller and weaker Greater Vancouver Regional District (see Figure 4). The regional district produced a growth management strategy entitled *The Livable Region 1976/1986* (GVRD 1975). This strategy advocated balanced population and employment growth in each municipality, reduced commuting and increased public transit, the development of five regional centres including downtown Vancouver, and the creation of an open space conservancy and careful resource-based analysis of greenfield development sites. Periodic revisions were made to the strategy in the 1980s, including the addition of the notion in 1986 that each municipality would be a largely self-contained community. A new plan with fifty-four action items was produced in 1990, entitled Creating our Future: Steps to a More Livable Region (GVRD 1990).

By the late 1980s the lack of a clear growth strategy for Vancouver was becoming problematic. As single-family neighbourhoods responded to intensification processes by demanding more restrictive zoning and design guidelines, council had little option but to grant them, simultaneously sparking criticism from the development industry and further contributing to the crisis of housing affordability. There was no forum for debating the role of each neighbourhood in the future development of the city, and there was a lack of consensus about what forms of development and in what locations would be acceptable. There was disquiet about the proposed high-rise megaprojects on the north side of False Creek and in Coal Harbour (discussed in Chapter 6), and it was clear that the Vancouver public wanted to be much more heavily involved in the preparation of these plans and in setting directions for the development of the city at large (Riera et al. 1993: 16-17). A series of planning reports on housing demand and the supply of land heralded the citywide plan initiative.

A number of housing projections made in the late 1980s concluded that the city needed to increase its rate of housing completions significantly and to more than double its existing supply of apartment units. The planners developed a housing opportunity strategy in 1990, the implementation of which would require additional staffing and funding. The strategy was aimed at providing more choice of housing types, improving the balance of jobs and housing within the city, and creating more housing close to workplaces to reduce commuting (Vancouver 1991l). There were four elements to the strategy:

- a residential streets program to revise commercial zoning (C-1 and C-2) to allow 2 storeys of housing above shops on arterial roads beyond downtown
- a new communities program focused on surplus or derelict industrial land
- a neighbourhood centres program to add new housing next to existing shopping and services
- a largely opportunistic new initiatives program to facilitate rezoning for rental housing.

As the city manager could not find funds for all four programs, the planning director, Tom Fletcher, set the new communities and new initiatives programs as priorities. At council Finance Committee, the Urban Development Institute spoke strongly in approval of the neighbourhood centres program, as did Councillor Libby Davies (COPE) who was in favour of financing the program over two years. However, the mayor and Non-Partisan Association councillors voted to take forward the commercial zoning study and asked the planning director to develop a half-cost program to progress the other objectives (Vancouver 1991l). The new communities program was kick-started by council releasing 110 hectares (270 acres) of surplus industrial land for residential development with the potential to provide 5,000 to 10,000 housing units. These lands included a former brewery site at Arbutus and 12th Avenue, the southeast shore of False Creek, Burrard Slopes (zoned for mixed industrial-residential uses), an area to the west of the Joyce SkyTrain Station (see Plate 31), and several smaller sites. The neighbourhood centres program

Plate 31 Joyce/Vanness neighbourhood from Kingsway, viewed from the south. This neighbourhood illustrates how a high-density node has been created around the Joyce SkyTrain Station. Just visible (centre) is the parkland provided to accompany this intensification.

was rejected by council in 1991 amid Non-Partisan Association councillors' fears that the demolition of 2,000 single-family homes to accommodate up to 22,000 apartments would provoke a storm of protest in their political heartlands (Tomalty 1998: 45-46).

Sustainable Development and Design Policies

Another important catalyst for developing a citywide plan – and a key driver for more comprehensive sustainable development policies in the city – was the 1990 report of the City of Vancouver Task Force on atmospheric change entitled *Clouds of Change* (Vancouver 1990a). This task force was set up by the city in the wake of a 1988 Toronto conference, which confirmed the threat to public health of air pollution and atmospheric change. In fact the City of Vancouver had a markedly better air quality than most of its urban region – the prevailing westerlies bring Pacific air in over the city and funnel and concentrate pollutants at the eastern end of the Fraser Delta where pollution levels can be 80 percent higher as a consequence. The report estimated that 80 percent of the pollutants were from transport sources, 65 percent of which came from cars, with about a quarter of all pollution (except for sulphur dioxide) emanating from Vancouver itself. The task force recommended that the city become a leader in addressing atmospheric change, listing thirty-five recommendations for action from setting targets at all levels of government to public education programs. While such bodies, established outside the city bureaucracy, usually find it difficult to get their recommendations incorporated in policy, this task force got a more receptive response from the Vancouver council. Some amendments were made by council in adopting the recommendations, such as removing the references to cement works and oil refineries as the main sources of CO_2 emissions, dropping reduced rate transit passes for higher education students, and not introducing a bylaw to enforce packaging recycling. But the vast majority of the recommendations were accepted by council. Proposals relating directly to matters of urban design included:

- energy-efficient land-use policies (recommendation 16)
- an international design competition to facilitate such policies in the Southeast False Creek redevelopment (recommendation 17)
- ecological development incentives (recommendation 18)
- proximity policies and incentives (recommendation 19)
- residential intensification (recommendation 20)
- local area planning, including traffic calming and neighbourhood centres (recommendation 22)
- energy conservation and efficiency in new and existing buildings (recommendation 25)
- urban reforestation (recommendation 28).

The international design competition (recommendation 17) was replaced by a commitment to a planning and design process in Southeast False Creek. The ecological development incentives, proximity policies study, and the requirement for energy-efficient interior lighting standards were dropped. Nonetheless, the report had a major impact on councillors, administrative officers, and public consultants. It increased the momentum for a citywide planning initiative, as well as supporting the neighbourhood megaprojects and particularly the experiment in Southeast False Creek (discussed in Chapter 6). Subsequent to the report, the Greater Vancouver Regional District data show that air quality remained only fair throughout the 1990s, with periods, usually winter, of poor quality. But downtown's air quality improved significantly throughout the 1980s and 1990s, with mean monthly levels of pollutants decreasing by about 40 percent (Vancouver 1999w: 4).

By 1993 environmental concerns had become a planning priority, and land use and transport planning were being brought closer together. The Greater Vancouver Regional District's 1994 *Livable Region Strategic Plan* to manage growth to 2021 had been drafted by Vancouver Mayor Gordon Campbell. It recommended a compact development option with increased densities of development and a "complete communities" concept to reduce commuting and journeys to services and to provide more diversified housing stock. It was endorsed by the city in June 1995, adopted by the regional district, and approved by the minister of municipal affairs in 1996 (Tomalty 1998: 39-44). While providing a strategic framework for regional development, in reality it followed Vancouver's philosophy of a livable city and a sustainable urban form supported by intensification, mixed land uses, and transit policies.

The Politics of CityPlan

One expression of citizen disquiet and of the need for an overall vision was a May 1991 conference sponsored by the political opposition, the Confederation of Progressive Electors (COPE), intended to elaborate earlier COPE election themes of the "livable inclusive city" versus the "executive city" espoused by Non-Partisan supporters. A Community Directions Conference sought to define a planning vision that would appeal to a wider constituency. The outcome, a commentary on the conference proceedings (Gerecke 1991c), contained important planning ideas and policy criticisms focused on the gap between architects' models of redevelopment schemes and the realities of urban experience dominated by increasing congestion, pollution, and noise. The downside of the burgeoning "executive city" was stressed in terms of the lack of affordable housing and jobs. The conference noted the drive for exclusive developments and posited them against the well-established preference for a livable city where amenities, facilities, and services were available to all. There were also complaints about public access to council meetings, a reduction in the right to address council, and council's failure to harness grassroots citizen views (Gerecke 1991b: 15-17).

COPE's conference had been prompted by a number of pronouncements by property interests concerned about the increase in neighbourhood activism, notably campaigns for affordable housing and urban environmental conservation. Vancouver developers commissioned a series of articles entitled "Future Growth: Future Shock" from the head of the UBC Planning School, for publication in the *Vancouver Sun* to emphasize the importance of urban growth (Mitchell 1996: 478, 489). These articles stressed international capital flows in the real estate market and international immigration, focusing on Vancouver's new synergy with Pacific Rim economies and societies. They stressed the benefits of urban growth and of higher densities, as well as public benefits recouped from developers through the official development plan process. On the other hand, the articles also criticized city zoning and planning controls as restrictions on the market and the cause of delays in development. They put forward the view that "a growing number of planners, developers and politicians [were] saying that popular sovereignty [had] become a euphemism for abandoning responsible representative govern-ment" (Seelig and Artibise 1990). These contributions articulated "a con-servative form of civic republicanism" (Mitchell 1996: 195) that provoked a lively correspondence in the newspaper. Other UBC academics joined the debate, the urban land economist Michael Goldberg citing the NIMBY (not in my backyard) factor as the biggest problem in cities and advocating the abolition of local government, seeing neighbourhood action as a reactionary, selfish response opposing the best interests of society at large (Gerecke 1991b: 18). But few Non-Partisan Association councillors shared these anti-planning sentiments.

A Participative Vision: CityPlan Phase One

In June 1992 city council finally responded to these pressures and initiatives to approve the preparation of a citywide plan. Mayor Gordon Campbell played a central role in defining its terms of reference. The key to his thinking was that council and planners should not become the "meat in the sandwich" between contesting residents and developers. It was his idea to ensure that the public talked together to resolve policy issues. From this concept was born the idea of "kitchen-table" circles where the public's ideas and energies could be harnessed to generate new approaches to long-standing planning problems, and through which public ownership of policies would be in-creased. Council knew that selling the idea of neighbourhood centres would be difficult, but had been quite unprepared for public antipathy to the deci-sion to rezone the land at Arbutus and 12th Avenue for residential develop-ment. The local residents complained of a lack of consultation. Council felt irritated by this complaint, as councillors were merely responding to needs expressed, particularly by the elderly, for more diverse housing across the city. So Mayor Campbell's idea was to get citizens to talk face to face to understand the issues and to find solutions in a non-confrontational way. He wanted free thinking about a citywide plan rather than a process stage-managed by the planning department. He reassured the planners that, if the outcomes were unworkable, the staff would then formulate an alternative plan. So city council established a program to "inform citizens about the issues ... and create, from their advice, a shared sense of direction for the city and its place in the region" (Vancouver 1995a: 4).

Council identified four key requirements for the consultation. They stressed the need to cover the full range of planning issues under the city's control, and to present a broad vision for the city's future, rather than a detailed policy document or a strategic land-use plan. The other two requirements empha-sized deep public involvement in the process, reaching out beyond conven-tional participation efforts to as many people as possible, and exposing citizens to the inevitable conflicts and necessary trade-offs required, and asking them to resolve the hard choices the city faced in planning matters. The result was a very ambitious public involvement program designed to collect ideas, to discuss them, to make choices between different alternatives, and finally to establish a vision of the future directions Vancouver should take.

Generating Ideas

The consultation was structured by a set of guiding principles that included parallel participation where the council, planners, and public would agree to each step in the process; ideas and solutions for "travelling together" so that consensus could be reached about values and solutions; public rather than planning-staff generation of a wide range of ideas; and multi-layered involvement where more people than ever before would read about the plan, attend meetings, comment on key issues, or develop ideas or solutions for consideration. In the first phase of participation, the public was presented with background information in seven languages on the proposed CityPlan process, its context, and the key issues. A "tool kit" of forty-eight background papers in the form of illustrated two- to four-page leaflets explaining policy development and key issues was made available to prompt and focus discussion (Vancouver 1992b). As regards design, the major issues were the preferred pattern of urban growth and consequently the location and form of new housing (see Figure 27). A series of questions also explored the level and extent of design review desired across the city; the level of and preferred mechanisms for heritage conservation; the extent of nature conservation within built-up areas; and the use of streets. The questions posed a considerable challenge to citizens without a background in such issues; opportunities were also available for experts and specialists to develop some very specific responses that might help shape future policy. A general impression of the responses is that few of the questions were answered directly because, understandably, they merged into associated issues of housing, employment, community, movement, and lifestyle, and into general preferences for particular types of neighbourhoods, streets, and building forms.

To develop collective responses to the questions and to solicit broader responses from residents, the public was invited to form circles of individuals with similar interests or similar identities. Planners facilitated this process and some 250 circles were formed from nearly 3,000 individuals. A further special program was organized to solicit the views of children and minority cultures. Facilitators were provided to help groups articulate their views, and these were summarized and published as an ideas book (Vancouver 1993d). Over 500 submissions were forthcoming – with a further 700 from youth – and these were drawn together through a series of "theme days" involving the

Figure 27 Vancouver CityPlan tool kit. The CityPlan team produced fifteen sets of leaflets to explain the CityPlan process, issues, and choices to the citizens. This extract covers some of the key design issues in the leaflet on the "Look of the City."

Look of the City

1. Issues and choices
   - Should we do more to protect public views?
   - Should we encourage more diversity of building types?
   - Should we extend the use of design reviews?
   - What do we value most from Vancouver's past?
   - How can we preserve our heritage, however we choose to define it, as the city changes?
   - What balance do we want between an "urban" landscape and a diverse "natural" landscape?
   - Should city council encourage access to other waterfronts, even though they are used for port or industrial purposes?
   - How should we design streetscapes?
   - Do we need more flexible standards for different types of streets?
   - How much do we want to invest in our streets?
   - Should we continue to foster traditional neighbourhood shopping areas?

2. New buildings
   - Should we plan skylines, or leave them to evolve over time?
   - What features make skylines attractive to Vancouverites?
   - Do we want them to continue to reflect the city's physical contours and areas of activity?
   - Which additional public views are important to catalogue and protect?
   - Should we create more opportunities to experiment with new building types, such as townhouses, rowhouses, and infill houses?
   - In which neighbourhoods would these alternatives be appropriate?
   - Is design review of new buildings worth the extra cost?
   - Should any area that wants design review be able to have it?
   - Who should bear the extra costs?
   - Should single-family houses be subject to design review, or should it be limited to high-density developments to ensure their sustainability and quality?

3. Heritage (selected 6 of 13)
   - What is of heritage value to different individuals and groups?
   - How should we identify and set priorities for what is of value?
   - How can regulation and incentives be balanced?
   - Should some aspects of conservation be mandatory rather than voluntary?
   - What kinds of additional incentives for heritage conservation are needed?
   - Should we protect more neighbourhoods as heritage areas?

▶

◀ *Figure 27*

4. Nature (selected 6 of 17)
- Should the city exert greater control over the character of the urban landscape?
- How much city regulation of tree replacement on private property is appropriate?
- Do Vancouverites want to encourage a diversity of wildlife in the city, or is its presence viewed as being a concern and perhaps a nuisance?
- Do the environmental, wildlife habitat, and aesthetic benefits of restoring Vancouver's hidden waterways justify the costs?
- Do we need to fundamentally rethink how we use, treat, and share our public streets?
- Should we consider new kinds of streets, such as the Dutch *woonerf,* which assigns vehicle through-traffic a minor role in the design and life of residential streets?

Source: Vancouver (1993b)

relevant consultation circles to distill common ideas and objectives. These were subsequently presented at a three-day "ideas fair" which represented the second step in the participation program.

Representations from property, development, and design professionals in the CityPlan ideas book were few, but those that responded generally tried to be creative and altruistic rather than self-interested; the Urban Development Institute, for example, presented the concept of a pedestrian village. The Building Owners and Managers Associations were more true to type, pleading for a rise in residential tax rates to halve the business rate, advocating business improvement areas, and arguing for a one-third increase in downtown floor-space ratios to discourage the proliferation of squat buildings (Vancouver 1993d: 374-76). But they also argued for separation of sanitary and storm-water sewerage, and universal secondary sewage treatment. One of the most valuable design contributions came from the Architectural Institute of British Columbia, which sought more innovation in housing through design competitions, demonstration projects, and prototype development; a greater variety of house types and densities; and an increased supply of medium-density ground-oriented housing.

There were surprisingly few site-specific proposals, but two were of special merit. The first was a proposal by an architectural practice to provide a pedestrian walkway underneath the Granville Street Bridge to connect Granville Island to Downtown South, tackling two of Vancouver's planning problems – the lack of pedestrian access between downtown and Granville Island and Fairview Slopes, and the need for stronger pedestrian flows along the length of Granville Street. The second, from the mysteriously named "Eighth Circle" (possibly politicians), proposed a new focal point for downtown – an animated urban plaza in front of the art gallery on Georgia Street to replace the existing lawn, fountain, and mature trees (see Figure 28).

An idea that received widespread support was the notion of greenways – landscaped or treed corridors with paths for pedestrians and cyclists – with some thirteen separate citations in the CityPlan ideas book (Vancouver 1993d). Proposals for greenways had arisen from the mayor's Urban Landscape Task Force appointed by council in 1991 to report on ways to manage, protect, and enhance the urban landscape (Vancouver 1992c). The task force made fifteen recommendations for developing policies, plans, proposals, and processes to enhance the city's landscape, but the one that especially caught the public's imagination was the creation of a system of linear parks and paths with a public trust to manage them. Once the idea was tested and won strong support in the CityPlan public consultation, it was taken forward jointly by city planning and engineering staff. Completion and adoption of the "City Greenways Plan" (Vancouver 1995l) by council in mid-1995, more or less simultaneously with CityPlan, provided a way in which council could demonstrate commitment to, and the credibility of, the plan (see Figure 29).

The 478-page "CityPlan: Ideas Illustrated" book provides a fascinating insight into the concerns of the public. There were many expressions of support for a city of diverse neighbourhoods where communities could determine the nature of redevelopment and simultaneously ensure a greater diversity of housing. Strong demands were articulated for enhanced transit to foster continued growth of the commercial core, for more mixture of uses, particularly residential and leisure, and for defined neighbourhood centres. Design concerns emphasized protection of the city's high-quality residential streetscapes and an endorsement of design review as a means of ensuring compatible redevelopment. The protection of green spaces, trees, and natural environments was stressed, as was the need to promote the development of more quality public space. There was widespread recognition of the need for a greater mix of more affordable housing in single-family neighbourhoods, and for a more positive approach to secondary suites, density increases, and design guidelines. Downtown residents endorsed building height and view controls, as well as firmer heritage provisions with greater protection for buildings listed in category B and tax incentives for building restoration and retention.

The three-day ideas fair brought 10,000 people to view the exhibition of the submissions. Artists had drawn exhibit panels for ideas from each city circle in a series of "co-design workshops," which were subsequently published (Vancouver 1993d). The exhibits were accompanied by a series of guest talks, panel presentations, and discussions. About 2,000 visitors evaluated the

* WHERE YOU CAN BE DOWNTOWN AND
  ENJOY A DAY OR EVENING OUTDOORS
  IN THE HEART OF THE CITY.

* WHERE YOU CAN MEET YOUR FRIENDS,
  WATCH THE PASSING PARADE, SAVOUR A
  BEER OR CAPPUCCINO AFTER WORK —
  AFTER A MOVIE.

* VANCOUVER HAS NO PERMANENT GATHERING
  PLACE WHERE THE URBAN CROWD CAN
  BRING LIFE AND CHARM TO CITY STREET.

* THE SPACE BETWEEN THE ART GALLERY
  AND GEORGIA ST. IS BARE AND UNUSED.
  LET'S TRANSFORM IT INTO A TRUE PUBLIC
  SQUARE WHERE WE ALL WANT TO GO!

- NORA KELLY   JOYCE CATLIFF
       REPRESENTING
  "THE EIGHTH CIRCLE"

NEEDED! A TRUE PUBLIC SQUARE

* REMOVE THE FOUNTAIN — IT'S TOO CHILLY
  FOR OUR CLIMATE.

* REMOVE THE GRASS — REPLACE WITH
  ORNAMENTAL PAVERS.

* ENCLOSE THE SPACE WITH A BORDER OF
  TREES AND ORNAMENTAL LIGHTING.

* ILLUMINATE THE ART GALLERY DOME
  AND THE LIONS ON THE STEPS.

* FURNISH THE SQUARE FROM MAY TO
  OCTOBER WITH SMALL MOVABLE CHAIRS
  AND TABLES FOR SHIFTING GROUPS
  OF PEOPLE.

* SERVE COFFEES, SOFT DRINKS, WINE, BEER,
  AND FINGER FOOD

* ENCOURAGE MUSICIANS, BUSKERS, STREET
  VENDORS WITH SPECIALTY FOODS.

CLARK WILSON

Figure 28 Vancouver "CityPlan Ideas Illustrated" book: example of a submission from a city circle, 1993. An illustration which articulates the ideas of small groups (circles) arguing for particular initiatives. The sketch illustrates proposals for a new animated, urbane city square to replace Courthouse Square. (Source: Vancouver (1993d))

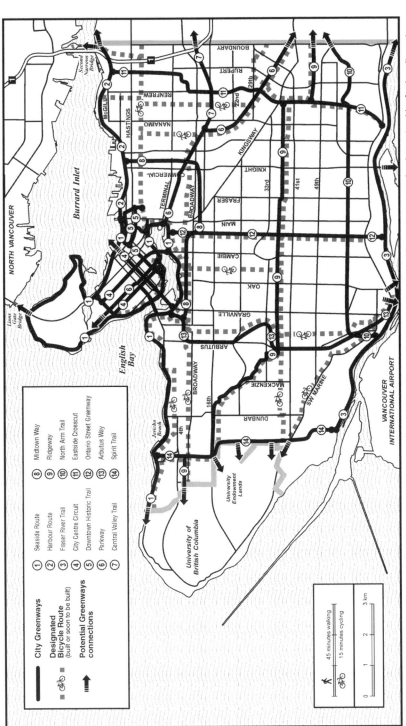

Figure 29 City Greenways Plan, 1995. This plan, approved by council in 1995, projected fourteen greenways, with exact routes to be determined by further discussion and study. (*Source:* Vancouver [1995])

ideas by filling out the "check book" provided to identify areas of agreement and contention.

Making Choices

For the third step of the CityPlan program, the planners synthesized and counterposed the key ideas and produced a forty-page booklet (Vancouver 1994g). This was organized into twelve themes and distributed to the 6,000 people on the CityPlan mailing list. It included a questionnaire to allow people to choose their preferred directions for each policy area. There was a consensus about policy directions in the areas of public safety, movement, public places, environment, art, and culture, but there were significant disagreements about housing, neighbourhood character, employment, community services, and decision making. To accommodate these differences, the planners articulated four alternative futures for the city, each in an eight-page "Making Choices" brochure (Vancouver 1994h), which was mailed to all households to allow them to choose their preferred option through an accompanying questionnaire. The four alternatives were encapsulated as: the city of neighbourhood centres, the city of mixed residential and main-street neighbourhoods, the central city, and the traditional city (see Figure 30). Over 15,000 people visited the subsequent exhibition explaining these choices.

Adopting the Plan

Of the four futures, it was the city of neighbourhood centres – the idea rejected by city council in 1991 as too controversial – that found the most favour with the public. It became the basis of the CityPlan vision (see Figure 31). The planners, who had expected that NIMBY (not in my backyard) attitudes would prevail, were collectively astonished that 80 percent of the participants supported the provision of more housing choice in the city and a reduction in regional sprawl (McAfee 1997b: 20-21). The public preferred to concentrate growth in neighbourhood centres that would provide a wider range of housing for the young, the old, and the less affluent – and impact less on existing low-density neighbourhoods. These same centres would also be the focus for community services and new employment opportunities, principally office jobs. Neighbourhoods would have a say in the design and fit of new housing within their areas and better local access to government services, while downtown and uptown would be reinforced by new residential populations and more lively streets and public spaces.

Drawing together the public contributions from the "making choices" consultation, the results of the city future questionnaire, and a supporting random survey of residents, the planners assembled a draft comprehensive citywide plan for the public to discuss with councillors. This draft plan embraced basic

Figure 30 The four futures for the City of Vancouver, CityPlan, 1994. The outcome of the "Choices" exercise was the distilling of four different possible futures for the City of Vancouver. The City of Neighbourhood Centres garnered an astonishing 80 percent of citizen support.

	1 Housing variety	2 Development character	3 Employment	4 Neighbourhoods	5 Decision making	6 Housing costs	7 Community services
City of Neighbourhood Centres	Neighbourhood centres	Traditional and contemporary	Downtown, neighbourhood centres, industrial areas	More village neighbourhoods	Networked city	Subsidies and regulation	Access and participation
City of Mixed Residential and Main Street Neighbourhoods	Scattered redevelopment	Traditional and contemporary	Downtown, main streets, industrial areas	More mixed neighbourhoods and main streets	Participatory neighbourhoods	Some regulation	Access and participation
The Central City	On industrial lands	Traditional and contemporary	Downtown offices	Traditional single family	Open city government	Subsidies and regulation	Range, some targeted
The Traditional City	Limited to existing and planned	Traditional	Regional centres outside city	Traditional single family	Participatory neighbourhoods	Some subsidized housing	Range, some targeted

Source: Vancouver (1994g)

Figure 31   Key aspects of "A Vision for Vancouver," CityPlan, 1995. The vision of "a city of neighbourhoods" was spelt out under six headings embracing form, community, economy, environment, and implementation.

A city of neighbourhoods: prepared options

Neighbourhood centres
- developed from existing shopping streets to provide a heart for each neighbourhood
- will provide jobs and services, reduce travel, and provide new housing in single-family areas

Housing variety
- more housing choice for older and younger people in neighbourhoods
- residents will have a say on how it looks and fits in

Distinctive neighbourhood character
- major changes in scale in neighbourhood centres and around downtown

Sense of community

Accessible, community-based services
- in neighbourhood centres and with coordinated problem solving

Promoting safety
- crime prevention and community awareness

Addressing housing costs
- promoting more low-cost housing in private and public sectors

Art and culture
- contribute to neighbourhood character

New and more diverse public places
- parks, greenways, nature protection, and more diverse public spaces

Healthy economy: healthy environment

Diverse economy and jobs close to home
- downtown growth but also new jobs in neighbourhood centres

Transit walking and biking
- widened transport choice and less need to travel as a priority

Clean air and water
- emphasizing alternatives to the car; raising user fees for garbage and water

A vibrant central area

Downtown Vancouver
- twin office locations downtown and Broadway; mixed use and diverse downtown for residents, employees, and tourists; range of living environments

►

◄ *Figure 31*

Making CityPlan happen

People involved in decision making
• neighbourhoods identifying and resolving local issues

Financial accountability
• relating tax increases to cost of living, more efficient services, and accountable financing

The city in the region

Vancouver and the region
• supporting GVRD's Livable Region Strategic Plan

Source: Adapted from Vancouver (1995a)

principles of sustainable development, rejected the continued conversion of industrial lands to residential use, and focused new housing supply on low-density neighbourhoods. The key changes of direction required in city planning policies were defined by CityPlan team leader Ann McAfee as follows:

• increasing housing variety throughout the city to meet people's needs and make better use of existing city services
• locating jobs closer to where people live to reduce travel
• maintaining a diverse economy
• moving people by transit, walking, and biking, and devoting some streets to the pedestrian/cyclist
• changing the delivery of services to a neighbourhood-based model
• supporting stronger neighbourhoods through the development of neighbourhood centres, local character zoning, community-based policing, and integrated service teams. (1997c: 246)

The major design challenges, identified as a series of "next steps," included:

• defining, with residents, the acceptable alternatives to single-family housing in neighbourhoods
• building demonstration projects for the same
• incorporating housing into neighbourhood centres and increasing housing choice in each neighbourhood
• developing area appraisal techniques, bylaws, and guidelines to help neighbourhoods create the character they want
• expanding heritage and tree regulations to protect existing amenities
• applying "crime prevention through environmental design" principles

- reviewing regulations that add to housing cost and incentivizing low-cost market housing
- including public art in developments and along the city's greenways
- pursuing greenways at large, and major public space developments in the downtown
- clarifying protected views, skyline, and public realm policies in the Central Area
- promoting a compact downtown
- involving businesses and residents in the planning of neighbourhood centres and the surrounding community. (Vancouver 1995a: 12, 14, 20, 22, 24, 26, 38, 42)

The draft plan was adopted by council as "a broad vision for the city [that would] guide policy decisions, corporate work priorities, budgets and capital plans ... and ... provide a context for developing partnership agreements" with the regional district (Vancouver 1995a: 1). Because of provincial legislation, the CityPlan document does not provide a policy for the city's development in the way that Toronto's 1993 CityPlan document does. It merely sets a broad citywide framework for neighbourhood planning and service delivery. Vancouver's CityPlan was based on the principle that each neighbourhood would develop its own detailed land-use plan, zoning regulations, design guidelines, and enhancement projects that would respond to the overall CityPlan directions.

Seen from the perspective of the neighbourhoods' clamour for restrictive zoning codes and tight design guidelines discussed in the previous chapter, the achievements of the CityPlan process were very positive. CityPlan helped make a large number of residents aware of the dangers of NIMBY thinking, and of the need both to allow significant diversification of the housing stock and to reinforce neighbourhood centres throughout the city. It helped to build support for a well-planned approach to intensification. Furthermore, it provided a valuable public endorsement of many of the planning principles that the city had pursued over the previous decade: promoting a broadly defined sustainable form of development, restricting building heights and protecting views, ensuring that development fitted into its context, and ensuring major redevelopment yielded a range of public amenities and facilities including an affordable housing component. However, it left unresolved other really difficult issues: the restrictiveness of single-family zoning, the restraints placed on secondary suites and other forms of low impact intensification, the acceptability of intensification along arterial roads (with commercial C-2 zoning), the rezoning for multiplex housing (RM zoning), and the design of neighbourhood centres. While each of these would be usefully explored through the second phase of CityPlan – the neighbourhood visions – ultimately, they could be resolved only by a citywide rezoning strategy.

Neighbourhood Visions: CityPlan Phase Two

In July 1996 city council approved the terms of reference for the second phase of CityPlan – community visions for each of the twenty-three neighbourhoods in the city. Each vision was not so much a plan but rather "a document which has words, drawings, pictures and maps to show how the community proposes to meet its needs and to move forward on CityPlan directions over the coming decades" (Vancouver 1996g: 7). Vision plans were to use a thirty-year time frame. An eight-month broad participation process in seven steps was envisaged within the neighbourhoods; the steps were later reduced to four: getting in touch; creating ideas; choosing directions; and finalizing the vision. The specific roles of the community, city planners, and council were described alongside that of a liaison group to represent a wide range of community interests and act as a watchdog on the process. A group of respected individuals from across the city was to comment on how each community vision met CityPlan objectives. The process concluded with a setting of vision priorities, their endorsement by city council, and subsequent implementation through various corporate and departmental initiatives. Each vision process would be tailored by each community and would specialize as necessary. Areas that had not had much planning activity were given first priority in the visions program. No targets for accommodating housing or population increases were set, although each community was expected both to make a contribution to find housing for an additional 60,000 people citywide over the decade, and to increase the variety of housing available in the neighbourhood (i.e., to rezone in part). Existing rezoning applications and inquiries that were underway before 18 January 1996 would continue to be processed, but subsequent applications that might prejudice different options or visions would not be considered.

As for the content of each vision, the planners drew up a list of possible CityPlan topics to include movement, community services, neighbourhood centres, new public places, housing variety and cost, distinctive neighbourhood character, and financial accountability. Communities could differentially emphasize these or other issues as they saw fit. They could locate and differentiate neighbourhood centres "but not necessarily [specify] exact size and boundaries"; suggest ways of increasing housing variety and what housing needs should be met; define under what conditions rezoning could be considered; state what aspects of neighbourhood character could be protected and by what means; and define the desired future character of neighbourhoods and centres. The status of these neighbourhood visions remained ambiguous, however, because the Vancouver Charter did not include provision for an official community plan as exists in many other BC municipalities. Nonetheless, the visions could be adopted as policy statements to guide council decisions, and council asked planning staff to proceed with neighbourhood centre plans to be implemented through rezoning and new capital commitments. There was no specific budget allocation for implementation in the early years, although a community could identify priorities for the disbursement of development-cost levies and community-amenity contributions produced by new developments if these were extended (see Chapter 8).

Dunbar and Kensington–Cedar Cottage Visions

The two neighbourhoods selected for the first visions were Dunbar (the northern half of Dunbar–Southlands) in the far west – adjoining the University of British Columbia Endowment Lands – and Kensington–Cedar Cottage in the east, straddling Kingsway. While Dunbar represented a middle-income neighbourhood of single-family houses on quiet tree-lined streets with many amenities, Kensington–Cedar Cottage had a much more varied socioeconomic and ethnic character, with fast population growth and obvious problems with crime, property maintenance, and traffic. Thus the two communities represented the long-standing west/east social and environmental polarities in Vancouver. Residents in each neighbourhood developed a comprehensive set of proposed directions for the community in a highly illustrated newspaper format and these were then the subject of a postal survey in which residents expressed their support, lack of support, or uncertainty with regard to each (Figure 32). Over 1,600 responses were received in Dunbar and over 1,200 in Kensington–Cedar Cottage, even though the latter had twice the population. A survey firm confirmed with a telephone random survey that these results were valid. Each proposal in the vision was turned into a direction and the votes for, against, and uncertain were recorded. All those for which there was a clear majority in favour in both surveys were taken forward as agreed directions, but all those where a majority could not be achieved were dropped. In a few cases votes were close or contradictory, and some of these directions were reformulated and retested (as recorded below). But the whole exercise was conducted with the utmost care to establish clear majorities before directions were accepted.

The broad topics covered in both surveys were similar. Kensington–Cedar Cottage residents gave a high priority to issues of community involvement and development, safety, service targeting, and accessibility, whereas Dunbar residents gave their greatest support for shopping areas, retaining neighbourhood character, and new housing, and greening issues (see Figure 32). The

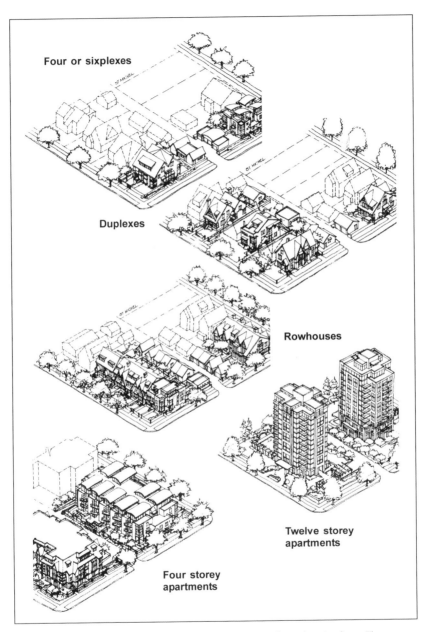

Figure 32 CityPlan neighbourhood visions: choices survey for future housing forms. These illustrations from a Choices Survey 'newspaper' show some of the different housing forms offered to residents. Each form was translated into a specific choice and the responses recorded and then checked by random telephone surveys for representativeness. Similar choices were offered to all neighbourhoods; the rejection of 12-storey apartments appears to be universal. (*Source:* Vancouver [1998m])

priorities reflect differences between those living in lower- versus middle-income areas, respectively. The design aspirations of each neighbourhood were also quite distinct.

Dunbar residents supported improvements to their three shopping areas, including traffic calming, public realm improvements, sidewalk shops, and on-street car parking, but rejected big-box or mall retail developments. They narrowly approved the idea of developing a community plaza close to the shopping centre as a focus for community life, but rejected the idea of extending the shopping centre south to link to it. While residents approved the provision of rowhouses and duplexes, and four- and six-plexes along Dunbar Street and parts of 16th and 41st avenues, they did not approve of the widening of this development corridor into adjacent blocks or of allowing such housing opposite public parks. Nor did they approve of apartment housing or any residential development above 4 storeys in height, rejecting the idea of a high-rise building (up to 12 storeys) for seniors in each shopping area (Figure 32). There was strong support (88 percent) for the retention of single-family areas and for design review being required for all new houses (71 percent). A small majority were in favour of more design diversity in housing than at present. There was support for smaller house sizes, for variations in yard sizes and orientations to allow sunlight access, and for allowing secondary suites across a larger area, but there was no consensus in favour of infill housing. Dunbar residents supported pedestrian and cycling improvements, and greening initiatives and view protection, as well as community involvement in decision making. So overall, and to no one's surprise, residents opted to preserve "the green village-like character of the community, while focusing most changes [and new housing] on short sections of Dunbar Street," making it in turn "more attractive and safer for pedestrians (and) transit" (Vancouver 1999c).

In Kensington–Cedar Cottage, residents strongly supported strengthening and improving the main shopping streets throughout the area and improving pedestrian comfort, but there was no support for shopping malls or big-box retail developments. Residents favoured better-designed mixed-use development on all major streets, but not additional height above 4 storeys. Only a narrow majority supported the spread of 4-storey mixed development along the main commercial arterial roads. As in Dunbar, a high proportion of Kensington–Cedar Cottage residents (82 percent) supported the retention of single-family areas, but acknowledged that secondary suite approvals should be easier to get and should be better designed (68 percent). But, unlike Dunbar, the eastside residents did not generally support design review, although they might retain it to protect the character of pre-1940 housing. Kensington–Cedar Cottage residents liked the idea of increasing rowhousing, duplexes, and four- and six-plexes, but rejected further intensification along arterials within single-family zones, as did Dunbar residents (Figure 33). Residents favoured housing for seniors but did not support apartment housing in 6- to 12-storey buildings, although the original neighbourhood vision had proposed up to twelve such buildings close to shopping streets and transit stops. Overall Kensington–Cedar Cottage residents were more amenable to physical change and less concerned to protect existing character through design review. Nonetheless, it was not possible to get a majority to accept either significant apartment development for seniors, or rowhouses, duplexes, or six-plexes on all arterial roads. The neighbourhood was much more concerned with community development, crime prevention, better maintenance and management, and more traffic calming.

Implementing Neighbourhood Visions
Both Dunbar and Kensington–Cedar Cottage neighbourhoods have set up residents committees to take forward the results of the visioning process and to maintain interaction with city officials and council. The Dunbar committee met more or less monthly after March 1999, with an attendance of between eight and thirty-five residents. It set itself some guiding principles: to be representative, accountable, interactive with the city, and cooperative with existing community groups in the area. The committee has a website and regularly publishes its minutes. It has had city officials speak to it on a range of planning, highway, and policing issues and has campaigned on the condition of particular streets, for a library forecourt beautification project, against large three-dimensional billboards, and for shopping street improvements. It is acting as a conduit for information on planning and highways initiatives and as a prompt for general neighbourhood management.

The Kensington–Cedar Cottage committee, which began meeting in March 2000, is a small committee of eight persons including a planner. As it has not established a website, its minutes are more difficult to monitor, but the committee has been very active with predominant concerns for traffic calming and safety for pedestrians. Three of the committee's initiatives are particularly noteworthy. The first is the planning of Kingcrest, a new neighbourhood centre at Kingsway and Knight Street, where an empty Safeway supermarket has been a long-running sore in the community and a restrictive covenant prevents its re-use as a food store. Proposals unsympathetic to the development of the neighbourhood centre, such as a 24–hour gas station, have been rejected, and a "pedestrian-friendly" development policy is being proposed. The second initiative is a new neighbourhood centre at Broadway and Commercial where a new SkyTrain loop has connected to the existing line and a new station and interchange built. A neighbourhood design charrette was used to generate a range of new guidelines to encourage the development of a "safe and vibrant" transit interchange and a mixed commercial development between the two SkyTrain stations (Vancouver 2000b). Draft guidelines (for C-2C and C-3A zoning) have been compiled to create a pedestrian-oriented neighbourhood strip with retail uses at grade and offices and housing above (Vancouver 2001a, 2000b). These guidelines focus on such issues as noise, safety, weather protection, active and narrow frontages, frequent entrances, and strong fenestration and articulation of facades. They also emphasize the importance of a wide range of improvements to the public realm, embracing landscaping, pedestrian safety, and comfort. Reduced car-parking standards have been approved for surrounding residential blocks and a precinct plan for a range of public realm improvements has been prepared, although funding will be incremental. However, no rezoning is proposed. The third initiative is a demonstration project for rowhousing in a city yard on Welwyn Street that might well yield some interesting prototypes for future housing in the neighbourhood and beyond.

Implementation of both neighbourhoods' visions was given major impetus in July 1999 when city council delivered extra staff and an additional budget. These included a traffic engineer to work on comprehensive plans for calming arterial roads and to develop pedestrian priority areas, and a planning post to coordinate implementation, monitoring, and communication. A $50,000 budget was created to support communications and outreach activities, and implementation funds were made available from the city's capital budget. Proposals for a community development worker to support activities in Kensington–Cedar Cottage await more discussion with the neighbourhood committee.

Implementation action plans have been prepared to reflect the vision directions set out in each community. These schedule and resource specific initiatives under each of the broad directions and indicate which city department will take the lead. The majority of actions identified are scheduled to be implemented in the next three years – such things as community involvement and development initiatives, safety, community centre improvements, greening, maintenance, and recycling actions – delivering tangible benefits to the area and undoubtedly helping to build community confidence in the process. But, from the perspective of the citywide strategy, the actions that are not yet scheduled nor resourced are the most significant. These include: two neighbourhood centre plans and related multiplex rezoning; traffic management plans for the three arterials in Kensington–Cedar Cottage; the revisiting of design review; and the facilitation of housing demonstration projects and view studies in Dunbar. But these actions are not as significant as the future pattern of development on the arterials (C-2 zoning being revised), the future of single-family zoning designations (on hold), and the rules for establishing secondary suites (revised zoning/construction codes). These issues impinge on all of the city's central residential neighbourhoods.

Future Housing Supply and Rezoning

A crucial planning issue for Dunbar and Kensington–Cedar Cottage is the relationship between the demand and potential supply of housing, specifically the housing potential of current zoning and the willingness of the community to accommodate, through rezoning, new forms of housing for smaller households. The statistics show that indigenous household growth over the next twenty years in both areas will be entirely accounted for by the increase in the number of mature, now mostly childless, couples of over fifty-five years, while the number of young and middle-aged households with or without children will steadily decline. Factoring migration into the neighbourhoods into the equation, using 1986-91 figures to estimate demand, adds about one-third to housing demand (see Figure 33).

The crux of the issue will continue to be strong demand for single-family housing – estimated at over 2,000 units in Dunbar and over 4,000 in Kensington–Cedar Cottage. But development opportunities for this type of housing in either neighbourhood are limited. The overall housing demand in Kensington–Cedar Cottage could be easily met because there is extensive capacity for apartment development within existing zoning, but only half the existing demand could be met in Dunbar largely through apartment provision. Further difficulties are created by the paucity of potential housing supply in rowhouse or duplex forms, or in secondary suites that are more likely to appeal to those unable to buy single-family units, although there is capacity on the arterial roads zoned C-2. A great deal of debate within the neighbourhood visioning process focused on the possibilities of creating new opportunities for townhouses and multiplexes, but the amounts that might be created in existing zoning designations will not meet significant proportions of the single-family demand – perhaps one-third in Dunbar and one-seventh in Kensington–Cedar Cottage. In Dunbar, despite initial opposition, residents have now agreed to consideration of infill development on large lots – but only where existing "character" buildings are retained – and rowhouses or duplexes to six-plexes on three arterial roads subject to further planning studies. In Kensington–Cedar Cottage, residents were in favour of more rowhousing or multiplex units rather than housing units above commercial uses on arterial roads in areas zoned C-2S, but getting agreement about the location of clusters of such units proved more difficult. Revised vision directions have accommodated some infill on larger lots, and defined two potential clusters for rowhousing or multiplexes around the neighbourhood

Figure 33 Housing demand, potential supply, and neighbourhood vision directions: Dunbar and Kensington–Cedar Cottage, 1999. These summary statistics demonstrate the demographic challenge to housing supply in these two quite different neighbourhoods. The unfulfilled demand for single-family housing is obvious in both. Also of interest are the different planning priorities in these socially distinct neighbourhoods.

CityPlan Visions	Dunbar	Kensington–Cedar Cottage
Demographic Trends	**Change, 1991-2001**	
Households		
1 Existing (1991)	6,770	12,700
2 First households (15-24 yrs)	–25	–150
3 Established childless couples (25-54)	–210	–220
4 Families with children (25-54)	–410	–330
5 Mature households (55+)	+2,195	+4,380
Housing Projections	**Projections, 2001-2021**	
6 Housing units required	1,550	4,141
7 Additional demand anticipated (6 × demand factor)	2,130 (× 1.37)	5,460 (× 1.32)
8 Potential of existing zoning	1,060	6,670
9 Housing shortfall/surplus (7 minus 8)	–1,070	+1,390
10 Possible new house types under Visions	280 –750	655
11 Estimated unfulfilled demand for single family	2,050	4,645

Vision Directions
In order of importance

Preserve single-family character
Strengthen three shopping areas
Multiple-unit housing on arterials
Improve walking and cycling
Preserving and enhancing green: recycling, etc.
Seniors/special needs housing
Community policing
Community involvement

Community involvement
Crime prevention
Cleaner and greener neighbourhoods
Taming arterial traffic
Local transit improvement
Walking and cycling, greenways
Community services (incl. drugs, alcohol)
Retain single-family but encourage secondary suites
Create three neighbourhood centres
More multi-unit housing in centres/ along arterials

Source: Information from Vancouver (1999c, 1999d)

centres at Knight Street and Kingsway and at Victoria Drive and East 41st Avenue for further study.

Changes to households and housing demand reveal the stark choices facing single-family neighbourhoods. Existing residents are the ones most likely to face reduced housing choices locally if they leave their existing single-family homes. While in Kensington–Cedar Cottage there is some possibility of a balance of housing supply and demand by 2021, in Dunbar there is likely to be a significant shortfall unless residents are prepared to take a more positive attitude toward rezoning. The ability of the visioning process to deliver more affordable and more diverse forms of ground-oriented housing as alternatives to single-family housing remains in the balance. It can be seen that significant numbers of residents recognize the challenges and are prepared to vote in principle for the necessary rezoning, but securing a consistent majority in general surveys and subsequent random surveys has proven elusive. Revised directions have had to be generated that will require more planning studies for rezoning in both communities.

The commercial zoning that allows housing over retail shops (C-2) is one of the main means of providing low-rise apartment units in single-family neighbourhoods. Revisions to the zoning, emanating from the consultants' 1990 study, removed disincentives to housing provision in commercial areas zoned C-1 and C-2 and created a potential 5,500 additional dwelling units in commercial districts. Within three years, some forty-five projects had been approved and, by 1993, the planning department had prepared new C-2 design guidelines for projects to improve both livability of units and neighbourhood fit (Tomalty 1998: 46). Key considerations were to minimize negative impacts on the adjacent housing, avoid monotonous facades, relate to the character of nearby buildings, and ensure appropriate unit configuration, access to daylight, and noise protection. Underground car parking, as well as private open space in the form of balconies, decks, and patios, was required (Vancouver 1996j). Several of these projects have been very successful, of which the Capers Block of retail, office, and residential units on West 4th Avenue at Vine is the most celebrated (Vancouver 1999v: 24-27) (see Plate 32).

The importance of these mixed commercial-residential strips to Vancouverites in general, and to their surrounding neighbourhoods in particular, should not be underestimated. Studies have shown that such strips as Commercial Drive between Venables Street and East Broadway, and West Broadway between Alma and Macdonald streets, are among the most valued parts of the city for their vitality, conviviality, and retail diversity (Vancouver 1992i: 10-11). Gentrification can take its toll on their social and ethnic diversity, as for example West 4th Avenue's transition from "freak" to "chic" (Ley 1995: 301-3). New locations emerge that take on the neighbourhood character alongside

Plate 32   Capers Block, 2211 West 4th Avenue. This positive example of C-2 zoned development breaks up the bulk and boxiness of the apartments, on a site that was less constrained by adjacent properties by virtue of the existence of a back lane. These are inherently more livable apartments because they have wide balconies and several aspects. The pavement courtyard (far right) provides south-facing outdoor eating space. Massing, materials, colour, and details are exemplary through-out the project. Its significant sustainability credentials are enhanced by its ground-source heat pump system.

some citywide retail or service specialization, such as the Punjabi market at Main Street and East 49th Street. The task for planning and design is to ensure that the new built forms enhance street safety and comfort, commercial diversity, consumer choice, and residential livability, all key design considerations in the conceptualization of CityPlan's neighbourhood centres.

But, just as C-2 zoning became essential to neighbourhood intensification in single-family districts, it came under a cloud. Neighbourhood groups, the city's Urban Design Panel, and the Development Permit Board all began to question whether the guidelines adequately ensured livability and, more critically, properly related to the adjacent single-family housing located behind the blocks or strips. Particular problems ensued with height relaxations and, in June 1998, city council required that all such relaxations be referred to council, allowing no further relaxations above 16.8 metres. At the same time council required that a general clause be inserted in the guidelines requiring "good architectural design," and that all C-2 projects be referred to the Urban Design Panel for advice. Subsequently the panel saw six C-2 proposals in westside Vancouver neighbourhoods, three of which they refused to support because they constituted overdevelopment, had poor parking layouts or landscaping, or poorly detailed elevations and inadequate private outdoor space.

Plate 33 C-2 apartment units, Dunbar Street. These new apartments epitomize a future pattern of intensification that was largely rejected by local residents. The reinforcement of the commercial functions of the street and the tree planting are to be welcomed, but the bulky, boxy forms allowed by the C-2 zoning need to be relieved with more modelling and stronger setbacks on the third floor. To the rear, there is a loss of privacy, light, and aspect where these properties abut single-family homes.

It was those in Dunbar that aroused the most significant local protest, and the panel had some success in markedly improving two schemes (see Plate 33 and Figure 34). At the time of writing, consultants are expected to report on ways to improve both zoning and guidelines. Their ability to resolve the design issues while retaining the economic incentive to redevelop will be critical to the provision of smaller, more affordable apartments in many single-family neighbourhoods throughout the city.

Three other initiatives are similarly crucial. First, experiments with the design of neighbourhood centres must accommodate significant commercial and community services while also providing housing forms that have good internal and external amenities, good aspects, and easy access. A second factor is the pressing need to undertake a review of zoning and building code regulations with regard to secondary suites to make them easier to achieve. (At the time of writing, this review was underway.) Finally, residential zoning must be made more flexible to accommodate conversions, additional units, and infill on larger sites, with more design diversity. As yet, there is no pressure from within the neighbourhoods for these kinds of change. A rethink of RS zoning is only a medium-term priority for the planning department and is not at all a political priority.

Figure 34 5629 Dunbar Street: reactions of the Urban Design Panel and Development Permit Board. This is an example of the problems with C-2 zoning and their impact on single-family housing to the rear. The board was reluctant to approve the scheme, but could not change the zoning. Although such examples signalled that a review of C-2 zoning was overdue, they also indicated powerful neighbourhood opposition to any intensification despite careful screening.

Address and Location
5629 Dunbar Street

Project Description
4-storey block with retail ground floor
and residential above (28 units)

Zoning and Bonuses
C-2 / 4 storey

Architect and Client
unknown / I.R. Capital Corp

Urban Design Panel
02/97 *2-5 no support.* Recognize that it meets zoning but concerns with its RS-1 interface – especially livability issues. Rear elevation needs attention – need to articulate with balconies, step backs. Attention to corners on the frontage. Key precedent, needs care.
03/97 *7-0 support.* Good response to previous comments. Rear facade softened and made more interesting. Entrance safer.

Development Permit Board
05/97 *Approve.* Board cannot rezone and application meets all zoning requirements. Board reservations on information provided and on consultation with residents. Significant neighbourhood opposition. Maximizing density compromises livability. Some improvements achieved with setbacks.

Source: Compiled from panel and board minutes

Neighbourhood Committees and Area Management

At the local level the democratic experiment continues, with the neighbour-hood committees helping to manage and monitor implementation of the visions they contributed to CityPlan. The committees contribute to day-to-day management of their neighbourhoods and coordinate community improvement projects. An evaluation of public involvement in the preparation of the first two visions, by consultants (Vancouver 1999g), concluded that participants found the program worthwhile and of benefit to their communities. Respondents also highlighted a number of suggestions for improvement, such as better definition of, and better communication within, visioning programs. They also suggested that councillors play a more active role in the process. There were criticisms that visioning is still too top-down – organized programs rather than dynamic processes – and pressure for more community outreach, more facilities, more training, and more active liaison with organized groups. Many felt that the community liaison group could be established earlier, represent wider interests, and be more effective. But the main reservations concerned implementation of the visions. First, residents felt that the process should deliver tangible improvements to the community, particularly in infrastructure – as, for example, the federal Neighbourhood Improvement Program (1975-83) had done. Second, they felt that, once the visions they had developed reached City Hall, they lost momentum and lacked official follow-through. These latter criticisms were somewhat premature, as they predated council's endorsement of the Implementation Action Plans in June 1999, the allocation of new planning and transport staff resources, and the new communication budget. But they emphasize the fact that, through the CityPlan visions, each neighbourhood expects to achieve major enhancement to services and amenities, if it is simultaneously to widen housing choice and meet its share of citywide housing needs.

Meanwhile, two new visioning exercises are underway in three southeast neighbourhoods of the city – in Sunset and in Fraserview–Killarney, a combined program. These areas were chosen because they had not been subject to any recent planning initiatives. The main issues emerging in both areas are traffic calming and crime prevention; in Sunset better street cleaning and garbage collection on Fraser Street is an immediate problem, and in Fraserview–Killarney, the redevelopment of the Champlain Mall as a neighbourhood centre is a priority. Neighbourhoods such as Sunset pose particular challenges to involve large populations of Punjabi- and Cantonese-speaking residents. In both areas the visioning process emphasizes two aspects of CityPlan: the need for better coordinated environmental management, and the need to win the confidence of residents who have until now had very little contact with, or awareness of, planning issues. Both neighbourhoods have plenty of affordable housing and are not predisposed against the proliferation of secondary suites or the intensification of development on arterial roads. They have much to achieve in terms of community development.

Opposition to Intensification

Kensington–Cedar Cottage may well be the first area to develop prototypes of the new neighbourhood centres, with its proposals for service concentrations and residential intensification. Some provisional redevelopment proposals are already suggesting how the market might respond positively to these initiatives. But city planners have much work to do to develop convincing models capable of accommodating significant amounts of attractive ground-oriented housing. C-2 commercial zoning and design guidelines have to be redefined to reduce impacts on adjacent single-family properties, and to improve the livability of the units themselves. Then new zoning has to be developed to accommodate rowhousing and multiplexes (i.e., duplex to six-plex units). Design challenges with traffic management, parking, and public realm improvements and with the design of retail streets are beginning to be resolved through the Broadway–Commercial guidelines (Vancouver 2001a, 2001b).

CityPlan recognized that accommodating significant new housing in existing neighbourhoods is not merely a matter of finding appropriate design prototypes. Each neighbourhood needs to be convinced that increasing and diversifying its housing stock is in local interests. The key factor in promoting housing diversification is the ageing of existing residents, which is the single most important demographic trend in the city: the number of mature households of fifty-five years or over is predicted to double in many neighbourhoods by 2021. A major question is what housing such households will need. CityPlan visions have brought the impending reality of this choice home to many people, particularly the elderly, and have helped to build a considerable constituency for change. But they have yet to achieve a consensus for rezoning to provide townhouses or multiplexes, or mid- or high-rise housing forms for seniors – decisively rejected in Dunbar. This is a major disappointment to city planners. Another factor in the negotiation process is equity between neighbourhoods. Each neighbourhood will be carefully assessing each other's projected housing shortfalls. Dunbar's shortfall is particularly interesting in this regard (see Figure 33). Getting neighbourhoods to agree to intensification depends on the ability of planning and environmental management to deliver a wide range of benefits – calming traffic, greening streets, improving transit, pedestrian crossings, sidewalks, parks, cleansing, garbage collection, and community services, as well as reducing crime and incidence of drugs and alcohol abuse. Many of these benefits are simply good housekeeping, but they require the city to work closely with police, the transit authority,

and numerous other agencies. The visioning exercises have clearly established priorities in neighbourhoods. The city now has to deliver on them to
build resident confidence and, to do so, it needs adequate capital investment,
some of which will come from development levies and community-amenity
contributions. But these take time to accumulate; desired improvements will
be expensive and there are especial funding difficulties in the short term.

CityPlan: Criticisms and Responses

CityPlan has received fundamental criticisms as well as accolades. The academic consultancy team of Michael and Julie Seelig criticized the process by
which CityPlan was developed as misconceived, over-elaborate, and a waste
of money. In an echo of the controversial technocratic planning articles in
the *Vancouver Sun* in 1990, discussed earlier, the Seeligs likened CityPlan to
the "Emperor's New Clothes." Arguing that the neighbourhoods were incapa-
ble of transcending NIMBY thinking and developing a citywide vision, the
Seeligs claimed that CityPlan offered no real mechanism for resolving conflicts and considering the real resource implications of choices and solutions;
they advocated instead referenda to establish clear policy choices. The Seeligs
argued that the first phase of CityPlan cost $4 million and that the second
phase of neighbourhood visioning and planning would cost a further $11.5
million, at a time when the city had a $27.5 million budget shortfall (1996).
They concluded that

> today it seems that planners are making it their particular expertise to produce
> wish lists. So we have the new notion of the planner as a "Department Store
> Santa" to replace earlier roles ... Planners and politicians may call the end result
> a "general, flexible blueprint" or a "first round in the dialogue with the public,"
> but what is it really? It is nothing more than a wish list prepared by some
> interested citizens, treated like children, that provides no insight into how to
> shape the future of the city. (Seelig and Seelig 1997: 21-22)

The CityPlan director rejected these criticisms and the cost figures cited –
actual costs were $3 million for Phase One and $4.5 million for Phase Two
– pointing to the real success achieved by CityPlan in getting 10,000 citizens
to contribute to the ideas process. She rejected both the idea that the plan
was an "unrealistic wish list" (McAfee 1997b: 19) and the professional elitism
implicit in the Seeligs' criticisms of the participation process. She quoted
Thomas Jefferson to support CityPlan's democratic aspirations: "I know of no
safe repository of the ultimate powers of the society but the people themselves; and if we think them not enlightened enough to exercise their control
with a wholesome discretion, the remedy is not to take it from them, but to

inform their discretion" (quoted in McAfee 1997b: 22). Surprisingly, the Seeligs' critical paper won a Canadian Institute of Planners Award in 1997, so it obviously struck a strong chord in the profession. Other Vancouver planning and development figures have similar doubts about the expense of the project, the loss of professional planners' vision, and the dangers of planners becoming mere advocates of citizens' views.

In general such critics were very much in the minority and CityPlan won provincial, national, and international planning awards (see Appendix 1). It attracted huge interest from other municipalities around the world who have sought details on how the ambitious participatory processes were established and fostered. A more progressive professional view would argue that the process and the principles on which CityPlan is based – and on which the city's general planning practices are deeply embedded – have a deep resonance with the alternative vision of city planning put forward in Leonie Sandercock's *Towards Cosmopolis* (1998). Her epistemologies of talking and listening, mutual learning, and the reflective practitioner as a "community ally," promoting community agenda-setting and empowerment but maintaining a critical distance and developing an awareness of wider planning responsibilities, are evident in CityPlan. These ideas are predicated on notions of multiculturalism, equal citizenship, and distributive justice, which all underpin the CityPlan process. In Vancouver, CityPlan won strong council backing. Non-Partisan Alderman Gordon Price welcomed the consensus established about the need for incremental change, responsiveness to context, better quality design and traffic restraint, and the "re-creation of the streetcar suburb," as Price characterized it. He remained optimistic about the capacity of relatively modest intensifications across the city to accommodate growth and was, like all Non-Partisan politicians, unwilling to fight neighbourhoods that did not want to increase building density. Like many of the city planners, he saw no possibility of imposing an intensified urban form on neighbourhoods without their consent (interview). To be successful, any citywide program of intensification must have the active support of neighbourhoods. This is the political imperative that underpinned CityPlan and would have driven it forward even without the deep professional commitment in Vancouver to neighbourhood participation.

A Verdict on CityPlan
Few cities have invested as heavily as Vancouver in community visioning as a foundation for citywide and neighbourhood planning, or established such thorough processes for assessing community preferences on built form. These are exemplary processes and procedures, but their outcomes have yet to fully endorse the deeper ambitions of progressive urban design to create

social inclusion, community well-being, sustainable development, and design innovation (see Figure 1). This was not likely to happen overnight, or even over the decade in which CityPlan has been in gestation. The plan's initiators take a much longer-term view of how planning and design might evolve through new forms of neighbourhood governance, development taxation, and decentralized service delivery and environmental management. This will comprise the principal planning agenda for the next decade.

What has the CityPlan process achieved? Has it defined a citywide planning strategy capable of accommodating an additional 60,000 persons beyond current zoning allowances by 2021, in a manner acceptable to the residents of the city's largely low-density single-family neighbourhoods? Has it established a system for the management of environmental change that is efficient, equitable, inclusive, and responsive to community needs? Ray Tomalty argues that, through CityPlan, "Vancouver has forged ahead of Toronto and Montreal in promoting neighbourhood change," and he concludes, albeit tentatively, that this may be "partially attributable to its strong programs of public participation" in making the necessary trade-offs between neighbourhood protection and citywide efficiency (Tomalty 1998: 186). Certainly CityPlan has established a citizen consensus in favour of a city of neighbourhood centres; the no-growth option has also been decisively rejected. The main street model, where the arterial roads would be the focus for intensification, won much professional and political support, but the single-family neighbourhoods still clearly fear the intrusion of 4- to 5-storey mixed-use developments, and the increased activity they would bring. The comparisons with Toronto's ill-fated "Main Streets" program (Toronto 1991c) are quite striking.

Another challenge for the implementation of CityPlan is the development of new forms of neighbourhood governance. One of the major benefits delivered by CityPlan has been the lesson in civics provided through visioning meetings and neighbourhood committees for large sections of the community. The city has embarked on a major experiment in neighbourhood management that is breaking new ground and involving sections of the community who have not previously participated in planning or other city services. In a multicultural city like Vancouver, where Anglo-Canadians are now in a minority, genuine community participation is essential for the future of successful planning and design.

Finally, it is useful to compare Vancouver's CityPlan with Seattle's first comprehensive plan adopted in June 1994, in the wake of Washington State's 1990 *Growth Management Act*. It too had an active participatory process and an internationally recognized sustainability dimension. It too adopted an "urban villages strategy" to resolve planning issues around growth and environmental quality, accessibility and congestion, urbanity and amenity, and neighbourhoods and citywide interests (Punter 1999a: 38-54). The plan concentrates three-quarters of the growth in a hierarchy of "village centres," each the subject of a neighbourhood plan that takes forward aspects of the comprehensive plan at the local level. These centres are to be the focus of public investment in services and amenities and improvements in bus transit. The main difference is that Seattle's comprehensive plan actually rezoned the city, significantly expanding commercial and especially multi-family residential zones to accommodate growth. The neighbourhood plans have to work within these parameters. If the neighbourhoods – led by planning committees of representative stakeholders, but engaging in wider public participation – accept these growth allocations, as almost all have done, then the neighbourhood plans will attract significant capital funds to ensure implementation. The city has devolved elements of design review to each neighbourhood, requiring negotiations between the community and developers as part of the decision-making process. The Seattle model has been much more of a top-down planning model than Vancouver's and more modest in its participatory program. Correspondingly, it has allowed the city to keep a tighter grip on the essentials of its intensification strategy. Time will tell how successful Vancouver's and Seattle's citywide plans have been in accommodating remarkably similar amounts of population growth and in promoting more sustainable urban forms and behaviour.

6
Megaprojects on the Waterfront, 1987-2000

In the 1980s, as city planners struggled to come to grips with commercial development downtown and high-rise residential development in Downtown South, they found themselves increasingly deployed to manage the redevelopment of industrial and railway lands on the north and south shores of downtown. The first redevelopment proposals for False Creek North were submitted in 1969, but it was not until 1990 that an official development plan was approved. Coal Harbour, on Burrard Inlet, had its official development plan approved in the same year. The negotiations for both official plans took close to a decade, partly because of the sheer scale of the projects and partly because of changes in land ownership, developers, planning climate and regulations, property markets, and municipal and provincial politics. The Coal Harbour project on Burrard Inlet, while more upmarket, has many similarities with False Creek North. The Southeast False Creek project, however, aims to create a much more sustainable neighbourhood that can serve as a testing ground for a range of more environmentally benign planning, building design, economic, and community development practices that can inform neighbourhood design in the twenty-first century.

The False Creek North project in particular illustrates how the city developed planning and design processes that could deliver high-quality residential neighbourhoods and major amenities for the Vancouver public. Four mechanisms are of primary interest: the development of the design principles; the regulatory framework of policy broadsheets (official development plan rezoning and guidelines developed in sequence); the imposition of public facility benefit provisions; and the invention of a cooperative planning process. Each of these mechanisms picks up on several of the best practice principles for progressive design review identified in Figure 1 in terms of substantive design principles, the integration of zoning, and the application of fiscal devices to support quality design and community visioning, respectively. The resultant forms of development and their design quality are also of major interest.

Development Negotiations on False Creek North, 1974-83

While False Creek South was under development in the 1970s, a rather different future for the north side of False Creek was being formulated. The land there was entirely owned by Marathon, the property arm of Canadian Pacific Railway, but when CP moved its railway yards to Port Coquitlam further east, the land became surplus. In 1969 Marathon proposed a substantial scheme in the style of "La Ville Radieuse," with nineteen towers, each 150 to 200 metres tall, set along the shoreline away from a major highway (Pacific Boulevard). The city countered with its own scenario but, by 1974, Marathon had elaborated its plans to define four distinct neighbourhoods and requested a rezoning for them. Despite criticism that the city was giving away huge increases in land value, the first phase for rezoning (of 38 hectares) was agreed, but Marathon did not proceed because council insisted that one-third of the residential space be allocated for low-income residents. The city required Marathon to provide subsidized sites for low-cost housing to be sold at non-market rates. The negotiations for Marathon with the city were being conducted by project officer Gordon Campbell (Gutstein 1975a: 84-87), who was to become city mayor between 1986 and 1993.

In 1975 the lands attracted the attention of the province when the minister of recreation commissioned a concept study for a second-rank world fair, a mini-exposition, to be a focal point of Vancouver's centennial celebrations. In 1978, the minister suggested that Marathon build a covered stadium to seat 60,000 in return for rezoning of land in the vicinity. Gordon Campbell confirmed that Marathon would sell the land for a modest $1.25 million for the development; however, nine months later, the province acquired some 71 hectares of False Creek North, paying Marathon $30 million in cash and an equivalent sum in downtown properties, along with other undisclosed assets (Gutstein 1986-87: 31-32). In January 1980, Premier Bill Bennett announced Cabinet's decision not just to build a new sports stadium but to hold a world transportation fair – Expo '86 – to celebrate the centennial of the city and Canadian Pacific. The premier also announced his intention to build "a great meeting place for all of our people that we would call British Columbia Place ... the focal point of our great province" (quoted in Ley 1987: 50). Also revealed were plans to build 10,000 residential units and 700,000 square metres of offices on the False Creek lands after the exposition, the profits from this venture going to finance provincial projects in other BC cities and towns.

The political rationale for these decisions was that the Social Credit government, suffering from a crisis of public confidence, saw Vancouver seats as the key to winning the forthcoming election and retain power. The provincial government envisaged that these massive investments would persuade undecided voters in the city to vote Social Credit. Major political tensions developed, with the Vancouver mayor supporting the New Democratic Party and the Social Credit provincial government strongly allied with the Non-Partisan municipal opposition. The province willingly subverted attempts to reform the city's voting system in the early 1980s, a change that would have provided for local ward representation instead of citywide councillors. In the process, it upheld the vested interests of business and commerce and improved Non-Partisan election prospects, helping them resume control of city council in 1986.

British Columbia Place Ltd. was established as a Crown Corporation in May 1980, with powers to raise and disburse funds, expropriate lands, and override all city planning powers. It was "established specifically to bypass municipal interference" (Ley 1987: 53). Thus began three years of acrimonious and openly adversarial negotiations between the province as developer and the city as regulator, the planning for the rapid transit SkyTrain being conducted in a similar fashion (Vancouver annual review 1980-81: 5-6). In 1981 the council adopted thirteen planning principles for the eventual redevelopment of the False Creek North site. Relationships with the province were strained at the political and administrative levels through 1983, although more realistic concepts were being drawn up notwithstanding disputes about densities, parkland, and non-market housing (Vancouver annual review 1982-83: 5). However, between 1982 and 1984, provincial initiatives were absorbing more than 40 percent of the total central area planning budget and staff time (Vancouver annual review 1982-83 and 1984-85). Meanwhile, the first development, the covered BC Place Stadium, which was to house the BC Lions football team, proved to be one of the biggest urban design failures of the previous twenty years. The distinctive air-filled quilted roof – described by design professionals as "a marshmallow in bondage" – was something of a technological marvel. But the huge bulk of the stadium and its awkward relationship with the changes of level on the site, its blockage of any extension of Robson Street to the shore of False Creek, and its separation of the two lanes of Pacific Boulevard have all created long-term urban design problems for the redevelopment of the area.

Expo '86 and Its Impacts

Plans for Expo '86 and its subsequent redevelopment were drawn up under the direction of the project's chief architect Bruno Freschi and, in 1983, BC Place commissioned five leading local architects to develop a series of distinct neighbourhoods with a mix of medium- to high-density housing. Subsequently, in what became known as "The Gathering of the Silver Knights," a BC Place conference brought in internationally renowned architects and planners from eastern Canada and the United States to develop the design (Boddy 1984a: 19). It provided a platform for Arthur Erickson and Rodney Friedman, the San Francisco urban designer, to argue for high-rise point towers all along the water's edge. Although they were awarded key urban design commissions for the megaproject shortly afterward, the project seemed to lose its momentum.

The city acceded to provincial arguments about the need for construction jobs and enhanced tax returns from the new development and in 1984 approved an official development plan for the Southeast Granville Slopes (see Chapter 3) so that some development could proceed. A policy plan was also agreed for the east end of False Creek in 1984 on land that was not owned by the province. The concept was for a dense mixed-use area concentrated around the SkyTrain station and looking out on False Creek, the waterfront park, and Science World's geodesic dome to the west, with the green square of Thornton Park to the east. In these discussions, the development planners established many of the urban design principles that would guide development throughout the rest of False Creek to better relate tall buildings to the streetscape, to protect view corridors, to strengthen street enclosure, to reduce shadowing of public and private space, and generally to improve solar access to dwellings and spaces. There was also guidance on ameliorating traffic noise and ensuring security in this potentially high-crime area. Maximum building heights were closely specified for the redevelopment sites. Tapered, relatively slender towers were recommended, with height exceptions considered only for well-designed landmark buildings. The ensuing CityGate development consisted of three tall apartment towers linked by medium-rise apartments enclosing the street and creating a series of surprisingly accessible, well-landscaped squares above the underground parking (see Plate 34). Even today CityGate remains isolated, largely surrounded by industrial lands and encircled by the elevated rapid transit line, awaiting the development of the southeast False Creek community to link it to other neighbourhoods.

In 1983 BC Place appointed as project manager Stanley Kwok, an architect with a keen understanding of development economics and fifteen years of experience in Vancouver. He fostered a much more cooperative approach to planning and design development, ably abetted by Downs and Lebofsky Architects. Instead of preparing yet more schemes for the entire site, they concentrated on the northeast corner of the site adjacent to Chinatown in Strathcona. Close joint working with the city and BC Place led to an agreement on a new plan for 28 hectares (70 acres) in what became known as North Park, immediately east of the stadium. The process involved close communication with the public, neighbourhood groups, and special interest

Plate 34 CityGate, 1100-block Quebec and Main streets. Three 28- to 30-storey apartments with white concrete frames and sea-green solar glass distinguish this megaproject at the east end of False Creek. The SkyTrain station is built adjacent to the VanCity office building (right). The site planning delivers a series of rectangular hard and soft landscaped squares accessible to the public, a surprising aspect of this still rather lonely development. The Science World sphere is a legacy of Expo '86.

groups. It embraced five well-advertised public meetings, six half-day workshops with special interest groups, and two evenings where council received briefs and heard delegations. Principles for public involvement were drafted to guide the program (see Figure 35). The result was a positive public hearing and unanimous adoption of the official plan by council in April 1986. Development did not proceed, however, because of the discovery of contaminated soils; in 1989 the eventual purchasers, Concord Pacific, were forced to come back to council to request the withdrawal of the official development plan and the rezoning of the site (Vancouver 1989g). But the enduring legacy of the North Park plan is its invention of a positive participatory and collaborative process with which to formulate agreed redevelopment plans.

As an event, Expo '86 was a resounding success, despite its overtones of "circuses before bread." Although its deficit escalated from a projected $12 million in 1980 to $311 million by 1985, a press survey of over 2,000 people who had visited the exposition was overwhelmingly favourable. The same respondents were sharply critical of those like Mayor Harcourt and Alderman Harry Rankin who had opposed the event. For the Social Credit provincial government, Expo '86 is credited with achieving a 15 percent swing in popular opinion in their favour and delivering an election victory. But for most Vancouverites the positive experiences of friendliness, happiness, excitement, partying, and meeting people were the dominant memories of Expo '86.

Figure 35 Principles and processes for public involvement in North Park. This approach, adopted in North Park, became the prototype for all the megaprojects.

Key Principles

- *Consult three publics:* general public, neighbouring communities, special interest groups
- *Purpose:* disseminate information, gather ideas, mutual learning, build support, create place
- *Processes:* display consideration, understanding, influence timely decisions, relationship to neighbours, wide outreach, open process, involve existing and specially created groups

Stages of the Process

1 *Policy Broadsheet*
   Public meetings in different communities (5)
   Half-day workshops for special-interest groups with corporate team (6)
   Council hears delegations/receives briefs (2)

2 *Overall Plan*
   Workshops with special-interest groups (2 rounds)
   Meetings with neighbouring communities (minimum 6)
   Monitor media comment: developer exhibition
   Bi-monthly newsletter (to all attendees)
   Public information meetings prior to public hearing
   Public hearing

3 *Area Plans*
   Meetings with immediate neighbours (each twice; additional as necessary)
   Comments from special-interest groups
   (To be developed in more detail)

4 *Rezoning*
   Developer meetings with special-interest groups (city staff in attendance)
   Developer meetings with adjacent community (city staff in attendance)
   Developer meetings with general public (city staff in attendance)
   Formal staff and Urban Design Panel review: summary of all consultations
   Public hearing

5 *Implementation*
   Normal permit processing; neighbour notification

Source: Adapted from Vancouver (1989g)

Even the most skeptical academics were forced to concede that "the manipulation of consciousness by mass culture [and] the cultural dupes posed by mass culture theorists are less visible on the ground than they are in nonempirical speculation" (Ley and Olds 1988: 209) – that is, local people genuinely enjoyed it.

Expo '86 is widely credited with marketing Vancouver to the rest of the world and reviving the city's economic fortunes. It had generated a series of major public works during an economic recession and left the city with some important tourist and cultural facilities: the Canada Place convention, hotel, and cruise-ship facility (see Plate 41), the geodesic sphere converted to Science World in 1988-89 (see Plate 34), the Plaza of Nations complex, and the vital rapid transit line, SkyTrain. The transit line precipitated a significant amount of commercial and residential development activity in downtown and around the suburban stations. More importantly perhaps, Expo '86 raised public expectations for street life, design quality, and amenities. It also gave the public access to all the False Creek North waterfront, and city planners enshrined this as a key redevelopment objective alongside their determination to "solidly connect the core of downtown to our coasts," to retain the full extent of water in False Creek and not to allow any further filling in, or at least to balance any cut and fill to the 1987 shoreline (Vancouver annual review 1987-88: 30). All previous development plans had shown significant intrusions into the water, the 1982 plans reducing it to one large marina.

A totally different verdict on Expo '86 might be drawn from the campaigns against it of the Downtown Eastside Residents Association. In the early 1980s, in partnership with the First United Church and the Chinese Benevolent Association, the residents association had proposed a warehouse conversion to residential uses to provide 450 rental units for Expo visitors, intending that the units revert to non-profit housing afterward. The Expo '86 Corporation rejected the idea, choosing instead to build student housing on the University of British Columbia campus, almost 10 kilometres (6 miles) away from the site. Further antagonized, the association developed an analysis of the impact that Expo would have on single-room occupancy hotels and on low-income housing markets, and following up its findings sought rent freezes and eviction protection in the run-up to Expo. A proposed bylaw to this effect promoted by the association twice achieved a tied vote in council, but was opposed by the Non-Partisan councillors. Early in 1986, with plenty of evidence of evictions and rent increases, the city agreed to the bylaw and petitioned the province for enabling legislation, but this was denied. In fact, the provincial premier supported such evictions arguing that clearing the "slums" – as the city had failed to do – would be one of Expo's major achievements. Over a thousand evictions ensued in the period prior to Expo, mainly from fifteen hotels serving as roominghouses, none of which actually made any money from their conversion even though their rents were increased tenfold (Gerecke 1991b: 10). The residents association gained international recognition for its campaign, its fears about the negative impacts of the megaprojects and rezonings on low-cost housing in central Vancouver proving well founded –

despite the fact that these concerns were ignored by a majority of both city and provincial politicians at the time.

The Sale of the Expo Site

Shortly after Expo '86, the provincial government announced its decision to sell the False Creek North site as part of its newly initiated privatization program. The province needed the money because budgets were very tight and the costs of redevelopment would be massive with limited immediate return. A second reason for the sale was it was clear that conflicts between the city and the province over the form of the development would persist throughout the planning and permitting process, the province having been cast in the public's mind in the role of rapacious developer. Third, the local development industry was opposed to the province playing a direct role in such a major scheme, arguing that the province's role was to stimulate, rather than to undertake, development (Gutstein 1990: 136-38). An international sale of the land was organized, based on a financial bid and a vision or concept design. Three bidders submitted proposals and the province selected that of Li Ka-shing, Hong Kong's wealthiest property tycoon. Li Ka-shing wanted to provide his son Victor, already established as a residential developer in the region, with an appropriately high-profile project to expand his capabilities and to diversify the Li family's property portfolio. His agent had expressed interest in the site during a dinner party organized by the premier during Expo '86 (Olds 1988: 374). The purchase was a dramatic expression of the globalization of Vancouver's economy and of Asian inroads into the city's commercial and residential property markets.

The price reputedly paid for the whole site was $320 million. Gutstein noted that only $50 million was required as a downpayment on the deal with no further payments until 1995, when $10 million was payable each year until 2000 (Gutstein 1990). The balance was due in 2003 and there were no interest payments. Critics argued that, with government financing toward clearing up contamination, the actual price was closer to $125 million (Olds 1995: 17-23); still, this was four times what the province had paid Marathon eight years earlier. Of the total area beyond the water, 30 hectares would become roads, parks, schools, and other public space. The remaining 36 hectares were to be developed at a modest floor-space ratio of just over 3.0. The developers paid $100 per developable square metre, which compared very favourably with the $250 to $350 market price for similar property at the time. By 1990, when the official development plan was approved, the development site was worth more than $1 billion. The land deal provoked much debate. Why was the site sold so cheaply? Why was it not sold by public auction? Why was it not sold in smaller parcels to gain a higher price? Why

did the province agree to pay the costs of remediating polluted land estimated at $60 million by 1991? Why did the province suddenly abandon its
own development project as uneconomic? Why did the BC minister of economic affairs meet with Li Ka-shing shortly after the deadline for offers? The
best explanation was that the province considered that the sale of the property to the wealthiest man in Hong Kong could stimulate massive Asian investment in Vancouver real estate (see Gutstein 1990: 135-40). This indeed
proved to be the case, but most experts considered that the land had been
under-priced and that it promised to be a "goldmine" for the developers.

The price was only one facet of the competition to buy the site, as the
developers also had to submit a design concept. During Expo '86, Stanley
Kwok had been working on the idea of a new master plan and considering
the involvement of outside developers. He interviewed a number of architectural practices, including at least one international name, in the end selecting
Rick Hulbert. Hulbert added Downs/Archambault and Davidson & Yuen to
his team to develop proposals. When the sale of the Expo site was announced,
Kwok was already working with Victor Li and his father to develop the bid,
and his design team worked for three months in total secrecy in Kwok's
offices to develop a new design concept for the site. Hulbert's scheme for
Concord Pacific – as the developers named their shell company for the project
– was distinguished by its intention to excavate much of the shoreline to
create two large islands extending further out into False Creek, accommodating clusters of residential tower blocks within parkland settings (see Plate
35). This dramatically increased the amount of valuable waterfront property,
as well as, for Asians, the amount of *ch'i* (i.e., positive energy) in the development. It allowed Hulbert to transform the requirement for a six-lane Pacific
Boulevard into a form of Creekside Drive and to put the housing in quieter
parkland settings on islands away from the road. On the northern edge of
Pacific Boulevard, a more modest scale of development was envisaged, completing the existing street grid. A major commercial node was projected above
the Stadium SkyTrain Station, with nine tall office towers linked under the
Georgia Viaduct to a cluster of hotels and a marina on False Creek. Overall,
what was now an 82 hectare (204 acre) site was projected to accommodate
1.2 million square metres (13 million square feet) of floor space. It was not a
master plan for the faint-hearted and it negated most of the extant planning
principles for the area.

The False Creek North Official Development Plan
Compared with the efforts of the provincial Crown corporation, Concord
Pacific's progress toward resolving planning issues was swift indeed. A more
pro-development council and a mayor who was a former Marathon employee

Plate 35 Concord Pacific's concept for False Creek North. This view northeast toward Cambie Bridge (upper right) from above the Granville Bridge (lower left) illustrates the initial conception of Pacific Boulevard as a marine drive alongside excavated lagoons that dramatically increase the valuable waterfront in the scheme. The George Wainborn Park is heralded (foreground) but the site planning looks rather unresolved and the deep-plan apartment buildings unmarketable. (Courtesy the Hulbert Group International, Inc.)

certainly smoothed the way. But much of the progress seems to have been the result of replicating Kwok's approach in North Park by resolving the large-scale conceptual issues before proceeding to specifics, and by ensuring public and private sector cooperation to develop the scheme. At the outset the developers were expected to pay all the costs of the city's planning and regulatory work, and this allowed the creation of a dedicated staff team of city officers – planners, engineers, park board members, housing officers, social planners, cultural affairs (for public art) – to work across departments and alongside the developers and their designers. While the Concord Pacific master plan certainly captured the imagination of many development and design interests, it conflicted with many of the key principles set out by the planners – especially that the base shoreline of 1987 should be maintained and that the project be fully integrated into the existing city pattern. City planners objected to the potential exclusivity of the project and city engineers worried about the complexity of servicing implied by the bridges and islands. However, Stanley Kwok was not going to let these difficulties impede the progress of the development. He retained Rick Hulbert and Barry Downs within the developers' design team and added the landscape architect Don Vaughan. They refined the partnership approach with the city's team to collaborate on site plans, floor-space allocations, and design guidelines, rather than having the planners merely respond to the developers' proposals (Blore and Sutherland 1999: 56). These principles of collaborative and corporate planning were of critical importance to the eventual success of the megaproject.

Following extensive public discussion, the council approved policy broadsheets for the area in 1988, setting out seven organizing design principles for the project that responded to its setting at the edge of downtown and on the waterfront. The principles would also frame the development of design guidelines, which were to:

1 Integrate with the city
2 Build on the Setting
3 Maintain the Sense of a Substantial Water Basin
4 Use Streets as an Organizing Device
5 Create Lively Places having Strong Imageability
6 Create Neighbourhoods
7 Plan for all Age Groups, with a Particular Emphasis on Children
 (Vancouver 1989d).

Early in 1989 the new city council adopted a public involvement program to support the planning of False Creek North and to enshrine a heightened participatory dimension in the planning process. A major consultation exercise had been undertaken to update the policies for the area, including five public meetings in different communities and six half-day workshops with special interest groups. For the preparation of the plan the city manager recommended an ongoing, open, inclusive planning process to consider both the megaproject and the surrounding areas. Three different public groups to be involved were identified: neighbouring communities and property owners, special interest groups, and the general public. A five-stage process was identified, the purpose of which was to inform the public, to receive its advice, and to build support for the plan through fulfilling community needs (see the North Park model in Figure 35). An eight-month timetable was set out into mid-1990 when the public hearing on the proposed official development plan would be conducted.

Another key facet of the Concord Pacific project was the early resolution of the levels of provision of community facilities and social housing that would be expected of the developer. The council was in the throes of introducing development-cost levies in Downtown South and refining its approach to community-amenity contributions for rezoning (see Chapter 3). By September 1989 the False Creek North planning group had prepared a paper setting out what facilities would be required area by area and how these would be achieved. This required the developer to convey land for schools, to provide space for libraries to lease, and to build and convey to the city community centres, daycare, out-of-school care facilities, family places, and multi-purpose rooms. Such specialty items as shoreline treatments, public art, walkways, and aquatic features were also built into the benefits. A notable requirement was that the developer provide sufficient sites for 20 percent of the residential units to accommodate core-need households, and that a quarter of all the housing units be suitable for families. The sites for the 20 percent affordable housing requirement had to be set against the requirements of 33 percent non-market housing imposed by the TEAM council in 1974 on Marathon, but not accepted by them. Another was the requirement for public parks at a standard of 1.1 hectares (2.75 acres) per 1,000 people. These essential provisions were to become the Major Project Public Amenity Requirements (Figure 36) subsequently imposed on all the megaprojects. They gave the megaprojects their quality facilities, their generous amenities, and the crucial possibility of some measure of social mix.

The official development plan for False Creek North was completed and approved in 1990 as a concept master plan accommodating up to 9,100 residential units (886,622 square metres) with floor-space maximums prescribed for each of ten sub-areas, and a quarter of the units to be suitable for families with small children, and one-fifth to be non-market housing (Figure 37). The mix of dwelling unit types was also regulated sub-area by sub-area. Office uses of up to 152,790 square metres were allowed on the eastern part of the site. Retail and service uses of up to 55,948 square metres were mandated on a central section of waterfront but could also be developed in four other locations. Three marinas were to be expanded. Community uses included

Figure 36 Major Public Facility Benefit Provisions for the megaprojects, October 1999. This table shows the list of public amenities that developers are required to provide in the waterfront megaprojects and their date of introduction into planning practice. It reveals how the requirements evolved and were differentially applied, with daycare operating funds still to be determined.

		Downtown Major Projects			
	Date started	FALSE CN	COAL HH	BAYSH	CITY G
Basic engineering services to meet city standards	Ongoing	P	P	P	P
Standard items					
Parks					
275 - 2.75 acres per 1,000 people	1982	P	P	P+PIL	PIL
Community centres					
229 sq. ft. per person	1988	P	P	C	C
Schools					
Approx. 200 children/ full elementary school	1974	P	P	C	
Social housing					
Sites for 20% of units for core-need households	1988	P	P	P	P
Shoreline pedestrian/bicycle system					
25 ft. walk + 25 ft. setback	1974	P	P	P	P
Childcare facilities					
# spaces + # family units × 0.3 × 0.6 × 0.72	1990	P	P	P	P
Library					
$41 per capita	1990	P	PIL	PIL	
Public art					
$1 per leasable foot	1990	P	P	P	
Specialty items					
Arts complex					
Provide site + some costs	1990		P		
Saltwater pump stations					
Variable 25% FCN	1990	C	C	C	
Special treatment areas	1989	P			
Police boat moorage	1990		P		
Items under consideration					
Childcare operating funds					
Pending council decision	To be determined				

Note: P = provided; PIL = payment in lieu; C = contribution
Source: Redrawn from Vancouver (1999aa)

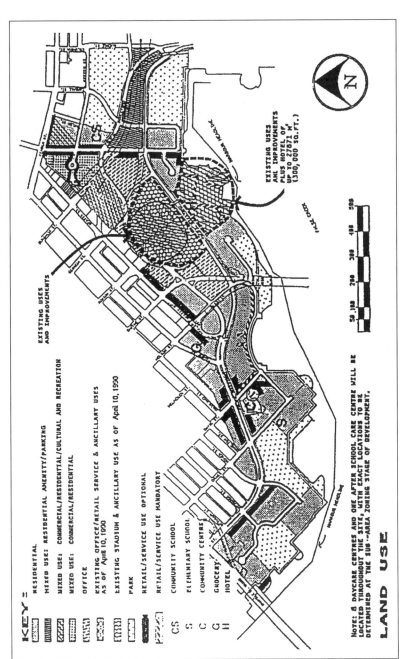

Figure 37 False Creek North official development plan, 1990: land use. This plan reveals the full extent of the project, the residential areas, the generous parkland, the specific disposition of commercial uses, and the location of schools and community centres. The official plan was sketchy regarding the uses around BC Place and the Plaza of Nations. (*Source*: Vancouver (1999e))

two schools, a community centre, eight daycare centres, a branch library, and eight separate pieces of parkland totalling 17 hectares.

A specific set of urban design guidelines was incorporated into the False Creek official plan. Views from Cambie Street and the bridge were protected, as well as those from six points on the walkway on the south side of False Creek (see Figure 16). Views southward down existing streets to False Creek, and vistas within the site, were also protected. A general height limit of 91 metres was prescribed, with one exception for a tower of up to 110 metres at the foot of Homer Street. Individual building heights would be determined according to five criteria. Tall buildings were required to orient themselves to the city grid, except on the eastern waterfront, and to be point not slab blocks. There was a strong emphasis placed on the design of a quality public realm. A paragraph of general description was provided to explain the design conception of each of the sub-areas, and an illustrative three-dimensional site plan was provided as "a general guide to the preparation of sub-area zonings and related development control instruments" (Vancouver 1990e: 13). This revealed some forty-six high-rise towers, most between 15 and 32 storeys, but largely linked by perimeter blocks of apartments and townhouses to retain strong frontages and to enclose and overlook the streets (see Figure 38). The final plans reduced the developers' original floor-space proposals by less than 8 percent. Fierce opposition was expressed during the first day of hearings on the plan but, by the second day, the developers had marshalled their supporters. The local press supported the development with extreme language born of civic boosterism. Apart from a spat about the time allowed for Canadians to buy the condominiums prior to construction – the twenty-four-hour deadline was extended to two weeks – the plan was approved without much controversy. The official plan represented a fusion of developer ambitions and council and planning department requirements. City planners insisted on continuous street-wall apartments and townhouses to provide a traditional streetscape, and the developers were able to accommodate the majority of their housing units in high-rise towers where the spectacular views would command premium values (see Figure 38). Some flexibility was built into the plan by allowing the developers to vary the number of dwelling units and floor-space areas by 10 percent phase by phase. The city's requirement of 25 percent family housing of a certain minimum size had to be located no higher than the eighth storey, while the 20 percent non-market component was to be accommodated in eighteen specific locations.

With official plan approval, the detailed design process could start. The developers used their internal design team and other architectural practices to work up the site plans to the stage where they could be converted into

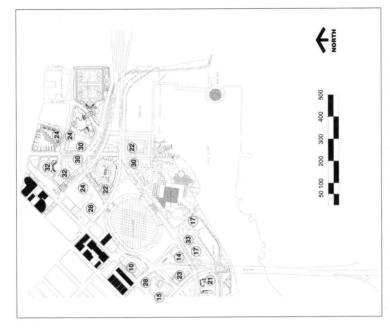

Maximum Tower Heights

KEY:

(23) Number of Storeys

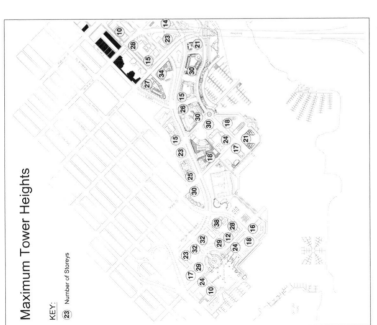

Figure 38 False Creek North official development plan, 1990: urban form. The 1990 plan set the basic characteristics of urban form, including the very sensitive issue of tower disposition and heights. Close examination reveals that the site plans were very schematic, but they would be refined through rezoning and the design guidelines for each phase of development. (*Source:* Vancouver [1999e])

zoning plans and regulations. These plans then provided workable parameters for the developers, but gave the city guarantees over key aspects of built forms in terms of height, volume, and massing. Then, to control detailed design, the architects and planners produced written design guidelines, for use by the architects commissioned to design individual blocks or buildings. It was a slow process of steady negotiation that provided both parties with the certainty they needed – the developers having guarantees on development quantities, the city having guarantees on urban forms and amenities. From the developers' perspective there was rarely enough flexibility. As things were tried and found wanting (e.g., locations for retail development) or as market conditions changed (e.g., demand for smaller dwelling units from first-time buyers), so changes in the official development plan were required, which re-opened some old controversies and political uncertainties. While the overall floor-space allocations remained the same, the developers negotiated an increase in dwelling units from 7,600 to 8,500 in March 1996, and up to 9,100 in November 1997, when a hotel site was rezoned to residential. As the market continues to demand small rather than large apartments, the total number of residential units may be renegotiated again.

To bolster the official development plan, two further design studies were undertaken. A shoreline treatment study (Vancouver 1991m) was commissioned to develop both generic and site-specific approaches to respond to Vancouver's large tide variations (up to 5 metres). The report recommended a variety of design solutions, but drew particularly on the Stanley Park seawall as a model: the use of stone masonry, the creation of natural habitats through the use of cobbles, the use of walls to below high-tide levels, and limited use of railings. A range of ways to improve access to the water and to create visual interest along the walkways – viewpoints, piers, floats, intertidal habitats – were also suggested, and these have been progressively refined as the megaprojects have proceeded. The planners also updated their general guidelines for high-density family housing; they were expressed as a series of largely quantitative measures to be used, not as rigid standards, but as evaluative criteria. They included such matters as privacy of entries and maximizing of private outdoor space, while ensuring that common amenity space could be accessed only by residents. Outdoor play areas with winter sunshine and with separate provision for pre-school and teenage play were specified with acceptable sizes. Multi-purpose meeting rooms were also required and indoor amenity spaces advised, including minimum bedroom size for play and study (Vancouver 1992e). These guidelines were comprehensive, well intentioned, and soundly based on experience, although some critics suggested that they were too detailed to be rigorously applied.

Yaletown Edge and the Roundhouse

Concord Pacific is developing the land in False Creek North between the Cambie and Granville bridges in four phases. The Yaletown Edge was the first phase to be completed, followed by the Roundhouse Neighbourhood in 1997. To the east the Quayside Neighbourhood saw the early completion of the Beatty Mews/Waterworks site in 1998 and then a forced abandonment of the design guidelines for the Marinaside, subsequently redesigned and largely complete at the time of writing. The Beach Neighbourhood guidelines were the last to be adopted in 1997, and the first of its buildings went through the permitting process in 2000.

The first phase of the project was the redevelopment of the three sites on the north side of Pacific Boulevard, a tidying up operation that rounded off the ragged edges of Downtown South and Yaletown. It marked a clear intention to make a major urban street out of Pacific Boulevard, with back-of-sidewalk apartment blocks above retail units. The buildings ranged from 4 to 8 storeys to enclose the street and to create varied massing and facade treatments (see Plate 36). While the middle apartment block on Pacific Boulevard used generous bay windows, and recessed and projecting balconies, the easternmost buildings (designed by Downs/Archambault) have a particularly

Plate 36 Yaletown Edge, Pacific Boulevard at Drake Street, looking northeast to BC Place Stadium and the Landmark Tower (see Plate 39). The complex massing and modelling of the apartments that provide the street-wall on the Yaletown Edge can be seen, as well as the careful treatment of the towers where they reach the street. Design quality is somewhat defeated by the excessive width of Pacific Boulevard, but the whole complex is unified by a limited architectural palette of red-brown brick relieved by bands and cornices of stone.

pronounced vertical emphasis, recessed windows, and clearly articulated base that is evocative of classical warehouse forms (Berelowitz 1995: 20-21). The towers behind are also predominantly faced in brick to respond to the brick warehouses in Yaletown behind (see Plate 66). Generally, 27- to 30-storey apartment towers dominate and anchor the corners of each block, descending straight to the edge of the side streets; to the east where they are a much deeper plan and more slab-like, they are only 15 storeys. What is especially satisfying about the site planning is the way in which the towers respond to the historic grid street pattern to the north, while the street-wall apartment blocks with their ground-floor retail units enclose Pacific Boulevard and provide both a human scale and vitality at street level. These forms were clearly prescribed as planning requirements and dimensional constraints. The advice on architectural expression, materials, and colours was equally precise and sought to ensure that the designs made a transition between the "heritage influence of Yaletown and the Roundhouse ... to a more contemporary expression at the waterfront" (Berelowitz 1995). Where the design fails is in the highway engineering of Pacific Boulevard where six traffic lanes plus left-turn lanes sever the urban fabric. While the density of development threatens to overwhelm Yaletown, in fact the massing is carefully articulated to enclose the axial view down Mainland and Hamilton streets, retaining the scale of these industrial roads and providing strong contrasts of form between the late nineteenth- and late-twentieth-century buildings, but using compatible brick colours.

An example of the process for refinement of design ideas is provided by the second phase of the development. The CPR Roundhouse and turntable, which were restored for Expo '86, were the only original buildings preserved in the whole project, and these provide the community focus and the circular open space at the heart of the neighbourhood. The rezoning, approved in July 1993, set out the maximum number, overall floor space and mix of units, and a range of other uses. Maximum floor areas, dwelling units, and building heights were specified for each sub-area, along with overall parking standards and allowable noise levels in rooms of dwellings. The twenty-nine pages of design guidelines, approved simultaneously, embraced site planning, massing, architecture, livability, and public realm and access; precinct guidelines set requirements for three public spaces and the shoreline. The twelve organizing principles repeated the design principles from the official development plan but emphasized the creation of a "family neighbourhood with a full range of community amenities and facilities" (Vancouver 1993j). The design guidelines were especially detailed on materials and colour; massing and height of the street-wall; and the architectural expression of townhouses, apartments, and tower blocks. There are guidelines on livability of family

Plate 37 The Crestmark, 1200 Marinaside Crescent. These townhouses front the seawall and are raised above a secondary walkway and cycle path to provide privacy and house well-designed seating. Each entrance is given a porch by a piloti supporting 2 storeys of angular bay windows to enhance the sense of a threshold, and to increase the views of the seawall and water. The public and private landscaping is simple but exemplary.

units, privacy, individuality, safety, views, and natural light. The precinct guidelines explained how the street and public spaces would be designed, including their relationship to buildings that front the public realm. Brick was required at the base of buildings around the Roundhouse, but concrete and stone cladding and metal frameworks could be used elsewhere. Adjacent to the water, the guidelines noted that "the brightness associated with the shoreline setting should be expressed in the soft, light, and subtle colours of the walls and intensity of accents and trims" (Vancouver 1993j) (see Plates 37 and 38). This transition from heavy brown brick street-wall buildings on the Yaletown Edge (see Plate 36) to gleaming white concrete and steel, and pale green glass townhouses and towers on the waterfront, was a strong contextual design theme and is one of the most successful features of the detailed design.

The residential developments in the Roundhouse neighbourhood were very successful, in particular the townhouse and tower complex between Marinaside Crescent and False Creek, which not only enclosed the street and seawall but also cleverly provided views of False Creek for units on the interior of the block (Vancouver 1999v: 10-11). The seawall townhouses are particularly well detailed and landscaped with small sitting spaces outside the front door protected by a porch overhung by two-storeyed crisply detailed bays (see Plate 37). The fact that Downs/Archambault wrote the guidelines and also designed the scheme, with Harold Neufeldt as landscape architect, helps explain how the guidelines could be so prescriptive.

Quayside, Beach, and False Creek East

To the east of the Roundhouse, the Quayside Neighbourhood consisted of a large waterside site between Pacific Boulevard and False Creek and three small sites to the north at the foot of Beatty Street. As with the Yaletown Edge, city planners were concerned to complete the grid and street enclosure to the north side of Pacific Boulevard. Design guidelines in 1987 had sought to ensure this, using a set of organizing principles for the public realm. The developers produced several sets of schematic plans in 1992 and 1993 to refine setbacks, heights, massing, and building orientation, with tower positions influenced by the Cambie Bridge view corridors. Compared with those for the Roundhouse Neighbourhood, the guidelines were much less detailed and the statements on architectural treatments and materials more concise, so a less prescriptive approach was being developed as the project progressed. As before, these guidelines were further elaborated in a set of precinct guidelines, but the design principles remained the same. However, each building was allowed a distinct identity and was designed to complement its neighbours. Simplified diagrams and maps helped to convey the basic principles. But on the site fronting the marina, the original design guidelines proved problematic. The proposed massing blocked views from many buildings and made the units less marketable, and the 6- to 8-storey street-walls made the streets oppressive. The towers were too slab-like and the architects could not resolve these issues to the developers' or the planners' satisfaction. So James Cheng was retained to prepare an acceptable redesign. He chose to reduce the height of the podium down to 3 storeys on the seawall and on the side streets, and to dispose more of the floor space in some six waterside slip towers, with a further three towers on Pacific Boulevard. Cheng treats the towers as a family of buildings restrained in design, elegant and quiet, and essentially as background buildings despite their size (see Plate 38). No revised guidelines were produced. Instead, use was made of the preliminary development permit process (discussed in Chapter 9) to ensure that the scheme was generally acceptable before it went to detailed design (see Figure 39).

Across Pacific Boulevard, on what is known as the waterworks site, Beatty Street was pedestrianized and enclosed by 3-storey townhouses fronted with rectangular brick screens framing recessed balconies. Both sites have major towers, and the southerly 90-metre (300-foot) flat-iron tower with a curved south elevation acts as a focus for the view down Pacific Boulevard (see Plate 39). Spaces for play and amenities have been provided in the upper levels

Plate 38 The Aquarius Project, Marinaside Crescent. The design guidelines failed on this project so James Cheng undertook the redesign. A
strong but restrained modernist aesthetic was delivered. The light-
coloured palette of materials works particularly well on seafront locations.
Cheng lowered the podium height to 3 storeys on the sea frontage and
the side streets to enhance the views, transferring the space to some six
slip towers. Coopers' Park (foreground) flows beneath Cambie Bridge.

behind the townhouses, and a large and rather open plaza has been created
at the foot of Beatty Street with a leaf-shaped pool and lawn designed by
Harold Neufeldt. Designed by Downs/Archambault, this is another scheme
celebrated as one of the city's major urban design achievements (Vancouver
1999v: 2-3) though its main space is not entirely successful. The Quayside
Neighbourhood is completed by the waterside Coopers' Park, an informally
landscaped space of trees, lawns, and meandering paths, which flows beneath the Cambie Street Bridge (see Plate 38).

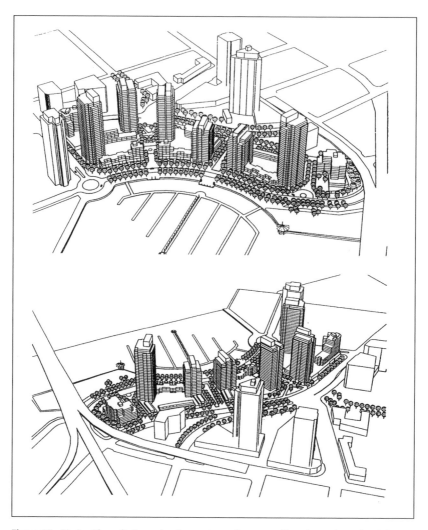

Figure 39 Marinaside preliminary development permit concept (Aquarius project, plate 38). When the Quayside Neighbourhood design guidelines proved unworkable on this site, the city agreed that, rather than re-write them, Concord Pacific could prepare a design conforming to the zoning, and utilize the Preliminary Development Permit route to establish an approvable scheme. James Cheng was retained to develop the design and two of his axonometric drawings are shown, lowering the street-wall buildings to improve views and allow more light into the interior courtyards. (*Source:* James K.M. Cheng Architects)

In the Beach Neighbourhood at the west end of the megaproject, the Hulbert Group developed a comprehensive rezoning submission to respond to the design guidelines (for CD-1) adopted in 1996. City council made only slight alterations to the preliminary submission, the main feature of which was another major park to act as the focal point for a series of largely symmetrically

Plate 39 Landmark Tower and Beatty Mews. Landmark Tower is the second tallest tower in False Creek North. There is some doubt as to whether the townhouses successfully enclose the parkette, which is open on the south side to Pacific Boulevard. The leaf motif (at left) is used for the design of the shallow pool in the parkette and is picked up on a series of glass screens that decorate the sidewalk. This is a space where form and function are not entirely successful.

arranged towers linked by 3-storey townhouses and medium-rise apartment blocks (see Figure 40). Again the guidelines were reduced in detail, a measure of the trust that now existed between city and developer, but a recognition, too, of the disadvantages of being too prescriptive. There were significant disputes about the height of the townhouses forming a crescent to face the park and the waterfront, and, as a result of residents' comments, these were lowered to 3 storeys to protect views from Downtown South, despite the objections of the Urban Design Panel and the architects who pointed out that

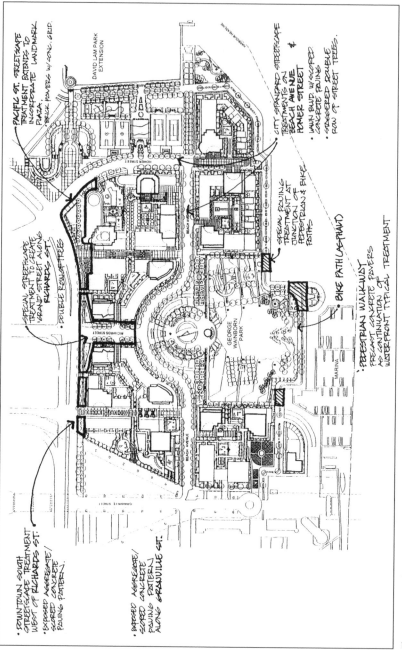

Figure 40 Beach Neighbourhood rezoning proposals. Beach Neighbourhood is focused on George Wainborn Park, and includes basketball and tennis courts as an extension to David Lam Park. This drawing explains the detailed treatment of the streetscape, including two mews on either side of the extension to Richards Street. The project contains five blocks of non-market housing. (*Source:* Concord Pacific Area 1 Beach Neighbourhood Rezoning Submission [1998])

this would weaken the sense of enclosure of the park. There were extensive debates too about the design and setbacks of the pedestrian mews that connect Pacific Boulevard and the park. The architects experienced some difficulties working within the zoning and guidelines, especially with the constraints set on tower design of height, width, and floor plate maximum. These "condom" constraints, as one architect expressed it, frequently need to be stretched at the detailed design stage when the developer decides exactly what disposition and size of units is required to suit market conditions. This can be difficult when adjacent residents and property owners object to what would be very minor changes, citing both regulations and guidelines.

Beach Neighbourhood is very much focused on the George Wainborn Park, which has been designed by Jim Lowden, the head of the Vancouver Park Board. This park has a complex design rationale utilizing a metaphor of broken continental plates (see Figure 40). The northern end of the park was designed to be very formal, with a promenade and crescent defined by rows of trees and contoured lawns around a yin-yang water feature. The promenade overlooks the wide open green that runs down to the seawall and narrows to a glade between informal groups of coniferous and deciduous trees. On the west side of the park a "contemplative garden room" formed by a tree bosque creates a series of smaller lawns while, to the east, lines of trees and statues create a series of avenues that will include a children's play area. Meanwhile, on the eastern edge of the site the extension of David Lam Park will add basketball and tennis courts to provide more intensive recreational use, along with a set of picnic and play areas traversed by tree-lined avenues leading to the seawall. Beach Neighbourhood will complete the development between the Granville and Cambie bridges and provide a rich public realm.

Mention should also be made of the investment in public art in all the False Creek North neighbourhoods. There are over a dozen works in the first three phases of the scheme completed as part of the development agreement. The Beatty Mews development's parkette with its leaf-shaped and veined pool has already been mentioned, but the botanical metaphor is carried through into a series of granite seats and an etched glass screen at the entrance to the mews by artist Barbara Steinman (see Plate 39). Particularly interesting are a set of installations at the foot of Drake Street on the seawall that include text applied to the railings in steel letters by artist Henry Tsang; and a modern shelter (one of three) with steel screen walls out of which are cut words and shapes that evoke the area's past, by artist Michael Davis. But arguably the best is a set of tall bronze poles, also by Michael Davis, that form a "constructivist scaffold" on the water's edge and evoke construction, industrial, or pier pilings (see Plate 40). To the west, a series of glass canopies grace a lookout, providing some shelter and evoking stunted cypress trees. These installations, all

Plate 40 Public art, False Creek North seawall. Here, Michael Davis's bronze poles suggest construction and pilings, the industrial past of False Creek, and support a series of etched screens evoking the area's past.

the result of international competitions, considerably enrich the public realm, providing stopping and sitting places on the seawall and adding to a sense of history and a sense of place.

Northeast False Creek

A major rethink of the nature of the False Creek North project east of the Cambie Bridge has been underway since 1997. The ill-fated North Park official development plan for the area north of the Georgia Viaduct was recast with a greater commitment to residential units (800), a major hotel, and considerable office space. The International Village, as it was called, recreated four city blocks south of Pender Street with strong street enclosure of 8 to 10 storeys of apartments punctuated by three pairs of 24- to 30-storey towers. To the east of Carrall Street, 4 hectares (10 acres) of award-winning parkland were developed as Andy Livingston Park, designed by the Kreuk Durante Partnership, containing a landscaped hilltop with all-weather sports pitches (Bula 2000: E11).

Over the last decade the future of the area around the BC Stadium has changed direction as a result of several adjacent developments – the Ford Centre for the Performing Arts, the Vancouver Public Library, and General Motors Place (an ice rink and former basketball stadium). Close by are the remnants of Expo – Science World and the Plaza of the Nations – and the Vancouver

Playhouse and the Queen Elizabeth Theatre. Proposals for a new convention centre and a hotel suggested a need to rethink the future of the area.

In 1996 the city sought to review the official development plan for the area around the stadium. The developers were reluctant, but after they were given assurances that the net value of their development rights would not be reduced, two charettes took place in June 1997 to explore a range of urban design issues related to the area's future use. At the time of writing, three architectural practices were working on the area with three different sets of developers. Concord Pacific retained James Cheng to coordinate these ideas and prepare proposals for their sites. Cheng's proposals were posted on the city's website in June 2001 (see Figure 41). He suggested more choice-of-use zoning to mix commercial and residential land uses, but otherwise stayed within the densities and land uses prescribed in the official development plan, save for additional commercial floor space to the west of the stadium. The main thrust of the proposals was to improve pedestrian movement and the public realm in the area and to restore the street pattern by extending Smithe Street to the water and containing the ramps of the Cambie Bridge. These plans have yet to undergo public consultation, but they start to resolve some of the urban design problems in this challenging location.

False Creek North is arguably Vancouver's most important urban design achievement. It is a complete and thoroughgoing example of the advantages of large-scale master planning as may be found anywhere. Its participative, corporate, collaborative processes have become the norm for large-scale

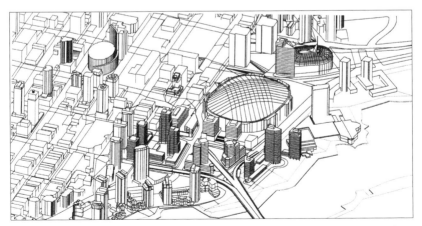

Figure 41 Urban design proposals for Northeast False Creek, 2001. Since 1997, Concord Pacific and the city have been working to rethink the area between the Cambie bridgehead and Pender Street. By mid-2001 James Cheng had produced a draft urban design plan (shown) restoring some coherence to the area, focusing on improving its livability and viability, and dramatically improving pedestrian movement and the public realm. (*Source:* Vancouver [2001n])

redevelopment in Vancouver, but remain the envy of other North American cities for their smoothness and sophistication, and for the design quality they deliver. In retrospect it all looks comparatively easy, given the favourable conditions of consolidated land ownership, cheap land, enlightened land-owner, highly accessible location, and waterfront potential, but one glance at the plans of the mid-1970s and mid-1980s (see Plate 35) shows how the project might easily have become a modernist nightmare and a place apart from the city.

The Coal Harbour Megaproject

The second official development plan approved in 1990 was for the Coal Harbour megaproject on the north side of downtown on the shores of Burrard Inlet. Coal Harbour shares a similar history and some of the same actors as the Concord Pacific scheme: Marathon as developer, Rick Hulbert Group as the architectural master planners, and key city planning personnel. But the project is only one-third the size of the False Creek megaproject. It has been developed much more slowly, with only one neighbourhood completed by 2000. As with False Creek North, the planning history for Coal Harbour was long and frequently abortive. Serious redevelopment planning began in 1973 and embraced the whole area between Stanley Park and Main Street. By 1978 a Central Waterfront official development plan had been adopted, carefully reconciling the ambitions of the main landowners: Marathon, CP Rail, the federal port authority, and the Greater Vancouver Regional District. The plan sought to encourage commercial development over the rail tracks and "urban water-oriented" uses on the waterfront. There were broad design guidelines for the physical form of development and these were accompanied by brief sub-area statements on density and physical form.

In the 1980s, one project related to Expo '86 was built on the central waterfront, defining the eastern end of the Coal Harbour site. A major conference venue and trade centre combined with a cruise-liner terminal was built on the edge of downtown, a perfect vehicle for a provincial megaproject and a prominent facility for Expo. However, by 1983 the project was in financial difficulties and had to be rescued by the federal government; it subsequently served as the Canada Pavilion at Expo '86. It has since proven to be a valuable commercial facility because of the continued growth of the cruise business. The city felt that it had not been properly consulted or involved in the design, although the area development process did set out the floor-space allocation in detail and agreed the broad disposition of uses, building massing, access, circulation, and parking. The project's massive 5-storey exhibition and function rooms and IMAX theatre were topped by a 20-storey hotel clad in mirror glass, and a similar office tower. But the most distinctive feature

Plate 41 Canada Place and 200 Granville Street. 200 Granville is modernist urban design of the 1970s, while Canada Place is an iconic postmodern response appropriate to a cruise-ship terminal. Also revealed are the urban design challenges that lie to the east of the terminal, both in integrating public transport facilities and in successfully relating to the waterfront.

of the design is the set of tall white sails, rigged from ten masts that top the convention centre throughout its length (see Plate 41). This entire project, designed by three architectural practices led by Zeidler Roberts Partnership, was massed to evoke a huge cruise ship with its prow facing out across the inlet. It has proved to be a signature building for Vancouver.

Coal Harbour is the name given to the project that occupies the former port lands between Canada Place and the Westin Bayshore Inn to the west, although only one-third of this area is within Coal Harbour proper. The land, originally owned by CP Rail, was transferred to its property company, Marathon, following changes in the provincial tax regime, and Marathon began to develop its plans for the area (14.5 hectares) in the late 1980s. The initial plans were for about 470,000 square metres of floor space, of which 150,000 square metres were to be offices and 50,000 square metres a hotel. The rest was to be residential, yielding somewhere in the region of 2,200 dwelling units. The Marathon proposals included a large marina and hotel at the west end of the site and a large festival market, backed by five major office towers at the east end. The residential uses were disposed along a central axis leading through the middle of the site to the shores of the marina, focused on a circular open space at the foot of Bute Street (Figure 42).

The city followed the same participatory procedures, plan development stages, and public facility provisions that were successfully emerging from the Concord Pacific negotiations for North Park. It responded to Marathon's proposals with the development of a policy statement, which drew heavily on extant Central Waterfront policies and was approved by council in February 1990 (Vancouver 1990d). It envisaged commercial development at the eastern end of the site closest to downtown, but residential over the greater part of the site (25 percent family, 20 percent affordable). It set an average net base density of 2.75 floor-space ratio, increasing toward downtown and away from the water. A density incentive of 0.5 floor-space ratio was suggested for the provision of smaller rental housing units. Extensive parklands were suggested – nearly 4 hectares for the area as a whole – including a waterfront walkway that would link a series of smaller parks and one large one. Built-form policies were a challenge, given the density required, the north-facing slope, the dense development behind, the need to retain views northward, and the desire to maximize the sunlight penetration to parks and walkway. The issue of a new ground plane for the development was a critical departure point: the policy statement allowed a raised ground level over much of the site to provide car parking and servicing underneath, but with a feature to be made of the existing escarpment where it was left intact or created anew. As with False Creek North, a street-wall building form of 10.5 metres was required, with a mix of low- and medium-sized towers up to 36 metres in the west, rising to 69 metres and some to 100 metres as they progressed eastward. Among other requirements were street view corridors, a full range of community services, a new interceptor sewer to prevent the release of raw sewage from pre-1956 sewers, and saltwater pumping stations to fight fires in the event of an earthquake.

The Official Development Plan

By November 1990 the city had produced an official development plan for the Marathon lands and it had been approved by council. It was not as precise as that for False Creek North, but the key planning principles were virtually identical. The plan specified land-use zones, including a major extension of downtown offices and retail east of Thurlow Street with a hotel and reserved site for a civic arts complex and public open space. Five residential areas were designated to the west, three behind a large park (Harbour Green) that occupied the central waterfront on the site, with a second smaller

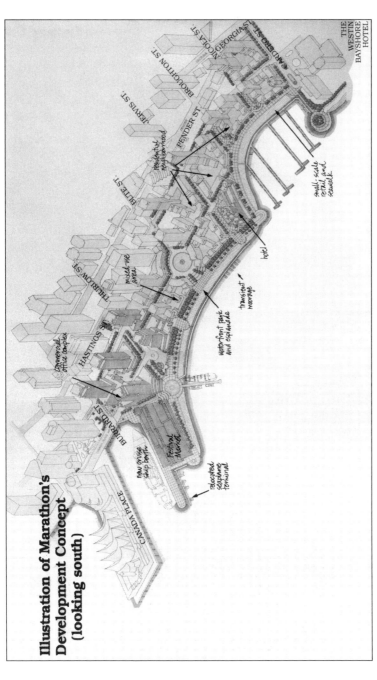

Figure 42 Marathon proposals for Coal Harbour megaproject, 1988. Marathon's proposals prior to an official plan extended the street grid to the inlet, leaving a boulevarded esplanade as public space across the site. Building heights were kept low toward the sea, with most of the residential floor space in seven tall and seven medium-height towers on a series of perimeter blocks at the back of the site. The north-south streets connected well to the grid, but the main east link was less satisfactory. (*Source:* Vancouver [1988g])

Illustration of Marathon's Development Concept (looking south)

CANADA PLACE

new cruise ship berth

relocated seaplane terminal

Festival Market

DURRARD ST.

commercial office complex

HASTINGS ST.

THURLOW ST.

mixed-use areas

waterfront park and esplanade

transient moorage

hotel

BUTE ST.

residential neighbourhood

JERVIS ST.

PENDER ST.

BROUGHTON ST.

NICOLA ST.

GEORGIA ST.

CARDERO ST.

small-scale retail and seawalk

THE WESTIN BAYSHORE HOTEL

park on the newly sculpted bay to the west. Maximum numbers of residential units and floor areas were prescribed for each site, and floor-space limits were set for the commercial sites. Pedestrian routes were indicative but view corridors were quite precise. An illustrative plan showing building forms, space design, and landscaping was included, along with maximum tower heights, to reveal a generous allocation of public space and a high level of visual and pedestrian permeability that would provide much-needed seafront and parkland for downtown.

The detailed plans for the first phase of development were drawn up and approved in 1991. The residential floor space proposed by Marathon had been reduced by 20 percent to 216,858 square metres and the number of dwelling units had been reduced by 10 percent to 2,034. But both reductions could largely be reclaimed by Marathon if they utilized incentives for the provision of smaller rental units (less than 70 square metres). In design terms, the key changes from Marathon's concept plan were the addition of a single large sunlit green space on the waterfront between the marina and the arts complex, a park board aspiration, as opposed to a series of small urban spaces; the extension of Cordova Street to serve the rear of the site; and the reliance on a dozen tall slim residential towers to carry the bulk of the floor space and not overshadow the park.

Three Neighbourhood Designs

Phase One of Coal Harbour, the Marina Neighbourhood, was designed in detail immediately after the approval of the official development plan and was accepted by city council early in 1992 (see Figure 43). It looked out on a recreational marina in a new bay created by the Coal Harbour landfill. To the west there was space to create two new city blocks between the extensions of Cordova, Nicola, and Broughton streets with a pair of 22-storey towers on each, and townhouses completing the block (see Plate 42). The western block included retail on the ground floor on the waterfront side, with 3 storeys of apartments above. Pedestrian walkways bisected the block north-south and east-west. The second block to the east had a single north-south route, but both blocks possessed semi-private green space that trapped sunlight. A low-rise 6-storey apartment block of non-market housing to be built atop a neighbourhood school and four daycare facilities that open out eastward into a small plaza and a one-hectare (2.35-acre) park completes this neighbourhood (see Figure 43). Several architects and planners have voiced disappointment with the design of the first block completed: perhaps the site plan was too tight and density too great for a relatively small block (see Plate 42). However, Richard Henriquez's award-winning park is very successful, as is

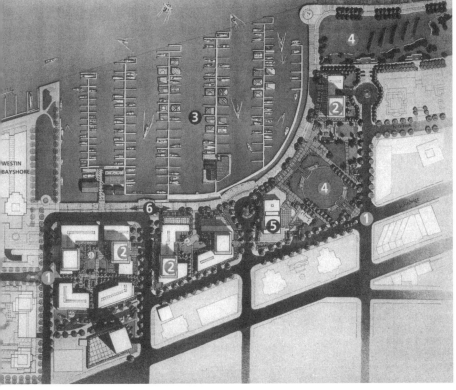

Figure 43 Marina Neighbourhood site plan. This site plan provided the basis for development of the first phase of Coal Harbour, focusing on the new marina (3). Richard Henriquez went on to design the award-winning park (4). The complex to the west (2) accommodates social housing at the rear, and community facilities (5) will be provided adjacent to the park. (*Source:* Marathon [1995])

the design of the waterfront walkway, picking up the Stanley Park traditions defined by the shoreline treatment study (Vancouver 1991m) (see Plate 43).

The plans for the commercial component of Coal Harbour – Phase Two, called Burrard Landing – were effectively an extension of downtown to the waterfront. Detailed design work began early in 1992, a detailed plan being agreed upon with city staff and subjected to public comment in a series of seventy-five meetings, exhibitions, and workshops. In these plans, three towers were to be oriented to face onto the extension of Thurlow Street, a due north aspect that would capture the view across Burrard Inlet to North Vancouver. A planted promenade stepped down through a civic plaza adjacent to an arts complex and onto the waterfront walkway, with retail and catering uses tucked under the promenade, and beneath a hotel tower overlooking Canada Place. Very different development proposals emerged, however, at

Plate 42 Marina Neighbourhood, Coal Harbour. The Marina Neighbourhood, viewed from the new park at the foot of Jervis Street to the east, is intimidating in its scale and battleship grey finish. There are also some awkward transitions to the apartments and townhouses at street level, and the social housing to the rear is rather nondescript. The towers look rather wide when viewed laterally but do allow upslope properties good views northward. To the right is the Bayshore Drive complex, developed in the 1990s, which generally fails to meet the city's high design standards.

the end of the decade to accommodate the extension to the Vancouver convention and exhibition centre on the site. Designed by convention centre specialist George Loschky of LMN Architects and a local architectural team, much of the exhibition hall would be placed at the seawall level with a circular landscaped "civic performance park" and a 2-storey meeting room above. A large ballroom and other function rooms above it on the second floor would be housed underneath a complex waved roof. Two of the three high-rise towers initially proposed would remain on the site, but probably for

Plate 43   Coal Harbour waterfront walkway. The waterfront
walkway, detailed design by Phillips Farevaag Smallenberg, marks
the close collaboration of park board, planning, and engineering in
its planning and implementation. It manages considerable changes
of grade successfully, separates cycle and pedestrians in an informal
way, and its art deco details are particularly successful and very
Vancouver.

development as hotels. An unusually large amount of work has gone into the
concept design of the public spaces, gardens, walkways, and promenades, to
emphasize the community benefits of the scheme. The arts complex initially
proposed would remain to the west of the convention centre. The design of
the convention centre has been explained with the following state-of-the-art
piece of aesthetic hyperbole.

> The design vernacular is built around the concept of landscape as architecture.
> All development to the upper ballroom level is conceived as landscaped ter-
> raced ground floor, rich in its context of northwest ecology, Vancouver culture

and history. Metaphorically above the landscape terraces will be a floating sculptured roof structure of waves washing to the shore. The rolling horizontality of
the structure will reinforce the maritime concept of Canada Place without copying or competing with the ship metaphor. (Marathon 2000: 7)

The convention centre was undergoing detailed design at the time of writing.

Phase Three of Coal Harbour, the central residential section, was worked
up in detail in 1993 and early 1994 as a set of seven 30-plus storey towers
containing 907 units placed above blocks of townhouses that define Cordova
Street to the rear. They were set slightly above a new pedestrian boulevard
acting as a promenade, which in turn looks out over the 3.6-hectare, 50-
metre-wide park that extends to the waterfront walkway (see Plate 44). Each
of the towers was separated by a pedestrian walkway lined with trees and
townhouse gardens and had small green spaces adjacent for residents' use.
Three of these walkways were shown as gated to provide semi-private space
for the residents. The 292 non-market housing units were to be accommodated in another tower and townhouse block behind the western towers at
Jervis Street and the extension of Cordova Street. Public consultation in the
nine months leading up to April 1995 resulted in some adjustments in the size
and number of dwelling units on each site and to the towers. The rezoning
plan was approved in June 1995 and design guidelines adopted in 1996. All
seven towers that look out over Harbour Green are to be designed as a
related cluster with the three to the east and two to the west of the Bute Street
extension fronting the promenade having near identical design (the Regatta
Group) (see Plate 44 and Figure 44). The towers were designed with slim
floor plates to ensure midday sunshine reaches the park and promenade –
critical on this cool, northerly aspect – and to provide a foil to the darker,
rather monolithic office towers behind.

Design Issues in Harbour Green
The detailed design of these towers has continued to be an issue, as more
and more occupants of office and, in particular, residential towers upslope in
Triangle West have protested about view blockage. Despite the thorough
consultation undertaken by the planning department, it transpires that many
apartment purchasers in Triangle West were not aware of the redevelopment
plans and the impacts they would have on their views when they purchased
their properties. This has led to demands for a rethink of the designs and,
failing this, for rigid enforcement of the existing guidelines, denying the architects the flexibility they need to refine their designs. Three of the towers
have been through the permitting process and the design of each project has
raised some interesting conflicts with the design guidelines and developer/

Plate 44 Artist's impression of the Harbour Green scheme, 1995. The first comprehensive plan drawn up for the third phase of Coal Harbour in 1995 created Harbour Green Park with the five towers set at the back of a promenade, with a sixth behind the tower to the west, and a seventh at the west end of Harbour Green and fronting the sea wall. Subsequently the whole approach to tower and podium design changed, and the buildings took on the regatta concept of white sail-like towers against the dark office-block background (see Figure 44). (Courtesy Marathon Developments, Inc., 1995)

designer aspirations. The westernmost tower, at the foot of Jervis Street on the seawall, designed by James Cheng, was applauded for its slimness and proportions and given a 10 percent height relaxation, although doubts were raised about its orthogonal grid. The top of the tower was to be designed as a piece of public art. The designer sought to substitute live/work units for retail at the base of the tower but the Development Permit Board was unable to alter the official development plan. A second issue concerned the Jervis view corridor requirement, which the architect considered impaired the relationship to the Harbour Green towers to the east and failed to enclose the park to the north properly. In the end the applicant did seek a view corridor relaxation, but council denied it.

Similar issues arose when different architects came to design the first two of the five towers on the promenade above Harbour Green. The architects undertook extensive view analyses and consultations with upslope residents, facilitated by the planning department, to help refine their designs. Both revised designs challenged the guidelines because they were creating slimmer towers on the east-west dimension but giving them a bigger floor plate overall and making one of them four metres taller. These changes recognized the desire to minimize the impacts on the views of the water from properties behind, but the biggest improvement to the views was achieved by removing the 12 storeys of apartments that fronted the Harbour Green promenade and replacing them with townhouses, similar to the changes made in Marinaside Crescent in False Creek North. Both tower designs employ more iconic sculptural forms with white, sail-like facades apparently tapering at their base, producing a regatta concept for the five towers to continue the theme of the Canada Place cruise terminal, but this time in 27- and 35-storey towers (see Figure 44). The Development Permit Board approved the scheme but insisted that the towers could not exceed the guideline height because of an objection by the owner of an adjacent office building.

The development of Coal Harbour is proceeding more slowly than anticipated and will take another decade to complete, not least because it is aimed at the top end of the market. The 50 × 375 metres Harbour Green Park alongside the seawall will be its biggest contribution to the city and, with the seawall, this will prove to be an enduring attraction for office workers, Triangle West residents, and tourists (see Plate 44). The design of the Burrard Landing complex will be critical, because it provides the first real contact point between the central business district and the sea. Councillors regard Coal Harbour as "the city's front door" and "the best waterfront development in North America" (interviews). Certainly it is a more exclusive development than False Creek North, but this is counterbalanced by the creation of a highly accessible major public space with a truly spectacular setting.

Criticisms of the Megaproject Neighbourhoods

Commentators and critics are largely agreed on the success of the megaprojects and the design qualities achieved. Visiting American planners, particularly those from the Pacific Northwest, are deeply envious of the achievement and of the political and planning regimes that can deliver high-quality development with considerable public facility benefits on such a scale and to a wide public (Blore and Sutherland 1999: 49). But not every Vancouverite is so convinced. Walter Hardwick and Ray Spaxman have expressed their doubts about the emphasis on apartment living at high densities and look for more neighbourhood diversity and a broader social mix. Housing experts are worried about the sustained delivery of the non-market housing and argue that developers should transfer such sites into public ownership or provide operating subsidies to improve development feasibility. In the CityPlan visioning processes, Vancouver citizens rejected the alternative "central city" model, with major residential development concentrated in megaprojects on industrial land. The Vancouver public remains unconvinced that the megaprojects offer a quality of life and a quality of neighbourhood that is appropriate for

Figure 44 1239 and 1281 West Cordova, Coal Harbour: reactions of the Urban Design Panel and Development Permit Board. This is an example of the refinement of the original conceptions for the five residential towers above Harbour Green and of the flexibility that exists in the permitting process. It also illustrates the unwillingness/inability of the Development Permit Board to compromise on key official development plan parameters (e.g., tower height). The sketch (top left) indicates the overall concept of the "regatta" that links the five towers.

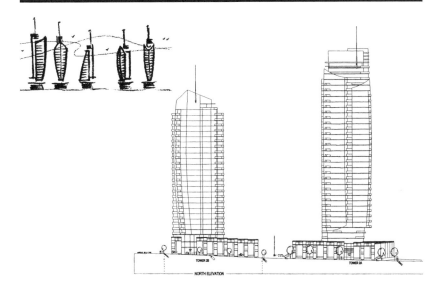

Address and Location
1239 and 1281 West Cordova Street, Coal Harbour

Zoning and Bonuses
CD-1 / 325-foot and 245-foot height limits

Project Description
35- and 27-storey residential towers with townhouses at grade

Architect and Client
Hancock Bruckner Eng & Wright / Marathon

Urban Design Panel
01/00 *5-1 approve.* Challenging the guidelines but approve of extra height; like slimmer sculptured designs and sail concept. Ambitious design and base/podium redesign improves visual access from upslope to Harbour Green.

Development Permit Board
05/00 *Approve in principle.* Slimmer towers but bigger floor plate allow removal of 12-storey terraces at the base and better views through. Bold innovative use of sail and regatta analogies, but heights of the offending tower to be reduced to the original guideline maximum. Also refusal to allow a play area to be added to a public park requiring it to be provided on site for resident use only.

Source: Hancock Bruckner Eng & Wright (drawings); text compiled from panel and board minutes

the future of the city at large, but this may be only the older generation's perspective.

Related criticisms have been made about the neatness and orderliness of the projects, and the sanitizing of city and public realm. Journalist Sean Blore sees in the Concord Pacific scheme the pursuit of a formal and behavioural perfection that he labels "Smileyville," a description of what he perceives as a Vancouver-wide "urge to use design to predict, program, and control all aspects of public behaviour" (Blore and Sutherland 1999: 58). There are times when it does resemble a high-density version of *The Truman Show* (Paramount Films 1998) with its pristine public realm, its exciting architectural backdrops, and its lightly populated stage-scenery feel (see Plates 36 to 40). That impression is heightened by the body-beautiful cyclists, joggers, and rollerbladers who glide past the tourists on the seawall. It is also projected by the Concord Pacific publicity, with its emphasis on "resort" living, gourmet cuisine, and passive and especially active recreation. Current Concord Pacific marketing of Beach Neighbourhood highlights nature – sky, sunsets, earth, sea, parkland – alongside the excitement and consumer choice of the urban setting. Predominant themes are "in it, away from it," in the sense of being within the city but detached from its negative aspects, and being able to (literally) "sail off into the sunset." Equally significant is the marketing of each complex's recreation facilities, which are now complemented by such facilities as private cinemas, bars, and entertainment rooms where residents can socialize in private. The planners emphasize that megaproject planning has brought all the advantages of suburbia into high-density inner-city living. The developers carry this ethos to its privatized extreme. Urban Design panellist and architect Lance Berelowitz identifies "the cult of the view" – one of Vancouver's defining characteristics – as the driving force of design and links it with the production of "highly contrived, ideologically controlled and economically commodified reality" in the waterfront zone, "a space of personal leisure and private gratification" (Berelowitz 1998: 6). He argues that "the city acts as a kind of mirror, or a vast display case for the aesthetic consumption of Nature. In the metamorphosis from a street-oriented and centripetal urban model to the outward looking centrifugal city, activity intensifies towards the edges. The centre is stilled" (Berelowitz 1998: 6). Berelowitz sees the attractions of the seawall draining downtown of its vitality and civic life and depriving it of truly public spaces. Blore and Berelowitz's conclusions might be viewed as a premature response to incomplete developments that lack a certain amount of vitality and diversity merely because they are so new. But their comments resonate with more sustained critiques of the introduction of postmodern aesthetics to urban life and the gentrification of the central city. David Ley postulates that Vancouver is becoming a city with a sanitized aesthetic, one where public life is driven by conspicuous consumption, where conviviality replaces community, and where aesthetics override equity (Ley 1996: 365-66; See Sorkin 1992 for a similar US view).

But the evidence provided by False Creek North and Coal Harbour suggests that they have created major public amenities that can be accessed and enjoyed by everyone and that cater to a wide range of tastes and recreational preferences. They have a quality infrastructure for everyday life with daycares, community centres, and library facilities. They are fully and carefully integrated into the existing urban fabric and they provide public facilities that can be enjoyed by neighbouring communities. And they accommodate a wide section of the community with their family housing and the 20 percent of affordable units. The nature of the social mix and the level of affordable housing provided in these projects are the subject of the liveliest debate. Skeptics note that even the 20 percent affordable housing may not be sustained without more subsidies from higher levels of government. Could the megaprojects have sustained substantially higher development levies or levels of public benefit provision? The problem for those who would extract the absolute maximum benefit from developers is that they can define what this might be only when the developer has walked away for good. There are also arguments that Concord Pacific and Marathon each acquired the land for their projects at such low rates that they could have afforded to contribute more to low-cost housing, and could certainly have conveyed the land for social housing to the city at no cost. In the context of the late 1980s, with the scale and longevity of the projects, with the uncertainties of the market, and with no extant experience on levies and amenity contributions except for parks and schools, on balance the city has achieved very high facility and amenity standards.

Planning Southeast False Creek: A Sustainable Megaproject?

Southeast False Creek, on formerly industrial waterfront east of the Cambie Bridge, is still in the planning stages. The evolution of this project provides a measure of how far the planning agenda has shifted over the last decade. For a while, there were possibilities that development practices – and more especially development economics – might dictate built forms little different from those created by Marathon and Concord Pacific. However, with the official development plan imminent, the die is cast for a major experiment in neighbourhood design, reminiscent of the 1974 plans for False Creek South. This time, however, the objective is the development of an innovative sustainable neighbourhood formulating entirely new approaches to site planning and urban design.

The southeast corner of False Creek was the site of lumber and steel industries, and the land remains heavily contaminated. The 32-hectare (80-acre) site was acquired by the city, which continued to run a garbage incinerator and an asphalt plant there. A 1992 survey put the costs of clean-up for redevelopment unhelpfully between $15 million and $150 million; it is the lower figure that has been adopted for most subsequent development appraisal exercises. The site was suggested as the location for an experiment in energy-efficient land-use policies in the 1990 *Clouds of Change: Final Report* (Vancouver 1990a), a recommendation that council accepted, committing itself to a raft of energy-efficient, ecologically appropriate, transit-oriented, residential intensification policies for the city at large. However, little was actually done until 1994 when council suggested that the Special Office for the Environment explore with the city's real estate division the potential for sustainable development on the Southeast False Creek site, a move that appeased both the environmentalists and development-oriented councillors. The city manager and the real estate division, given their preoccupation with maximizing the returns to the city's Property Endowment Fund, had more conventional aspirations for the site. In mid-1996 they retained Stanley Kwok, who had been so instrumental in developing the master plan for False Creek North, to prepare a master plan for this area that could then be used for marketing individual sites – a clear signal of their intention to maximize development potential. The terms of reference for the master plan did not mention sustainable development. Kwok's first task was to undertake a development appraisal – the city uses the term "pro forma analysis" – to establish the feasibility of development, given the contamination costs. This revealed a project on the margins of profitability – a 4.5 percent rate of return was estimated – and opportunity costs of holding the site were put at nearly $3 million a year, emphasizing the need to proceed quickly if the city was not to lose money. Sustainable development was interpreted as that which maximized the returns to the city's Property Endowment Fund, or, as Kwok and his city employers cleverly put it, to minimize medium-term financial losses. The sustainability principles in the project, which Kwok renamed "Creekside Landing," were largely derived from a workshop held – not with the academic and professional sustainability experts for which the city was renowned – but with mainstream development and architectural interests and planners. The workshop outcomes led Kwok to conclude that

> sustainable development is difficult to define ... It would appear [it] should be applied in a macro sense and in a regional context [and] urban intensification should be viewed as supportive of sustainable development. On a micro level, sustainable planning and design, not only involving compact, mixed use, transit supportive development but also advanced applications in the management of energy, waste and natural ecological systems, including water and landscapes

should be looked into, taking into account costs and benefits. (Kwok Consultants, Inc. 1997: 24)

Kwok's pro forma analysis went much further than the brief suggested to produce a concept design and even a model for the site. This illustrated a by-now familiar approach – a dense residential neighbourhood of 3,750 varied dwelling units for 5,000 people, with a generous park and green space system on the waterfront penetrating deep into the site in a series of wedges to bring all units within easy reach of the parkland. A commercial "village" of 7,600 square metres of retail created a focus for the development alongside a marina. Both these elements were reminiscent of the design concepts underpinning the False Creek South development of the 1970s, but the site planning and density were much more similar to the False Creek North development of the 1990s. Gross and net floor-space densities were set slightly above those of the latter (1.6 gross/3.13 net floor-space ratio) and there was a mix of 2-storey townhouses and terraced 4-storey apartments fronting the park, with six high-rise and as many as ten medium-size apartment blocks mainly at the east end of the site closest to the Main Street SkyTrain Station. While a stream was exposed in the southeast corner of the site, and a new stream was to be created to meander through the project, there were few concessions to any ecological principles of site planning. However, through-traffic was excluded and the mews concept was used to create pedestrian-friendly urban design. The concept plan incorporated all the standard public amenities expected of a megaproject.

In contrast to the city's real estate department's expensive and sophisticated financial analysis and master plan, the city planning department could initially fund only a summer student to research the policies and precedents for sustainable development. Mark Holland's review ably summarized the physical and ecological aspects of sustainability, but the social dimension was not part of his brief (Vancouver 1996a). He looked at ecosystems, energy, water production and management, land use and transportation, landscape, construction, services, and agriculture, as well as costs in use and the economics of resource use. He developed a matrix as a framework to assess each in terms of water, soil, air, habitat, and energy resources, and waste production impacts. The report embraced both the science of the issue and its relevance to urban development, mentioning precedents where these existed. It provided a solid basis for subsequent drafts of a policy statement for the area.

As the tensions between conventional and sustainable development intensified, the Vancouver Planning Commission stepped in to sponsor a two-day conference on urban sustainability that attracted six councillors and some

300 delegates. It was the self-appointed Southeast False Creek Working Group – a diverse collection of professionals, students, and social activists who had been debating the project for a couple of years – who convinced council that sustainability was something worth pursuing in the project (Blore 1998). Belatedly council recognized that their sustainability objectives from the *Clouds of Change* commitment had been derailed. They shelved the Kwok report and agreed to pay for a consultants' study to refine sustainability indicators and targets for the development that would inform the production of an official development plan. Subsequently Kwok was retained by the city manager to do a second-phase study writing up development proposals as a contribution to the official development plan (Kwok Consultants, Inc. 1997).

Sustainability consultants Sheltair reported to council a year later with a set of goals, objectives, and targets and full cost accounting processes to guide the planning of the site (Vancouver 1998ii). Each sustainability objective defined for Southeast False Creek was compared on a linear scale with other exemplar projects or with municipalities with strong sustainability policies (see Figure 69). Sheltair's performance targets have been appended to the 1999 policy statement, which will underpin the official development plan, providing valuable criteria with which to evaluate the plan's commitments and an agenda for detailed development planning for the next decade.

Preparing the Policy Statement

Public participation in the preparation of a policy statement for Southeast False Creek began in the summer of 1997 when an advisory group was established to represent interested parties, local businesses, and adjacent communities. Formal public review was conducted in the summer of 1998, through workshops and open houses to establish consensus. The advisory group drafted a set of its sustainability principles to guide the development, emphasizing equity, education, participation, and accountability alongside adaptability, community, and livability (Vancouver 1999p: 80-81). Meanwhile, in October 1998, the city planners held a multi-disciplinary, three-day design charrette to pursue alternative designs for the site. Their commonalities can be encapsulated in four themes:

- *incrementalism/phased development:* to take advantage of evolving technologies and incorporate "lessons" in later phases
- *flexibility/adaptability:* especially in built forms
- *working green:* to work in concert with natural systems making them visible
- *multi-functionality:* of spaces, infrastructure, and buildings. (Vancouver 1998gg: 3)

The Holland and Sheltair studies, the synthesis of the design charrette, and various real estate studies, including some more sustainability-conscious costings, were progressively fed into drafts of the policy statement through 1997 to 1999. Two problems emerged. First, senior staff in city engineering, and to a lesser extent parks, were taken aback by many of the ideas in the statement and required further reassurance and information. A 700-signature petition, driven by a few residents of Mount Pleasant, advocated turning the entire site into a park, using the argument that the wider area was deficient in neighbourhood parks. The result was a compromise facilitated by further studies on soil contamination and remediation. The parkland was extended to 11 hectares, resulting in a loss of 100,000 square metres of floor space, but this reduced remediation costs from $30 million to $15 million to make such changes "economic." The policy statement (Vancouver 1999p) was unanimously adopted by council in October 1999. Unlike previous city policy statements, it carefully considered how each policy related to different stages of the planning process (official development plan, zoning, and guidelines), extending these into postdevelopment management initiatives, including demonstration projects. The policy statement was Vancouver's first to embrace ecological, social, and economic aspects of sustainable development, with substantive sections on environmental concerns (i.e., energy, water, waste, soils, air quality, and agriculture), economic development, and stewardship (i.e., cost accounting and management).

The policy statement promised a dense diverse mixed-use and mixed form neighbourhood. The development and design principles were very similar to those espoused for False Creek North, but there was more of an emphasis on creating a continuous green-space system and incorporating a range of ecological devices and some natural features into the site planning and landscaping. More attention was given to creating quite distinct neighbourhoods, in terms of density, height, form, social mix, and mixes of land uses. The western side of the project had much lower building heights, more akin to those in False Creek South. The more innovative aspects of policy remain to be articulated at the official development plan stage, particularly the requirements for separate energy, water management, waste management, air quality, and urban agriculture strategies. This is in addition to the development of such demonstration projects as the community centre to promote environmentally responsible business or, crucially, financial strategies for affordable housing. One notable innovation is the proposed transformation of the advisory group to provide guidance to the city on stewardship issues throughout the development process and beyond, using sustainability indicators to monitor performance. To help manage the area in the future, this advisory group is intended to become a neighbourhood integrated service team (see Chapter 7).

City planners and building regulators still have important studies to complete, including policy and guideline preparation, and green building guidelines, which are also being considered by the region and the province on a broader front. A final component will be a monitoring exercise to be conducted on False Creek North to test the demographic projections and community satisfaction with the area's facilities and amenities. This will be of much broader value to the planning department and will replicate the evaluations undertaken of False Creek South in the 1980s (see Chapter 2). It will have a specific relevance to the official development plan as a contribution to a "Community Facilities White Paper," rethinking the standard public facility benefit requirements developed in 1989 and considering what the area and its immediate environs need as regards social, cultural, and environmental facilities (see also Chapter 8).

How do the current proposals compare with Stanley Kwok's conventional megaproject development proposals for Creekside Landing, prepared in 1996? The overall floor-space ratio has been reduced from 3.75 to 3.0, the residential and retail floor space has been reduced by one-third, and the official policy statement has clearly tempered the real estate division's ambitious financial return targets in the interests of an experiment in sustainable neighbourhood design. The potentially major concession to "consider" the use of full cost accounting – to include longer-term and environmental impacts – along with a suggested seven-year time frame to measure how capital costs can be recouped from operating efficiencies produced by enhanced environmental performance, remain unresolved (Vancouver 1999p: 77). Much will depend on the soil remediation study to meet federal government requirements and its costings. There has been discussion of requiring the project to clean up the silt in False Creek, which would be a major financial burden. A full environmental study is being completed, and the stewardship committee has been reconvened. The timetable for the official development plan, rezoning, and guidelines has slipped by at least two years and, given the quantity of residential development already in the pipeline in the city, the project is very much on hold. The best opportunity for developing Southeast False Creek may be as an Olympic village for the 2010 Winter Olympics, should the Vancouver/Whistler bid be successful and the federal government offer some funding for remediation.

Verdicts on the Megaprojects

Although the False Creek North and Coal Harbour projects are unlikely to be completed much before the end of this decade, there is a widely held view that they are among the most successful large-scale redevelopment projects anywhere in North America over the last two decades. The targets of over

12,200 housing units and 20,400 residents for the two projects combined – and a further 4,000 people in Southeast False Creek – make them collectively the most ambitious high-density residential neighbourhoods on the edge of a downtown anywhere in North America in the 1990s (see Figure 45). Also significant are the 25 percent family and 20 percent non-market housing targets, the four-and-a-half kilometres of seawall walkway and cycle path with extensive public art and seating and viewing facilities, and the 25 hectares of public parkland. The "living first" strategy for downtown, established in the 1991 Central Area Plan, will be largely delivered by the waterfront megaprojects, which will allow its residential population to double between 1990 and 2015. However, to emphasize the scale of the problem confronting Greater Vancouver, these 25,000 new residents constitute only one year's population increase in the region.

These quantitative achievements would mean little without the high design quality achieved. This quality is the outcome of a range of design principles that were defined at the outset of the projects. The seven design principles enshrined in the False Creek North 1989 policy statement have been progressively refined to embrace particular urban design principles for mixed-use neighbourhoods, livable streets, a linked open-space system, a tower and townhouse form that gives privacy with urbanity, and the use of architectural treatments and materials that differentiate neighbourhoods and encourage them to respond to their context (see Figure 46). The parks also demarcate the neighbourhoods, relieve the high net densities, and create an extraordinary feeling of spaciousness that is enhanced by the seawall and the expansive views across the water. They do so not only for the new neighbourhoods, but also for the margins of downtown, Downtown South, and Triangle West (see Plate 44). Previously provided with narrow view corridors and glimpses of water and mountains at the ends of claustrophobic streets, Vancouverites can now escape to urbane settings that are sunlit and well landscaped from which to enjoy panoramas of water, urban hillsides, and mountains.

City engineering, parks, and planning departments have worked together closely to ensure that the public realm is intricate, well landscaped and furnished, traffic-calmed, overlooked, and safe. Planners ensured permeable layouts, insisted on townhouses and apartment buildings to overlook and enliven the street, and reinvented the mews, promenades, and other pedestrian street forms. Their quality has been reinforced by high standards of paving and landscaping, by unobtrusive elegant street furniture, and by generous public art installations (see Plate 40). The urban form and architecture have refined the new Vancouver vernacular, the townhouse and apartment-and-townhouse perimeter blocks punctuated by slim towers – the former recreating the traditional inhabited street and private courtyards, the latter

Figure 45 The megaprojects: land use, density, floor space, and public facilities

Description	False Creek North Concord Pacific	Coal Harbour Marathon	Coal Harbour Bayshore	CityGate	Southeast False Creek	Fraser Lands	Creekside Landing
Gross land area	166 acres	46.4 acres	17.8 acres	9.2 acres	81.2 acres	≈38.6 acres	46.2 acres
Parks	42 acres	10.4 acres	2.4 acres	cash contribution	16.2 acres	≈8 acres	18.6 acres
Gross land area less parks	124 acres	30 acres	15.4 acres				27.6 acres
Pro-rated land area: non-residential space excl. parks	30 acres	13.2 acres	1.7 acres				0.7 acres
Pro-rated land area: residential space excl. parks	94 acres	16.8 acres	13.7 acres				26.9 acres
Pro-rated gross residential land area with parks	136 acres	37.2 acres	16.1 acres				45.5 acres
Residential land area after park	94 acres	16.8 acres	13.7 acres	9.2 acres	65 acres	30.6 acres	26.9 acres
Residential land area after park and roads	≈75.2 acres	≈14 acres	≈11.4 acres	≈8.7 acres	≈52.7 acres	≈24.5 acres	≈23 acres
Residential building floor area	9,185,450 sf	2,645,000 sf	1,490,700 sf	1,424,000 sf	2,100,000 sf	1,558,000 sf	3,138,400 sf
Floor-space ratio (FSR): on gross residential land area	1.55	1.63	2.13	3.55	0.59	0.93	1.58
FSR: on net residential land area	2.24	3.61	2.50	3.55	0.74	1.17	2.68
FSR: on net residential land area after parks and roads	2.80	4.34	3.00	3.76	0.93	1.46	3.13
Number of housing units: market and non-market	8,500	2,250	980	1,000	1,850	1,400	3,750
Unit per acre: on gross residential land area	63	60	62	109	23	36	83
Retail space	385,000 sf	165,000 sf	39,300 sf				76,600 sf

Hotel space	600,000 sf	400,000 sf	150,000 sf more			
Commercial service space	265,000 sf	included in retail	included in retail			
Office space	1,700,000 sf	1,500,000 sf	included in retail			
Total non-residential space	2,950,000 sf	2,065,000 sf	189,300			76,600 sf
Park and public open space	yes	yes	yes	yes	yes	yes
Social housing in units	1,700	370	196	200	no	750 co-op, rental, etc.
School site	2	cash contribution	no	no	False Creek School	yes
Daycare	8 daycares	yes	yes	no	no	180 spaces
Community centre	yes	cash contribution	multi-purpose room	yes	yes	can be provided
Out-of-school facility	yes	cash contribution	no	no	no	included in daycare
Library contribution	yes	cash contribution	no	no	no	yes
Public art	yes	yes	no	no	no	yes
Public waterfront walkway	yes	yes	yes	yes	with park	yes
Specialty items:						
Stadium parking	yes	no	yes	no	no	no
Saltwater pumping station	yes	yes	no	no	no	no
Pacific Blvd treatment	yes	yes	no	no	no	no
Police boat moorage	yes	no	no	no	no	no
Arts complex	no	yes	no	no	no	no

Note: These statistics were prepared by Stanley Kwok as part of his Creekside Landing (Southeast False Creek) proposals in 1997. Kwok designed a scheme consistent with the central area precedents and also provided a valuable statistical comparison for posterity.
Source: Kwok Consultants, Inc. (1997)

Figure 46 Megaproject design principles (False Creek North). Many of these design principles can be traced back to the False Creek South official development plan, but they reached their full expression in the long gestation process of False Creek North (Concord Pacific).

1 **Livable downtown neighbourhoods**
Proximity to downtown employment, services, culture, transit
High net, medium gross project density
Social mix: 25 percent family, 20 percent non-market
Private livability: quiet, private, safe, views, amenities
Public amenity: seawall linking substantial parks
Protected view corridors

2 **Neighbourhood facilities in the "third place"**
Community centres
Primary schools
Leisure facilities (interior)
Active recreation space
Park space
Neighbourhood shops and offices

3 **Livable streets**
Extend grid to water's edge
Eliminate through-traffic
Reduce street parking
Pedestrian/cycle streets: mews, promenades with public art
Well-landscaped/furnished public realm
Weather protection
Active commercial strips

4 **Generous park system: "necklace of green pearls"**
Regional parks for citywide use
Differentiated functions: active/passive, formal/informal, children/adults
Public seawall: 35 feet (13 metres) of cycle/promenade/sitting space
Children's play space
Neighbourhood focus spaces/parkettes

5 **Urban form**
Perimeter block and green courtyard
Townhouse and street-wall apartment
Slim articulated tower and top
Clear gradations of public, semi-public, and private space
Underground car parking

6 **Elevational treatment**
Neighbourhood differentiation: different designers
Families of towers in each project
Articulated towers: orientations, floor plans, balconies, solariums
Active street frontages: steps, porches, bays, balconies, patios
Contextual materials and elevations
Waterfront palette: light colours and glass

accommodating most of the floor space. The prototype has been adapted to maximize views from block interiors and to minimize overshadowing and reduce blockage. With underground car parking, the block interiors can be lushly landscaped to provide quality communal space, while the public streets can seem remarkably lightly trafficked as a result.

With only four neighbourhoods complete and commercial facilities yet to become fully established, it is still a little early to assess the sense of community in these megaprojects. They have provided extensive public social and leisure facilities that are well designed, with daycare, play space, internal and exterior recreation space, community centres, and the occasional primary school. The family and social housing components have helped to create a mix of inhabitants (see Plate 45), and the early opening of the primary school testifies to the attractiveness of the area to young families. There was concern at the slow delivery of the social housing projects, because of the withdrawal of federal funding in 1993, but only one such site in the first three False Creek North neighbourhoods remains to be developed.

If the principles of development were right from the outset, it still took a very long time to establish the much-vaunted cooperative planning process. Credit must go to Stanley Kwok who brought a new spirit of cooperation and collaboration to the development side. Many of the principles of cooperative planning had been deeply rooted in the Spaxman approach to neighbourhood

Plate 45   Social housing and daycare, Marinaside Crescent. A social housing project east of Quayside and adjacent to the Cambie Bridge viaduct faces directly onto Coopers' Park. It has a daycare centre carefully integrated into and animating its ground floor. This medium-rise building, largely for families, contrasts with the much taller market rental and condominium towers.

planning, but the Central Area planning team overcame the departmentalism and turf wars that had characterized the Spaxman era. The cooperative planning process (see Figure 47) is characterized by a clear demarcation between political decision making, which sets the overall parameters of the projects, and the technical resolution of development forms and designs that is delegated to city officials. The emphasis is on joint working by teams comprised of developer and city staff to prepare master plans and convert them into official development plans, rezoning plans, and design guidelines, rather than planners preparing concept plans and guidelines on their own. The developer pays for the creation of a dedicated planning team to work full time on the project preparation, while the city works corporately, linking the planning function with other departments as necessary (Beasley 2000a).

This approach is complemented by sustained public participation at all stages of project development, achieving consensus and translating this into agreed facilities, amenities, mixes, and three-dimensional forms. This resulted in over 200 public meetings with 25,000 attendees on the Concord Pacific scheme between 1988 and 1993. To many in the development industry, this is overkill. They find staff workshops and formal meetings with public committees the most useful consultation vehicles, and open houses, public meetings, and hearings on each of the project phases largely unhelpful (Stamp 1999). But the consultation process has delivered a high level of certainty to the developers once the official development plan was agreed over the fifteen years or more of each megaproject. It has allowed them to proceed neighbourhood by neighbourhood, progressively developing their designs, gaining their permits, constructing and marketing their properties, managing their cash flow, and minimizing their risk. Critical to both development certainty and project quality are the public facility benefits that are stated at the outset and that can be built into the basic development costs and allocated according to neighbourhood composition (see Figure 36).

From an urban design perspective, one of the key dimensions of the process is the role of the architectural practice that acts as the master planner, and then the associated practices that develop rezoning plans and design guidelines. Not only do these practices prepare the developer's concept proposals but they respond to all the city's comments and criticisms and translate these into three-dimensional forms. They then play a major role translating these forms into planning documents and design guidelines to ensure that what has been agreed on gets built, the important reference points when it comes to processing development permits. The collaborative process makes the best use of the developer's architectural expertise to establish effective design guidance. Gradually the guidelines have become much briefer and less constraining, without becoming less effective.

Figure 47   The "cooperative planning model" for the megaprojects. The director of current planning distilled these principles, which have become known as the "cooperative planning model" that underpins the planning of Vancouver's megaprojects.

Established practices (False Creek North, Coal Harbour)

Establish parameters
- Council decides policy, planners set guidelines and decide permits
- Early resolution of major issues: Major Projects Steering Group
- Gross floor-space allowances defined by official development
- Clear statement of public-facility benefits required

Team working
- City and developers/designers work as a team
- Developer pays for dedicated planning team
- City works corporately: planning, engineering, parks

Public participation
- Extensive, continuous public participation at each stage (see Figure 35)

Design skills
- Skilled private architectural practices prepare master plans, rezonings, design guidelines

Steady progression
- Long-term certainty (15 years) offsets slow speed at the outset
- Clear stages of policy broadsheet, official development plan, rezoning, guidelines, permits
- Move from concepts to specifics to details over time
- Smooth permitting with development planner managing the process: refusals almost non-existent

Emerging practices (Southeast False Creek)

Sustainability and flexibility
- Simpler guidelines focus on essentials
- Increasing sustainability agenda: energy, water, waste, movement, ecology, urban agriculture
- Extending participation into stewardship
- New forms of social housing provision?

Source: Adapted from Beasley 1997

Finally, of course, the process is always changing, not just in the refinement of guidelines but in the adoption of new planning ideas. The 1990 processes were content to embrace sustainability in terms of reduced commuting, high-density living, and mixed-use and mixed-tenure neighbourhoods. But the current process in Southeast False Creek is formulating future planning policies and taking on considerations about energy, water, waste, ecology, and urban agriculture to reflect more profound sustainability concerns.

These should in turn lead to closer integration of more environmentally benign requirements for the building code and planning standards in the pursuit of sustainable structures. It is already resulting in experiments extending the participatory planning process into notions of stewardship and subsequent area management. There are also profound implications for development appraisal methods, public facility benefit calculations, pro forma analysis, and project life-cycle costing that could transform development economics themselves. The megaprojects, and their exemplary characteristics of community involvement, excellent public amenities, social and family housing, substantive and comprehensive design principles and guidelines, innovative and diverse design, and highly skilled and efficient permit processing (see Figure 1) continue to evolve.

7
Downtown Vancouver, 1991-2000

While the cooperative planning process managed the redevelopment of the waterfront megaprojects, the 1991 Central Area Plan redefined a much more differentiated future for the various sub-areas and fringe neighbourhoods of downtown. It did this principally by reducing the size of the central business district and its projected commercial zone, in its stead creating a variety of mixed-use and high-density residential areas while conserving the heritage character of Gastown and Chinatown, Victory Square, Yaletown, and Granville Street, to diversify the townscape, economy, and society of the central area. As these plans unfolded, a recurrent theme was how to ensure the quality of the public realm – whether in urban design guidelines for downtown streets, another facelift for Granville Street, or securing the dangerous streets of the Downtown Eastside.

The 1990s was the decade when Vancouver's livable downtown became a reality, when residential development on downtown's margins eclipsed all commercial development – with the partial exception of hotels – and when office construction stagnated. The livable downtown was confirmed by the 1996 census, which demonstrated a dramatic population increase in the first half of the decade. Downtown South's population grew by 141 percent, Triangle West by 92 percent, and downtown east to Main grew by 60 percent between 1991 and 1996. While the pace of residential development slowed in the second half of the 1990s, it is still very rapid by most North American city centre standards and projections suggest that the number of housing units in downtown neighbourhoods will increase by 125 percent from 1996 to 2008. Each of the emerging central residential areas is taking on a distinctive character, a product of different morphologies, heritage legacies, density differentials, and market forces, but also fashioned by different zonings, design guidelines, view corridors, and streetscape policies. But against all these design achievements, the deprivations of the Downtown Eastside are stark reminders of the fact that while some of the worst excesses of gentrification have been ameliorated, social exclusion is still rampant.

Preparing the 1991 Central Area Plan

The 1987 planning department's annual review noted that the 1975 downtown official development plan needed updating, having been prepared in a period of very rapid commercial growth (Vancouver City Planning Department Annual Review 1986-87: 7) (see Chapter 3). The rate of commercial development had been significantly overestimated, even with an office boom underway in 1986-89, and the city needed to readjust its zoning to fit recent patterns of floor-space demand and development activity. Surveys identified a number of desired actions in different localities, including diversification of the downtown area, the revitalization of East Hastings Street and Granville Mall, opening up both waterfronts to public use, and creating a mixed-use area in Yaletown. Some of these objectives were being addressed by the waterfront megaprojects, but while the 1975 plan had been successful in encouraging some residential development downtown, it was now time to secure an "adequate complement of residential services to ensure a satisfactory residential environment" (Vancouver City Planning Department Annual Review 1986-87: 10). To take the downtown plan forward, early in 1988 the Vancouver Planning Commission and the planning department jointly sponsored a symposium attended by over a hundred interest groups from which new planning objectives for downtown were derived. These included enhancing the appeal of the prestige office area along Burrard and Georgia, widening the area of retail prosperity, and ensuring that new developments did not prejudice street vitality (Vancouver 1988c). In the event, only the latter was to be of major significance in the subsequent document.

Although nominally a plan, the 1991 Central Area Plan was in fact a goal statement and a land-use policy framework for the whole of the central area north of Broadway, west of Main and east of Arbutus, including the downtown peninsula. It demarcated some thirty-four sub-areas, two of which had official development plans recently approved – the megaprojects in False Creek North and Coal Harbour – and four of which had plans approved in the mid-1970s or early 1980s. Seven general goals expressed a desire for downtown pre-eminence, downtown vitality, a place for all to live in and visit, protection of the spirit of place and the natural setting, and a walkable and accessible area – collectively reaffirming the ambitions of the mid-1970s. Significant changes were made to the proposed land-use structure of the area, aimed at producing a finer-grained pattern of land uses. New categories were added for "choice-of-use/mixed-use" areas and "heritage character" areas, the latter not fully fledged historic districts but nonetheless having protective

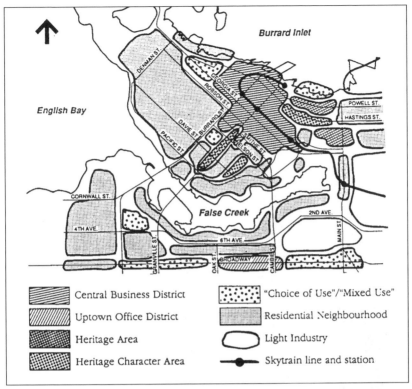

Figure 48 This map, taken from the 1991 policy statement, shows how the whole approach to planning in the central area had become much more fine-grained to create distinctive heritage and residential sub-areas, and significantly shrink the commercial core (compare with Figure 10). (*Source:* Vancouver [1991e])

zoning. So the broad zones of the amended 1975 plan gave way to a much more variegated pattern of smaller district areas, particularly in Downtown South and along Broadway (compare Figures 10 and 48).

The strategy was to consolidate a more compact central business district for offices downtown, and secondarily uptown on Broadway around Cambie, in those locations best served by transit to match office growth to transport capacity. Elsewhere office allocations were reduced in favour of residential uses or heritage buildings. There was a similar intention to focus retail activity on streets designated pedestrian-only and to limit underground or mall development, in part a recognition that the demand for retail uses had been overestimated previously. The protection of "support service" areas was also a notable part of the strategy, although the only designations to achieve this were the choice-of-use/mixed-use areas or the heritage character areas where low-rent "incubator" premises might be retained (e.g., Yaletown). New heritage protection areas were discussed for East Hastings Street in the Downtown

Eastside and Granville Street, as well as for Gastown, Chinatown, and Yaletown. Choice-of-use/mixed-use areas tended to be those formerly zoned for office development where hotel and residential uses would now be allowed, with commercial replacing the housing bonus provisions that had previously operated in most of these areas. Finally, a main plank of the strategy was to create neighbourhoods with a mix of lifestyles, life-cycle stages, and income levels, and with a high level of livability. This policy, and the designated residential areas, remained largely unchanged from the repeatedly revised 1975 plan.

A set of livability policies tackled the design and spirit-of-place issues, focusing on the new opportunities to achieve more housing, a wider choice of lifestyles, and more diverse and dense neighbourhoods within the central area. The policy statement recognized that increases in density could greatly affect livability, noting that for the first time residential floor-space ratios of up to 6.0 were being proposed in some areas, and that residential development might not be compatible with some environmental aspects of busy mixed-use central locations. The 1991 plan explored the housing form implications (see Figure 66), arguing that, as densities increased, the quality of design became more important, especially in matters of views, privacy, sunlight, safety, and usable open space. It also reduced the scattering of different uses to develop a set of distinct precincts where the land uses were compatible with residential use (Vancouver 1994a: 25). The policies retained design review as an instrument to ensure livability, but sought to make it more explicit through the specification of qualitative criteria. But there remained important policy work to be done on built form, view studies, and public realm planning, as well as matters of affordable housing and public facilities. No immediate changes were made to the zoning. Instead the policies would be "applied through area studies, rezoning, and project planning" (Vancouver 1991c). Revisions were made to the downtown official development plan to accept these policy shifts.

While downtown remained very quiet with little building activity in the 1990s, it was a very different story in Triangle West and Downtown South, where high-rise condominium development continued apace. Rates of construction were much faster than projected and seemed unaffected by the recession of the early 1990s and by the 1998 "Asian flu" in the property market that followed the crises in Asian economies. Developers were able to adjust their residential buildings to market conditions, varying apartment sizes and costs to maintain sales. In Triangle West and Downtown South an added impetus was created by the need to complete condominiums before the towers of Coal Harbour and False Creek North, respectively, began to intrude on the views of the shoreline and water, thereby reducing rental and sale values.

Triangle West

The slopes of Triangle West, looking over the new Coal Harbour development, provide particularly stunning views northwestward across Burrard Inlet and Stanley Park to the North Shore mountains. It had long been considered that the central business district would extend westward and, from the second half of the 1960s onward, a large concentration of major office buildings was erected in the north of the area. However, by the early 1980s, the first high-rise residential condominium tower had appeared; by 1992 there were four towers of luxury condos and seven more seeking approval, so that a high calibre housing future was assured. Council initiated a planning study of the area in 1990, and in the 1991 Central Area Plan designated it a choice-of-use area in recognition of the tension between established commercial land uses and current residential development trends. The planning study posed a set of land-use, heritage, and public realm questions. Considerable attention was devoted to built-form controls and how the 4.0 floor-space ratio (with 1.0 residential and 1.0 commercial bonus) could best be accommodated, along with the 15 percent hotel bonus. City planners defined approved tower locations, favouring the idea of two towers per rectangular city block to retain wider views northward, while minimizing shadowing on the north-facing slopes. They posed questions as to the best height for street-oriented buildings and whether tower heights should be reduced toward the water. They recognized that the built-quality of the area would depend on the siting, form, and architecture of the towers and the quality of the public realm, while substantial parks and play space would be provided in the Coal Harbour development.

To consider the public realm issues, design consultants (Matrix and Don Vaughan) were retained to prepare a streetscape study. Because both Georgia and Robson streets had been the focus of urban design studies in the 1980s (see Chapter 3), and had clear design guidelines that had achieved some success, the consultants focused on the enhancement of the five north-south streets that slope sharply northward, offering spectacular views. The consultants recommended that setbacks of about 3.6 metres should be designated to create a wide sidewalk with a series of terraces linked by short flights of steps. These would have low walls for sitting, be bordered with low hedges and groundcover, and planted with two lines of trees, creating viewing and resting places. A concept design was included in the study, approved by city council in July 1994, and incorporated into two projects already under design. On the award-winning Pacific Palisades development the project architect, James Cheng, enhanced the Bute Street frontage with a stream, large boulders, waterfall, and reflecting pool that flowed around and under the residential tower. On his award-winning block to the south (1200 West Georgia), he

Plate 46 The Residences on Georgia, 1200-block Georgia Street. The two towers on this block are linked by a row of townhouses fronting elegantly on Alberni Street (top), which create a delightful, privately accessible but publicly visible landscape, pool, and waterfall on Georgia Street. The townhouses have private patios and roof decks. The Bute Street terrace (bottom) has the Heritage Banff Apartments (1909) as a focal point and – as well as pools and small fountains – has seating, integral lighting, and a splendid piece of public art – Dale Chihuly's display case of brightly coloured glass florets.

continued the water feature, but in a more formal way, providing a series of small fountains bubbling up from a pool on each terrace (see Plate 46). The latter development, The Residences on Georgia, is *the* exemplary piece of urban design in Triangle West. Bringing together James Cheng Architects and Phillips Farevaag Smallenberg as landscape architects – the same team who had designed 888 Beach (see Plate 23) – this project exemplified a number of the design principles adopted for Triangle West in both 1984 and 1994. These included the creation of a green oasis on West Georgia Street, a row of townhouses fronting Alberni, a rather over-restored heritage building, Abbott House (on Jervis Street), and two elegant 34-storey green-glazed towers sited at either end of the block to minimize view impacts on upland properties (see Plate 46).

Slim green towers with mostly glazed exteriors and set in expanses of private landscape have become a hallmark of West Georgia, repeated in The Lions (1350 West Georgia), Georgia Towers (1450), and The Pointe (1331) (see Plate 65). The Lions allows public access to its landscaped area, having a public footpath diagonally bisecting the site and squeezing dramatically under the pilotis of the west tower – again with distinctive public art. Otherwise, only visual access is allowed to each scheme's green space, so George Baird's 1982 concept has been only half-realized. As compensation, the improvements to the public realm of the north-south streets have created some sitting and socializing space but these public amenities do not appear to be particularly well used as yet.

Downtown South

Downtown South was earmarked as the main new residential area downtown with a capacity of 11,000 people by 2016. A community plan (1991), design guidelines (1991), and a streetscape manual (1994) were all prepared to shape its character and built form (see Chapter 3). The take-up of residential development was 50 percent quicker than expected and more than half of the anticipated housing units have now been built (Vancouver 2001h). The area will have been largely rebuilt by 2007, although many of the redevelopment sites that are left are encumbered by view corridors from False Creek South and may be developed more slowly. A large quantity of moderately priced units have been built, which have helped to reduce price inflation in the housing market generally. There are mixed verdicts on the design quality of development achieved. The middle-income condominium towers of Downtown South lack the elegance of those in Triangle West, and the wide one-way streets, utilitarian back lanes, and often undistinguished existing commercial buildings make it a more challenging environment to humanize. The members of the Urban Design Panel have collectively commented that they consider the developments in Downtown South to be too similar. Certainly the planners and the panel have been kept busy trying to ensure that the massing of base and towers is well considered, that there is some stylistic consistency within each project, that there is adequate private open space on the podium roofs, that all suites are livable, and that the street level and streetscape are properly detailed and provide adequate amenities. A good case in point is 1221 Homer, a 14-storey tower the panel saw three times to resolve these issues. At 955 Richards, the guidelines suggested one tower, but two towers higher than 20 storeys were designed, the townhouses were overwhelmed by the towers, and the multiplicity of architectural styles employed had to be resolved. At 940-990 Seymour, the developer and architect argued for a single 33-storey tower and a 6-storey street-wall but, after they failed to convince either planners or panel, reverted to two towers of 30 and 22 storeys (see Figure 49). This project never gained more than marginal support from the panel, and doubts about massing, elevations, and materials persisted, although the private amenity space was improved. However, overall the townhouse and tower form, with back-of-sidewalk aligned housing, has been successfully adopted in Downtown South, and on Seymour and Richards in particular the re-emergence of the residential street is becoming a reality.

Unfortunately, development in Downtown South has been largely unable to deliver green spaces that are enclosed and protected, because the blocks are split by back lanes, creating parcels 142.5 metres long but only 36 metres wide. There is some evidence that rooftop gardens on the townhouses and above car parking and service access are providing good communal sitting out spaces. However, the back lanes have not been civilized in the way that the guidelines suggested they might (see Plate 47), but they do stop service vehicles and residents' cars from having to cross the sidewalks. The streetscape guidelines have worked well on the main streets south of Granville. Here double rows of tree planting at the front and the back of the sidewalk were implemented, and the private landscaping in front of the townhouses enhances the public realm.

A major concern has been the long-standing city policy to retain or replace – but not to add to – the 1,400 units of low-income housing. This policy is statistically consistent with the 20 percent affordable housing required in the megaprojects but is clearly inadequate, given the housing needs in the central area. The social housing bonus enshrined in the 1990 rezoning failed to deliver any new provision. So far a policy of one-to-one replacement of lost single-room occupancy units has been implemented, mostly funded through provincial housing programs. Two recent social housing projects have attracted interest. At 1221 Seymour, a distinctive medium-rise block in a contemporary

Figure 49 940 Seymour Street: reactions of the Urban Design Panel and Development Permit Board. At the very highest residential density, the tower dimensions and placement of this project created considerable difficulties, as did the six-storey street-wall apartments. This was one of the schemes the Urban Design Panel was least enamoured with.

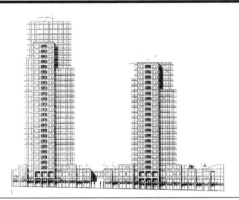

Address and Location
940 Seymour Street,
   Downtown South

Project Description
33-storey residential tower, 6-storey
   podium, commercial at grade

Zoning and Bonuses
CD-1 / 5.0 / 230 feet. Heritage
   TDR of 1.71 floor-space ratio

Architect and Client
Buttjes Architects/
   Wall Financial Corp.

Urban Design Panel

08/98   *3-4 no support.* Single tower solution, but massing needs to be reduced – slimmer, notched, sculpted. Relationship to Dufferin Hotel needs to be considered and lane improved. Strong support for 6-storey street-wall. Clarity of expression welcomed but more colour needed. More amenity space.

09/98   *8-0 support.* Helpful massing studies and considerable improvement. Asymmetrical floor plate works well and low-rise mass reduced. Retail works well and lane improved. Corner and the facade facing the hotel need reworking.

06/99   *4-2 support.* Return to two-tower solution but doubts about it and 6-storey street-wall. Nelson-Seymour corner is weak. Weak colour palette. More greening required on second level. Auto-court should be opened up to Seymour.

Development Permit Board

11/98   *Approve in principle.* Concerns over massing and location of towers, particularly the maintenance of 80-foot separation between towers for privacy. Also concerns about height and mass of street-wall. Heritage TDR will be used. Need to consider in relation to 955 Richards development also seeking permit.

08/99   *Approve.* Twin tower scheme meets the CD-1 chequerboard ideas for tower placement / massing. Concerns over the design of the podium. More work needs to be done to create private amenity space, e.g., over driveway. Has 15 percent in smaller units but 10 percent is the maximum.

Sources: Buttjes Architects (drawing); text compiled from panel and board minutes

Plate 47 Downtown South back lanes. The back lanes in Downtown South make it difficult for high-density developments to create attractive, enclosed amenity space behind the street-wall building. But they do allow the rear servicing and access to underground car parking that make the main streets more civilized. Guidelines suggesting how to improve their design have not been particularly successful. Retention of the old hydro lines, which are expensive to move, does provide a memory of the more commercial/industrial past.

European style has been built on city land leased free to a housing society, where specific units have been incorporated for persons with AIDS and for mental health patients, and a drop-in centre has been included (see Plate 48). Another city-initiated project, at 1265-67 Granville Street, with sixty-two similarly sized units for low-income urban singles, won unanimous support from the Urban Design Panel and has recently been approved. This is one of a dozen such developments planned citywide to help reduce a lengthy waiting list for such accommodation.

Downtown South is facing a shortfall in projected development-cost levy revenue to fund social housing, parks, and childcare facilities because a significant amount of development was approved in 1989-92 prior to the introduction to the development-cost levy. As a result, funds have been slow to accumulate, despite the unexpected speed of development. No childcare facilities or parks have yet been provided in Downtown South. Land acquisitions for the two projected parks are still to be made, although some progress is evident with the first half of the southern park that will eventually occupy most of the block formed by Richards, Davie, Seymour, and Helmcken streets. Development-cost levy funds are being used to develop the Richards Street side of the park, the design of which is the subject of consultation through the Vancouver Park Board to see if it should accommodate children's play.

Plate 48 Low-income housing, 1221 Seymour Street. Designed by Davidson Yuen Simpson, this complex has a 2-storey podium that houses various support services and facilities, while the tower has been broken into individual volumes to reduce its scale. A roof deck, terrace, and balconies provide outdoor sitting space for residents.

The current concept, the result of public design workshops in 1997 and 1998, has a linear treed plaza and water features and could include a large oval lawn, but the design may change. The northern park is still proving difficult to fund.

Downtown South is rapidly emerging as a socially diverse area, as had been envisaged in the 1991 Community Plan (see Figure 17). South of Granville Street in "New Yaletown" the tower and townhouse projects are rapidly transforming Seymour and Richards streets and the west side of Homer Street. A diverse physical and social transition is evident from the new Concord Pacific megaproject; across historic Yaletown's converted warehouses, live/work units, and café/club culture; to Granville Street's hotels, retail, and entertainment establishments and its stronger heritage character. To the west of Granville a much more mixed-use area has evolved with numerous hotels, some office developments, and a variety of condominium projects as the zoning intended, although it rather lacks character. As a new population is established, so retail uses will expand and Granville and Davie streets will be able to re-establish themselves as animated strips of neighbourhood shopping, eating, and drinking. New residents' reaction to the nightclubs and bars in Downtown South has led to greater scrutiny of their design, licensing, and management, and the city has used its licensing powers to encourage their transfer to Granville Street to reduce these conflicts.

Revitalizing Granville Street (Again)

Some of these Downtown South planning issues are related to attempts to speed up the revitalization of Granville Street. Throughout the last thirty years Granville Street has been offending certain sensibilities – such as those of the Vancouver Business Association – as it is home to many street people and drug users (see Figure 50). The street has stubbornly refused to become respectable or to wither away at the hands of international hotel chains. During the day, Granville Street seems tawdry and drab but, at night, its bright lights continue to draw large numbers of Greater Vancouver young people as the destination for a weekend night out. The attempts to revitalize Granville Street in the 1970s and 1980s were largely replayed in the 1990s as the city attempted to develop design guidelines for the street, to consolidate the 700-900 blocks as an entertainment district, to stimulate the 1100-1300 blocks as a neighbourhood shopping centre for Downtown South, and to define its transportation role. In the 1991 Downtown South rezoning, density could be transferred off Granville Street to elsewhere in Downtown South and heritage bonuses were made available for the street's twenty-two heritage buildings. Its single-room occupancy accommodation in eleven hotels – nine of them heritage protected – was also safeguarded by a one-for-one replacement provision bonus. Given an overall 3.5 floor-space ratio and a 27-metre height limit (21 metres at back of sidewalk), the street was protected as a relatively low-rise corridor through Downtown South (see Plate 49 and Figure 17).

Plate 49 Granville Street, looking north from Helmcken. The retention of Granville's character is evident from this photograph. About 90 percent of the 1,900 daily transit movements are by quiet, clean trolley buses. The clock in the Vancouver Block is a key Vancouver landmark, offsetting the 1970s towers of darkness and the white box of the former Eaton's store (left).

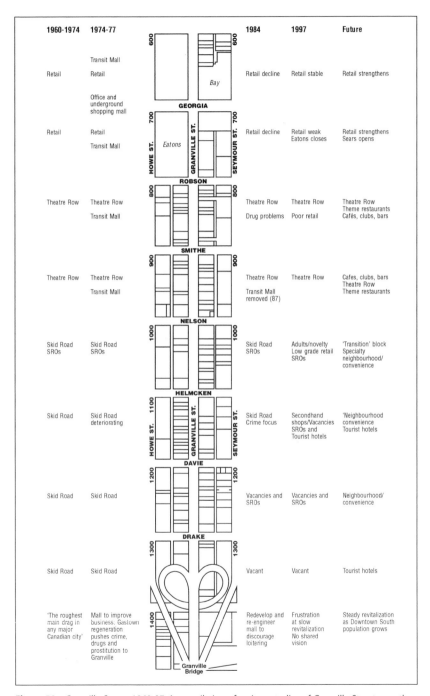

Figure 50   Granville Street, 1960-97. A compilation of various studies of Granville Street over the last three decades, noting land-use changes and planning intentions. (*Sources:* Drawn by Jan Edwards; information from Vancouver [1997i])

Two consultant studies of Granville Street were commissioned in 1996, one a business revitalization by Urbanics, the other a building and street design by architects Hotson Bakker. The business revitalization study was a mixed bag, combining sound analysis of the existing situation with ill-advised commercial solutions such as the introduction of large-format retailing and "category killers" whose retail offer impacts on a wide range of small shops. Worse still was a frightening list of potential theme restaurants, cafés, bistros, and specialty retailers guaranteed to destroy the street's identity. The study reaffirmed the entertainment district for the 800 and 900 blocks, the latter now much more viable because of the extent of residential development in Downtown South. This left the 1000 block as a "transition zone" between the two – dominated by adult sex and novelty shops, convenience stores, and video arcades, with a significant presence of these in the 1100 block alongside pawnbrokers and second-hand dealers. These uses were, of course, the target of many of those seeking to sanitize the street. By the mid-1990s – when a greater degree of tolerance for the street's seamy side had set in, perhaps because much of the drug trade, prostitution, and alcoholism had moved into the Downtown Eastside – selected Granville Street merchants were vigorously defending them as legitimate businesses.

To guide the early stages of building design and to supplement the design guidelines produced in 1991, Hotson Bakker were commissioned to produce a handbook for detailed design of building frontages on Granville Street. The guidelines were updated in 1998 to cross-reference the new handbook. Their design concept, predicated on Allan Jacobs's concept of a great street (1993), delivered a vision, ten design principles, and criteria and illustrations of how they might be applied. The final section of the report presented short- and long-term possibilities for various sections of each block (see Figures 50 and 51). The vision – an irritating stage-cues and choreographed audience-performance theme – did recognize the need to retain the street's brash and gritty raw energy alongside its entertainment glitz and heritage buildings. The ten design principles stressed the street's role as "a primary civic approach" with important heritage buildings. They emphasized striking corner buildings at the intersections, and dramatically sculpted buildings to animate the street throughout. Key concerns were the retention of the 7.6-metre (25-foot) shopfronts, the vibrant signage, and the creation of animated upper storeys that would look out on and enliven the street. Pedestrian comfort, safety, and coordinated signage and street furniture were also stressed. Each principle was then supported by a set of criteria and policies, and illustrated with examples from the street. Architectural critic Robin Ward was unconvinced by the approach:

The building-frontage guidelines ... attempt to impose an architectural order and 1990s planning orthodoxy on a street whose essential personality ... is linear, disorderly, and diverse ... The choreographer here seems to be the Vancouver planning department. As well as the 1990s let's-make-the-new-buildings-refer-to-the-old mantra, the handbook presents all the coy clichés of 1980s "festive" urban renewal that on Granville Island Hotson Bakker managed to avoid ... The intention, if an artist's impression is accurate, is to tidy up a tacky but eccentric street and turn it into a downtown theme park. (1998b)

What Hotson Bakker were suggesting was highly unusual in design guidance. Trying to encourage overdesign, they sought a commercial brashness and tackiness in the new development in the street while simultaneously urging developers and their architects to recognize some of the qualities of the Edwardian buildings, particularly the theatres, with their art deco signs and elaborate entrances. Whether these two approaches are reconcilable is debatable. Many of the long-term design solutions Hotson Bakker have suggested appear like the worst excesses of postmodernism from the early 1990s, and they are all too believable as composite products of the whimsy, festivity, and heritage that dominate the guidelines and developers' kitsch (see Figure 51). Currently, city planners are considering the street's future traffic role and are working on a sign bylaw to attract larger, more colourful, and especially neon signs to the buildings on Granville.

In fact, Granville Street seems to be steadily regenerating as a consequence of reinvestment in the clubs and live venues on the street, and the replacement of single-room occupancy hotels with budget American-owned tourist hotels with the subsequent upgrading of their bars and restaurants. The Orpheum and the Stanley theatres have been recently restored. There is the emergence of neighbourhood shops and a restaurant strip that also extends along Davie Street. Significant land assemblies have taken place in both the 1100 and 1200 blocks, which suggest some large-scale redevelopments that will need to be carefully controlled. A long-term planning goal has been achieved with the attraction of a dance centre in a former Bank of Nova Scotia building at Granville and Davie, although the facadist treatment of the heritage-protected building caused considerable antipathy (see Figure 52). The debate was over whether this project merited the heritage bonus necessary to accommodate the rehearsal space, but with Arthur Erickson working with Architectura, the design quality of the scheme defrayed some of the criticism. The director of current planning noted at the Development Permit Board hearing that approval of the scheme "was a highly unusual circumstance involving a priority cultural amenity [and] did not set a precedent."

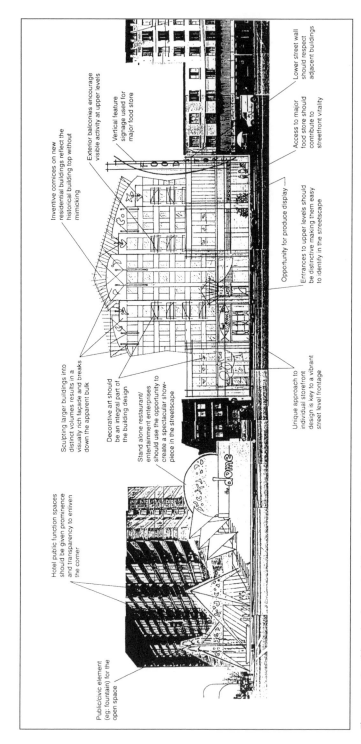

Hotel public function spaces should be given prominence and transparency to enliven the corner

Public/civic element (eg: fountain) for the open space

Sculpting larger buildings into distinct volumes results in a visually rich façade and breaks down the apparent bulk

Decorative art should be an integral part of the building design

Stand alone restaurant/ entertainment enterprises should use the opportunity to create a spectacular show-piece in the streetscape

Inventive cornices on new residential buildings reflect the historical building top without mimicking

Exterior balconies encourage visible activity at upper levels

Vertical feature signage used for major food store

Lower street wall should respect adjacent buildings

Access to major food store should contribute to streetfront vitality

Opportunity for produce display

Entrances to upper levels should be distinctive making them easy to identify in the streetscape

Unique approach to individual storefront design is key to a vibrant street level frontage

Figure 51 Possible redevelopment of Granville Street/Helmcken corner, southeast side, 1997. The Hotson Bakker study trod a fine line between the need for heritage conservation and the creation of "entertainment" buildings with neon signs and highly expressive façades. (*Source:* Vancouver [1997b])

Figure 52 1196 Granville/677 Davie streets: reactions of the Urban Design Panel and Development Permit Board. There were major conflicts over the desirability of the dance facility in this location and over heritage considerations. The quality of architect/ architectural design was crucial to winning the permit. Getting the right use in the right location is a major consideration in planning/design and can justifiably override conservationist imperatives.

Address and Location
677 Davie Street, Downtown South
  1196 Granville Street

Project Description
7-storey dance centre with studios, offices, and ancillary partly behind heritage facades

Zoning, Height Limit, and Bonuses
DD / 3.5 / seeks heritage bonus of 2.0 for retaining B-listed Bank of Nova Scotia

Architect and Client
Arthur Erickson with Architectura / unknown

Urban Design Panel
02/99 *5-2 support.* Panel split on whether heritage bonus is earned with only the Granville facade of the Heritage-listed bank saved. But they regard the "stage set" approach as audacious and exciting.
05/99 *9-0 support.* Positive response to the previous comments and to upper level massing changes and setback of mechanical areas. Concern over wall facing the hotel. Prefer simpler weather protection on Davie Street facade.

Development Permit Board
06/99 *Approve.* Three retention options considered but Dance Company plead hardship. Nonetheless facadism on B-listed heritage building is a poor precedent and historic groups oppose it. But dance facility has been a council priority on Granville since 1993 and council clearly supported the trade-off with conservation objectives.

Source: Compiled from panel and board minutes

Council approved both the amount of the heritage bonus and the relaxation of parking and setbacks.

Another application that was taken to city council for approval in 1999 posed a major threat to the future of Granville Street. A proposal for a sixteen-screen cinema and IMAX theatre at 900 Burrard, three blocks to the west, was hardly consistent with a determination to revive Granville Street. As a piece of urban design, the concept for this "urban entertainment centre" was extremely well received, with Busby Architects putting its distinctive stamp on the project. Notwithstanding its sophisticated design it was still a drive-in leisure megabox whose raison d'être was to capture its patrons' expenditure for the night, and it was difficult to see it doing anything but undermining vitality on Granville Street. Fortunately, the multiplex scheme did not proceed and Granville Street continues to be the focus of city nightlife and a vital service street for Downtown South.

Urban Design and Downtown Development

In 1991, when the central area policy statement was finalized, office development in downtown Vancouver was collapsing in the wake of the 1989 recession, and a large surplus supply was being built up as a result of the late 1980s construction boom. Office vacancy rates, as high as 15 percent in 1992, dropped only gradually down to 7 percent by 1997. The last major office building to be completed in downtown – the new BC Hydro building – was in 1992 and very little new development was discussed until a new tower at 564 Granville was approved late in 1997 and the fifth and final Bentall Centre tower was approved in May 2000. The new BC Hydro building, on Dunsmuir at Homer Street on the eastern edge of downtown, constituted something of a gross intrusion on the margins of Gastown and the Victory Square historic districts (see Plate 50). Widely regarded as one of Vancouver's worst eyesores (Blore and Sutherland 1999: 51), it squats over the Victory Square area to the north and west and intrudes on the Edwardian towers from numerous vantage points. Overweight and dated, the intrusion is made more poignant by the retention of the Del Mar Hotel with its decorative classical facade, whose owner refused to sell to the developer, forcing the tower to be resited (Kalman et al. 1993: 62). The offices drew inevitable comparisons with the first BC Hydro building, the fate of which was a testament to current downtown development trends. Conversion of the building (renamed the Electra) from commercial to residential use exemplified the huge oversupply of older office space and a correspondingly high demand for apartments on the edge of downtown.

The Electra, on Nelson at Burrard, was the first postwar building to receive heritage designation to save it from demolition. It was sensitively converted

Plate 50 BC Hydro, 333 Dunsmuir Street. This postmodern pile, one of the very few 1990s office buildings in the city, has attracted the ire of many commentators because of the way it looms over the Victory Square historic district to the rear. Designed by Musson Cattell Mackey Partnership, its generous landscaped plaza along Dunsmuir has both admirers (Bula 2000) and detractors (Ward 1993b).

into 242 condominium flats by Paul Merrick, using its heritage cachet as a marketing device. The Electra escaped the fate of the other key 1950s modernist buildings, the Burrard Building and the Vancouver Public Library, which were saved by heritage designation but converted very insensitively. Hotel development filled some of the vacuum created by the demise of office construction and was evidence of the increasing tourism importance to the downtown economy. There were extensive conversions of older hotels, many of which had become single-room occupancy, the last bastions of cheap housing in the city. During the early 1990s some of the larger new hotels were built on Burrard and Howe streets in Downtown South, the most obtrusive being Peter Wall's blue/black mirror-clad Wall Centre Hotel at Burrard and Helmcken (see Plate 60). By the late 1990s Triangle West and downtown proper were the targets for hotel construction; slim white towers, including the Delta Pinnacle (1128 West Hastings) and the Coal Harbour Hotel (1178 West Pender) were shoehorned into tight sites with spectacular views. The generous 15 percent floor-space bonus for hotels certainly eased development finances, and the demand for hotel rooms increased steadily, with hotel occupancy rates rising through the 1990s to reach 77 percent in 1997. Cruise ship sailings also increased (800,000 passengers), more than doubling the 1990 figure, and the convention trade reached 500,000 visitors a year (Vancouver 1999w). By 1994 the province had recognized that expansion of the convention centre at Canada Place could be a substantial generator of economic growth province-wide with its tourist spin-offs.

Pressure was being exerted by developers to relax the height limits in the downtown area, presumably in the belief that the opportunity for taller buildings might encourage some new commercial or hotel development, and this idea gained some support from city council. A discretionary limit of 450 feet (135-metres) was being discussed in 1996, and the planners decided that it would be useful to consider whether the skyline of the city could be shaped more effectively and aesthetically and still accommodate taller buildings. The brief asked the consultants, led by Ray Spaxman, to consider whether there were sites where buildings of more than 135 metres might be accommodated to good effect. The consultants defined three viewpoints from which to consider the skyline – Lonsdale Quay on the North Vancouver waterfront, Jericho Beach in Point Grey, and Boundary Road at Hastings. They also defined five skyline scenarios, including a build out to existing limits. Two forms of "landmark skylines" were modelled, one with two towers of 180 metres and the other with two towers of 225 metres (see Figure 53). The other two scenarios were a gap-toothed model with several towers up to 135-65 metres, and a dome-shaped skyline with a maximum height of 165 metres. When the public was consulted, a majority expressed a preference for a maximum height between 104 and 135 metres, but a quarter of respondents were prepared to consider heights as great as 294 metres, similar to Toronto or Seattle (Vancouver 1997g). The recommendation adopted by council was to create the possibility of a building up to a maximum of 180 metres in part of the downtown core, with council's preference for these tallest buildings to be on the city's primary streets – Georgia, Burrard, or Granville. Such a tall building had to achieve architectural excellence and deliver other community benefits, include an observation deck or other public amenity, and not adversely affect the microclimate. Five probable sites for development were identified,

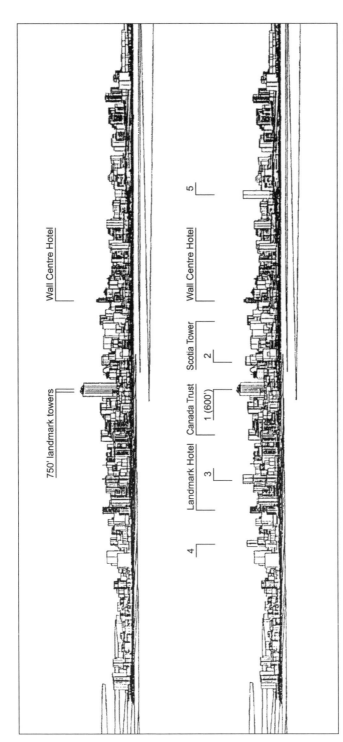

Figure 53 Downtown Vancouver Skyline Study, 1997. This excerpt from the skyline study (Vancouver 1997g) conducted by Ray Spaxman Associates looks at two of the five alternative skylines they posited, as seen from the North Vancouver Lonsdale Quay SeaBus terminal. The two line drawings illustrate the impact of 180- (top) and 225-metre (bottom) towers on West Georgia west of Burrard, creating new landmarks. Note how the Coal Harbour towers (middle right) were planned and developed in conformity with the existing skyline. (*Source:* Vancouver [1997g])

largely unaffected by existing view corridors. Three were on or adjacent to Granville and two on Burrard. Three sites for buildings of up to 120 metres were also demarcated just outside the core area. Proposals for a 45-storey, 135-metre tower behind the heritage-listed Hotel Georgia were approved as a preliminary application at the end of 1997. Because the developers wished to preserve the hotel, they have been given a 5.8 floor-space ratio bonus, which some suggest will give a total ratio in the region of 14.0 when the hotel bonus is added in. The proposals for a tall slim tower behind the heritage hotel were strongly endorsed by the Heritage Commission and the Urban Design Panel, although the size of the bonus was debated at the Development Permit Board. So, while view corridors remained intact, council was creating the possibility of a new generation of taller, probably mixed-use, towers in the downtown core.

Downtown East and the Library Precinct

Like the revitalization of Granville Street, the revival of the east side of downtown was problematic. Vitality and variety had been reduced by large single uses across entire city blocks for the post office, Vancouver Community College, the CBC building, and the Queen Elizabeth Theatre. Low levels of pedestrian movement were maintained by the blockage of east-west movement by BC Place Stadium and the swirling Georgia and Cambie Bridge viaducts. The demise of the office market in the 1990s left the east side of downtown very much in limbo, while protecting it at least from further insensitive incursions of the BC Hydro variety. One idea emerged for a cultural and entertainment area linking the theatres, the CBC, the Ford Centre for the Performing Arts, and the stadium. Another idea was to relocate the city's public library to a city-owned block between Georgia and Robson to act as a major people attractor. The old library, the modernist masterpiece at Robson and Burrard, was far too small for contemporary needs and occupied a prime retail location, so it could be sold to fund the redevelopment. The planners' intentions were to use the library to create a multi-purpose civic focus with a variety of public spaces and facilities (Vancouver 1993h).

The notion of holding an architectural competition for the library design was a first for the city in modern times and it proved a fascinating experience for the design professions and the public. The result is an iconic postmodern building very much at odds with Vancouver traditions. A Selection Advisory Committee was formed to choose architects, and in March 1992 three schemes were exhibited for public comment, then for review by the Urban Design Panel and the Selection Advisory Committee. In April 1992, a design by Moshe Safdie partnered with Downs/Archambault was chosen by the committee and, after the scheme was revised, formally accepted in June 1992. Two other finalists produced buildings that scored much more highly on the library planning committee's criteria, but 70 percent of the public liked the Safdie scheme as a "unique, imaginative, exciting, interesting building" (Ledger 1992: 23). The Urban Design Panel voted almost unanimously for the Safdie scheme, subject to changes that included refinement of the elevations with more contemporary detailing and, importantly, the moving of the federal office tower to the northeast corner of the site where it would not overshadow the public spaces.

The library's form and elevations resemble the Roman Colosseum in its ruined state, including a remnant of an outer wall to create a full height screen to parallel one side of the oval form that encloses the rectilinear library stacks and services (see Plate 51). The 4-storey colonnaded facade – with rectilinear rather than arched openings – completes the allusion, although Safdie himself denied resemblance of the scheme to the Colosseum. A second outer elliptical wall creates two grand entrances into a tall narrow atrium that functions as a public lobby to the library and provides a safe, climate-controlled, and comfortable, albeit commercialized, space for visitors to take a break from reading. The two entrances, at either end of the semi-circular atrium, face west, cleverly drawing in pedestrians walking from downtown along both Georgia and Robson streets. The steep slope of the site was

Plate 51 Vancouver Public Library from Robson Street. This extraordinary building has withstood architectural criticism to enjoy great public acclaim. Its atrium, through the entrance to the right, houses useful shops and cafés and is a comfortable meeting place, while the curved steps of the southern plaza provide great sitting spaces for reading, sunning, and people watching. The benefits of having re-sited the tall office tower to the northeast corner of the site are obvious from this picture.

well handled (after the revisions), with the library set into the slope and reducing its bulk on the northwest corner. Two plazas have been created in front of these entrances, the northern one being rather exposed and windswept. The southern one, sheltered by the library itself and sloping to the south, is a very animated and successful space when the weather is kind.

Two major debates ensued about the symbolism of the architecture and the public-private space of the library. One critic argued that Safdie had used the Colosseum motif deliberately to satisfy "the public's thirst for drama and an easily grasped image" (Ledger 1992: 21), knowing that public support would be vital to winning the competition. However, most professional opinion and critics saw the building as a piece of Disneyland with good urban design but poor architecture made worse in some eyes by the modernizing of the classicism requested by the advisory committee (see also Lees 1999).

The library, while the most expensive capital project ever undertaken in the city, has proven to be an enormously popular building, its design fiercely defended by the public against its critics. Library visitors increased by 800,000 in the year following its opening, and it continues to accommodate over two million visitors annually, equivalent to the annual attendance at all professional sport events in the city (mid-1990s figures: Vancouver 1999w). The library project prompted city planners to recommend a consultants' study of the blocks around Library Square, to consider adjacent building massing and design, and to update the area's character guidelines, principally because the latter did not encourage unified designs in the vicinity (Vancouver 1993h) (see Figure 54). A new character area description sought to take advantage of the pedestrian activity that the library would generate to encourage selective redevelopment of the eight surrounding blocks, and to create a unique precinct focusing on the new public amenities of Library Square. There was a desire to develop complementary spaces on adjacent sites and special tree planting, paving treatments, furniture, and lighting were proposed, along with specific massing recommendations for each block.

These guidelines have not exerted much positive influence on subsequent developments. The biggest disappointment was the design of the Ford Centre for the Performing Arts facing the west flank of the library, another postmodern parody by Moshe Safdie. This used the idea of a hypothetical section through the theatre to define the elevations, with auditorium, stalls, balcony, and stage expressed in a stylized form in what are otherwise blank elevations. No plaza was developed, but a 20-storey hotel was built adjacent to it and facing onto Robson. To the south a condominium development at least provided complementary ground-floor retail uses to face the library's main plaza.

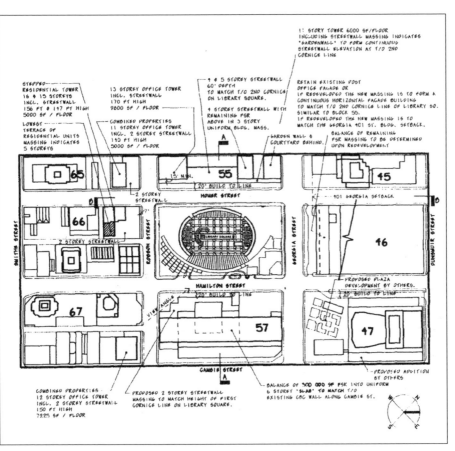

Figure 54 Library Precinct design guidelines, 1993. With the design for the new library approved (centre), city planners developed guidelines for the adjacent blocks to ensure that site plans and building forms complemented the new landmark. These were incorporated into the character area guidelines. They have influenced new development on block 66 but not the new hotel/theatre complex on block 55. (*Source:* Vancouver [1993h])

A footnote to the library's success as a generator of development in the east of the central business district is provided by the proposals to redevelop The Plaza, a single-room occupancy hotel at 488 Robson, half a block away, as a condominium development (see Figure 55). This offered a music gallery on the ground floor as a means of securing a floor-space bonus for a cultural facility, allowing it to achieve a 5.0 floor-space ratio and to use the full 90-metre height limit. The Urban Design Panel suggested redesign of the corner, top, and pedestrian level of the building, which was duly executed. But the issue that worried both the Urban Design Panel and the Development Permit

Figure 55 488 Robson Street: reactions of the Urban Design Panel and Development Permit Board. This is a case where the loss of single-room occupancies (SROs) negated the value of the arts use and where the whole bonusing system was questioned by panel and board. The architects significantly improved the design, but it became clear that the bonusing policy encouraged gentrification rather than social inclusion.

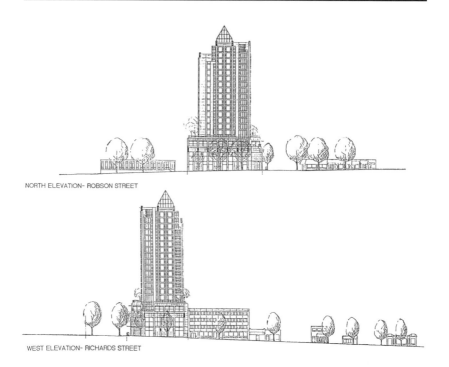

NORTH ELEVATION- ROBSON STREET

WEST ELEVATION- RICHARDS STREET

Address and Location
488 Robson Street, Downtown

Project Description
18-storey mixed-use tower, 84 dwelling units, and 3,000-square-foot music library

Zoning and Bonuses
DD / 5.0 / 300 feet: seeks 2.26 bonus (on music library)

Architect and Client
Downs/Archambault / unknown

Urban Design Panel

10/97 *5-2 non-support.* Object to tower location, corner treatment, rigidity of design of retail plinth; livability of small units. Negative comments on loss of single-room occupancy units and doubts about value of the proposed music library as a cultural facility eligible for bonuses.

11/97 *6-0 support.* Redesign improves corner and top; public realm improved with seating and landscape; third-floor roof deck for residents.

▶

◀ *Figure 55*

Development Permit Board

12/97 *Prelim. approved in principle.* Major debate about loss of single-room occupancy units and parking failures as opposed to arts gain. Concern with shadowing impacts, encroachment of cornices of building, and design of the top. Good mix of uses and space design good.

04/98 *Full approval.* Housing Centre satisfied with relocation of single-room residents. Cornice encroachments made demountable but retained to improve visual interest.

Sources: Downs/Archambault (drawings); text compiled from panel and board minutes

---

Board was the obscenity of the loss of the low-income accommodation set against a floor-space bonus for a music library. While the Development Permit Board was powerless to change the zoning – and could content itself with the satisfactory relocation of the single-room occupancy residents – the issue graphically demonstrated how the zoning could be manipulated to ensure wholesale gentrification. Everyone participating in the decision on behalf of the public felt uncomfortable with the outcome.

Trade and Convention Centre Proposals

While the new city-initiated library proved to be a major pedestrian generator for the east side of downtown, proposals for a new trade and convention centre initiated by the province for the Burrard waterfront promised to deliver a much bigger economic boost to downtown and to tourism at large. The project was aborted in 1999 by the provincial government for financial reasons but its planning history established principles that will influence future deliberations on the central waterfront. During the planning process initiated in 1992 by the city, the Vancouver Port Authority, and the federal landowner, the possibility was aired of including a casino in the waterfront scheme; a concept plan produced a design resembling a pinball machine in site plan. Extensive public participation was undertaken, which revealed citywide disquiet about the idea, especially strong among residents of the Downtown Eastside, and the casino element was dropped. It was agreed that people from the Downtown Eastside would be involved in the planning of the site and offered training and preferential employment within the completed project. Public benefits of $5.36 million were agreed for off-site social housing and recreation. The policy statement defined three primary uses for the site – a transportation interchange, tourism facilities, and community activities – and established basic design guidelines (Vancouver 1994b). In January

1995 the province and the city agreed to seek expressions of interest from developers for the project, the province looking for an innovative public-private partnership to minimize its financial contribution (Vancouver 1995g). The city was not a financial partner. In contrast with the development of Canada Place in the early 1980s, the province and city cooperated fully in the planning process.

Three developers responded to the brief. Marathon's "Discovery Place" proposed a convention centre to the west of the existing one at Burrard Landing at the east end of Coal Harbour. It would be linked underground to the extant convention facilities and have close integration with existing hotels, while a public park would be developed aboveground. It was clearly a proposal with much merit, notwithstanding the fact that it did not conform to the 1990 official development plan for the site (Vancouver 1995i). The second scheme, Greystone's proposals for "Portside," developed the wharf to the east of the existing trade and convention centre and incorporated the existing sea bus terminal. It had the advantage of being able to link directly into the existing convention centre, although it had to bridge the rail lines to connect effectively with downtown. This project provided a major civic plaza above the exhibition hall to open up the waterfront to public use, but had not thought through all the transportation interchange possibilities with the SkyTrain and the West Coast Express services. Unlike the other two proposals it addressed the important question about partnerships with the active involvement of the federal port authority and Marriott Hotels in the scheme, but it would clearly impact heavily on Gastown and the Downtown Eastside. The third proposal, from Concord Pacific, was in some ways the most intriguing because it selected a "distant" site between the Georgia and Dunsmuir viaducts at the eastern edge of downtown. It linked GM Place to the Queen Elizabeth Theatre with a new park at the viaduct level with the exhibition centre below. It was fully integrated with the Stadium SkyTrain Station and entertainment and sports facilities, but it was too far from the existing convention centre to be viable.

Only the Greystone proposal proceeded beyond the first stage of submissions. Their project was thoroughly evaluated for financing and planning, the report giving clear instructions as to how each of its urban design problems might be obviated. The project proceeded and development and financial agreements between city and province were signed. By July both had been approved, the project design refined, and the plans unveiled to the public. Robin Ward, architecture critic at the *Vancouver Sun*, noted that the design "still looks like a big barge drifting in search of an elegant superstructure ... [and] the project still seems to float offshore, adrift from Gastown and the city centre" (Ward 1998d). The Urban Design Panel saw the project nine times over the following year as the scheme was refined and a second phase was added to extend the project as far east as Cambie Street. The dissent at these meetings culminated, in November 1999, in the panel voting unanimously against support for the way in which the scheme was progressing, even though some of the main design issues were subsequently resolved. Shortly after, council approved a comprehensive development agreement with the developers that was similar to a rezoning. Each element of the development then went through the Urban Design Panel and the Development Permit Board without any difficulties, but with an extensive set of conditions. The board raised the issue that the Downtown Eastside would likely lose up to a thousand units of low-cost housing to tourist use, and that a one-for-one conversion bylaw was necessary to protect the area. The eventual demise of the Portside scheme was something of a blessing for the city because its urban design left a lot to be desired. On the whole, integrating the facility into Marathon's Coal Harbour project would have had fewer negative impacts on adjacent areas, notably Gastown and the vulnerable communities of the Downtown Eastside.

To avoid negative impacts on the Downtown Eastside, a provincial study led by activist Jim Green argued the case for provision of non-market housing, the introduction of single-room occupancy conversion, demolition controls for five years, the creation of meaningful local training, employment opportunities in the development, and a community development strategy to accompany any convention centre (British Columbia, 1999). The New Democratic provincial government accepted the case for ameliorative measures, learning from experience on the US west coast. However, once an eastward extension to the project had been incorporated into the design and Cambie Street had been selected as the main point of eastern access, the traffic and housing impacts on the Downtown Eastside would have been intense. While many politicians and businessmen considered that massive gentrification was the best thing that could happen to the Downtown Eastside, the prospects of those who relied on the area as the main locus of low-income housing, shelters, emergency medical care, and crisis support would have been bleak indeed (see Figure 56). The predictions of progressive encirclement and gentrification made by Jim Green and others in the run-up to Expo '86 would have been realized had the convention centre been approved. But only the area's drug and health problems, crime, and antisocial behaviour stood in the way of major property investment by hotel and condominium developers, intensifying community suspicions and resentment about the real commitment of the city to ameliorative programs for the area.

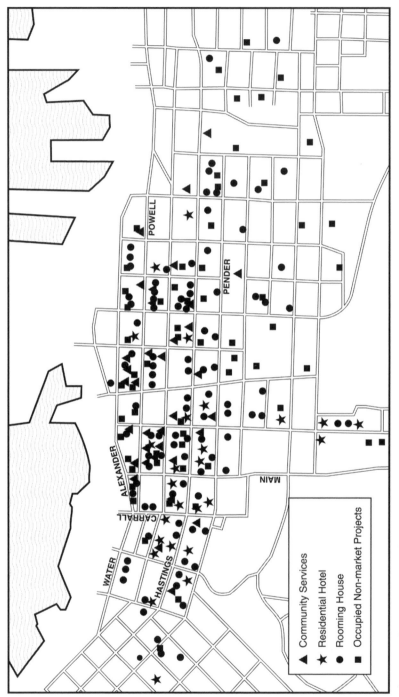

Figure 56 The Downtown Eastside: low-income housing and community service facilities, 1998. This map illustrates the particular concentration of residential hotels, rooming houses, and non-market housing projects in the Downtown Eastside, and the attendant community services (shelters, food, health, community centres, daycare) to support its low-income population. There are seven such services in the block southeast of Powell and Main. (*Source: Redrawn as composite from Vancouver* [1999z])

Legend:
▲ Community Services
★ Residential Hotel
● Rooming House
■ Occupied Non-market Projects

Map labels: WATER, HASTINGS, CARRALL, ALEXANDER, POWELL, PENDER, MAIN

Revitalizing Downtown Eastside: Heritage and Social Concerns

The Downtown Eastside has far more than its share of the city's social problems and deprivations but it also has more heritage buildings than any other neighbourhood, amounting to 17 percent of the city's total. Both the Victory Square Concept Plan (Vancouver 1998ll) and the Gastown Land Use Plan are preoccupied with revitalizing this stock of heritage buildings. In Victory Square, where more than 40 percent of the buildings are designated as heritage, policies seek to perpetuate street-wall developments, the fine grain of frontages, and varied building heights, while ensuring that the sidewalk on the north sides of the streets remains sunlit (see Plate 52). A vertical emphasis in the elevations of new buildings is sought, along with an avoidance of facadism and "compatible but distinguishable" building character, and active street-level uses. In amendments to the zoning, density increases will not be permitted where these involve a loss of heritage value, and building heights will be assessed for their shadow impacts on the street (Vancouver 1998ll). Transfers of density are to be encouraged to protect heritage quality. A variety of amendments to the building bylaw are proposed to make conservation and re-use of heritage buildings more feasible. Relaxations of density and height are proposed for schemes that include low-cost housing and single-room occupancy retention and upgrading.

Plate 52 Victory Square (with cenotaph) and the Dominion Building (left). The heritage character of Victory Square – evident in this view from Terminal City Club Tower – includes the restored Architectural Institute of British Columbia building (upper right), the Pendera social housing complex (upper centre), and Woodward's (upper left). The heritage Dominion Building commands the Cambie/Hastings corner, where the city's grid changes.

The Gastown Land Use Plan (Vancouver 2000l) was a sketchier interim plan that focused on the conflicts between entertainment and residential uses, the need for more flexible application of seismic standards to facilitate heritage conservation, and the provision of more residential condominium units. No limits for condos were proposed, although the threat that this poses to low-income housing was noted. There was no expectation of an increase in low-income housing in the area and single-room occupancy replacements would be encouraged. Small-scale development was preferred, with a broad mix of uses and with retention of the architectural character and the strong pedestrian orientation of the area. Heritage planning issues that have been festering for some time include the relationship between new and existing structures, general traffic management and street treatments, particularly on Water Street, and bonuses or transfer of development rights for heritage conservation previously not available because of the provincial rather than municipal designation of the area. Other building issues include the impact of the 36.5-metre (120-foot) bonus limit and the utility of the 23-metre (75-foot) height limit. Criticism by Robin Ward and fellow conservationists of the height limit, and the general practice of adding extra floors to existing turn-of-nineteenth-century buildings, persist. The latter has created a uniform enclosure of the street completely at odds with Gastown's traditionally saw-tooth skyline, where 2-storey domestic buildings might well be juxtaposed with 7-storey high-ceilinged warehouses (Ward 1996a) (see Plate 53).

The height limit issue was prominent in the late 1990s in the proposed refurbishment of the Malkin Warehouse and redevelopment of adjoining vacant sites to provide retail, office, and residential floor space. Three development scenarios were prepared. Public consultations with the planners, neighbours, the Vancouver Heritage Commission, and three Gastown groups, including the local historic area planning committee, took place over the summer of 1997. There was support for most of the development principles espoused, but not for the new 14-storey residential unit proposed on the small vacant site to the east. Concern was expressed over breaching the 23-metre (75-foot) Gastown height limit. Paul Merrick Architects argued that a uniform height limit was contrary to the historic character of the area, and that the additional residential space was required to pay for the restoration and seismic upgrading of the warehouse; the three levels of underground parking would yield a surplus of fifty spaces for adjacent businesses (see Figure 57). The Urban Design Panel gave the scheme firm support as did the Development Permit Board, noting enthusiastic approval from the community and the local historic area planning and business improvement committees. The project was approved by the board despite some planning reservations, particularly about height; but the director of current planning

Plate 53   Alexander/Carrall streets and the Hotel Europe (far right). An examination of the facades on Alexander Street reveals that the sawtooth skyline of Gastown is almost a thing of the past as developers have retained heritage buildings but have added new residential space above. The globe lamps to which some conservationists object are prominent.

subsequently used the provincial Heritage Conservation Act to remove the two additions to the roof and this, along with market conditions, put the project on hold. Planners later concluded a heritage revitalization agreement to include some live/work units, reduce parking requirements, remove the 3-storey roof addition to the warehouse and to take one storey off the condominium tower. However, they allowed the development to transfer the density elsewhere as a cross-subsidy to ensure the project's viability (Ward 1999b).

Other proposals for market housing have aroused similar controversies, as might be expected, given the divisions in the community (Ward 1996f, 1996d). One such building is the Van Horne loft complex, angled back from the southeast corner of Carrall and Cordova streets to leave the old CP Rail right-of-way as an open space between it and a small commercial building on the corner (see Plate 54).

The Malkin Warehouse conversion demonstrated an essential principle in heritage conservation, most clearly articulated by conservationist and critic Robin Ward, that what is original should be retained and what is new should be expressed in a contemporary manner. The best example of this is Peter Busby/Robert Lemon's conversion of the early-twentieth-century printing plant of the *Province* newspaper on Victory Square (Ward 1999d) (see Plate 52). The client being the Architectural Institute of British Columbia might lead one to

Figure 57 65 Water Street: reactions of the Urban Design Panel and Development Permit Board. The architect probably knew he would not get his initial ideas accepted, so he proceeded to a full design to demonstrate that his ideas could be made to work. This is a fine example of creative conversion, with new additions in modern forms to complement the old. The project was on the edge of commercial viability.

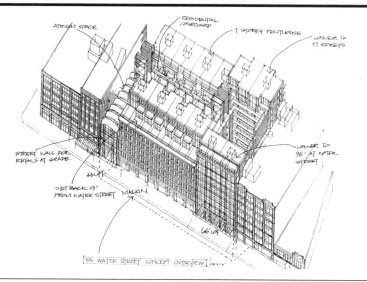

Address and Location

65 Water Street

Project Description

Refurbishment / Conversion of B-listed Malkin Warehouse with additional atrium and 9- to 11-storey residential units

Zoning and Bonuses

HA-2 / No maximum floor-space ratio / 75 feet: seeks height relaxation

Architect and Client

Paul Merrick / Reliance Holdings

Urban Design Panel

08/98 *3-1 support*. Should have been a preliminary application, but a well-crafted, innovative, and positive addition "framing" the warehouse. Exciting design that sets the standard: 75-foot height limit produces undesirable "table-topping" so the additional height sought should be allowed for refurbishment / conversion.

Development Permit Board

11/98 *Approve*. With deletion of three conditions and amendment of three others. Allow height of 120 feet instead of 75 feet; strong staff and board support for exciting, provocative scheme. Some negative but mainly positive local reaction.

Council subsequently overrules the board to remove the additional floor space / height. They subsequently agree that this floor space can be sold to another site as Heritage TDR (transferred development rights) to ensure project viability.

Sources: Paul Merrick Architects (drawing); text compiled from panel and board minutes

Plate 54 The Van Horne lofts at Cordova/Carrall streets. The Van Horne is angled back from the corner to protect the old Canadian Pacific Railway right-of-way which is preserved as a gated public space because of the area's current drug problems. The architects Kasian Kennedy took advantage of the amenity bonus to add extra floor space to the project. Critics have suggested that the elevations need more depth, and better and more varied materials, but the architects subsequently designed almost identical elevations for the adjacent corner building (left).

expect a restored classical facade and a dramatic modern interior – which has been delivered. One of the secrets of the success of the conversion is that the heritage bonus has been transferred off-site – in this case, in an especial architectural irony, to the much-reviled Wall Centre tower (see Chapter 9).

A further heritage issue in Gastown is the appropriate treatment of the area's streets. Water Street does not set a good precedent with its theme-park Victorianism (Ward 1998e) (see Plate 11). The globe lamps are now working their way onto other streets in a move characterized by at least one critic as a mockery of the area's industrial warehouse past (Ward 1996b) (see Plate 53). The planning documents talk about distinctive public realm treatments, which have yet to be developed. Certainly, it is to be hoped that more robust and urbane treatments that avoid prettifying are selected. On a positive note it is now city policy that the back lanes, with their hydro-poles and wirescapes, are treated robustly.

These and other heritage issues are being tackled by a Gastown Heritage Management Plan, which was commissioned by the city from Spaxman Associates, using Robert Lemon and Don Luxton of the Gastown Historic Area Planning Committee – a very experienced team. This promises a fresh and comprehensive approach to set priorities for "authentic heritage conservation." It proposes regulations to favour conservation of existing buildings with only minor rooftop additions, while ensuring that new buildings reflect "the built form of the area in ... height, scale and density" (Vancouver 2001k). It offers a choice between three alternative street treatments – beautification, authentic restoration, or a new "look and feel," and it suggests a more sensitive set of height restrictions and design guidelines "tailored to the architectural character of Gastown." As interesting are the various financial incentives, expedited processes, and relaxed regulations proposed to aid project viability. The funding incentives have been derived from a trawl of the best ideas in other Canadian jurisdictions, but the scale of the task is epitomized by a recent pro forma analysis of an office conversion in the locality. This shows renovation costs almost doubling acquisition costs and break-even rentals nearly twice the highest rent achieved in the area (Vancouver 2001k). Nonetheless the plan is encouraging in its clarity of vision and its technical sophistication, and it heralds a much more positive approach to heritage conservation, which has generally not been one of the main areas of achievement for Vancouver's planning system.

The vanguard of gentrification is already apparent in the eastern edges of downtown. City planners propose new zoning to encourage a broader range of associated cultural and light industrial uses and to formalize live/work suites in a flourishing artists' community in and around Victory Square. The establishment of several higher-educational institutions in the west of the area offers some support for these uses but will likely also bring demands for student housing. There are plans to improve the public realm along East Hastings (see Plate 55) and the major cross streets of Richards, Hamilton, Cambie, and Abbott with tree planting, weather protection, and new paving, as well as restoration of existing historic street features. Some of this will be financed through a public-benefits strategy under consideration to encourage heritage retention, low-income housing, public realm improvements, and facilities for the arts, culture, daycare, and community activities. Unfortunately, these strategies will also have the effect of adding a financial burden on developers already struggling to finance heritage building conversions and seismic upgrading.

Downtown Eastside: Strategies for a Neighbourhood under Siege

Since the 1980s, the Downtown Eastside has been in a state of deep crisis. With a long-standing high concentration of elderly single men – seasonally employed at logging and mining jobs when they were younger, but now permanently unemployed – came concentrated alcoholism, homelessness, and vagrancy. A population of heroin-dependent young people moved in during the 1980s, bringing with them a rise in crime, prostitution, hepatitis, and HIV-AIDS – soon at an epidemic scale. During the 1990s, the arrival of crack cocaine as a cheaper and more addictive drug, deepened these problems.

Plate 55 Hastings Street from Carrall Street, looking west to the Woodward's store, with its distinctive "W" pylon sign in the background. It is hard to believe that twenty years ago this was a busy shopping street. Save-On-Meats still attracts a lot of customers, but a strong retail draw, such as Woodward's once was, is vital for the street's future.

With an associated rise in crime – particularly thefts from cars – came an invasion of drug dealing into the area's cafés and bars. Increasing drug use led to a further deterioration, and occasional destruction, of the stock of single-room occupancy housing. As crime and antisocial behaviour increased, businesses closed, customers became scarcer, and the spiral of economic decline intensified (Vancouver 1998ff: 3-4). New businesses tended to be pawnbrokers, second-hand dealers, and convenience stores open late into the night, some of which supported various aspects of illegal activity. The area has always been the focus of Vancouver's cheapest housing and has also become a locus for Aboriginal families. With the phasing out of provincial mental-health institutions, such as the one at Riverview, many former patients have also sought cheap places to live in the Downtown Eastside.

While the Downtown Eastside has only 3.2 percent of Vancouver's population, it has 79 percent of all single-room occupancy and 22 percent of non-market housing (see Figure 56). Given this concentration, a high incidence of social and health issues might be expected. Residents of the Downtown Eastside include 20 percent of the city's welfare cases, as well as 18 percent of mental-health care cases, and generate 21 percent of medical-emergency service calls. Crime statistics indicate that the area has long been in danger of imploding: 11 percent of thefts from cars, 17 percent of all fire responses, 19 percent of violent crime, and 22 percent of the city's police calls – as well as a staggering 74 percent of all drug arrests and 32 percent of all homicides (Vancouver 1999f). Murders of women, in particular those reported missing from the area, have been consistently making national headlines. Control of many of these issues is impaired by the fact that the area has a concentration of lounges, hotel bars, and cabarets that are open much of each day and sell alcohol for consumption off-premises. Some politicians and interest groups presume a causal relationship between the high proportion of low-income housing and the high crime rate, but police statistics for 1999 noted that 55 percent of the crime in the area is committed by non-residents and 68 percent of the drug addicts using the area live elsewhere.

The Downtown Eastside has a concentration of emergency shelters (five), free or low-cost meal centres (six), and specialist health agencies (seven), which support the poorest and most vulnerable residents from throughout Vancouver (Figure 56). The concentration of these facilities – and more especially the fact that they are not being provided elsewhere – were contributing to the area's spiral of decline. Residents were coming to recognize that the area could not house any more such facilities. In 1993 two further blows hit the community: the ending of federal housing subsidies and the closing of Woodward's department store at Hastings and Abbott, the anchor for retail business (see Plate 55). City planners had already started work on a plan for Victory Square embracing heritage character retention, revitalization, and the consolidation of low-income housing – but clearly a much broader effort was required of all levels of government.

Fortunately the mayor, Philip Owen, took a special interest in the Downtown Eastside issue, providing very powerful leadership for a revitalization program. In 1995 the city established the Vancouver Caucus to bring together government and agencies to discuss approaches to managing the area, beginning with a housing plan, discussed later. In 1996 a Neighbourhood Integrated Service Team was established to coordinate the work of city and provincial agencies in combating crime and social disorder and improving living conditions. It began a more intense inspection program for single-room occupancy housing and businesses, revoking licences of substandard and criminal, or criminal-tolerant, operations. New policies were devised to control the locations of, and activities within, pawnshops, second-hand stores, and liquor establishments. In October 1997 city council formed the Vancouver Coalition for Crime Prevention and Drug Treatment, with the police and more than sixty community organizations. In 1998 council prepared and approved a strategic program for the Downtown Eastside to target drug addiction and drug-related crime, alcohol abuse, mental-health care, business revitalization, housing provision, community participation, and street programming

(Vancouver 1998c). The federal government early in 1999 agreed to provide the city with $1 million in each of five years to support a community crime-prevention and revitalization program. The provincial government signed a three-year housing agreement with the city to fund two single-room occupancy hotel acquisitions/renovations and two low-income housing projects on East Hastings Street. Between April 2000 and 2003, forty new officers are to be added to police the area, in particular to strengthen community policing and to target drug dealers. A detox centre with outreach services to replace one that had been closed years earlier was planned, and, to reduce drug dealing, the city restricted the classes of business able to operate twenty-four hours.

Arguably the mayor's greatest achievement was to develop the Vancouver Agreement, signed in July 1999 by federal, provincial, and city governments as well as the Vancouver/Richmond Health Board, for "sustainable economic and social development and community capacity building." It reaffirmed the drive for collaboration across hugely complex bureaucracies to improve service delivery in the Downtown Eastside. Under the Vancouver Agreement, in mid-2001, a four-pillar approach was agreed upon to tackle the city's drug problems by combining prevention, treatment, enforcement, and harm-reduction initiatives as an enlightened and even-handed approach to balance public order with community safety concerns and public health measures. Community consensus was reached over the goals (80 percent support), a phenomenal achievement given the previous dissension. In 2001 community policing levels were increased to twenty-seven officers to tackle drug dealing and to work with health agencies to help addicts. In the same year the front of the Carnegie (Community) Centre at the corner of Main and Hastings was redesigned to get rid of the open drug trade that prevailed there. This pro-posal will relocate bus stops, reduce the public area on Main Street, improve visibility, and create an enclosed patio and controlled access for the community building to bar entry to people under the influence of alcohol and drugs.

Meanwhile, community groups and residents in the Downtown Eastside and Strathcona had formed a Community Directions coalition to ensure that any initiatives benefited neighbourhood residents, putting the most vulnerable people's needs first. Their program stressed community involvement in planning, outreach programs to embrace all residents, improved health treatment, housing and economic opportunities, and long-term sustainable quality-of-life strategies. The mayor stood firm when this coalition was fiercely critical of the early implementation of the drug program, but gradually the collaborative four-pillar approach has won community support. Progress is slow and painstaking, with many conflicts among different constituencies to be resolved by corporate working. There are enormous challenges, but the process has huge potential to address the area's most intractable problems.

Downtown Eastside Housing Plan, 1998

The plan for Downtown Eastside housing is a vital element of these programs, as it attempts to deal simultaneously with local shortages of cheap
housing, community fears about over-concentrations of people with drug/
alcohol addictions and mental illnesses, and low-income housing displacement by redevelopment (Vancouver 1998y). A steady provision of market
rental housing is foreseen with protection of 100 to 200 units per year doubling
the amount available by the end of the decade and supporting new retail
operations by bringing more affluent people into the community. About 100
units of low-income housing will be built annually to replace single-room
occupancy, along with about 100 new units of social housing. The latter
would meet only half the projected need for low-income singles housing
over the next decade, and implies the development of more such housing
elsewhere in the city, notably in Downtown South, leaving a pitiful allocation
of ten to thirty units per year for the rest of the city. Hastings Street and the
heart of the Downtown Eastside are likely to be the focus of most of the new
low-income housing. The housing plan sees most of the market units being
built in Gastown and Chinatown; it notes that there may be some difficulties
replacing losses of low-income housing in these areas.

The housing plan also explores the question of a minimum size for self-
contained dwelling units and its relationship to housing affordability, in terms
of both rental levels and numbers that might be built for the same investment. The minimum size set by the zoning bylaw is 37 square metres (400
square feet), which can be relaxed to 30 square metres (320 square feet) –
although council has considered the possibility of reducing the size to 25.5
square metres (275 square feet), pending discussions with the community.
Previous exhibitions and surveys have shown considerable community support for units as small as 17 square metres (180 square feet) and a consensus
for minimum sizes of 28 square metres (300 square feet). Social housing
providers like the prospect of offering a greater number of suites at lower
cost, thereby increasing the rental return from their properties, with up to 40
percent more units with small suites of 25.5 square metres (275 square feet)
or 80 percent more with micro suites of 17 square metres (180 square feet).
Demonstration projects to explore these possibilities are being considered
along with a reduction of minimum unit size to 25.5 square metres (275
square feet), as recommended by the plan. But these initiatives do little to
address the needs of the 10,000 households waiting for housing. Simultaneously, there are concerns that rising land and property values in the area
could make it difficult to develop housing within existing provincial budgets.
The proposal that the city purchase one site a year for social housing – with
additional subsidies over the normal sixty-year lease at 75 percent of market

Plate 56 Central City Lodge, 415 West Pender Street. This special-needs housing and alcohol-recovery unit designed by Neale Staniszkis Doll Adams (1996) uses a series of contextual references to blend into the Edwardian downtown, looking as if it could have been there for at least seventy years. It is particularly cleverly designed on its sloping Homer Street entrance, where a sheltered private courtyard provides sitting out space for residents.

value – may be a realistic target but will do little to meet wider affordable housing needs (Vancouver 1998y).

Despite the shortages of funds, the quality of design of social housing projects continues to uphold the standards set in the 1980s and to enrich the city's architectural heritage (see Chapter 3). Among recently completed projects, plaudits and architectural medals have been awarded for the Central City Lodge (Neale Staniszkis Doll Adams) (Plate 56) at 415 West Pender Street and for VanCity Place (Nigel Baldwin) on Victory Square, praised for its appropriate scale but refusal to copy adjacent Victorian styles (Ward 1998g). Bruce Eriksen Place is a particular joy for two reasons. A slick Richard Henriquez design, it commemorates a key Downtown Eastside figure of the 1970s and 1980s, with his credo on the facade. Here is public art at its most meaningful (see Plate 57). Other notable projects include the renovations of the New Portland and Metropole hotels and the new mixed-use complex at Alexander and Main, The Edge. Richard Henriquez has designed another exciting social housing project at 65 West Cordova, much commended by the Urban Design Panel.

The failure of the proposed redevelopment of Woodward's department store for social housing was a major disappointment to Downtown Eastsiders

Plate 57 Bruce Eriksen Place, 370 Main Street. Richard Henriquez
has created a monument to the former leader of the Downtown
Eastside Residents Association in this modernist social housing
project. The latter's credo is engraved on the balcony, and cartoons
of his exploits create a frieze above the recessed ground floor. It
has a delightful roof garden.

(see Plate 55). Each of the three redevelopment proposals has caused huge
controversies, splitting the community along tenure lines. A market condominium conversion proposal was rejected in favour of a mixed-market project
negotiated through financing from the city and the New Democratic provincial government, which was willing to subsidize 200 low-income units. That
project fell through and was followed by an approved scheme for 5 storeys
of 417 market residential units above three lower storeys of small-unit commercial space grouped around a courtyard cut out of the old store. At the
Development Permit Board hearing, an unprecedented fifty members of the
public – organized by the Downtown Eastside Residents Association – spoke
against the scheme, although support for it came from the Gastown Business

Improvement Society and the Gastown Homeowners Association, exemplifying the divisions in the community. But, since the proposal conformed to the zoning, the board had to approve the project. Proposals had Simon Fraser University taking half the space, with the rest being residential, retail, or office space. Whether it is implemented is up to the Liberal provincial government, guided by former mayor, now premier, Gordon Campbell, assuming support continues from a broad section of the community.

The housing plan debates how much more new social housing should be shoehorned into the Downtown Eastside, what kind of social mix should be attempted to ensure commercial vitality for small businesses and shops, and the ability of community services to cope. But the real issue is to ensure that much more social/lower-income housing is built elsewhere in downtown and in the city's new neighbourhood centres so that the Downtown Eastside is not further ghettoized and its health and welfare services are not further overwhelmed.

In the Downtown Eastside it is clear what has *not* been achieved in Vancouver in the last thirty years. The multiple exclusions induced by the gentrification and aestheticization of the city at large reinforce deeper and more pernicious social, economic, and political processes that have set the Downtown Eastside on a spiral of social decline. These processes include globalization, labour-shedding, senior government withdrawal from welfare provision and social housing subsidies, municipal fiscal crises, and deep civic indifference to problems of poverty collectively. These have produced a concentration of social problems arguably unequalled anywhere else in Canada. Many of the proposed solutions have no relationship to issues of urban design, but issues of low-income housing provision, housing design, street safety, heritage protection, and area character all have a critical role to play in recreating a safe and habitable neighbourhood on the eastern edge of downtown Vancouver. This is the biggest challenge that Vancouver's planning and urban management faces over the next decade, and a major test of the city's social conscience.

The Quality of the Downtown Public Realm

Key issues in the quality of the public realm in downtown Vancouver present new challenges to city planners at the start of the twenty-first century. The 1991 central area goals and policy statement did not directly embrace the creation of a quality public realm, although six of the seven goals contained some facet of it, including the "public street [as] the primary scene for public life," "active public spaces," "connection to the natural setting," and enhancing pedestrian and other accessibility (Vancouver 1991c). There is evidence that residential and mixed-use developments are delivering much more widespread pedestrian vitality and many more interesting commercial and cultural destinations, but there is a recognition that the public realm is rather impoverished and lags behind such cities as Portland, Oregon, which is widely admired by Vancouver's urban design experts. It is a generally held view that the downtown public realm has not lived up to Vancouver's other urban design achievements, and that it lacks the civic spaces, great streets, and pedestrian experiences that it deserves.

Downtown has been the subject of a number of interesting design studies that might contribute to public realm improvements, including the streetscape policies already mentioned in Triangle West, Downtown South, and the Library Precinct. Weather protection policies, for instance, were first developed in 1978 to further enhance pedestrian movement and comfort and to improve the shopping experience. These policies actively promoted provision by property owners and developers on the most heavily trafficked downtown and uptown streets and encouraged them in adjacent streets. The policy has been amended to extend the network to Davie south of Burrard, Robson east of Seymour, and Hamilton between Robson and Pender (Vancouver 1993b). In 1984 a major study of downtown plazas was conducted by consultants Buchan and Simmons (Vancouver 1984b) for the social planning department, in recognition of the fact that many were not well used and that "unsuccessful plazas are a waste of precious public spaces and opportunities." It analyzed twenty-eight downtown plazas and concluded that Vancouver's public spaces were predominantly a set of sunny and sheltered office plazas located at grade on arterials. They were generally noisy and many were predominantly bare and minimally landscaped modernist designs attracting little use or pedestrian movement (Vancouver 1984b). Drawing heavily on this report's recommendations, another consultant developed the city's plaza design guidelines, adding a preference for distant views from the plaza, clear links into pedestrian networks, and, above all, a clear design concept (Vancouver 1992f). By the time they were approved in 1994 the guidelines had been rendered practically redundant by the collapse of downtown office development, but they remain relevant to new public realm initiatives. Also relevant is the public art program in downtown, although most of the best pieces predate the installations program begun in 1994.

Transportation and the Public Realm

Two studies of importance to the downtown public realm are currently underway. A downtown transportation plan, initiated in 1999, is a comprehensive review of the areas in the wake of a citywide plan completed in 1997. The latter set goals of not increasing the number of private vehicles on city streets through to 2021, and limiting commuter parking spaces to 34,000, to encourage commuting by transit, cycling, or walking. Other suggestions were a free or low-fare zone, more transit stops, expanded ferry services, a range of pedestrian and cycle routes, and adding a downtown transit loop. The downtown plan is a collaboration between city planning and engineering services to take a broader view of transportation and movement than previously. The survey for the plan sought users' views on ways to improve transit ridership, reduce noise and air pollution, and encourage demand management. A range of options are to be set out for certain city streets, including the selection of specific greenways as cycle and pedestrian links across the downtown, the future roles of Pacific Boulevard through False Creek North and the transit mall on Granville, and the future of the one-way street system on the east side of downtown. The possibility of at least a partial street classification system to identify specific functions for particular streets has also been mentioned.

Another city engineering and planning partnership initiative is the proposed historic streetcar loop. A consultant study (Baker McGarva Hart et al.) examined thirteen possible lines and loops (Vancouver 1998jj). An extension from terminal SkyTrain station to the Waterfront SkyTrain Station along Quebec, Columbia, and Cordova streets was shown to recover all operating and capital costs, and an extension along Pacific Boulevard to Davie could recover 88 percent, assuming employment growth with commercial development in that corridor. Both routes were recommended as first-phase options, and an extension to Stanley Park from Waterfront station was recommended as a viable later stage, with an estimated 80 percent cost recovery. Simultaneously, city planning and engineering departments have completed a study and a policy for street furniture and amenities. They are developing a streetscape design standard to draw together existing design policies and technical guidelines for all street paving, landscaping, furnishing, and weather protection. These include contracts with advertising companies who will provide and maintain a coordinated range of well-designed street furniture in return for the rights to use them to display advertising, an "innovation" now sweeping most major North American and European cities, with mixed results.

Much depends on the future of the Granville Street transit mall, which still attracts some of the largest pedestrian flows in the city between Hastings and Smithe. One question being studied is how much of this flow is a result of concentrated bus routes down this street. It is clear that improvements for pedestrians are long overdue and will benefit all downtown users. Two excellent innovations embodied in the CityPlan ideas are relevant to the downtown public realm in general and to Granville Street in particular (Vancouver 1993d: s.7,6). The first was a revival of an idea to build a low-level pedestrian-and-cycle link under the Granville Bridge. This would provide an excellent commuter link from uptown to downtown while making Granville Island much more accessible on foot from downtown, and would strengthen pedestrian flows at the southern end. The second is to make radical improvements to Courthouse Square and Robson Square, an idea that has already been discussed as part of an extension to the art gallery that might well go underneath Robson Square. The province retained Architectura with Arthur Erickson to prepare some design ideas in 1997, but these were not taken forward. The remodelling of these central public spaces is of immense importance to downtown for creating a civic focus, providing meeting and resting places for shoppers and downtown workers, and strengthening the pedestrian flows at this critical junction of the main shopping, promenading, and people-watching streets of the city (see Plates 13 and 14).

The creation of major new or remodelled civic spaces in the city needs to be very carefully related to current and projected patterns of movement, to detailed land-use changes, and shifting patterns of active frontages. Lance Berelowitz (1998) has drawn attention to the centrifugal pull of the new seawall, which will be greatly intensified when Burrard Landing is developed. The city's principal streets and spaces need a coordinated strategy if their appeal is to be assured and their urbanity enhanced. What is striking is the dramatic change in pedestrian movement patterns since the 1970s and the shift in peak flows westward with the demise of East Hastings Street and the rise of Robson Street in the west. It will be interesting to see if new surveys show a maintenance or decline of the high movement levels that characterized Granville, West Georgia, and Dunsmuir in the early 1990s, and the strengthening of the Robson-Granville dogleg as the downtown passeggiata. It will be equally important to analyze night-time movement patterns in relation to Granville Street's footfall and vitality, and wider patterns of entertainment, culture, and hotel locations.

Social Exclusion, Gentrification, and the Public Realm

The rapid creation of quite distinct sets of high-density mixed-use neighbourhoods on the very margins of downtown is a major planning and urban design achievement. By the end of the 1990s, the formerly disparate and dispersed neighbourhoods and pockets of vitality and interest on the downtown peninsula had begun to cohere. Much of this change was anticipated in the 1975 character area guidelines and the 1991 central area policy statement (see Figure 48). However, cheek by jowl with the newly livable downtown is the markedly unlivable skid row, to which have been added crack cocaine,

HIV-AIDS and hepatitis outbreaks, and serial homicides. Compared to many similar-sized American cities, Vancouver has contained and confined its crack alley but, by Canadian standards, its problems are very severe and spectacularly concentrated (British Columbia 1999: 14). The problems of the Downtown Eastside are accentuated by the proximity of so much wealth, investment, and environmental quality in the rest of the downtown peninsula.

The Downtown Eastside is a testament to rampant processes of social exclusion and gentrification that operate not just in the downtown peninsula but citywide. Similar processes impact upon the public realm and, specifically, attempts to improve the city's streets. This is evident in the *Vancouver Sun*'s characterization of the Downtown Eastside crisis as "The Battle for Hastings," to reclaim the streets and public spaces from dealers, drug users, pushers, prostitutes, and drunks (Mulgrew 1998a-e). The enhancement of the public realm as a key component of the regeneration and redevelopment of central Vancouver is normally treated unproblematically by planners and by proponents of urban renaissance who regard themselves as defenders of democratic streets and public space. But many planners and councillors have an urge to domesticate the vitality, diversity, freedom, and choice of the busiest city streets and urban spaces to make them safe for middle-class inhabitation and investment. The geographer Loretta Lees draws attention to this phenomenon in the attempts to clean up Granville Street and to create safe spaces for women and children in the new city library, summing up the urban designer's dilemma: "Simultaneously embracing and withdrawing from the public spaces of city streets, gentrification is deeply ambivalent in its stance to urban life. Its attempts to foster genuine public culture in the street subvert that very goal, as efforts to secure urban space stifle its celebrated diversity and vitality" (Lees 1998: 251). So, in the city's efforts to improve the downtown public realm, planners and councillors need to recognize the dangers of sanitizing and prettifying city streets, and the absolute necessity of reinforcing pedestrian movement and ensuring that downtown attracts the widest possible population. As the residential population steadily increases and more people occupy downtown streets, more vitality will naturally accrue. Now is the time to consider where strategic interventions might be made and where traffic might be calmer to create a truly pedestrian- and cycle-friendly downtown.

Part 3
Regulating Development and Improving Design

8
Reforming Permit Processing and Development Levies, 1980-2000

Our focus now turns from the broad planning and design of neighbourhoods to the detailed aspects of contemporary planning practices that deliver neighbourhood amenities and design quality. This chapter looks at ongoing reforms to permit processing and development financing, and Chapter 9 analyzes the design dimension of the processing of major development permits. The debates and reforms that have accompanied the progressive reform of the permitting system since the early 1980s are now analyzed, and how these have shaped contemporary practice and the "due process" dimensions of design review is explained. Also examined are the current reforms of permit processing, which are nearing completion and their potential is assessed. As important as these reforms are the fiscal instruments for delivering a quality urban environment, and the city's current initiatives to restructure development levies and community amenity contributions.

Both issues are part of an administration-wide *Better City Government* initiative launched in 1993 and aimed at delivering pivotal services more effectively and more efficiently within a tight municipal budget. And both issues provide an opportunity to look at how the development industry has shaped planning and design processes in Vancouver, whereas previously the focus has been on the role of the public and neighbourhood groups, and council and planning department in determining policy and guidelines. Since 1974 the development industry and architectural profession have continually lobbied for the lessening of controls and for more predictable, less discretionary zoning, for more efficient permit processing, and for less onerous development levies (see Figure 58). Council has often echoed their criticisms and sought to make the system more predictable, more efficient, and less onerous, respectively.

How a permit application is processed, and how much of a development charge is levied on an approved scheme are highly technical but also deeply political matters. Their complexities have to be understood if sound democratic processes are to be established and significant design and amenity value is to be added to contemporary development (see Figure 1). Permit processing is a complex system of consultation and decision making (see Figure 59) whereby each permit is checked against extensive rules and guidelines, and a wide range of expert and technical advice sought on major applications. The process has to satisfy the developer's desire for speed, predictability, and fairness on the one hand, and the public's desire to minimize development impacts and externalities and improve design on the other. The quality of the processes, processors, and procedures is critical to the quality of the decisions and the "value-added" to design in its broadest sense. The same is true of the system of development levies that delivers the physical and social infrastructure necessary to support urban growth, and neighbourhood amenities and facilities to serve existing and new populations. Both are critical to progressive design review and a successful urban design policy.

Reviewing Permit Processing

As in the 1970s developers, architects, and Non-Partisan councillors in the early 1980s put pressure on Vancouver's planning department to deliver a more efficient, quicker, and less onerous system of permit processing. Comprehensive reviews of permit processing had been undertaken in 1976 and 1979 but, by 1981, heavy development pressures and a three-month civic strike had produced a major backlog of applications. A doubling in the success rate of developers' appeals on decisions between 1982 and 1984 – to 56 percent – emphasized the difference of perspective between the Board of Variance (council appointees) and the Development Permit Board (department heads). City planners monitored what they considered to be a series of irrational decisions by the Board of Variance and, fortunately, that problem diminished. In 1983, in response to renewed complaints from architects and developers, city council retained consultants to review the development permit process to identify areas of concern and potential improvement, and to assess the overall level of permitting performance. Fifteen issues were identified focusing on the uncertainties, complexity, and amount of discretion in the process; the variation in the interpretation of design guidelines; the lack of early advice to aid applicants; the interventions into architectural design detail rather than urban design; and the speed of the process. Thus began a sequence of reports, reforms, and monitoring exercises at roughly four-year intervals.

The Chilton Report, 1984

The 1984 Chilton Report suggested a standard regulatory system as an alternative, but focused most of its attention on ways to reduce discretion and uncertainty in the existing system (Vancouver 1994k: 22) (see Figure 58). It advocated a general move toward a more clearly defined legalistic approach to permit processing, but it suggested that the architect-trained development planners should be delegated authority to administer the bylaws and the permit process. There were specific suggestions about the desirability of pre-design conferences, and of adding the city manager or deputy to the Development Permit Board. Despite criticisms of the process, there were strong endorsements of the abilities of both the planning director, Ray Spaxman, and the two recently hired development planners who were negotiating major applications. Some did criticize the director for his desire always to be flexible, his unwillingness to delegate, and his determination to ensure that each application was "rigorously challenged by the process" (Vancouver 1984a: 5), but he survived a council motion that he should relinquish the chairmanship of the Development Permit Board. Surprisingly, the Urban Development Institute, the developers' lobby organization, supported the director, as did the Urban Design Panel; the Architectural Institute of British Columbia wanted him to have a non-voting role. Overall, city council continued to endorse the existing system, while making recommendations to speed up and simplify the process. As a result of the Chilton Report, most decisions were delegated to senior planning staff in the Land Use and Development Division, with fewer applications going to the Development Permit Board and the Urban Design Panel. Pre-design conferences for major applications were introduced. Leaflets were produced to explain the rationalized permitting processes and guidelines. Monitoring of applications and liaison with the development industry were both improved.

The Campbell Task Force and the Hardwick Report, 1986-88

With the arrival in 1986 of a new mayor to lead the Non-Partisan council came intensified pressure on the current system of permit processing. Mayor Gordon Campbell announced in his inaugural speech that a task force would be established on the development permit process, chaired by himself and comprised of councillors Baker and Price. This was hardly surprising, given the mayor's developer backing, his long-standing antipathy to the planning director, and a boom in development. For six months the task force heard conflicting representations from all participants in the process, leading the two aldermen on the task force to produce rather different position papers. The city manager undertook to resolve these but, encountering difficulties, took the unusual step of asking ex-TEAM Alderman Walter Hardwick, by then back in academia, for help. Hardwick's report upheld some of the complaints of the Urban Development Institute. It considered that, notwithstanding the increase in delegation of decision making implemented in 1984, too

Figure 58 The key points of controversy in permit processing, 1984-90. This table, prepared by the planning department, summarizes the main criticisms of the five main studies/submissions on the performance of the permitting process. It shows the persistence of some criticisms, but the resolution of others, particularly those relating to uncertainty and, to a lesser extent, the exercise of discretion.

	1984 Chilton Report	1988 Urban Dev't Institute Brief	1988 Hardwick Report	1988 Architectural Society of BC Survey	1990 Urban Dev't Institute Survey
1. Uncertainty of Process					
1.1 Too much uncertainty	×	×			
1.2 Lack of clarity in guidelines	×	×			
1.3 Staff interpretations not documented	×				
1.4 Inadequate access to staff	×				
1.5 Lack of coordination between departments	×	×			
1.6 On-going staff requests for more information		×			
1.7 Inadequate notification of staff recommendations prior to DPB meeting		×			×
2. Complexity of Process					
2.1 Process and requirements are too complex	×	×	×	×	
2.2 Too much detail required for preliminary application	×				×
2.3 Excessive number of prior-to conditions	×	×			
2.4 Too many forms and reports required				×	×
3. Length of Process					
3.1 Process is too long	×	×		×	×
3.2 Excessive time required to notify by letter			×		×
3.3 Excessive processing time for minor applications			×	×	
3.4 Need for improved performance tracking			×		
4. Amount of Discretion/ Influence					
4.1 Excessive amount of discretion/ influence vested in staff, director of planning, DPB, and UDP	×	×			
4.2 Too much staff influence in building design	×		×	×	

►

◄ *Figure 58*

	1984 Chilton Report	1988 Urban Dev't Institute Brief	1988 Hardwick Report	1988 Architectural Society of BC Survey	1990 Urban Dev't Institute Survey
4.3 Inequitable treatment of applicants		x			
4.4 Excessive "amenity extraction"		x			
4.5 Inability to negotiate early in the process			x		
4.6 Lack of clarity of roles and authority of staff				x	
4.7 Lack of impartiality of the DPB			x		x
4.8 Too many applications sent to DPB			x		x
4.9 Excessive influence of UDP		x			
4.10 Too many applications sent to UDP			x		x
4.11 UDP meetings not public					x

Note: DPB = Development Permit Board; UDP = Urban Design Panel
Source: Vancouver (1994d)

many applications were still being sent to the Development Permit Board – which seemed to lack impartiality – and to the Urban Design Panel (see Figure 58).

Hardwick's report was more specific in its criticisms of the length and complexity of the process, the slow processing of minor applications, and the need for better monitoring. Hardwick made eleven recommendations capable of immediate action. He affirmed the role of the planning director in the process, but suggested including the city manager in a leadership role on the Development Permit Board. The planning director was to set up a team to simplify the zoning and development bylaws and to prepare a particular zoning schedule as a model. Intervention in building design was to require the demonstration of clear public benefit and the Urban Design Panel was to report to the planning director in the first instance, rather than directly to the Development Permit Board. In effect, fine tuning of the process was proposed but no radical change. The inclusion of the city manager on the Development Permit Board and the reporting of the Urban Design Panel to the planning director were implemented. However, the biggest change that occurred to permit processing was the resignation of planning director Ray Spaxman in February 1989, robbing the Development Permit Board of its driving force and its main source of expertise.

An Internal Review, 1989-91
In 1990 the Urban Development Institute was pressing again to reduce the

number of applications sent to both Development Permit Board and Urban Design Panel, and still complaining of the dubious impartiality of the former, and the lack of transparency of the latter's proceedings (see Figure 58). So one of the first acts of the new director, Tom Fletcher, was to ask the associate planning director responsible for permitting, Rick Scobie, to consider how the planning department might best undertake a review of the major application process. Scobie went back to 1956 to trace the roots of discretionary control. He charted the increase in the number of major applications, their complexity, and the time taken to discuss and process them. Against these findings, he set the facts that many applications were incomplete and hence delayed, and that generally the acceptability of the final submission was increasing, so by implication their quality was improving. His report recommended a quicker service with more delegation to the planning director in return for higher fees, arguing that no one wanted to compromise the quality of advice or decisions by speeding them up (Vancouver 1989h). His report was taken to council, recommending a comprehensive review of the system (Vancouver 1994k).

This time, more significant reforms were made to the regulations, as well as to the permitting system. New zoning standards were implemented with more outright approvals and standardized guidelines. They included new zonings for new multiple-dwellings (RM-5/6), for commercial districts (C-5/6), and for historic area controls in Yaletown (HA-2). Numerous minor changes were made to the process, such as streamlining of procedures, entering information into a computerized system, improving public information, and allowing counter staff to approve minor changes of use and amendments (see Figure 59). Particularly important were two changes: more development planner positions to increase design expertise in-house, and the establishment of a liaison committee to provide more sustained contributions from the development industry to the continued reform of permit processing (Vancouver 1994k: 23).

Further Reports and Reforms, 1991-94

City council approved the planning department's proposal for a thoroughgoing review of permit processing in March 1991, to proceed in collaboration with other city departments and with the newly established Development Permit Process Liaison Committee. Members of the new committee represented developers, provincial architects and landscape architects societies, the Urban Design Panel, the Development Permit Board Advisory Panel, and the Vancouver Planning Commission. The review made ongoing incremental recommendations. Eleven changes were effected in 1991, to make the work of the Urban Design Panel more transparent, such as adding a development

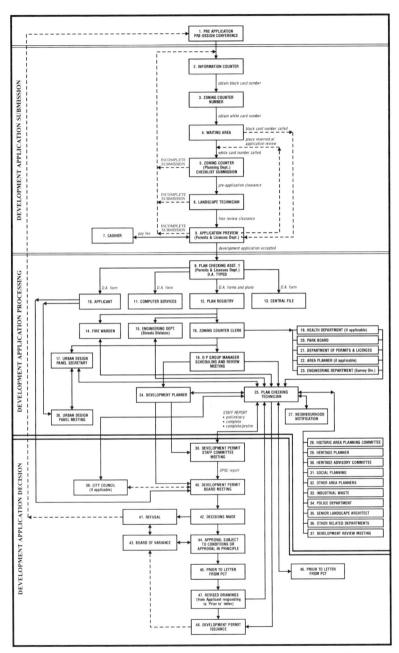

Figure 59   The development permit process, ca. 1991. This flow chart describes the permitting process as it existed through much of the 1990s. It covers both minor and major applications; note that although minor applications proceed from the plan-checker straight to the permit, major applications must progress through the Development Permit Staff Committee report and the Development Permit Board before gaining "approval subject to conditions." (*Source:* Vancouver City Graphics [redrawn])

representative, allowing applicants and planners to make representations, instituting a clearer voting system, and recording full minutes. The committee produced a series of reports on the Development Permit Board in 1992, to clarify the role of the chair and the Development Permit Board Advisory Panel and, in 1993, on applications in two- and multiple-family districts. In 1993 consultants' studies looked at how the Zoning Counter, where the public could consult checkers and planners directly about zoning, was working. Until 1994, there was constant scrutiny of, and adjustments to, the system to improve its transparency, rigour, and efficiency, and the Development Permit Process Liaison Committee had an active splinter group that was continually seeking to extend its terms of reference.

In January 1993, the planning department reported to council on three arguably more fundamental issues about the effectiveness and resourcing of permit processing. These included the achievement of urban design objectives in downtown, the expansion of discretionary zoning into lower-density districts, and the costs of permit processing – it had been discovered that only 35 to 50 percent of processing costs were being recovered. Another staff report to council suggested the establishment of a fully-fledged centre for development application and information with additional staffing.

Early in 1994, as well as criticizing the emerging single-family zoning and permitting system (discussed in Chapter 4), the committee recommended a much wider use of computer-aided design by controllers and applicants, the appointment of an advocate to ensure that development applications were efficiently processed, and the reassignment of design-skilled development planners from the review process to bylaw, policy, and guideline drafting (Vancouver 1994k: Appendix C). The committee's proposals provided a focus for a public forum and workshop, in which the development industry raised questions about the clarity and level of prescription of the guidelines, their appropriateness and contemporary relevance, the scope for design freedom, and architectural as opposed to urban design controls. As the planners responded to each of these concerns, the inherent conflicts between neighbourhood and community desires for effective controls and development industry desires for flexible and simple-to-apply guidelines and procedures became clear (see Figure 60). In particular, on matters of building detail, residents firmly supported interventions based on neighbourhood character and architectural treatment while the development industry favoured regulation of only the basic matters of urban design – massing, safety, privacy, and shadowing (Vancouver 1994k: 20). The main criticisms of the development industry and design professions were still the excessive amount of discretion vested in the Development Permit Board, and the pervasive influence of the Urban Design Panel, the deliberations of which were not open to the public.

Figure 60 Planning department's response to Development Permit Processing Liaison Committee's criticisms of discretionary zoning and permit processing, 1994. This shows planners' responses to developers' criticisms, the tensions between private and public interests, and the difficulties of reconciling these.

Industry concerns	Planning department's response
Philosophy and Role of Discretionary Zoning	
Too much policy making/ discussion at the application stage. Guidelines lack clarity and produce unpredictable interpretations.	Numerous guidelines have deliberately been designed to be flexible and qualitative rather than prescriptive and quantitative, in order to provide maximum design latitude within the zoning intent and to respond to site-specific contexts.
Scope of discretion is too wide. Some guidelines are too prescriptive and are interpreted as regulations. End point of community inputs is not clear.	Much of the perceived over-regulation and inflexible interpretation has been the result of undesirable development occurring within the parameters of flexible guidelines. Community complaints about loopholes or inadequate responses to guidelines often result in council-initiated rezoning or guideline amendments that are seen by the industry as reducing flexibility.
Discretionary Zoning in Lower-Density Districts	
Application of discretionary zoning in these districts imposed economic and other costs that are out of proportion with any benefits realised.	In response to requests from communities for more input and control over the scale and design of development in their communities, the city has been expanding discretionary zoning into lower-density areas. Recent examples include Strathcona RT-3 and South Shaughnessy RS-6.
Architecture versus Urban Design	
Design guidelines, and staff inter-pretation of the same, address too many detailed architectural issues (style, shape, materials, details).	Comprehensive neighbourhood planning programs with extensive community input (e.g., First Shaughnessy, Kitsilano, and Mount Pleasant RT districts) have resulted in council-approved design guidelines which contain community-supported building character and architectural treatment provisions.
Guidelines and interpretation should be limited to urban design (massing, compatibility, safety, privacy, shadowing). Excessive involvement in detail particularly felt in lower-density areas.	The boundary between architectural and urban design aspects of development is often difficult to define.

▶

◄ *Figure 60*

Industry concerns	Planning department's response
Complexity, Uncertainty, Length, and Cost of Processes	
Complexity, uncertainty, delay, and cost affect project viability, particularly small projects.	While staff continue to streamline the process, it continues to become more complex. There are a large number of participants, public objectives, inter-departmental coordination, public input, and review-body components.
Expanding number of planning considerations lengthens, complicates, and increases costs of process. Uncertainty of having to earn discretionary density adds to risk.	Recent added complexity is the result of new council-approved policies being implemented through the development application process. Examples include provisions relating to tree protection, soil contamination, rate of change, demolition control, bicycles, and heritage. These additional conditions are "layered" onto the process, increasing uncertainty, length, and cost.
No effective tracking of applications and performance measurement.	Staff are proceeding in 1994 with a computerized process tracking and performance measurement system.
Increased fees to meet current costs perpetuates a complex system.	If less costly alternatives are approved and implemented, then application fees would be reduced accordingly.
Role of Staff	
No effective conflict resolution mechanism to deal with extent of staff discretion.	The Development Permit Board offers a conflict resolution mechanism for major products.
Absence particularly felt by residents in lower-density districts. Appeals to Board of Variance take too long.	The large number of projects in the lower-density districts works against a "mini-development permit board format" for decision making and appeal.
Inconsistencies, inadequate information, flawed coordination in the process.	The new Development Information and Application Centre includes facilitators who are responsible for removing roadblocks and resolving process conflicts in the case of lower-density district applications.

►

◄ *Figure 60*

Industry concerns	Planning department's response
Accuracy of Information	
Provisions within guidelines do not reflect the zoning (which is often obsolete and inconsistent).	While updates of some guidelines have occurred, staff resources have not been available to review and revise guidelines on a regular basis. Bylaw and guideline revisions often flow from costly and time-consuming public consultation processes.
Some guidelines are inconsistent. These are treated inappropriately as checklists.	
Important interpretations/precedents are not communicated to the design community.	Staff must rely heavily on the quality and completeness of development application submissions. Not infrequently, these submissions are lacking, making review of the applications difficult and lengthening the process.

Source: Vancouver (1994l)

Underpinning these concerns was what the industry perceived as the excessive influence of the planning representative on the board. That representative, co-director of planning Larry Beasley, consistently echoed Ray Spaxman's view that each application should be "rigorously challenged by the process," and many developers and architects fretted about his interventions, which dominated board debates.

The Development and Building Regulation Review, 1994-98

By late 1994, reform of the permitting process became part of the *Better City Government* initiative aimed at flattening the city bureaucracy and reducing departments to improve service delivery. The fifteen former city departments were reorganized into eight work groups. Planning, Social Planning, Cultural Affairs, Permits and Licences, and Housing were clustered together to form a Community Services Group (see Appendix 3). The impetus for this change seems to have come from the city manager rather than council. Budget cuts and financial stringency resulted in some directors not being replaced, including those in the former planning, social planning, and building permits departments. More important, the changes reinforced interdepartmental working and reduced lobbying by directors for individual departments which worked at the expense of corporate thinking.

In May 1995, fifteen services were targeted for improvement, the highest priority being a review of development and building regulation on grounds that permitting is "a complex, politically charged and flawed process that impacts communities, applicants and much of the city organization" (Kostuk

1997: 1). These criticisms were continually voiced to councillors and the city manager by applicants and developers who regarded the planners as uncoordinated and "out of control," making negative changes to developments often quite late in the process. While some planners saw the service as very much policy driven, those in permit processing saw themselves as hamstrung by a vast range of arcane regulations and guidelines. During 1995, Community Services staff were consulted to develop principles for new processes and the guidelines they hoped to create. In the view of permitting staff, the key requirement was to identify potential problems at the pre-application stage, and resolve these before proceeding with the approval process. This was seen as the best means of injecting more efficiency into decision making without compromising the desire to improve the design of development.

Toward an Integrated Permit Processing System

The first phase of the Development and Building Regulation Review was conducted by consultants with a thirteen-person staff team specially trained for the purpose. It was quickly recognized that the regulations were just as much in need of reform as the permitting process, particularly as regards single-family housing (see Chapter 4), but it was considered that reforming the process might be easier and quicker, and would deliver more tangible improvements in the short term. The team reaffirmed that the codes and bylaws were complex, conflicting, unresponsive, and uncoordinated, while the permitting process was inconsistent, fragmented, too slow, too prone to error, and too adversarial. The solution was thought to be the creation of an integrated permitting process, with a single point of inquiry, staffed with highly trained personnel, and with policy and regulation more effectively integrated. There was pressure for less complex regulations and a better public review process, a quicker enforcement system with a more cost-related system of fines, and a coordinated performance system for all staff.

In mid-1995, Community Services began a series of service improvements to streamline processes, review zoning codes and bylaws, and improve enforcement. A comparison of twelve other cities' performance was undertaken, and benchmarks from this comparison convinced the team that they could equal and surpass their performance (Kostuk 1997). A visioning conference held in September 1996 successfully brought together perspectives from neighbourhood groups, the development industry, and planners. Subsequently, an advisory committee was set up to meet bi-monthly, with council-appointed members and an equal number of community and design and development representatives. From these initiatives came a set of principles to guide the restructuring of the permitting process as follows:

- stream inquiries by complexity, location, and applicant expertise
- provide project facilitators or coordinators for complex and simple projects to manage the application throughout
- provide different regulatory processes to fit the needs of project, applicant, and community
- decentralize services
- ensure early community involvement
- allow third-party appeals at the concept stage, with conflict resolution mechanisms
- provide one-stop assistance, expertise, and decision by knowledgeable staff
- eliminate work that does not add value or quality to proposals
- encourage customer feedback, as well as process and team evaluation
- empower and train staff.

It was recommended that applications be handled through one of four streams (see Figure 61).

- The express stream would provide over-the-counter service within a week – the same day, where possible – for sign, tree, and trade permits.
- A coordinated stream would deal with minor development applications, handled by a project coordinator.
- A facilitated stream would manage major development applications, handled by a project facilitator working with a team including an area generalist. Facilitated applications would then proceed to conceptual design and a decision before moving on to detailed design.
- A managed stream would deal with very complex developments, rezoning, or heritage rehabilitation agreements, drawing in specialist planners as necessary.

Critical to these new processes were the new roles for project coordinators, scopers, and facilitators (see Figure 61) through revised job descriptions for plan-checkers and planning staff. Driving the reforms was a desire to reduce the time required for permit processing by 80 percent for simple permits and for major applications by a third, both very ambitious targets.

A pilot project for the Development and Building Regulation Review was approved in March 1997. A team of nine staff was recruited and trained with the intention of assuming one-fifth of the permit-processing workload by mid-1998 and all of it by the end of 1999, when another nine members would join the staff. The team almost met the initial target and suggested that it

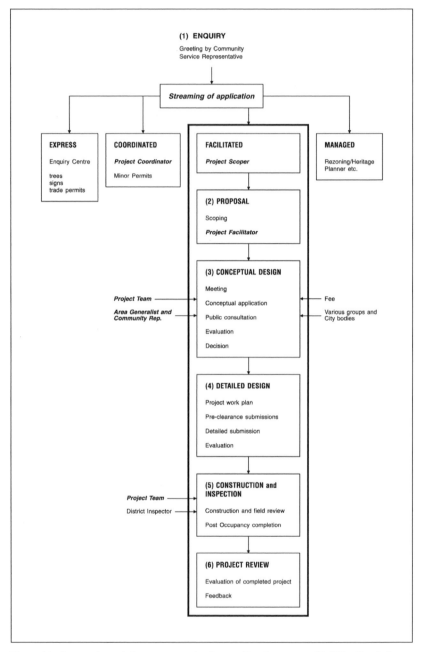

Figure 61 Proposed permitting process under the new Development and Building Regulation Review, 2000. This simplified diagram explains the review's four routes to a permit, with express and coordinated routes for minor projects. The facilitated route requires the project scoper to define the process and the project team, and the project facilitator to positively manage the process. (*Source:* Drawing by Jan Edwards)

could achieve an overall reduction of one-quarter the processing time. Evaluations of staff and user satisfaction with the new processes by the advisory committee and by external assessors conducted in mid-1998 were generally favourable. When reporting to council in July 1998, the service improvement manager was optimistic about achieving further economies in the $6.5 million allocated for the project, most of which was to pay for information technology. New targets were set to reduce processing times by 10 percent on simple projects, and by 25 percent on complex projects. An estimated 10 percent fee increase would be levied to recover departmental costs, once service improvements could be clearly demonstrated.

Problems of Implementation

By late 1998, problems were looming with the computer system, with community involvement, and with the lack of action on the simplification of planning and zoning regulations. Most worrying was the concern expressed by pilot team members that they did not possess "the tools and environment to do their work with excellence" (Vancouver 1998p: Appendix 6: ii). Implementation of the Development and Building Regulation Review was struggling, as other issues had become more significant. Many staff were finding it difficult to adjust to their new workload and role, and the loss of their contribution to broader planning activity. The dissatisfaction engendered union complaints about staff recruitment and about how the new Enquiry Centre and space for review teams would impact on departmental workspace at large. Three of the management team left, including the general manager – either fired or moving to other jobs – and council lost confidence in the way the review was being managed.

By mid-1999 a new management team suggested that, while the principles of the ongoing review were sound, its implementation strategy needed major revision. They suggested that it should focus on only five of the original twelve priorities. These included the development of the Enquiry Centre, the detailed procedures for project review, the formalization of new staff roles and organizational structures, an appropriate management structure, and building alterations to house the new processes. But further progress was dependent on advancing some elements of the other priorities, notably the investment in information technology. In September 1999, the Enquiry Centre was established with new procedures, including a telephone-inquiry component and, in February 2000, the new permitting system was introduced across the city. By that time, most of the work had been completed on a process guide to explain the new procedures. But it was becoming clear that staff could not cope with the introduction of the new processes, a backlog of applications, and a simultaneous increase in the number of applications –

without risking a return to increases in delays. So, although one of the original tenets of the reforms had been that there would be no net increase of staff in the Community Services Group, in mid-2000 a report to city council (Vancouver 2000i) requested that thirteen new staff be appointed over the next six months – five to the building permits and the rest to the development permits departments. The report suggested that new appointments would reduce the time for processing permits going to the Development Permit Board from fourteen-sixteen weeks to ten-twelve weeks, and for permits decided by the planning director from eight-twelve to eight-ten weeks, with a near halving of times to process building permits.

From a design perspective the request for two positions in the Urban Design and Development Planning Centre was particularly important because since 1997 the staff complement had been reduced from 7.5 (4.75 professional planners) to 5.75. The centre's workload in the late 1990s averaged 25 major applications annually going to the Development Permit Board, requiring the involvement of one staff person full-time and half the time of another. Some 650 other applications, in addition to 35-60 rezoning applications, required urban design assessment. It was estimated that single-family house applications zoned for RS-5 alone tied up one development planner's time, while all major projects like the trade and convention centre were especially problematic in terms of staff resources. The centre team had also lost its landscape architecture expertise. Some of the shortfall had been made up by the project facilitators in the Development Information and Application Centre, but they had found themselves spending three-quarters of their time on general urban design matters – rather than an anticipated one-quarter – at the expense of their application facilitating responsibilities.

By mid-2001, the Development and Building Regulation Review had weathered a lack of staff resources, a prolonged period of low staff morale exacerbated by the loss of the four-day week in 1999 and a municipal strike in late 2000, to begin to improve its service. The new Enquiry Centre was in place and working well, a new management structure was proving more responsive to staff, and the project facilitators were establishing their roles in the process, although not always without friction. The project coordinator posts had been filled and a guide had been written to explain all the stages and procedures in the new process. Some work had been completed on improvements to public notification; the development of a draft guide for public involvement, another component of the *Better City Government* initiative; and the development of monitoring measures of time allocated to customer inquiries. There were ongoing problems with the information system, which was to become web-based, and with the disaffection of plan-checkers, who felt their roles had been diminished. Processing times had improved but not as much as had been hoped. The five priorities defined in 1999 had been largely met, but the question of the broader goals of the review to ensure early community involvement, third-party appeals, and a broader decentralization of services remained outstanding. It will take a great deal of staff commitment to make the Development and Building Regulation Review work as intended.

Systematizing Development Charges to Finance Growth

Despite the implementation difficulties of the Development and Building Regulation Review, its relevance did not diminish, as evidenced by the continued support from the public and the development industry for a sophisticated, complex, design-sensitive, and relatively inexpensive system of permit processing. Successful development outcomes depend on all participants in the permitting process adding value to permit applications by improving their design and amenities and reducing their neighbourhood impacts and other externalities. Other major policy instruments that play a vital role in ensuring the latter are development-cost levies and community-amenity contributions that pay for parks, daycare, replacement housing, and other amenities and "soft" infrastructure. At the same time that the city managers and planners were reforming the permitting process, they also began pursuit of a more comprehensive system for financing growth, in response to both financial stringencies and the need to fund CityPlan's neighbourhood improvements. This meant working out a citywide system of development-cost levies on each permit, and community-amenity contributions on each rezoning, to pay for the necessary infrastructure to service major employment and population growth, and to ensure improvements in the urban environment, neighbourhood amenities and facilities, and citywide services. The public-amenity benefits accrued from waterfront megaprojects had demonstrated what could be achieved. The task was to set appropriate levies for all development that would cover infrastructure costs and not significantly impair the health of the development industry (see Figure 19).

By 1996 city officials had begun to investigate the question of how future growth might be financed and how inconsistencies and inequities in the current system might be eradicated. CityPlan recognized citizens' demands for new services and, simultaneously, senior governments' downloading of service costs to the municipality. It emphasized council's long-standing commitment not to raise the property tax above the level of inflation, but projected needs for more subsidized housing, more parks and open space, and better transit facilities by enabling rather than providing transit (the latter is a regional responsibility). CityPlan rather ducked the issue of how it was going to pay for the neighbourhood facilities, services, and environmental improvements that were necessary to accompany urban intensification. But it did set down some important principles under the banner of financial accountability, which emphasized "a cautious approach" to future expenditure and more public consultation on budgeting matters. CityPlan promised that its directives would lead to a re-allocation of funding. It mentioned development-cost charges, user charges for environmental services, and road pricing as potential new sources of funds, and it emphasized the need for a strategy to fund amenities and local services to support the development of neighbourhood centres (Vancouver 1995a: 44-45).

It was generally assumed that CityPlan Neighbourhood Visions would provide area-specific public-benefit strategies that would vary according to how each community chose to accommodate growth. This was what had happened in the Arbutus Neighbourhood in south Kitsilano between 1989 and 1992, and in Oakridge–Langara in 1996. In the former, the redevelopment of the brewery offered the opportunity to develop a mixed-use neighbourhood at higher densities. Direct provision of social housing and park space was anticipated – or community-amenity contributions would be levied. In the remainder of the Arbutus Neighbourhood, development-cost levies at $43 per square metre ($4 per square foot) were set for daycare (90 percent) and street improvements (10 percent). The park board expressed its dissatisfaction that no funds were to be provided for parks despite the proximity of Connaught Park, but planners were more concerned to ensure provision of social housing and more residential units (see Plate 58). The experience in the Arbutus Neighbourhood and in the Joyce/Vanness development around the SkyTrain station (see Plate 31), suggested that perhaps the major project amenity standards were too high and should be reduced to ensure more viable projects, particularly where the city was seeking to promote schemes for low-cost rental and, therefore, reducing developer profit. Communities were learning through pro forma analysis what amenities cost and what could be afforded through different densities.

A major issue for the city was that these area-specific designations for the collection of development-cost levy or community-amenity contributions covered only selected small areas (see Figure 19). Furthermore, development-cost levies applied only to larger developments, emphasizing the inequities of the system. There were clear needs for, first, a citywide study to assess development costs and, second, the preparation of a policy to collect adequate funds to meet them. The provincial government had produced *Development Cost Charge: Best Practices Guide*, in 1997 which provided valuable parameters and criteria. As the city formulated its approach, a major row blew up over suggestions that it might consider recouping all increases in land value produced by rezoning, and the Urban Development Institute wrote to the

Plate 58 West 11th Avenue, Arbutus Neighbourhood. This neighbourhood, planned 1990-91 on an old brewery site, was developed primarily with 4- to 6-storey apartments that respond to the existing grid pattern of streets. The grid was broken on 11th Avenue (pictured) to reinforce the neighbourhood centre on Arbutus Street and create a continuous retail frontage above underground car parking.

mayor to oppose this idea, which, they argued, would "confiscate private property rights" and "remove all incentive" for redevelopment (Urban Development Institute 1997). The city drafted the proposals in a discussion paper entitled *Financing Growth in the City of Vancouver* (Vancouver 1998v). The basis of its calculations and subsequent proposals are worth exploring in some detail.

Exploring Growth Costs and Potential Development Levies

During 1997 the policy options became progressively refined, as a better understanding of the city's growth costs and the implications of different types and levels of development and taxation emerged. Estimates were made of new service demands using the 1994 *Livable Region Strategic Plan* figures of 120,000 new residents and 76,000 new jobs in the city by 2021 (GVRD 1994). Rough costing of those items covered in existing development-cost levy policies that were allowed under the Vancouver Charter – such as replacement housing, parks, daycare, water/sewerage, and highways – suggested some $969 million in capital costs over the next twenty years (Vancouver 1998f). More detailed subsequent studies have put the capital costs at $1.2 billion, with the cost of parks lower than projected, and housing and engineering costs higher. Meeting these costs could be achieved through a 12 percent increase in the tax base maintained over a twenty-year period – not an attractive proposition to any council, but particularly not to the Non-Partisan council, which was committed to keeping increases at or below the level of inflation. It would be particularly unpopular with businesses, which already paid the highest taxes.

Estimates suggested that 50 percent of the projected population growth and development would not be subject to development-cost levies or community-amenity contributions because it would take place in areas where charges were not applied. A further one-sixth of the total population growth would be exempt from levies because it was in housing of less than four units. The case for citywide application of development-cost levies and community-amenity contributions was obvious, but the identification of significant financial shortfalls, even with this change, suggested that their projected levels needed to be raised significantly. Alternatively, standards of amenity and service provision could be reduced, not a popular suggestion from the perspective of residents, the park board, engineering, or housing departments.

The co-director of planning, Ann McAfee, addressed these issues in her February 1998 discussion paper, which proposed a comprehensive study of financing growth and interim citywide levies (Vancouver 1998f). Three alternative levels of development-cost levy were discussed:

- full cost recovery – $170 to $200 per square metre
- average levels in the regional district – $80 to $100 per square metre for residential uses and $15 to $30 per square metre for industrial and commercial uses – which covered about half of growth-related costs
- existing development-cost levy rates – $25 per square metre for residential and commercial uses and $10 per square metre for industrial – which covered about 15 percent of growth-related costs. These would add $2,125 to the cost of a standard condo as compared with 1997 levies of $11,073 in the suburban municipalities of Richmond and $15,980 in Surrey.

Ann McAfee's report also argued for citywide imposition of community-amenity contributions on private rezoning. Four different approaches were considered: (a) using existing community-amenity contributions ($30 per square metre, allowing for citywide development-cost levy); (b) taking a percentage between 50 and 100 percent of the increased land value; (c) calculating the value of standard requirements site by site (as in the megaprojects); or (d) combining all three methods into a blended approach.

The planners preferred the blended option because a simple flat rate could be used in most cases, but the capture of significant increases in land value where these occurred was also allowed (Vancouver 1998f). A strong argument in favour of this approach was that much higher development levies were established practice in other municipalities of the Greater Vancouver region. There, policies or proposals for rezoning bonuses varied from taking half of the uplift in values – in the City of North Vancouver – to all of it – in Burnaby's town centres. But site-specific zoning policies were not in existence in those jurisdictions. Development charges throughout the region ranged widely but 1999 median values were $45 per square metre for residential, while those levied in Vancouver varied from $32.50 in Oakridge–Langara to $93.60 in Triangle West (1998 figures: Vancouver 1998ff). In reality, each municipality was struggling to develop a rational policy that responded to actual growth costs and to levy equitable rates across the full range of development. The highest levies had begun to have an impact on development activity.

The city manager's discussion paper was debated by the leading members of the Urban Development Institute in January and March 1998. The institute maintained its opposition to the "subjective and arbitrary charge on development that is unrelated to real community needs," arguing that "the city's proposed policy sends an emphatic 'anti-business' message to businesses operating in an already fragile economy" (Urban Development Institute 1998). The institute argued that the current levies for major projects were seriously flawed and, while in need of review, could not form the basis for the current review. The institute was willing to consider "a system of known fixed charges, provided the cost calculations and their application are part of a transparent public process where the industry is a major participant" (Urban Development Institute 1998). Most developers regarded the development-cost levy as a necessary evil to meet basic infrastructure costs and, so, accepted reasonable levies. However, community-amenity contributions on rezoning were much more controversial because they were regarded as arbitrary, imposed project by project, and often prejudicial to development feasibility. While planners and politicians pointed to the achievements in False Creek North and Coal Harbour, developers regarded these megaprojects as special cases where cheap land had enabled the developers to meet community-amenity contributions and still make healthy profits. Where land values were nearer market rates, or where remediation costs were high, developers considered community-amenity contributions to undermine development viability. They cited as examples CityGate and Southeast False Creek, where the original development proposals could not bear these costs and major adjustments had to be made to ensure viability (see Chapter 6).

Pro Forma Analysis and Community-Amenity Contributions

There were two interesting examples of the problems of trying to recapture increased land values on site-specific zonings. One of these was in Arbutus

Village, a Westside neighbourhood in Arbutus Ridge. For a proposal to build a residential tower on a 4-hectare (10-acre) site in the car park of the local shopping centre, the developer offered $1 million to the city for an upgrade to the community centre and local recreation facilities. City staff had the project independently appraised and suggested $5-6 million. The cost of meeting park standards in an area already well endowed with parks was put at $3.5 million. The project was abandoned. A second rezoning application in adjacent Arbutus Gardens sought to replace 450 rental units with 750 condominium units, and the city proposed a $3 million levy for various public benefits, traffic calming, and adaptable housing for seniors. The community-amenity levy was calculated at $150 per square metre, about three times the rate suggested by city policy, but the city also wanted to own the 20 percent affordable component required, valued at $10 million by the developer. For his part the developer noted that the neighbourhood was actually opposed to such housing. The design of the development, an important issue in this affluent neighbourhood, elicited concerns about tree preservation, rooflines, and elevation treatment (i.e., mock Tudor), as well as adaptable life-time housing. While the developer argued that the costs of meeting the design requirements in this affluent area should reduce the community-amenity contributions, the city manager questioned whether the "gold-plating" of the development justified reduced payments for other community amenities. Once the developer's financial contribution was agreed during negotiations, there was a notable diminution in the quality of the detailed designs submitted for approval.

The potential conflicts between pro forma analysis and design review, and between neighbourhood amenities and design quality, are particularly clear in this example. Even though both community-amenity contributions and design review are principally aimed at protecting the character and amenities of the neighbourhood, the problem remains of ensuring that development makes a wider contribution to city livability – in the latter case offsetting the loss of 450 rental units – beyond merely fitting in well with its immediate surroundings.

Approval of Financial Review and Interim Policies

In December 1998 city council approved a study of growth-cost financing and proposals for an interim citywide development-cost levy bylaw and community-amenity contributions policy. This was to be included in the city's next capital plan, a financing strategy for replacement and upgrading of the city's infrastructure and facilities. Seven major tasks were defined for the study, including a review of existing standards that had evolved largely from the megaprojects, and a review of options for financing growth, embracing property taxes and utility charges, and development levies and their economic impacts (Vancouver 1999k). Legislative changes to the Vancouver Charter were to be considered, including removing the development-cost levy exemption from projects for single-family, duplex, or triplex housing – a potential reform identified by the province – and adding in street expenditures for transit, pedestrian, and cycling improvements. The whole process was to involve the province, regional bodies, municipal boards, and civic departments, as well as the development industry and the public. The review's working methods were to include "small, intensive working sessions and surveys," following Vancouver's tradition of collaborative policy making.

In January 1999, following a month of public review, council approved an interim bylaw for a citywide development-cost levy (Vancouver 1999i). This was set mostly at $27 per square metre ($2.50 per square foot) to be implemented in January 2000, so as not to interrupt current developments. Council also approved an interim policy for citywide community-amenity contributions for private rezoning at a flat rate of $30 per square metre on the increase in allowable floor space, with immediate effect; the sole exemptions were social housing, churches, and heritage projects. Developers had been given significant concessions. They were to pay community-amenity contributions only on the net gain in floor space and the payments became due not when the rezoning was made but when the development permit was issued. They were also granted a year's grace on the implementation of the new bylaw. The report acknowledged that developers had lobbied against recouping land value uplift on private zoning and the implementation of citywide development-cost levies, but noted that they had "previously confirmed [their] ... willingness to accept a set of development-cost levy and community-amenity contributions charges" (Vancouver 1999k: 4). Overall, the adopted interim bylaw and policy were a very conservative and inadequate response to the problems.

It would appear that the development industry fought a successful rearguard campaign against the interim bylaw and policy, which will collect only between a quarter and half of the estimated growth-related capital costs over the next twenty-five years. Developers were aided in their arguments by the economic slowdown, by the acknowledged long lead times in development projects and their susceptibility to changes in costs, by the recent introduction of regional development-cost charges for sewerage, and by provincial proposals for a levy of $1,000 per residential unit to contribute to the restoration fund for leaky condominiums. As there were also hints of regional water and transit levies and provincial school levies, it was not an opportune time to increase levies and contributions. The fact remains, however, that developers with projects in the City of Vancouver are paying substantially less than those with projects in adjacent municipalities. Some of this difference can be accounted for by the need for suburban municipalities to create brand new infrastructure for development on previously undeveloped lands (i.e., greenfield development), whereas in Vancouver basic infrastructure already exists. As unit-by-unit redevelopment is generally more expensive than greenfield development, this argument is hard to sustain.

Vancouver's pursuit of the full recovery of city costs for development projects goes on. The Interdepartmental Team, coordinated by CityPlan staff, is developing policies for public review in 2002 (Vancouver 2001j). Working alongside a resource group of developer and construction interests, resident business interests, and infrastructure interests, the team has estimated growth costs until 2021, based on an additional 100,000 people and 93,000 new employees, at $1,227 million. Over half of this, $720 million, is to be met by senior governments and various dedications. Of the remaining $507 million, nearly 90 percent is in projects eligible for development-cost levies, of which parks could receive $197 million, replacement housing $156 million, pedestrian and cycling facilities $66 million, and childcare $25 million. To recover these costs, the city will have to raise its development-cost levy rate from $25 to $60 per square metre. The rate to be levied is the key policy choice.

Whether to include all minor residential development in the development-cost levy, perhaps at a low rate of $10 per square metre, is another major issue, as is whether to charge different development-cost levies for commercial and residential. Council will have to decide which land uses would be exempt from development-cost levies and establish advance allocations for how revenue will be spent. The latter is important to the establishment of long-range facilities plans for neighbourhoods as part of CityPlan visions. Challenges to community-amenity contributions policy on rezoning include whether to provide a flat rate – currently $30 per square metre – or a percentage of the uplift in land value – two-thirds has been suggested – or to negotiate site by site. There is debate over whether to include sites smaller than 4 hectares (10 acres), the current threshold within the system. One important discovery by the consultants (Coriolis Consulting) is that most of the cost of the levies and contributions comes off the land price and does not raise house prices. They acknowledge that this may change if levies are raised above 10 percent of land value, and if market prices level off. Clearly, much political work remains to be done to establish an effective and equitable growth-financing system.

Adequate Neighbourhood Infrastructure and Efficient Processes?

The socio-environmental quality of Vancouver depends on the adequacy of the infrastructure, facilities, and amenities provided, and the establishment of a fair and effective citywide system of development taxation to meet the costs of growth. The interim charges, operational across the city since the start of 2000, will not meet expected needs. Unless council is prepared to set higher rates for development-cost levies or take a higher proportion of the uplift in land values created by rezoning through community-amenity contributions – 67 percent has been suggested – then planners will be unable to deliver the strategic objectives of CityPlan. They will be unable to finance the specific amenity, environmental management, service, and facility improvements that will be necessary to make intensification acceptable to the neighbourhoods. If the neighbourhoods do not see adequate benefits coming from additional development, or if the property tax has to be used to meet the shortfall in revenues to finance growth, then the entire CityPlan strategy may become untenable, NIMBY attitudes may intensify, and the problems of housing affordability and social exclusion will deepen. A frustrated development industry, under- or over-protected neighbourhoods, or inadequate public benefits and infrastructure to accompany growth, or a combination of all three, could easily unpick the progress made in the last decade. The success of the CityPlan strategy depends on effectively addressing all three issues simultaneously.

The Financing Growth Initiative and the Development and Building Regulation Review are works in progress. Both have made significant strides to 2001, but neither has yet achieved the fully reformed process initially anticipated. Development control processes are notoriously difficult to reform and the planners aimed very high. The debates about permit processing reveal just how contested Vancouver's discretionary planning system has been over the last two decades. They reveal the downside of the ever more complex zoning bylaws and design guidelines. The litany of complaints is familiar to all those involved in development control wherever they are practiced – but each complaint has a justifiable planning riposte (see Figure 60). One could be forgiven for thinking that little has changed but, year by year, small innovations have been made to permitting processes that have improved the system considerably.

Many of the development industry's most constructive suggestions for improvement have become components of past and current reforms. The key improvements include the introduction of a pre-design conference; more transparent Urban Design Panel procedures; reduced numbers of applications going to the board and panel; the appointment of more skilled development planners; the establishment of the Enquiry Centre; and most recently the creation of project facilitators and streamed applications. The system has been under constant siege, but while the debates of the 1980s were whether the city could tolerate a discretionary system, the debates of the late 1990s were about how such a system could be made more effective and efficient. Much remains to be done, both within the existing reform program, and then addressing the broader issues of community involvement, third party approvals, simplification of regulations, and single-family zoning. But what is impressive about the Vancouver system is the way that it has improved its permit processing, managed administrative discretion, and established a constructive and effective design negotiation process with highly skilled inputs from the development planners and the Urban Design Panel. Simultaneously it has also sought to ensure the citywide provision of a high level of neighbourhood facilities and amenities that will complement design quality and ensure social inclusion and community development. Whether there is the political will to take these agendas through to their logical conclusion is another matter.

9
Discretionary Control and Design Quality, 1997-2000

Having examined the persistent criticisms and resulting reforms of the permitting process, we can now analyze contemporary permit-processing practices and evaluate their outcomes. The focus remains upon "due process" as a key component of progressive design review. The current deliberations of the Development Permit Board and Urban Design Panel are examined to reveal the way in which plans, policies, zoning, and design guidelines are employed to control the nature, content, form, and external appearance of development. Particular attention is focused on the way in which different actors and agencies on the planning side operate, the advice they give, and the responses of architects and their clients. Their collective views on both the processes and their outcomes are explained to provide rounded evaluations of the approved designs and, where possible, the completed scheme. Four distinctive characteristics of the permitting process will be examined. These include the absence of political intervention into permit decisions and the full delegation of decisions to a Development Permit Board composed of senior city officials; the use of a Development Permit Board Advisory Panel to advise the board in its deliberations and to provide an all-important balance to its decision making; the use of an Urban Design Panel to provide specialist architectural input into the permitting process at both the outline and detailed design stages; and finally the use of a group of architect-trained and private sector experienced development planners to positively manage major permit applications throughout the process. These are all slightly unusual features of permit processing that have taken thirty years to refine. How well these elements work collectively is the subject of this chapter. It should be remembered that this is a system undergoing reforms (see Chapter 8), but the procedures and decision making described here, as applied to twenty-five or so major applications annually, are unlikely to be radically altered by the Development and Building Regulation Review. As a preliminary, the process for assessing minor applications will be explained and contrasted with the processing of major applications.

Review of Minor versus Major Applications

An important part of Vancouver's permitting process is the distinction made between major and minor applications and the different processes that have been developed for each. Development permits are required for all development except minor accessory buildings, interior alterations or non-structural maintenance and repairs, fences under 1.2 metres (4 feet) in height, changes of use except within retail or office buildings, and residential demolitions. The application process for minor developments (i.e., individual houses conforming to existing zoning) is simple and quickly handled by plan-checkers in the permits and licences department of the Community Services Group. Permits take a few days to be processed, and development and building permits can be combined. Decisions are taken by staff in the Development Information and Application Centre. More complex minor applications go to a development application group. Again, a plan-checker reviews the application for conformity to bylaws, plans, policies, and guidelines, and circulates it for comment to various city departments, health, and fire services. If design guidelines are involved, then one of the architecturally trained development planners will review the project and carry out any necessary negotiations. Under the new organization of Development Services its director has the authority to take all permit decisions (on behalf of the general manager of Community Services: see Appendix 3). The Enquiry Centre will handle all inquiries, and the Processing Centre will take the decisions.

The review process for major applications is much more complex and involves various different bodies and procedures. Major applications are those that are considered to have a significant impact on their surroundings by virtue of their location, scale, and context. They include most significant developments in downtown and its margins, multiple-dwelling districts, and comprehensive development districts, the latter covering redevelopment areas that are given site-specific rezonings. Any application that is likely to prove controversial will also be taken through this process. A major development requires a great deal of supporting documentation, is assigned to a development planner, is subject to a wide range of consultations with a number of expert bodies (i.e., the Urban Design Panel), and is reviewed by the Development Permit Staff Committee, chaired by a senior official from the planning department with representation from engineering, park board, and housing.

The first step in the process is a pre-design conference with a development planner. This 1985 innovation is required before a major application can be submitted. This establishes all the relevant bylaws, plans, policies, and guidelines that apply to the site and the general urban design considerations that will come into play. To ensure that planners get their views across at the formative stages of a design, and that architects and their developer clients do not waste their time with ideas that are contrary to policy, applicants are advised to analyze the site, its context, and relevant policy and guidelines before the pre-design conference, but not to embark on design or even sketch schemes. A preliminary development application is recommended but not required to determine basic use, density, form, site, massing, and contextual impact issues, and to gain approval for the basic concept of a proposal. The complete application can then proceed with a greater degree of confidence.

A complete application requires, among other things, a written design rationale and demonstrated compliance with zoning, official development plan, and design guidelines; a list of requested relaxations or variances; a description of the site and its heritage resources; a statement about how the scheme fits into its context and with other adjacent developments; existing streetscape photographs and photo-montages of the project; view, shadow, and microclimate analyses and daylight angles; full landscape plans; coloured elevations; and a model at a scale of 1:2,000 metres ($^1/_{16}$:12 inches). This long list of application requirements ensures that architects have fully considered all design parameters and that all parties have the information they need to evaluate the design. It is one of the best practice features of the Vancouver system.

Once the pre-design conference has been held, the application can be made and the fee paid. A plan-checker will circulate the drawings to all relevant consultees, check the history of the application, and notify neighbours. The applicant must erect a site notice advertising the application. The development planner then contacts the applicant to discuss relevant planning and design issues and responses from consultees, and conducts all design negotiations. Key consultees are the Urban Design Panel, the neighbourhood planning committees, and, if relevant, heritage advisory committees. The development planner then presents the application to the Development Permit Staff Committee, with the relevant plan-checker and an engineer in attendance. The staff committee reviews the application and prepares a report, including advice from persons consulted, and an overall summary with recommendations. Appended to the report are copies of the applicant's design rationale and reduced copies of the drawings. The report is reviewed and forwarded to the Development Permit Board and its advisory panel members three days prior to the scheduled meeting. Under the new permitting system, project facilitators take on much of this administrative and management role, liaising with the real estate department over pro forma analyses and the like, leaving the development planners to concentrate more on urban design (see Figure 61).

The Role of the Development Planner

At the heart of the discretionary process are the city's development planners, who are responsible for piloting all the major applications through the permitting process and ensuring that they meet all the zoning regulations and design guidelines. They also ensure that, as far as is possible within the rules or guidelines, development proposals meet with approval from residents, lobby groups, and the Urban Design Panel. The development planners are qualified architects, with private-sector experience. In 1980, two development planners were appointed for the first time. In the mid-1990s, four more were added and, now, there are seven to manage the discretionary process throughout the city. Each also has responsibility for a particular type of zoning, and the monitoring of its effectiveness; to enhance the planners' experience, the responsibilities are rotated. Development planners are now part of an Urban Design and Development planning section alongside rezoning, heritage, and current neighbourhood projects (see Appendix 3). Both central area planning and current planning initiatives are under the control of the director of current planning, Larry Beasley, who has opportunities as a member of the Development Permit Board to ensure that design matters are fully considered and resolved. So the development planners now stand outside the permitting process, though they conduct the negotiations over interpretations of the zoning and guideline requirements, presenting the application to the Urban Design Panel, and pursuing the latter's comments with the applicant. They are also largely responsible for the preparation of the comprehensive report to the Development Permit Staff Committee, which is also used to brief the Development Permit Board and may include a long list of conditions. A full report is included from the Urban Design Panel on the design of the proposal, noting areas of concern. There are also summaries of public comment and staff responses, and a brief report from the Development Permit Staff Committee on its deliberations. Included with each report is a list of staff committee conditions tailored to the application; a set of notes regarding deadlines for completion of the application, and the development; and a set of reduced drawings illustrating plans, sections, and elevations of the proposals with the design rationale written by the architect. Having been through the Development Permit Staff Committee, the major issues on the permit application should have been resolved, and the Development Permit Board can focus on the conditions to be applied, as has been the case for every application since January 1997.

Any board approval is subject to a list of conditions that have to be fulfilled *prior to* the issuance of the development permit, and to achieve this revised drawings and supporting information have to be submitted to the satisfaction of the director of current planning, in practice the development planners themselves. Most schemes are still being designed in detail when they go to the Development Permit Board and much work still remains for the development planner to do afterward. They must ensure that the conditions are fulfilled and that all the design details are implemented satisfactorily. A recent dispute over building materials on a major project, discussed later, has emphasized how vital this task is, and how much it relies on trust between city planners and developers.

Development Permit Board and Its Role

The Development Permit Board, comprised of the director of current planning, the city engineer, and the director of social planning (the latter replaced in 1998 by the deputy city manager), take the decisions on all major applications through voting. The Development Permit Board was always chaired by the planning director until the position was vacant in the early 1990s. Then, the role was performed first by the successive associate directors of Land Use and Development and, after Development Services was separated from planning, by Larry Beasley, the director of current planning. In November 1998, when a fourth member of the board was appointed as an independent chair, the role was given to Rick Scobie, the director of development services, in his capacity as the manager of the permitting process. Now, the chair has no vote and plays no decision-making role but is able to manage and facilitate decisions, while the director of current planning remains one of the three voting board members. This idea of an independent chair was a reform urged by the development industry in 1981 and 1984 when Ray Spaxman chaired the board and again in 1996-97 when Larry Beasley assumed the chair, and is a response to the powerful interventions that these individuals tended to make in the discussions.

Council delegates all decisions on applications to the Development Permit Board, although the board occasionally refers matters to council for advice, where major policy questions are debated or where the legitimacy of a decision might be questioned (e.g., stretching a heritage bonus, intruding on a view corridor). The Development Permit Board's decisions are free from political interference – one of the most important features of Vancouver's permitting system and one which contributes enormously to its technical proficiency and consistency of decisions. In most instances the Development Permit Board approves the development permit with conditions or occasionally defers the application. If an applicant's proposal is refused, or if the applicant wishes to have certain conditions modified or waived, then he or she can appeal to the Board of Variance. Between January 1997 and July 2000, no major applications have been refused and therefore there have been no major appeals.

The Development Permit Board's proceedings commence with a presentation from the development planner responsible for the application, outlining major issues and staff recommendations. The board and its advisory panel then review the drawings and models of the application displayed in the meeting room. This is followed by a presentation from the applicant – often the architect and the developer/applicant – responding generally to the development planner's recommendations, specifically the conditions identified in the Development Permit Staff Committee report. Often the architect or applicant will seek to have particular conditions deleted or amended, perhaps because further design work has rendered them obsolete or because of their impacts on other aspects of the scheme.

Meetings of the Development Permit Board are held in public and members of the public can address the board after the applicant has presented his/her response to the development planner's recommendations. To emphasize the board's independence, politicians do not attend its meetings. Minutes of meetings from 1997 to mid-2000 do not reveal much public comment, but there are occasions where the public turn up in force to oppose or support an application. In recent years these have included condo owners aggrieved by view blockages created by new residential towers; residents associations criticizing the provision – or not – of non-market housing; neighbours alarmed by the location of health, social, or residential facilities for the sick or addicted. Even if resolution of these issues is beyond the remit of the board, their importance as planning matters is not diminished.

Members of the board and its advisory panel may ask questions through the chair to clarify issues in any presentation. The advisory panel is then invited to discuss the application, usually hearing first from the chair of the Urban Design Panel, who reports on panel deliberations and details its concerns. The chair then invites each member of the advisory panel to speak. Finally, board members review the staff recommendation and conditions, and vote on the overall decision; they may also make amendments to individual conditions. The decision of the board and minutes of the discussion are subsequently posted on the city's website and sent to the applicant and other participants.

The Board's Advisory Panel

Appointed by city council, the Development Permit Board Advisory Panel includes two representatives each from the design professions and the development industry, and four representatives of the general public, creating a balance of development and public interests. The chair or deputy chair of the Urban Design Panel is one of two representatives of the design professions. The opinion of each member of the advisory panel is sought by the chair of the Development Permit Board on every application, but they do not vote on the decision. The purpose of the advisory panel is to ensure that the discretion allowed to city planners and officials is exercised appropriately.

The chair of the Urban Design Panel is usually the first member of the advisory panel to speak, explaining the Urban Design Panel's decision to support or not support an application. The chair's remarks are invariably the most substantive and wide-ranging comments made on the design of the development by the advisory panel, and they set the tone and direction for much that follows. The second design profession representative, who is not a member of the Urban Design Panel, can offer some additional comments on the application and the conditions to be imposed but his/her views are rarely at odds with those of the panel chair. Development industry representatives do not generally have a lot to say about the application beyond indicating their broad support (i.e., approve in principle). They occasionally pick up on particular design issues, such as density, massing, open space, or public realm treatments. Surprisingly, their intervention can be as much to question whether a project has really earned a particular increase in floor space (i.e., the discretionary component), as it can be to assert that certain conditions are unnecessary. They are markedly less critical in their comments than the Urban Design Panel chair and less inclined to get into matters of detail. Very occasional barbed comments are forthcoming over, for example, the need to subject social housing agencies to the same scrutiny as private developers, planners being over-prescriptive, or the need to consider project viability as well as planning requirements. But it is more common for the development representatives to support the conditions being imposed and not to question them. Occasionally the chair of the Development Permit Board will ask development industry representatives to comment on aspects of commercial viability or development practicality where their experience can help the board in its deliberations. Overall the development industry representatives have no apparent criticism of the process, decisions, or the conditions imposed.

The public's representatives have more to say than the development representatives and they are more inclined to talk about liking a development or finding a project "distinctive," "beautiful," or "exciting." In the past, however, individual members of the public have developed particular preoccupations

that they have consistently contributed to discussions. The most readily identifiable of these have come from women interested in the provision of recycling facilities, cycle racks, good lighting, and general personal safety
concerns, as regards the design of development. But otherwise, rather like
the development representatives, comment from the public picks up on one
or two particular issues (i.e., tower dimensions, landscaping, or public realm
treatment) but leaves substantive debate on conditions to the board itself. In
1999, council implemented a request from the advisory panel to have a young
person on the advisory panel to represent a broader spectrum of opinion; as
yet, it is not possible to detect any distinct perspective emerging from this
representation. Overall, the advisory panel has been successful in providing
a consumer's view of the permitting process and a check and balance on the
planners' exercise of discretion and the Development Permit Board's internal
deliberations, but it does not appear to make decisive interventions.

Board Deliberations

Advisory panel deliberations are followed by the Development Permit Board
discussion. Board members frame the motions to alter conditions or to approve, refuse, or defer a project. One of their roles is to provide expert
contributions on matters of infrastructure, streets, community facilities or
amenities, and city decision making. They also have to identify the points of
consensus among advisory panel members and to translate these into amendments of conditions as necessary. The members of the board who are not
planning staff are there primarily to ensure that the planners administer the
policies, regulations, and guidelines accurately, fairly and efficiently, and use
their considerable discretion in an appropriate manner.

The city engineer and the director of cultural affairs, who served on the board
until June 1998, often voiced well-informed judgments on planning and urban
design issues and participated fully in quite technical discussions on particular conditions. The city engineer and now his deputy offer their professional
expertise on such issues as street treatments and landscaping; public realm
improvements; traffic management; and access, servicing, and car parking.
The deputy city manager, who has replaced the director of cultural affairs on
the board, is very planning literate, and keeps an especially keen eye on
matters of administrative efficiency and the implementation of the broader
corporate goals of the council. He seems equally at home as his predecessor
in discussing details of conditions and the substance of applications.

The return to the board of Larry Beasley in November 1998 as co-director
of planning in a voting capacity has changed the dynamics of the board's
deliberations. Gone is the rather gentle dialogue between the city engineer
and the director of cultural affairs, replaced by a much more intense and

deeper assessment of the content and quality of schemes and the conditions to be imposed on applicants. This is reflected in a tougher questioning of the development planner and, to a lesser extent, the applicant, following their presentations. It is also reflected in the fact that the co-director tends to take the lead in framing motions to amend conditions. From Larry Beasley's perspective, an important aspect of his job description is ensuring that the development planners are performing at a high level and that as much design value as possible is added to a development (interview). As an expert himself on board practice, having frequently chaired it over the last decade, and as director of central area planning for much of the 1990s, he has an almost unrivalled knowledge of the interface between permitting and policy and guidelines. He also has a clear vision of overall planning strategy and an especial interest in the urban design qualities that each piece of development should achieve. Ensuring that he is extremely well briefed for each meeting, he visits the site of each application with the development planner, rehearsing his questions, and spending time poring over the drawings and the model. Other board members and developers consider him to be a master tactician in managing discussions and directing arguments.

Some architects and developers perceive a return to the 1970s and 1980s, when the planning director was able to control all the outcomes of the board's deliberations. This is much less of a threat than in the 1980s because the director of development services occupies the chair, but concerns about the conflicts of interest inherent in the system remain. The co-director of planning has assumed a double role, managing much of the work of the development planners and then commenting on their work as a voting member of the board. There are complaints about excessive interference in the work of development planners and attempts to re-do their work by the board. But the current co-director's view is that it is his professional duty to ensure both that maximum value (i.e., better design, facilities, and amenities) has been added to an application through the negotiations, and that major discretionary decisions are fully weighed and tested in a public arena.

Many architects and developers who have presented applications under both Ray Spaxman and Larry Beasley note numerous similarities in style and influence. However, Spaxman's control over proceedings was absolute as director of the former planning department and chair of the board, despite frequent tussles with city engineers. Spaxman had more influence over the whole approval process and rarely compromised his opinions. Beasley's influence is more subtle and his interventions more calculated, and his role has not really been diminished by loss of the chair. Now he has more freedom to pursue his planning and urban design agenda and to argue more forcefully, unencumbered by the even-handedness demanded of the chair. These issues of personality, expertise, and personal influence, while important in Vancouver's development arena, must not obscure the carefully structured processes of the board and its advisory panel. These have been designed and repeatedly refined to ensure that the enormous discretion provided to city planners is exercised according to prescribed regulations and guidelines in a fair and efficient manner. Current evidence suggests that this is being achieved.

Decisions of the Board, 1997-2000

Reviewing the deliberations and decisions of the Development Permit Board over the last four years, one can make a number of general observations. The board sees only about twenty-five applications annually and, with bi-weekly meetings scheduled, it has plenty of time to discuss the substance of each application in detail. The board approves virtually every application it receives, only occasionally deferring its decision. Members of the board themselves are almost always agreed on a decision, although occasionally a motion on a particular condition is defeated or not supported unanimously. Similarly, the advisory panellists are rarely at odds with the board in their views or with a report's recommendations, suggesting that a high level of consensus is achieved. The board rarely makes a major amendment to a condition, and it will delete a condition if it is convinced, through discussion, that the applicant is resolving the issue. It is inclined to make a number of minor revisions, adding conditions relating to such matters as cycle stands, garbage facilities, safety matters, or particular detailed design failures, often responding to concerns voiced by the advisory panel. While applicants frequently seek to be released from particular conditions, only very rarely does their response to the written or oral reports or discussions spill over into strong disagreement or dissent. Finally, the board occasionally experiences difficulties in making decisions as a result of being constrained by an official plan, zoning regulation, or design guideline. The board chair occasionally has to remind the advisory panel that only council can change policy and the panel is bound to follow existing regulations and guidelines. Issues that have aroused spirited debate include the protection of single-room occupancy properties, the floor-space generosity of C-2 zoning, apparent failures to consult properly on applications, or overgenerous interpretation of heritage bonuses (see Figures 55, 34, and 52, respectively). Such debates send messages to planners and council about the need for policy reform. But they have not prevented the board from performing its decision-making duties in an efficient, effective, and fair manner. (Various other examples of the board's decision making are illustrated in Figures 49, 55, 57, 64, 65.) While board decisions largely take the form of amended or new conditions for the development planner to follow up, they also highlight the major design issues that the board wishes resolved.

Urban Design Panel and its Role

The Urban Design Panel origins as an Architectural Advisory Panel in 1956 and its revised brief (1973) have already been established (see Chapter 3). Because the Panel was frequently a focus of developer antipathy, key changes were made in 1984 to reduce the number of permit applications it saw, and in 1991 to open panel meetings to the public, allow applicants to present their designs, and to remove the planning department representative. These changes have helped to make the Urban Design Panel's procedures more open and transparent, and its role in decision making clearer. The panel is composed of twelve members appointed by council. Half are members of the Architectural Institute of British Columbia, while two panellists are drawn from each of the Association of Professional Engineers and the British Columbia Society of Landscape Architects. One member represents the development industry and one represents the Vancouver Planning Commission. Members, who receive no remuneration, serve for two years and the chair is appointed from among the members to serve for one year.

Prior to meetings, members of the Urban Design Panel are sent sets of drawings to familiarize them with the scheme, with display materials, and, usually, a model made available at the meeting. The chair manages the meetings, summarizes discussion, and sits on the Development Permit Board Advisory Panel, where he or she can explain the Urban Design Panel's position in detail. Design and development teams may attend to hear discussion of their projects. A secretary records full minutes on each discussion, which are sent to the architects and developers whose schemes are discussed and posted on the city's website for public consumption. Meetings are public but regrettably very few people or local media attend, so any educative value of panel deliberations to the wider public is largely wasted. The public cannot speak at meetings, but opening them up to the public has raised the standard of debate and criticism and made participants more professional, consistent, and constructive in their comments (interviews).

At each meeting, the Urban Design Panel usually has three or four projects to discuss, so they have to be brisk and well chaired to ensure in-depth coverage of issues. A standard procedure sees the development planner managing the application present the proposed development and the main design issues on which the panel's advice is sought. Most applicants make a presentation, although they are not required to do so. Panel members then peruse the display materials and the model, often engaging one another – and sometimes the development planner, architect, or developer – in discussion to clarify points. When the panel reconvenes, the chair requests discussion, and allows everyone to make a comment. After discussion, the chair again asks individuals to summarize their views and a vote is taken. One of three outcomes – support, non-support, or deferral – is possible and only this decision is subsequently reported to the Development Permit Board. As the panel chair is a member of the Development Permit Board Advisory Panel, he or she can highlight design issues and explain the panel's thinking.

The Urban Design Panel sees some twenty-five to thirty new major rezoning or permit applications a year, commenting on some twice – very occasionally three times. The panel may also see some twenty minor applications annually that do not go to the Development Permit Board. These are selected by development planners who consider that they would benefit from the panel's advice. Some of these, such as proposed rezoning for C-2 development where residents' opposition has been intense, can constitute the panel's most important work. The Urban Design panellists' criticisms are expert and well articulated, tending to reflect their individual area of professional expertise, and it is a considerable task for the chair to draw them into a coherent whole.

Peer review by the Urban Design Panel is a very sensitive issue for many design professionals, as in most such evaluations (Scheer 1994). Not all architects who come before the panel are comfortable with it, but most acknowledge the value of the comments to their design thinking. It is also interesting to note that certain architects seem able to gain unanimous support from the Urban Design Panel the first time, although from time to time every architect has a project whose brief is likely to cause design controversy or dissension. Few applicants take issue with, or exception to, the Urban Design Panel's comments. Doing so would probably intensify rather than diminish the criticism. Panel chairs have noted that this is an unwritten convention, despite the fact that the panel is ultimately only an advisory body. The minutes record one or two examples where an architect has expressed frustration at the advice. This may be because of conflict between development planner and panel advice – for example, the proposal for 1400 West Georgia, where development planners wanted to retain townhouses and the panel sought a better tower design and landscaping – or because of conflicts between the client's brief, residents' views, and panel comments – for example, the application for Traders restaurant at Bayshore Drive, where the architect could not achieve the necessary architectural refinement with the floor space the client required on such a tight site. These very rare exceptions prove the rule that the panel's constructive advice is generally well received by applicants.

Panel Votes and Advice, 1997-2000

A detailed analysis of the minutes of the Urban Design Panel decisions taken between January 1997 and July 2000 establishes the impact of the panel's advice on development schemes. The schemes the panel examined were grouped into neighbourhoods with distinct design policies, in an attempt to control for sites and context. Figure 62 shows a breakdown of the pattern of panel voting according to the level of support for each scheme, and provides a measure of how generally support increased for schemes, because an applicant followed panel advice. Several general conclusions can be drawn. About half of the schemes presented to the panel gain unanimous support at their first presentation. These are schemes where the panel has no significant reservations about the direction the design is taking, although it will make comments that the development planner will translate into conditions on the development permit to be resolved at the detailed design stage. A further 16 percent receive "strong support" (i.e., have only one dissenting vote) at the first presentation, and in these cases there is a stronger likelihood of panel reservations finding their way into conditions. A quarter of submissions, including many from the latter category, gain unanimous support at their second or subsequent presentation. These are schemes where the developer/designer has taken on board previous reservations of the panel and successfully addressed them. Half of these cases (13 percent) were not supported at the first presentation; the other half represent cases where the developer/designer has sought to get unanimous, as opposed to mere majority, support. Again points raised by the panel may be translated into conditions to guide detailed design. Overall, three quarters of the schemes the panel vetted over the period received unanimous endorsement, a reassuringly high figure that suggests that the city has succeeded in getting a high standard of design in its major development applications as a matter of course.

Some eighteen schemes (12.5 percent) are not supported when first presented, but are unanimously supported at a subsequent presentation. Figure 63 identifies these "most improved" schemes and explains the changes made by the project architects in each case. Of the remaining one-fifth of schemes, some make do with a simple majority at first or second presentation (7.5 and 4.5 percent, respectively) and the remaining 9 percent are not supported at the second presentation. The fate of most of the latter cannot be determined without interrogating other data sets (the panel comments on many applications that are not within the Development Permit Board's jurisdiction).

In almost all cases the panel's views are echoed in both the Development Permit Staff Committee (officer's) Report and the Development Permit Board's discussions and minutes. The 1997 panel chair noted that during his tenure five non-supports were ignored by planners, but only one such case seemed to reach the Development Permit Board. Here the panel chair himself considered that the conditions imposed on the application in the committee report covered the panel's reservations, and voted to support the scheme at the board. This was a particularly prominent case, a 32-storey residential tower at

Figure 62 Urban Design Panel: votes and issues, 1997 to mid–2000

	No. of submissions	First or subsequent	Support			Non-support			Dramatic improvements	% not supported	Key design concerns
			Unanimous	Strong	Narrow	Unanimous	Strong	Narrow			
Downtown	19	1	7	1	2	–	2	1	2	16	Elevations and public realm
		2	4	–	2	–	–	–			Weather protection and entrances
Downtown South	17	1	4	1	1	1	1	1	3	29	Tower and street-wall: position and refinement
		2	3	1	2	–	1	1			Ground-plane treatments and public realm
Triangle West	14	1	1	1	–	2	1	–	2	36	Massing and private view obstruction; slimming towers, refining elevations
		2	3	4	–	–	–	2			Public and private landscape
Downtown Eastside	16	1	10	1	1	1	–	–	0	13	Refining elevations and materials, private space, security
		2	2	–	–	1	–	–			Lighting
False Creek North	17	1	10	3	–	–	–	–	0	6	Refining podiums, private space
		2	2	–	1	–	–	1			Public realm and open space
Coal Harbour	13	1	8	3	–	–	–	–	0	0	Refining towers and townhouses: private space
		2	2	–	–	–	–	–			

Area	n		1 / 2						Comments
Uptown (around Broadway)	34	1	9	3	3	1	3	1	4 — 21 · Tower massing and views, corner massing, streetscape elevations
		2	9	3	–	–	2	–	Courtyards and sidewalks
Westside (west of Cambie)	37	1	18	3	1	3	–	2	5 — 19 · C-2 zoning, intensification issues
		2	6	2	–	–	1	1	Residential elevations and massing: neighbourhood impact
Southside (south of 41st Ave.)	24	1	4	4	1	2	3	–	3 — 33 · Design of commercial/residential on arterials: SkyTrain stations and lines;
		2	6	1	–	1	2	–	mall intensification
Eastside (east of Cambie)	24	1	4	4	1	3	2	2	2 — 33 · Major hi-tech office park application
		2	3	1	3	–	1	–	
West End	12	1	5	2	–	2	–	–	0 — 25 · Bayshore projects – little comment
		2	–	2	–	–	1	–	One restaurant problem
									(excludes consideration of Convention Centre [7 submissions])
Sub-totals:		120	40	18	17	20	12	21	27
Totals:	227		178			49			

Figure 63 Urban Design Panel: most improved submissions, 1997-2000. These are the applications that, over a three-year period, were strongly criticized and voted against on their original submission, but which subsequently won unanimous approval. They epitomize the value of the panel as a peer-review system.

Dates	Address	Area	Type of Development	Voting 1	2	Key design changes executed
11/97	488 Robson	D	300-foot residential tower and gallery	2-5	6-0	Improved tower design, top, and especially corners; improved landscape and private space
6-12/98	1001 Hornby	DS	450-foot hotel tower	1-7	9-0	Improved caps, elegant tower, reduced podia; impact-transparency
11-12/97	1221 Homer	DS	14-storey residential tower	1-5	7-0	More refined, simplified elevations; broken-up base; improving ground plane
9-10/98	940 Seymour	DS	230-foot residential tower and 6-storey street-wall	3-4	8-0	Reshaped tower and asymmetric floor plate; increased tower separation; height reduction of low rise
8-10/98	1138 Melville	TW	16-storey office	0-5	6-0	Taller, slimmer tower; better daylight; materials and lighter colour palettes
2-4/00	1400 W. Georgia	TW	Residential tower and townhouses	0-7	8-0	Softened tower base; improved townhouses; improved landscape connections; reconfigured open space
3/97	428 W. 8th	UT	Live/work studios	3-4	8-0	Improved street frontage; enclosed staircase (complete model)
12/97 & 2/98	1768 W. Broadway	UT	2 towers	3-5	8-0	Complete revision, relocated tower at corner, strong street-wall; improved lane
4-7/98	1742 W. 2nd	UT	45 residential units above retail	0-7	5-0	Light industrial character: improved lane elevation and parking

Date	Address	Area	Description			Comments
11/97-2/98	3330 S.E. Marine	W	Church gymnasium	1-4	9-0	Improved height and form; reduced car parking
6-7/98	3585 W. 40th	W	3-storey live/work studios (C-2)	0-7	5-0	Reduced by one storey; good massing and fit now
9/98	2079 W. 42nd	W	4-storey residential above commercial (C-2)	3-4	4-0	More compatible townhouses; improved drugstore treatment
2-3/97	5629 Dunbar	W	4-storey residential above commercial (C-2)	2-5	7-0	Rear facade softened, more interest and more in scale; improved entrance; friendlier street frontage
6-7/97	2176 W. 10th	W	4-storey residential	0-5	7-0	Minor changes, major improvement; moved closer to street; better amenity space
7-9/98	990 W. 41st	S	5-storey residential and institutional	0-6	9-0	Increased massing at corner; positive landscaping
9/98-1/99	Champlain Mall	S	Mall refit and major residential	1-4	5-0	Improved site planning: generous open space; better relation to context
4-7/98	5605 Victoria	E	2-6-storey residential and revamped drugstore	2-5	4-0	Improved residential/livability; store roof improved; improved pedestrian environment
2-3/98	3550 Van Ness	E	Residential tower	1-7	10-0	Relocated tower; reduced floor plate; reconfigured street relationship; redesigned cornice

Note: D = Downtown; DS = Downtown South; TW = Triangle West; UT = Uptown; W = Westside; E = Eastside; S = Southside
Source: Compiled from panel minutes

501 Pacific Boulevard, where the scheme met the Downtown South guidelines (see Figure 64). Panel and development planners were slightly at odds with their advice about conflicting geometries of the tower form and the quality of space at street level. However, the members of the public on the Development Permit Board Advisory Panel voted to support the scheme. Overall, instances where panel advice is ignored are extremely rare. In most respects its advice effectively guides both the applicant preparing the permit application, and the development planner preparing the list of conditions for the permit approval.

Panel Design Concerns Area by Area

Turning to the area-by-area analysis reveals different patterns of support and non-support, different patterns of scheme improvement, and also distinct urban design issues (see Figure 62). For example, where the megaproject planning process has carefully prescribed basic built forms, and there are detailed design guidelines (in False Creek North and Coal Harbour), there is strong panel support for the design of the proposed developments and virtually no instances of non-support. Here the relatively few controversies relate to the panel wishing to modify the design guidelines in the interests of a particular architectural solution. Also, in downtown and the Downtown Eastside, where the design guidance is much less explicit, there are comparatively few examples of non-support (but there were no major office schemes over the period of study, and only a few hotel schemes). The social housing schemes in Downtown Eastside were well received by the panel, maintaining their tradition of retaining good designers.

Substantial panel criticism has been evident of schemes in the mixed-use, formerly largely commercial areas of Downtown South and Triangle West. Here the absence of a master plan (within an official development plan), and relatively high floor-space ratios (5.0-6.3) set to encourage redevelopment, have encouraged the insertion of tall residential towers and street-wall apartments and townhouses, and raised a range of design controversies. In Downtown South the guidelines encourage a diversity of architectural expression as well as a consistency of architectural form, but there are particular problems with view corridors that limit tower positions, and the high floor-space ratios put pressure on slim tower floor plates and drive up heights. There are also many differences of opinion about the disposition of floor space between tower and podium, about the treatment of the building at street level, and about how the tower and base should be treated architecturally (see Figure 49). Downtown South is also the area where the panel find themselves most at odds with the design guidelines, arguing that they are tending to produce "an undesirable sameness," despite the stated encouragement of

Figure 64 501 Pacific Boulevard: reactions of the Urban Design Panel and Development Review Board. This is the only clear example of the Development Permit Board discounting Urban Design Panel advice in the last three years. The building is permitted by the zoning even if it seems too tall for the area, but it will merge with the new Beach Neighbourhood towers to be built in the next few years.

Address and Location
501 Pacific Boulevard,
 Downtown South

Project Description
32-storey market residential on
 3-storey commercial (11 units) /
 residential amenity podium:
 248 units

Zoning and Bonuses
DD / 5.0 / 300-foot height relaxation
 to 307 feet: predominant unit size
 relaxed from 400 to 327 square feet

Architect and Client
Hewitt Tan Kwasnicky / unknown

Urban Design Panel
03/97 *0-8 non-support.* Great potential of elliptical floor plate but weak where it hits the ground: needs to define public and semi-public space and improve landscaping. Should have been a preliminary application.
05/97 *1-7 non-support.* Weakened by presence of two geometries: entrance too weak but courtyard improved. Need to soften orthogonality. Significant tension with development planner's advice.

Development Permit Board
06/97 *Approve.* City values small market suites and concierge system to manage it. Welcome open space on townhouse roofs: conditions to express the Urban Design Panel's concerns. Advisory panel likes it and counteracts Urban Design Panel's disquiet.

Source: Compiled from panel and board minutes

Plate 59 Downtown South apartment towers. Various tower forms have been adopted in Downtown South, where the guidelines encouraged "creative architectural expressionism" and sculpted tower tops. This view east across Nelson Street at Granville shows the 13-storey building, The Spot (left), on Seymour and the 34-storey Pinnacle on Homer Street (centre), between the more recent 955 Richards tower to the right.

architectural diversity (see Plate 59). In Triangle West there are particular problems with new towers blocking private views from adjacent towers and townhouses, and the need to dispose space in such a way that views north over Burrard Inlet are preserved. Slimming the towers and refining their elevations are the major concerns of the panel.

In uptown, where a mix of commercial, residential, and institutional (medical) uses is intensifying, all the above-mentioned issues have been aired by the panel, largely because of the diverse character of the area and its particular topography. The design constraints include the admixture of floor-space ratios and land uses, the importance of views northward, the more difficult lighting conditions on north facing slopes, the adjacency of much low-rise residential development, and the C-3A zoning that permits a wide range of commercial uses and compatibly designed residential. These pose considerable challenges to both an acceptable streetscape and a quality public realm.

In the outer neighbourhoods at large, a very diverse set of major proposals has been vetted by the panel. In the less affluent eastern and western residential neighbourhoods, some 40 percent of first submissions are not supported. In all the neighbourhoods there are particular problems with intensification on the arterials, where because C-2 zoning allows 3 storeys of residential above a commercial ground floor, overlooking problems and view blockage are created for single-family housing areas to the rear (see Figure 34 and Plate 33). The panel has had particular success in refining both the elevations and the massing of these low-rise apartment blocks, and encouraging the reformulation of the zoning code.

The Panel's Preoccupations

What is most noticeable about the Urban Design Panel's advice is the way it has embraced the essential principles of the city's regulatory system. This is evidenced by panellists' insistence that applications must earn their maximum floor-space ratio and additional density or bonuses through better design or amenities. These issues came to the fore in debates about heritage bonuses for the Dance Centre on Granville Street, where only one facade of the heritage-listed Bank of Nova Scotia was saved, and where panellists had to weigh the "audacity and excitement" of the Architectura/Arthur Erickson scheme against the loss of integrity of the historic bank (see pages 255, 258, and Figure 52). The principal design concerns of the Urban Design Panel, derived from frequency of mention in the minutes, can be summarized as follows:

- height, bulk, and massing, particularly tower width and shadowing impacts
- public and private views across the site and down adjacent streets
- enclosure of the street and its environmental comfort
- the design of the street level and ground plane to provide richness for the pedestrian
- concern with active uses and windows and doors on the street to support activity, safety, and surveillance
- the design of public space to ensure that it is sunny, well-lit, safe, and likely to be well-used
- the design of private and semi-private space so that it provides adequate amenity space for residents and especially children
- the livability of smaller units, low-income housing, and residential units on busy streets
- the need to minimize the impact of car-park and service access on pedestrian environment
- the adequacy of landscaping as an integral part of urban design
- elevational treatment, tower tops, and stylistic continuity throughout the scheme
- the choice of materials – especially weathering and wear – and the selected colour palette.

Although many of these considerations go beyond traditional urban design concerns into matters of architectural treatment and interior layout, most participants in the process seem comfortable with this. There are critics, including some panellists, who consider that the Urban Design Panel is continually drawn into discussion of matters of architectural detail at the expense of major urban design issues. But the development planners in particular value the deliberations on details because it helps develop an informed view on what would be best on the site.

The advice the Urban Design Panel offers tends not to be prescriptive about solutions. Instead, it clearly identifies design elements that would benefit from further consideration and makes suggestions about how such improvements might be achieved. Panellists themselves note that they are not in the business of redesigning projects. This perhaps explains why they are prepared to give some schemes unanimous support while still offering a long list of comments that might otherwise suggest disapproval of a project or a range of design problems to be rectified. If an architect can make a good presentation and convincing argument for a particular approach, the Urban Design Panel seems willing to support the proposal despite reservations about particular aspects of the scheme. A good example is provided by the second review of the rezoning for the Wall Centre, where the Urban Design Panel reversed firm non-support of the scheme to offer unanimous support for the final Peter Busby design, noting that: "[T]here is a tendency for some applicants to expect the Panel to explain what to do on a project. Architects must take responsibility for listening to advice (from both staff and the Panel) and making a strong argument" (Vancouver Urban Design Panel minutes: December 1998).

The relationship between the views of development planners and panellists regarding different schemes was the subject of a panel discussion in May 1997, and a number of their comments have already been noted. One statement in particular identifies a tension between panel advice and the extant zoning and design guidelines: "There is potential for planning staff to operate somewhat dogmatically in terms of requiring rigid adherence to guidelines rather than the underlying principles, which could lead to an undesirable sameness in buildings. There must be diversity within the guidelines" (Vancouver Urban Design Panel minutes: 21 May 1997). While the panel's perspective can be appreciated, there are clearly legal restrictions on relaxing guidelines that have been through public consultation and adoption processes. Activist members of the public and adjacent property owners are particularly concerned to ensure that any guidelines are respected, even when city development planners consider that a more relaxed interpretation is appropriate. An example is provided by the westernmost tower on Harbour Green, part of Coal Harbour at 301 Jervis. There, the panel wanted to allow townhouses to intrude into the view corridor down Jervis Street, which would have required a text amendment to the guidelines – a process likely to take about eight months. The developer and architect were understandably cautious but decided to go ahead to a council hearing where the director of current planning argued vociferously against it and won the day.

The Urban Design Panel has also sought regular briefings on emerging city policies and guidelines, and opportunities to discuss differences of opinion with planning staff. Correspondingly, the panel's advice is frequently sought by planners through workshops on major development schemes in their formative stages – where advice is provided but no vote is taken – such as the Southeast False Creek's sustainable development aspirations, the convention centre at Canada Place, and the Pacific Press redevelopment (see Figure 65). In the last four years the Urban Design Panel has been asked for its views on the design of SkyTrain stations, the downtown skyline study, public parks (Burrard), area-design guidelines (Beach Neighbourhood), hospital precincts (Vancouver General), high-tech office estates, and the future of the Cambie bridgeheads, so its advisory role is considerably broader than that of commenting on the design quality of specific permit applications.

Finally there are two other dimensions to the panel's deliberations that act to raise design standards in the city. Those architects who have served on the panel have noted how valuable they have found it personally to "sit on the other side" in design review deliberations, not least because it immerses them in the city's complex regulatory system, and forces them to come to terms with its realities. Serving on the panel implies a belief in the discretionary processes operated by the city and requires a considerable time commitment (unpaid) to make sure that it works. The existence of the panel, service on it, and rotation of membership all help to make discretionary review in the city much less adversarial, and help to build consensus about design issues between private-sector architects and public-sector planners in the close-knit design community that is Vancouver. This is especially important given the highly contested nature of the permit processing system over the 1970s and 1980s. Second, there is evidence to suggest that the panel has become a peer-review system in its own right. It seems to have become a matter of professional pride for developers/designers to seek a unanimous endorsement of their proposals when only a majority in favour is actually required, so a virtuous cycle of design improvement is further embedded in professional practice.

The Sad Story of the Wall Centre Tower

It is tempting to think of the Development Permit Board's decision as the final point in the permitting process. But a glance at the extensive conditions imposed on any major application reveals that a great deal of work still has to

Figure 65 2198-2298 Granville Street: reactions of the Urban Design Panel and Development Permit Board. Two blocks of major development provide a new landmark and contribute substantially to a new park (foreground) to the east of the Granville Bridge ramps. The architects recognized that not maximizing the density was the best approach to a permit. Design discussions were managed in exemplary fashion by the architects. Innovative design and bold use of colour and glazing set a precedent for this area.

Address and Location
Pacific Press, 2198 /
   2298 Granville Street

Project Description
Residential with retail (on Granville).
   South block with 360 dwelling
   units, 3-20 storeys. North block
   with 275 dwelling units, 5-11
   storeys

Zoning and Bonuses
C-3A / 3.0 with conditions:
   only seeking 2.81

Architect and Client
John Perkins / Bosa

Urban Design Panel

   Panel had workshop to discuss design approach and particularly explored the view blockage issues.

04/97 Phase 1 *7-1 support.* Strong support for a very successful scheme that conforms to C-3A zoning and earns the additional floor space. Does not maximize available floor space: support for the idea of a mid-block spine connector.

11/97 Phase 2 *9-0 support.* Very high-quality scheme and exceptional presentation. Liked asymmetry of scheme but felt NW corner had lost some strength. Mid-block pedestrian link liked but further detailing important. Need to better link architecture and landscaping.

Development Permit Board

6/97 (2198) *Approve.* Have allowed height relaxations. Still concerns about the position of the towers and view blockage. Strong public opposition: considerable relaxing of other conditions to improve views. Parkland given to city.

01/98 (2298) *Approve.* Loss of views are inevitable but there are possibilities of improvement by shifting tower 6 feet to west. Strong opposition from neighbouring properties but an exemplary scheme.

Source: Compiled from panel and board minutes

be done to ensure that the final design meets the expectations of the board and the Urban Design Panel. Resolution of the conditions is delegated to the director of current planning, whose advice is always available; effectively, the responsibility falls to the development planner who has handled the application from the outset. The process of finalizing the detailed design is largely unproblematic. It is based in large part on a system of trust between planner and developer and architect to fulfill conditions in the spirit of the board's approval and the Development Permit Staff Committee report. By a singular irony, this final step in the permitting system broke down with the city's tallest building, completed in 2001, causing enormous consternation to the development planner concerned, the city administration, and council. The city investigated the possibility of legal action against the developer, prompting the threat of a countersuit from the developer. The case threatened to undermine the entire discretionary system.

During its controversial permitting process, the Wall Centre went through many design guises as the developer sought to produce a building that would have maximum impact on the downtown skyline and could be marketed as the city's tallest structure. The developer, Peter Wall, is Vancouver's most bullish developer. His reflective glass towers are indicative of his general distaste for design guidelines (see Plate 60). His architect, Peter Busby, is regarded as one of the city's most accomplished and innovative. The man responsible for guiding the scheme through the process, Ralph Segal, has been a bastion among city development planners for more than a decade and has been largely responsible for building up their expertise and their working methods under the more recent guidance of Larry Beasley, director of current planning. So the actors in the process could not have been more experienced.

Peter Wall had acquired the city block that was almost the highest point in downtown, and which had only limited view corridor restrictions. He first approached the city with a scheme in 1993 but withdrew from negotiations when it was clear that the council was considering new height restrictions for downtown (see Chapter 7). By 1995, he had submitted a conception for a 45- to 48-storey tower clad in gold refracting-glass curtain walling. Later in that year, the notion of allocating one-third of the block to the creation of a square was discussed and the building had acquired considerably more architectural elegance with Peter Busby's proposal for a light grey, transparent, all-glass cladding. In August 1996 the proposal was considered by the Development Permit Board because the developer was impatient to get approval before the Vancouver Skyline Study was completed. Bonuses for a hotel and transferred density from the Stanley Theatre were used to gain the extra floor space to increase its height from 91 to 137 metres (300 to 450 feet) or 45

Plate 60 Wall Centre Tower, 1000 Burrard Street. Peter Wall's two earlier towers (at left and right in the photo) on this block exemplify his preference for dark reflective glass. On the new tower (centre), the difference between the glass in city-approved (upper storeys) and developer-selected (lower storeys) can be seen clearly, creating a monument to developer intransigence. Fortunately, the dark glass base of the tower is not seen from most distant vantage points.

storeys, using a deadline for the theatre purchase as a lever to encourage a quick approval. As the tower would intrude into the Queen Elizabeth Park view cone, the board referred the matter to council for a decision.

Council approved the scheme in February 1997 after hearing from the director of current planning on the compatibility of the tower with the prototypes then being considered as part of the Downtown Vancouver Skyline Study. Artists' impressions and publicity photographs of the scheme – described as "a slim shining shaft of light" – revealed a foil for Peter Wall's two existing dark blue/black reflective glass towers on the same block. However, as the cladding went on the frame, it became clear that – rather than the light transparent glass approved – a dark opaque had been chosen by the developer. This change was made despite the objections of the developer's own architect, and contrary to the expectations of everyone involved in vetting the scheme. One of the singular features of the scheme, and critical in gaining its approval, had been the promise that the building would be sheathed in "airy translucent" glass to reduce its impact on the skyline and the locality. Instead, the emerging tower was characterized by the press as the "Death Star" and its developer Peter Wall as "Darth Vader" (*Vancouver Sun*, 29 January 2000). Comparisons were made with the ominous, exclusive, impenetrable black towers like those that grace the corner of Granville and Georgia – the 1960s "towers of darkness" that had encouraged TEAM councillors to launch discretionary design controls.

Written specification of the approved glass could not be matched to the glass the developer was using, although the developer insisted that sample materials had been approved. A legal opinion suggested that there was some risk the city might not win a costly lawsuit and so a compromise was negotiated – by the director of current planning, with advice from the city engineer and architect James Cheng – whereby the bottom two-thirds of the tower would be completed in the dark glass but the residential top third would be finished in the light translucent glass anticipated by those approving the building. From many long-distance vantage points the tower appears much as intended (see Plate 60). Closer – from Robson Square, the West End, or up Nelson Street – its two-toned finish is a lasting reminder of the developer's ego and is a blight on a fine architectural statement.

The developer has subsequently revealed that he always intended to use the materials of his choice, whatever anyone else might say (Weder 2001). The business and development communities were appalled by his approach. Peter Ladner, president of *Business in Vancouver,* noted: "For the sake of one man's ego, a curse has been cast over not just one building, but over the whole process of trust between the city, its citizens, and its builders. Opponents of any new or daring addition to the city's architecture will always be able to point to the Wall tower and say: 'How do we know we can believe you?'" (Ladner 2000). However, Vancouver's major development permitting process has survived this setback. The process continues much as before, even though, regrettably, development planners now have to take greater care to tie down final scheme details to prevent a repetition. Everyone involved in this experience has been sobered by it, with the exception, it would appear, of Peter Wall.

Evaluating Processes, Skills, and Design Outcomes

The Wall Centre experience, fortunately, was an anomaly in Vancouver. In all other instances between 1997 and mid-2000, the Development Permit Board, its advisory panel, and the Urban Design Panel have worked toward a set of positive consensual decisions to approve close to 100 major developments in the city with no refusals of major schemes at the board. Given the highly contested nature of major permit processing over the last two decades, this is no mean accomplishment. Dissatisfaction on the part of the development industry and architects with the processing of major schemes had been long-standing, but nowadays there are few complaints about the system. The process, which delivers permits smoothly and steadily regardless of complexity, offers developers the high degree of certainty that they need. The innovation of the pre-application design conference has proved beneficial, as have the greater precision of the zoning and accompanying design guidelines, the thorough public consultation, and the wide use of conditions to allow detailed design to be resolved after the permit has been granted.

Overall, the major development permitting process in Vancouver and its design review component is transparent, rigorous, highly skilled, and consensus-seeking. It meets all the best practice due-process principles for progressive urban design review set out by Richard Lai and others (in Figure 1). There are clear a priori rules for intervention, sophisticated procedures for the management of officer discretion, constructive and effective permitting steps, and abundant provision of skilled advice to support the process. While the process is time consuming and resource intensive, it is also predictable. Success can be guaranteed if designers follow the regulations and guidelines and fully exercise their skills and imagination. Most importantly, it is a process that consistently delivers a quality product and that ensures developments worthy of their setting. Occasionally, when conditions are right, it delivers architecture and urban design that are excellent and innovative prize winning schemes that are providing valuable modern prototypes for medium- and high-density housing from which other cities can learn (see Plates 23, 32, 37, and 46) (see also Vancouver 1999e). A list of recent award-winning buildings appears in Appendix 1.

The Urban Design Panel is a model that could be widely copied. In Canada only the National Capital Commission in Ottawa has a similar body, but Vancouver's model has already been copied by Adelaide in South Australia (Brine 1997). Numerous features could be adopted by aesthetic committees and architects' advisory panels in North America and Europe. Most impressive is the way in which the Vancouver panel has become a peer-review mechanism in its own right, almost independently of its reports to the Development Permit Board. Serving on the Urban Design Panel changes architects' attitudes, enhances their presentation skills, and improves their understanding of guidelines, all of which help them when they come to submit permit applications. Incorporating them into the review process encourages them to share the same design goals as the planning department. The comments of the Urban Design Panel are also valued because they, in the words of one leading architect, "break the monopoly" of planners' views in the permitting process and provide instead an independent view.

The Urban Design Panel's views balance the pervasive roles of development planners and the director of current planning in the process, and the general power and precision of the guidelines. But the role of development planners is critical to quality outcomes. It has long been recognized that the planning department must recruit staff with appropriately high levels of design skill and private-sector experience who can command the respect of the architectural and development communities. Furthermore, they must be given the time to focus on the relatively few major projects, each year, and not be overloaded with minor applications. Their accomplishments are fully celebrated in a recent Vancouver planning publication, which argues that the achievements are the result of a "true public/private partnership" (Vancouver 1999v: i).

One leading architect has assessed Vancouver's permitting process as resulting in "medium high quality products." The guidelines and processes are deemed to be good at producing safe "background" buildings but cut out the truly innovative risk-taking design that might break the mould and/or provide those highlights of townscape so valued by postmodern urban designers and architectural photographers (interviews). This seems a fair verdict, but one slightly at odds with the summary statistics of Urban Design Panel decisions, which indicate that more than half of the schemes vetted by the panel receive their unanimous support, and another quarter have the support of all but one panellist. Arguably it is an evaluation for which any other city's design review process would settle.

10
Conclusion: Assessing Vancouver's Achievement

In the Introduction of this book reference was made to the popular local cliché that Vancouver is "a setting in search of a city." This is no longer the case. It is now a city worthy of its setting. Vancouver can justifiably claim to be a compact, proto-sustainable city with a livable downtown surrounded by a series of distinct high-density, mixed-use residential areas, whose residents need not commute by car but can walk, cycle, or use transit for many of their urban trips. Vancouver has protected most of the best qualities of its late-nineteenth- and early-twentieth-century suburbs, with their valuable legacy of Craftsman vernacular, their mature treed streets, and rich private landscaping. It has reinforced the commercial arterials of these suburbs to provide neighbourhood foci, pleasant meeting and strolling places, and a constantly changing pattern of services and shops. It has reclaimed its derelict industrial waterfront for public recreational use, completing the links in more than 20 kilometres of seawall and walk/cycleway encircling downtown, and linking urban and suburban beaches, parks, and leisure and recreational facilities. These amenities are transforming the city into a resort in its own right, quite apart from enriching the quality of life for its citizens.

Vancouver has significantly increased its vitality and civility and largely retained its safety as it has achieved its urban renaissance. In the words of its co-director of planning, it has sought to "bring out the competitive advantages of the urban lifestyle in preference to a suburban lifestyle ... to create an attractive surrogate for the single-family dwelling in the single-family suburb ... to facilitate a life experience even more exciting and convenient, yet equally as safe and secure" (Beasley 2000a).

In this concluding chapter, four different syntheses are executed. First "the Vancouver achievement" is summarized on three dimensions: the urban renaissance/regeneration in demographic and housing stock terms; the quality of urban form category by category, referring to different zonings; and its overall built-form quality. Second, the plans, policies, guidelines, and processes that have delivered these urban forms are assessed against the twelve principles of good practice urban design established at the outset of this study (Figure 1), and their strengths and weaknesses are identified. Third, the key contextual factors that have made this "achievement" possible are discussed. Finally, some of the future challenges to urban design and planning in Vancouver are identified, picking up on some of the weaknesses discussed earlier in the assessment of current practices.

An Urban Renaissance

The quantitative measures of Vancouver's urban renaissance are impressive. First, the city has reversed the population decline that began in the early 1970s. Between 1971 and 1991 the city's population grew by 70,000 people, but has subsequently increased more rapidly, adding another 50,000 between 1991 and 1996. Projections suggest a further 100,000 to 160,000 new residents will be accommodated between 1991 and 2021 and perhaps 93,000 jobs. The higher population figure would represent a 54 percent growth over 1971 totals. The most dramatic residential growth has been in the central area around the downtown core, a product of the Vancouver's "living first" policies on the margins of downtown and in the waterfront megaprojects where 40 percent of the city's growth has been accommodated. By 2021 the central area population is expected to increase another 50 percent over 1991 levels. Population density citywide has also increased markedly from 38 persons per hectare in 1976 to 49 in 1998, and may reach 60 by 2021.

With population growth has come citywide intensification. Seventy thousand new dwelling units have been added to the city's stock since 1971, which represents an increase of nearly 50 percent, or one-third of the current stock. Declining household size has been as much a factor as population increase in creating this residential demand. The nature of the housing stock has changed considerably. Whereas condos were only 20 percent of the market in 1951 they were running at 80 percent by the second half of the 1960s and returned to that proportion in the late 1990s, with single-family housing remaining at about 13 percent of completions (Vancouver 1999w). Rowhousing was significant between 1973 and 1994, but is now a very minor part of completions everywhere except downtown, where 1,000 townhouses have been built recently. The nature of the physical changes wrought by intensification must not be underestimated, with a large proportion of the central area growth being accommodated in high-rise housing. Despite this, Vancouver remains a predominantly low-rise city; about half is zoned for single-family residential use and very strong neighbourhood pressures exist to keep it that way. A 60:40 ratio in favour of owning a home in the early

1950s had shifted to a similar proportion in favour of renting by the late 1990s.

A substantive issue in relation to this population change and the accompanying patterns of development is housing affordability, expressed as the proportion of renters who can afford to buy a starter home. In 1998, when national indicators recorded 31 percent affordability, Vancouver was the most pressured metropolitan area at just below 20 percent. New house prices in the city rose 25 percent in real terms over the period 1986 to 1994 but, by 1998, that increase had fallen back to 10 percent as the housing stock increased. Single-family house prices have trebled and condo prices have increased by a third on the Westside, while single-family housing and new condo prices doubled on the Eastside in real terms over the same period. Housing rental levels have increased more modestly – less than 20 percent in real terms over the last fifteen years, despite low vacancy rates throughout the period. Social housing completions have fallen steadily, declining to a quarter of their 1989 level by 1997, although the city has helped provide nearly 7,000 new social housing units – about a tenth of the overall increase in housing stock – through owning, operating, or leasing land. Some measures of the current housing affordability crisis are the 10,000 people awaiting low-income housing in the Downtown Eastside and the estimated 10,000 single people looking for low-income units. Affordability is critical for young singles, and older single-room occupants: 42 percent of the former and 60 percent of the latter are estimated to spend more than 50 percent of their income in rent. So the poorest pay the highest rentals per square metre in the city. For these residents, it is no exaggeration to speak of a housing affordability crisis. Although occasionally Victoria claims the title, Vancouver has recently been the most expensive major urban housing market in Canada.

Housing affordability is one measure of livability on which Vancouver does not perform well, and a number of other indicators give mixed results. Only 150 heritage buildings are protected, up from 60 in 1986; about 1,800 are still unprotected, but demolitions of protected buildings have slowed to about 10 per annum, about a quarter of the level in the 1980s. Transportation and traffic measures are ambiguous. Car commuting grew by about 25 percent in the 1980s but, in the 1990s, has remained largely static into and out of the downtown peninsula and throughout the city at large. Transit ridership has increased by about a third since the 1980s (prior to the recent SkyTrain extension) but bus use has hardly increased at all. For its population density, Vancouver has low public transport use. The city has not built any freeways since the 1960s and made only very minor additions to its road capacity, but traffic growth has continued steadily. Nonetheless, downtown air quality has improved notably, monthly mean indices falling by half since 1981. More positively, planting of trees along streets has more than doubled since 1976 and the city has projected the creation of 140 kilometres of greenways. Cycle paths have increased by nearly 100 kilometres and 5 kilometres of new seawall walk and cycle paths have been built in the downtown peninsula, backed by more than 26 hectares of new waterfront parkland and another 9 hectares to come in Southeast False Creek.

Distinct Neighbourhood Character and Quality

But Vancouver's achievement in creating one of the world's most livable cities does not rest solely on its repopulation statistics, its "living first" downtown, its intensification and compaction, its increasing transit orientation and reliance on walking and cycling, or its clean air and commitment to green spaces. Arguably more important to environmental quality has been the consistent excellence of new residential development achieved by the city and the way that this has consolidated existing neighbourhoods and created entirely new ones. When discussing the city's urban design, most commentators focus on the high-density residential megaprojects that have been developed on the waterfronts. But good-quality residential design has been much more widespread, and the city has invented a variety of zoning designations, densities, and guidelines to deliver, and perpetuate, a wide range of housing forms and neighbourhood types. The 1991 Central Area Land Use Plan (Vancouver 1991c) set out a typology of residential forms over a range of densities, as part of an attempt to formulate livability policies (see Figure 66). This diagram has been annotated to show the key residential zonings, floor-space ratios, and locations that deliver these built forms. A simplified zoning map identifies their locations (Figure 67). The six housing types identified in Figure 66 are now discussed in turn to evaluate Vancouver's urban design achievement.

Single-Family Housing

The single-family areas are the exception in the typology because, by and large, they have severely restricted if not excluded intensification. There has been redevelopment of smaller houses to provide larger ones, and extensive provision of secondary rental suites, mainly on the eastside of Vancouver. The city went through a monster home invasion in the 1980s and the response was the invention of RS-5 zoning, which allowed larger houses only if applicants followed elaborate contextual design principles for architectural treatment and landscaping. The design guidelines produced a major improvement in the design of single-family housing in the eyes of the community (80 percent positive) and the planning department, and significantly increased levels of architectural patronage (from 10 percent to 50 percent, even to 75

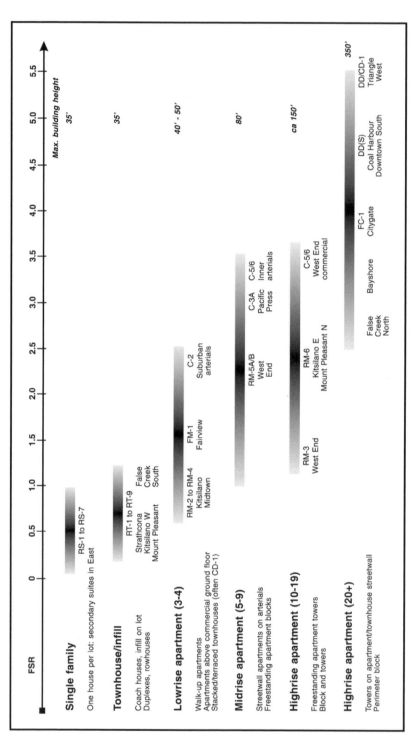

Figure 66 Residential density, building type, and zoning in Vancouver. A version of this diagram was included in the 1991 central area policy statement to illustrate planners' thinking about the relationship between zoning types, floor-space ratios, built forms, and neighbourhood character. It provides a concise description of the various forms of development that have been promoted by planning practice since the 1970s. (*Source*: Extended and redrawn from Vancouver [1991c])

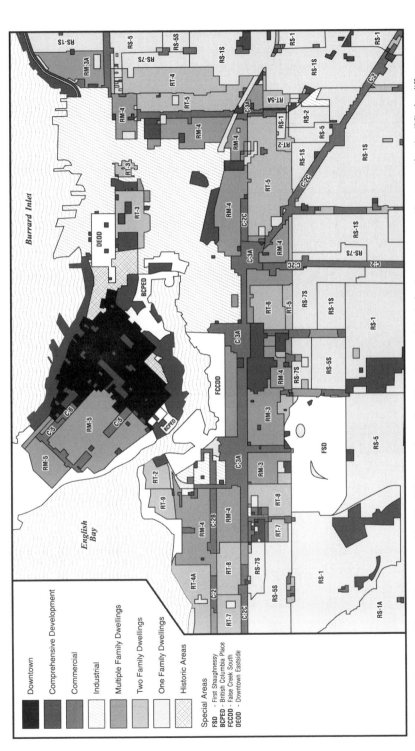

Figure 67 Zoning map of Central Vancouver (simplified). This map shows the different types of single-family zonings operating across the city (RS), the different intensities of residential development (RT/RM), and the commercial (C) zonings on the arterials. *(Source: Cartography by Jan Edwards)*

percent) (Vancouver 1999l; 1999c; 1999d) (see Plate 61; also Plate 30). Architects are less enthusiastic about the new zoning because of the constraints it imposes on their creativity. Most residents in single-family neighbourhoods, however, are convinced of its value and requested similar controls, sixteen neighbourhoods requesting them in 1996, and five more requesting the RS-7 zoning variant in 2000. From the perspective of ensuring contextual designs and protecting neighbourhood character and amenity, RS-5 zoning was a great success. However, the reinforcement of single-family character at a time when the city was facing high demand for small units of affordable, ground-oriented housing was a retrograde step and furthered an already dramatic inflation in single-family house prices. So the system delivers very high-quality housing design, and a careful contextual approach to development, but at the cost of housing choice and affordability. The new zoning and its discretionary process requires much more staff resources for what are numerous but individually minor applications. Housing design quality and neighbourhood character have been enhanced but in many locations, social exclusion has been reinforced and the RS-5 zoning has become a neighbourhood protection service for the more affluent.

Townhouses and Infill Housing

Areas with townhouses and infill housing span a greater range of floor-space ratios than do single-family units, and generate substantially more dwelling units. Many, however, were former rooming-house neighbourhoods that were gentrified in the 1970s and early 1980s, so they are only slowly regaining previous densities. The RT zoning that covers these areas was devised with the "intent ... to permit side by side two family dwellings," thereby encouraging selective redevelopment, but at the same time it aimed at retaining existing character buildings and conserving neighbourhood character. One might include variants of RM zoning in this same category because these emphasized the retention of existing buildings and good design (RM-4/4N), neighbourliness and respect for streetscape character (RM-5/5A, B, C), and for the Craftsman vernacular homes. The emphasis varies from a heritage preoccupation in west Mount Pleasant, to retention of family character in east Mount Pleasant and Grandview–Woodland, the encouragement of affordable housing in Strathcona, or the promotion of redevelopment of small houses in west Kitsilano. Only in Kitsilano Point on English Bay is there more of an emphasis on new building. So, while these zonings can retain neighbourhood physical character, they allow for conversions and extensions and the creation of a range of smaller housing units to take advantage of the back lanes that exist on most city blocks (see Plates 28 and 62).

Typical new house: no design review

Older house: example

Partial design review: example

RS-5 house, full design review: example

Full design review: example

RS-1 house, no design review: example

Modern design: example

Modern style house: example

Plate 61 Recent single-family house designs in Dunbar (right) and Kensington–Cedar Cottage (left). These photographs from their respective vision documents illustrate the architectural freedom that traditionally existed and the increasing tendency to copy the vernacular that has been encouraged by RS-5 zoning in Dunbar.

These zoning designations and their comparatively simple design guidelines have been very successful in retaining the character of the street, the boulevards, front yards, and traditional house forms. The major changes occur in the back lanes, which are being urbanized by new 2-storey structures, incorporating garages for both old and new properties. To a considerable extent, these developments are tidying up and organizing what are often rather neglected, run-down garages and rear fences. Where development is well designed, a new vernacular is emerging in which building frontages enliven and overlook the lane. But regrettably many lanes may well lose their greenery and become dominated by blank garage doors and carports, with the housing looking inward. Nonetheless, such neighbourhoods can provide large numbers of new housing units in well-serviced, accessible areas and they are good examples of new urbanist ideas in practice (Toronto 1991c).

The emphasis on maintaining "existing external character" and "compatibility" of new development has produced widespread historical reproduction stylings that have aroused the ire of the heritage conservation lobby (see Plate 62). They argue that it is now very difficult to tell what is original and what is new in these areas. While this is undoubtedly the case, it may be a price worth paying to ensure that the overall environmental quality and visual character of the neighbourhood is maintained, while significantly increasing the number of households that might be accommodated. Vancouver needs

Plate 62 RM-4 infill at Yukon at West 13th Avenue. Intensification in multiple-family zoning areas in Mount Pleasant is taking on the character of full historical reproduction. The solution here is similar to that employed at the back of the mayor's house (Figure 23) with a private second-floor deck above car parking space and garage.

more of this zoning in single-family areas to allow modest levels of intensification and expansion of the stock of small unit, ground-oriented housing.

Low-Rise Apartments and Stacked Townhouses

Low-rise, street-fronting apartments have been built in the city since the turn of the century, some having been developed to 6 or 8 storeys. The RM zoning was largely applied in the 1970s to the innermost neighbourhoods just beyond the old industrial belt to permit apartment development, but medium- and high-rise housing was allowed where large sites could be assembled. The RM zoning spans the range of 0.75 to 2.5 floor-space ratio and can be usefully linked with C-2 zoning, which allows for 3 storeys of apartments over commercial ground-floor units on many arterial roads. Walk-up apartments began as rather functional, flat-roofed rectangular buildings, their plain elevations relieved only by balconies. Occasionally they would be given some architectural treatment such as "moderne" stylings, "shingle" finishes, or, later, some postmodern flourishes (see Plate 9). Their saving grace was the requirement for underground car parking that obviated the problem of cluttered streets and paved lots on-site. A popular Vancouver form that emerged in the mid-1980s was the stacked or terraced townhouse, particularly in areas zoned RM-4, but the same form also evolved in many small comprehensive redevelopments (zoned CD-1 with densities between 0.75 and 1.5 floor-space ratio). The form adopted all manner of domestic stylings from the Tudor revival through Craftsman to more neo-moderne forms, always with underground parking, sometimes with small private gardens and/or balconies (see Plate 63). The best designed projects fitted unobtrusively with their lower-density vernacular neighbours, but whole streets of such developments often lacked the on-site landscaping necessary to soften and screen the more derivative architectural styles. In Fairview Slopes, a special zoning encouraged multiple units at a smaller scale to respond to topography, views, and mixed uses (FM-1). While the units, often townhouses, continued to address and enclose the street, there was much experimentation with semi-private courtyards and pedestrian lanes linking off the street to provide intimate entranceways and semi-private spaces within each complex (see Plate 64). While they can create interesting townscapes, they can also result in quite claustrophobic interiors and private spaces (see Plate 7).

Regrettably, many of these housing units – largely those built between 1983 and 1998 – have proved to be defective, mostly because they were inadequately weatherproofed and penetrating damp has rotted their wooden frames. The "leaky condo" phenomenon of the late 1990s was the result of poor quality construction, cutting corners to maintain profitability. However, a range of building science failures can be traced to poor interpretation of the

Plate 63   Multi-family townhouses, 2315 West 10th Avenue. This development overlooking Connaught Park was designed to look like two large Craftsman houses. The eastern block (pictured) takes advantage of its corner lot location to create a new frontage on Vine Street. This design by Nigel Baldwin Architects, with Phillips Farevaag Smallenberg as landscape architects, shows how intensification can be achieved with no loss of livability (Vancouver 1999v: 30-31).

Plate 64   Emerald Court, Fairview Slopes. Here in Fairview Heights in the early 1980s great ingenuity was shown to manage the slope, create usable communal spaces, and protect the views, all with the obligatory underground parking.

building code, lack of understanding of the implications of complex designs, lack of understanding of local traditions, and the use of inappropriate materials (British Columbia: 1998). The contextual and domestic architectural styles were popular with planners, neighbours, and consumers but were not well enough designed or detailed to resist water penetration. The result has been years of misery for people trapped in such buildings by lengthy reconstruction and depressed prices.

Different design issues have arisen with the walk-up apartments constructed on three floors above the shops and small offices on the city's arterial roads (zoned for C-2). Because they were concrete framed and less intricate in their roof forms and balconies, they have not been as susceptible to water penetration. They have helped to reinforce one of Vancouver's greatest pleasures – its diverse inner-city neighbourhood shopping strips, with their proliferation of small shopkeepers and businesses, mixed in with cafés, restaurants, and bars. In some projects, the commercial functions have been intensified by adding second-floor offices, or creating small outdoor eating spaces by widening and landscaping the pavement, or by introducing weather protection. Residential livability has been increased by carefully massing and modelling the upper floors to provide bay windows, balconies, and decks (see Plate 32). CityPlan and its neighbourhood visions pin much hope on a revised C-2 zoning and design guidelines as exploiting the least line of resistance to affordable housing in the single-family neighbourhoods. However, such development can impact severely on single-family housing to the rear, particularly where it overlooks gardens and the backs of houses (see Plate 33). Some critics doubt the livability of deep-plan apartments on busy arterial roads. Certainly, many more stretches of arterial roads could be intensified in this manner, providing much needed housing, increasing local commercial services, creating livelier streets, and reinforcing the use of transit.

Medium-Rise Apartment Buildings

The medium-rise apartment is not a particularly popular building form in Vancouver and its location is sporadic. It has not been specifically encouraged in zoning designations, although it has been allowed in districts zoned for RM-3/4/5/6. The single free-standing block can achieve considerable architectural distinction (for example, neo-moderne buildings in the West End at 1345 Burnaby Street and 1225 Barclay Street), where it can address and enclose the street, and retain the sense of a street-wall of apartments. Often the side and rear elevations are more problematic and have poor aspects. Elsewhere, medium-rise apartments tend to be quite obtrusive, as in east Kitsilano where they create green space that has little use or value, have anonymous architectural treatments, and make no attempt to enclose the street. Where postmodern eclecticism meets builder schlock, by contrast, the results are often particularly ugly: "hat roofed, Palladian-windowed, gaily coloured, mish-mashed or otherwise under-considered and over-decorated buildings" (Blore and Sutherland 1999: 51).

Wider use is now being made of street-wall apartments, 5 to 9 storeys in height, in uptown south of Broadway, above ground-floor retail on inner arterial roads (with C-3/5/6/7/8 zoning), and in Downtown South as part of much denser development. The physical bulk of these buildings can create urban design problems with shadowing, overlooking, and view blockage. They require considerable care with the site planning and elevations if they are not to appear faceless and overbearing (see Figure 34 and Plate 33). Cambridge Gardens uptown provided an excellent prototype in the late 1980s, because it created usable private green space in interior courtyards enclosed by smaller towers and townhouses (see Plate 21). Increasingly, inner-city social housing is adopting the medium-rise street-wall form; private-sector loft developments are following suit in Gastown (see Plate 54).

High-Rise Towers and Perimeter Blocks

The free-standing high-rise apartment was first developed in the West End in a series of largely undistinguished tower and point blocks that took advantage of the spectacular views – but blocked them for many other people. In the early 1980s Richard Henriquez pioneered the slim, highly glazed tower with a more complex floor plan and unit disposition, determined by the need to capture the best available views for each apartment (see Plate 20). His differential treatment of the tower facades created buildings with much more interest and identity. Henriquez also pioneered more imaginative use of landscaping, although the ground-floor plane was always a limited amenity for residents or neighbours. The tall free-standing tower continues to be built on infill sites in the West End and Triangle West (see Plate 65), but the vast majority are now linked to blocks of townhouses or street-wall apartments in megaprojects or Downtown South. These towers have become part of mixed-form development that rejects the modernist tower's uncompromising, and largely negative, impact on the street and neighbourhood and seeks to have a positive effect on both.

If Vancouver has invented a new residential form, then it is this variant of the high-density perimeter block, embracing the tower and townhouse or tower and street-wall apartment forms in Triangle West, Downtown South, and False Creek North, and the open block variant of CityGate. The floor-space ratios of these developments vary hugely from the surprisingly low net floor-space ratios of 2.8 in False Creek North to the very high floor-space ratio of 6.0 or more on selected sites in Downtown South and Triangle West.

Plate 65 Apartment towers, Jervis Street, Triangle West. Three luxury all-glazed complexes are pictured here: the Lions (left), The Pointe (middle), and the twin towers of Harbourside Park, all with prestigious addresses on West Georgia Street. They, and the relandscaped sidewalk of Jervis Street, look out over Burrard Inlet.

The essential principles, however, are the same (see Figure 46). The tall, slim tower boosts the density and capitalizes on the views without blocking either public views, as designated by view cones, or private views of adjacent property owners. They do not overshadow large parts of the street or the private landscaped space of the interior of the block. Traditional streets of domestic townhouses or apartments (see Plate 23) are created, with ground-floor commercial often included in the latter to service the population and animate the street (see Plates 34 and 36).

The design of the megaprojects, both at the neighbourhood and building block levels, is based on a set of principles that had been emerging since the early 1970s from politicians, planners, and the public. But these principles had to be translated from the low net density of False Creek South in the 1970s into much higher densities on successive megaprojects because of land prices and the city's desire to become more compact and transit-oriented (see Figure 45). In comprehensive redevelopments, there was an opportunity to espouse and implement a set of integrated neighbourhood design principles:

- Each project extends the fabric and character of the city.
- Each neighbourhood has a full range of services and amenities from a local "high street" through to the essential "third place" between home and work of community centre, café, or park.
- Each neighbourhood has a diverse mix of housing types and costs.
- Cars are stored underground, servicing is discreet or from back lanes, and streets are designed for slow traffic and pedestrian amenity.
- A continuous seawall dedicated to public use is linked to a series of lookouts, art installations, and new waterfront parks.
- The street is carefully landscaped and furnished and decorated to express community identity and each neighbourhood has its own distinctive park.
- A land-use mix or proximity of residence, workplace, leisure, and community services is sought.
- A "humane, domestic building form" for high-density housing is sought. (adapted from Beasley 1997)

The "humane, domestic building form" works well at floor-space ratios of 2.5 (Plate 38) and even 3.75 (Plate 34). It is severely tested at the higher floor-space ratios of 5.0 and over – as the 1991 Central Area Plan acknowledged it would be (Plates 23 and 46) – where environmental quality depends almost entirely on architectural skill. But the city carefully researched many of these qualitative factors and developed its multi-family high-density residential guidelines to ensure livability (Vancouver 1992e). In the end the critical standards are those for safety of the street and access, privacy, noise, private and communal landscaped space, recreational facilities, and play space.

Beyond the principles of neighbourhood design there is the question of building form, which is largely dependent on the size of the site and the size and disposition of the city block. In the megaprojects, the planners and developers could design new city blocks. In False Creek North, Concord Pacific has used a mixture of closed and open blocks – the latter to maximize water views but also to provide passersby with views into communal spaces. But in the central area at large, the block morphology generally provides long slim blocks (about 40 × 160 metres) because the back lanes bisect the city block on the short side. This prevents developers from creating enclosed communal sitting out areas as an urban oasis – James Cheng's 888 Beach Avenue, developed at a floor-space ratio of 5.94, being the exemplar (see Plate 23). Regrettably, there are relatively few opportunities in the central area to create these squarer perimeter blocks, and architects have been forced to compromise on communal amenity space. There, the best that can be achieved seems to be the creation of an enclosed street with townhouses between the towers and a private landscaped area to the rear that is set above but invisible from the back lane. The Residences on Georgia, also by James Cheng, is the exemplar (see Plate 46), but while its beautifully landscaped "front garden" (this block has main streets on both long sides) provides an excellent visual amenity, it is not a usable space for either residents or citizens. In other locations, communal gardens have been provided on townhouse or apartment roofs, but few developments have been able to create any urban design quality in the back lanes whose hard surfaces and service orientation remain unrelieved. The major components of this high-density "humane" domestic form are:

- underground car parking with unobtrusive entrances and minimal curb cuts
- continuous street-wall buildings of a domestic character with carefully detailed rowhousing that overlooks and animates the street
- quality, coordinated public and private landscaping and furnishing of the street
- tower bases carefully integrated with ground-oriented housing
- slim and elegant, highly glazed, view-articulated towers that catch the light and minimize shadow and wind vortex
- private, highly landscaped courtyards within or on top of the block
- ground-floor commercial uses separated from residential to manage noise
- internal adult recreational facilities (e.g., swimming pools, gymnasia) and children's outdoor play space.

Would this model work as well in cities without magnificent views from every apartment tower? Would the high-rise apartments be so marketable? The answer is that the model might work, but demand for the apartments might be less – with obvious implications for project viability. Everything would depend on the quality of the project and the neighbourhood – its amenities, facilities, and design quality.

The Coherent City
The essence of the Vancouver achievement then has been to create a series of coherent but distinct inner-city neighbourhoods offering high-quality living environments, attractive, safe, and lively streets and parks, a full range of

residential services and amenities, and a high level of accessibility to downtown, uptown, and a revived waterfront. These neighbourhoods are now merging one with another to create a coherent city with fewer and fewer vacant sites and dead areas. One of the real distinctions of the downtown peninsula is the seamless transition between downtown and the West End, into Triangle West, or Downtown South; or from the latter into Yaletown and the Concord Pacific neighbourhoods (see Plate 66). This is a testament to the achievement of the goal of the livable downtown with a series of coterminous fine-grain, diverse neighbourhoods set out in the 1991 central area policy statement (see Figure 48). In the northern and eastern parts of downtown itself there is still a strong feel of late-nineteenth- and early-twentieth-century character, and enormous potential to create a mixed community and business area with a strong heritage character extending into Gastown and the Downtown Eastside. But in downtown and on the west side of the downtown peninsula, except in Triangle West, the office towers and plazas create a largely anonymous townscape that could be in any North American city. The public realm is clean and functional, and the streets are well used and pleasant but, with one or two notable exceptions (see Plates 17 and 18), the downtown architecture and public realm are disappointing, and there is much work to be done to raise its quality to approach that of the megaprojects. As the central area population grows, and as its rapid transit connections are extended further east, downtown anticipates new commercial, retail, and leisure investment, having had little for a decade (see Plate 67). However, the city's record with regard to control of commercial development downtown has not been particularly distinguished, in contrast to its residential achievements. Much thought needs to be given to this in conjunction with the plans for the improvement of downtown transportation and the public realm.

Beyond downtown and uptown, much of the early twentieth-century character remains intact in the single-family and two-family neighbourhoods, and in some of the multiple-family housing areas. It is now strongly reinforced by both zoning and design guidelines, offering very high-quality but generally expensive living environments in accessible and well-serviced neighbourhoods. Back-lane developments are beginning to make meaningful increases in housing stock at the expense of reduced garden size. They are creating new small-scale, intricate living environments for smaller households. In a number of areas, the invasion of walk-up apartments and stacked townhouses has completely transformed neighbourhood character and the level of amenity is entirely dependent on the quality of the individual project because the streets have not been relandscaped as they have in the central redevelopment areas. Some provide excellent private and communal amenities, but the streets that contain them have often lost their coherence and quality. In residential

Plate 66 False Creek North and Yaletown interface, Hamilton Street. The rear of the Yaletown Edge complex carefully complements the well-preserved industrial heritage of Yaletown through sensitive massing, good choice of materials, and retention of the idiosyncratic street pattern. A good example of how careful planning is creating seamless transitions between distinct neighbourhoods in the central area.

Plate 67 Robson Street, west of Burrard. Robson Street retains its rather chaotic, undesigned feel despite having clearly established its retail supremacy. The heavy traffic adds to the bustle, but the sidewalks are not wide enough for comfortable shopping at busy times. Can significant retail intensification be far away?

Vancouver, more profound physical changes will come in the next half century as arterial roads are intensified and the neighbourhood centres establish themselves as nodes of commercial and residential redevelopment. With well designed development, these changes do not have to diminish neighbourhood quality. Rather they could enhance it because, as the Urban Landscape Task Force Report emphasized, the most diverse, lively, and distinctive commercial strips are among the most cherished places of Vancouverites (Vancouver 1992c: 9-11).

Assessing Urban Design Policies and Practice

Vancouver's achievements in urban environmental quality are the result of its sophisticated planning and urban design policies, guidelines, and processes and procedures, its detailed and design-skilled negotiation practices, and its partnerships with the design and development industries. These policies and practices are of particular interest to planners and designers seeking to improve their own planning and design review practices, and to find new ways of balancing accountability and efficiency, the value added to design and the resources required to achieve it, and the positive benefits of growth and the negative externalities.

In this book, principles for evaluating design review practices have been introduced (see Figure 1) and reinforced chapter by chapter, providing a basis for examining Vancouver's design practices. Now they can provide a means of systematically evaluating Vancouver's design review process and summarizing its strengths and weakness (see Figure 68).

Urban Design Based on Community Visions

At the outset two key principles relate to the overall need to establish community and corporate commitment to design quality, expressed perhaps through a community design plan, or a series of urban design plans, that can build consensus within the city bureaucracy and enthuse the development industry and community at large. Evidence of community commitment to design quality and a comprehensive coordinated effort to promote good design can be found in initiatives the city has undertaken to promote environmental quality more broadly. Foremost among these initiatives has been the city's corporate improvement of the public realm, which was fully integrated into planning practices in the cooperative planning model developed in the official development plan process of the 1980s for False Creek North and Coal Harbour. This brought together long-standing concerns regarding the creation of urban parks and livable city streets: the former focused on waterfront parks, beaches, and public access to the seawall; the latter stressed the use of quality landscape, furniture and paving, as well as traffic management and a program for public art. It brought together the departments of planning, engineering, and cultural affairs with the park board to deliver the full range of improvements to the public realm. To this comprehensive, coordinated approach should be added such specific planning and engineering policies and programs as heritage protection, view and skyline protection, greenways, street tree planting, green streets, and long-standing transport planning policies to reduce car commuting, promote transit, and encourage more walking and cycling. For evidence of community commitment and assent to all these goals, one need look no further than the CityPlan consultations (see Figure 27) or the findings of the mayor's Urban Landscape Task Force (Vancouver 1992c). It is important to emphasize that the planners' commitment to environmental quality extends beyond the purely aesthetic concerns of townscape or landscape to livability in its deepest collective sense, embracing the quality of internal and external space, privacy, noise, view, aspect, and microclimate, and the specific social concerns of safety, community facilities and daycare, and affordable housing. The latter brought the departments of social planning and housing into the cooperative planning model.

There are several examples of urban design plans, each of which has been based on thoroughgoing public participation to establish community support for policies, development form, and design guidelines. Clearly CityPlan – itself a product of extensive and innovative consultation – developed a citywide planning strategy that had clear urban design implications both in terms of its choice of "a city of neighbourhood centres," and in its catalogue of "next steps" for design and planning initiatives. Closely fitting the notion of a citywide design strategy, it achieved a remarkable 80 percent support from the public, though the implementation still looks problematic. Beyond the CityPlan strategy, neighbourhood visions provide the mechanisms for establishing detailed approaches to rezoning, design guidelines, and environmental management, and for formulating the future pattern of urban development at the local level. These visioning mechanisms are exemplary participatory processes, the establishment of majority opinion checked through random surveys of residents being particularly rigorous and fair. They are fundamental to Vancouver's approach to developing neighbourhood design policy.

Other exemplars of urban design plans in the Vancouver system are to be found in the city's official development plans, particularly those that were products of the cooperative planning model. The master plans that have been prepared for these communities, and their supporting guidelines, are models of their type both in their precision of future patterns of development and their three-dimensional forms, and the guidance they provide for the detailed design that comes much later. Their smooth and precise implementation over

Figure 68 Progressive urban design review: Vancouver achievements and continuing challenges

Principles	Successes		Continuing challenges
Community Vision			
1 Building a comprehensive, coordinated, community commitment to environmental beauty and design (Brennan's Law)	1	Corporate working: cooperative planning model Diversity of design initiatives: community assent	Downtown public realm Effective heritage conservation Greenways implementation
2 Developing and monitoring an urban design plan with community and development industry support and periodic review	2	CityPlan as shared vision Neighbourhood visioning Megaprojects vs. other official development plans	Citywide needs versus neighbourhood aspirations Establishing neighbourhood centres
Design, Planning, and Zoning			
3 Harnessing the broadest range of actors and instruments to promote better design (tax, subsidy, acquisition, etc.)	3	Development-cost levies Community-amenity contributions Public-facility benefits	Financing Growth Review Community Facilities White Paper
4 Mitigating the exclusionary effects of control strategies and urban design regulation	4	20 percent affordable units Replacement single-room occupancy units 25 percent family units "Third place"/public realm	30 percent affordable target How to increase supply of small units
5 Integrating zoning into planning and addressing the limitations of zoning	5	Incentive zoning for design quality Regulations or guidelines (choice of process)	Exclusion of single-family zoning
Broad, Substantive Design Principles			
6 Maintaining a commitment to urban design that goes well beyond elevations and aesthetics to embrace amenity, accessibility, community, vitality, and sustainability	6	Livability: especially at high density Neighbourhood amenities, facilities Vitality/safety Sustainability	Sustainable design policies

7	Basing guidelines on generic design principles and contextual analysis and articulating desired and mandatory outcomes	New urbanist design principles Downtown character areas Residential contextual design (RS-5, etc.) Regulatory versus discretionary distinction	Creating comprehensive and easy-to-administer RS systems
8	Accommodating organic spontaneity, vitality, innovation, and pluralism and not attempting to control all aspects of community design	Not elevation control but urban design Private architects prepare megaproject guidelines Urban Design Panel supports design innovation	RS-5 and RS Rethink: less prescription

Due Process

9	Identifying clear a priori roles for urban design intervention	Zoning regulations: mandatory Design guidelines: discretionary Guidelines clearly published	RS Rethink and more efficient mechanisms
10	Administering procedures with written opinions to manage administrative discretion, and with appropriate appeal mechanisms	Public consultation Checks and balances in permitting processes Few appeals	Implementing new permitting process Public Involvement Review: third-party appeals
11	Implementing an efficient, constructive, and effective permitting process	Partnership Early identification of design problems Rigorous examination Quality outcomes	Project facilitators Outstanding objectives of Development and Building Regulation Review
12	Providing appropriate design skills and expertise to support the process	Development planners and supervision Urban Design Panel	

ten to fifteen years is a testament to the mutual understanding that has been established through the process, and the confidence all parties have in it. More flexibility has been introduced into both plans and guidelines as development has progressed and quality outcomes delivered.

Thus, the first two principles of community commitment are fully met by the Vancouver system. The second group of principles embrace the wider context of design regulation and how it fits into broader planning practices. They look for the harnessing of a broad range of fiscal and policy initiatives to support good design, for mitigation of the exclusionary effects of urban design initiatives, and for the full integration of zoning into planning policy.

Fiscal Devices to Support Good Design

Beyond its system of plans, incentive zoning, and design guidelines, Vancouver has adopted fiscal measures to ensure that a wide range of amenities are added to each development. The issue of land policy and development taxation in Vancouver has been couched as a question of community-amenity contributions (on residential rezonings since 1989), development-cost levies (on development permits in major redevelopment areas since 1990), and public amenity requirements (in waterfront megaprojects since 1990). While community-amenity contributions cover such amenities as parks, community centres, and social housing, development-cost levies cover parks, daycare, replacement housing, and basic infrastructure. Public amenity requirements in major projects cover all of these plus schools, libraries, public art, and specialty items determined area by area. Collectively, they ensure that community facilities, replacement and social housing, and parks and public art can be funded to enhance neighbourhood quality in the broadest sense. Development planners concentrate on ensuring each project is as responsive to the zoning and design guidelines, and as architecturally refined as they can be, including the design of the adjacent sidewalk and public realm.

Public amenities in the megaprojects are delivered simultaneously with the completion of each neighbourhood and are distinguished by the sheer quality and generosity of amenities, especially parks. But elsewhere the city still has some way to go to catch up with other regional municipalities in ensuring that adequate levies and amenity contributions are forthcoming from the development industry to maintain these standards. Outside of the megaprojects, funds have to accumulate before investment can be made. In Downtown South, while replacement housing is keeping pace with losses of single-room occupancy units, the provision of parkland lags behind. Similar difficulties will be faced by each neighbourhood as it seeks to implement its CityPlan vision.

Urban design initiatives and environmental improvements are often associated with gentrification processes that progressively price out low-rent uses and households. There is plenty of evidence of this in Vancouver, whether it is the discretionary zoning to protect single-family neighbourhoods, or the affordability of the new high-density residential areas on the edge of downtown. But the issue was never disregarded. The city has tried to address it since the 1970s with its affordable housing policies, and it has used its land ownership powers to provide leasehold land at below market prices, sometimes free, to enable non-profit and cooperative groups to deliver social housing. In 1989 it committed itself to providing affordable housing equally among all neighbourhoods, and one-to-one replacement of single-room occupancy in Downtown South and subsequently in the Downtown Eastside.

A key provision was made in the megaprojects whereby the city ensured that 20 percent of the residential units were for "core need" households, while 25 percent of all residential units had to be suitable for families. Some city officials have questioned whether it was sufficient for the developers of major projects simply to set aside sites for such housing. They have suggested that, instead, they should have been required to donate the land to the city, as the main social housing land providers, or to provide construction or operating subsidies. Against the background of the withdrawal of federal housing subsidies, the securing of the 20 percent affordable housing in False Creek North is a major achievement. But, as the recent planning process in Southeast False Creek has suggested, a 30 percent target for affordable housing would now be more appropriate and socially sustainable.

A quite different dimension of social inclusion is exemplified by the investments made in such facilities as community centres, libraries, and daycare. This is encapsulated in the concept of the creation of "a third place" in the megaprojects, somewhere between home and work where people can freely associate with their neighbours and the wider community, and enjoy noncommercial services. A similar fundamental objective has been to create a fully accessible, high-quality public realm for use by everyone, including those whose mobility is impaired. This has focused on quality street furnishing, landscaping, and tree planting; the provision of seawall public art and paths for cycling and walking; and generous parks with a wide range of active and passive recreational facilities. Urban design has not been used to privatize or fortify space or to manipulate social behaviour, as it has in so many American cities (see Loukaitou-Sideris and Banerjee 1998). Rather it has been used to extend and improve the public realm and increase pedestrian accessibility at every opportunity.

Design-led Zoning

Best practice principles necessary to accompany design regulation address the limitations of zoning and its general lack of relationship to planning for the future. Discretionary zoning, as an integral part of the Vancouver planning system, is the key mechanism for achieving intensification and creating a predictable urban form. Zoning bylaws are a critical part of the official development plan process in areas of major redevelopment, as the means of translating general planning and design principles into regulations controlling land use, floor space, massing setbacks, and building height. A clear set of mandatory requirements is provided. But in the official development plan process, as elsewhere, the Vancouver approach has been to parallel the regulatory element – the zoning bylaw – with a discretionary element – design guidelines. Rather than make the zoning bylaw extremely complex, as has been done for example in San Francisco, design guidelines carry a wealth of advice about all matters to do with building forms and the public realm. The genius of Vancouver's system lies in providing the incentive of additional floor space in return for compliance to the guidelines, so the applicant benefits financially from following them. Thus, an essentially negative control system is given an attractive positive element with incentives for good design. For development planners, the Development Permit Board and its advisory panel, and the Urban Design Panel, the always-asked and decisive question is whether a proposed development has earned its full allocation of floor space through the quality of its design.

From the mid-1970s to the early 1990s, zoning changes were used to encourage and manage significant intensification in the inner neighbourhoods, establishing mostly low-rise apartments (RM zoning) or two-family dwellings (RT zoning). In the 1990s, as single-family neighbourhoods in the more affluent areas came under pressure, rezoning for RS-1A to RS-6 and accompanying design guidelines were used to maintain "single-family character," but also to ensure that all new housing and landscaping was "similar in character," "neighbourly," or "compatible." The exclusionary tendencies of single-family zoning became obvious, and the sheer complexity of zoning schedules and guidelines began to overwhelm permitting staff and development planners. The remedies of simple administrative rules-based zoning and more permissive zoning to allow subtle intensifications remained politically unacceptable.

Vancouver has made major advancements in terms of harnessing a range of actions and instruments to promote design quality, generally mitigate social exclusion, and integrate zoning with planning. Turning to the policy aspects of design review, we find that the principles embrace a commitment to a substantive version of urban design policy reinforced by guidelines rooted in accepted design principles and contextual analysis, but capable of accommodating innovation and pluralism.

Adoption of Substantive Design Principles

As for substantive design issues, the city has been able to define a set of
community goals embodied in the concept of the "livable city" that have
required little change over the last three decades. It has translated these into
a set of socially relevant urban design issues that have progressively embraced considerations of accessibility, vitality, safety, community, and
sustainability. So while the system has been preoccupied with the protection
of mountain and sea views, with conserving Craftsman-style single-family
neighbourhoods, and with ensuring a high quality of architecture and
streetscape, these aesthetic aspirations have been accompanied by equally
deep concerns with issues of "livability." In housing, the latter encompass
issues of visual privacy and noise protection, adequate yard size and children's play facilities, private and communal landscaped space, the microclimate
of private and public space, and crime prevention through design. Each has
been incorporated into guidelines, and many have found their way into conditions imposed on development permits. Concerns with neighbourhood
amenities and facilities, already mentioned in the context of development
levies and public facility benefits, are an expression of the same breadth of
concern for community life, social mix, public health, and recreation. So too is
the program for ensuring a high-quality public realm. Underground car parking has been one of the most important requirements in medium- to high-
density neighbourhoods so that vehicles do not visually intrude onto properties
and take up space that can be landscaped for communal use. All these considerations indicate that Vancouver's notions of urban design go far beyond a
concern with the external appearance of development.

Concerns for sustainable urban forms in Vancouver have tended to be
subsumed in neotraditional or new urbanist planning goals: dense, compact,
street-oriented and mixed-use neighbourhoods within easy walking distance
of downtown or neighbourhood services and employment centres. But more
recently, such issues as the extent of impermeable site coverage and associated runoff problems, and the extent of tree planting have become part of
residential zoning concerns. An injection of much deeper sustainability concerns into detailed design will come with the development of the Southeast
False Creek project, which will be a prototype for subsequent neighbourhoods. Sustainable design principles will influence the entire regulatory framework of building and planning regulations over the next decade (see Figure
69). So while Vancouver's concept of urban design is "the design of the city
in all its components" (Vancouver 1999v), it has dynamic community, livability, accessibility, and sustainability dimensions to set alongside its concerns
for visual delight.

Figure 69 Sustainability performance targets for Southeast False Creek. The Sheltair Consultants' study established best practice indicators for a range of key sustainable design features and suggested appropriate targets to be adopted in the development.

Performance Factors	Measure	Quantitative target	Best practice figures (Canada/USA)	1996 city or GVRD levels (%)
Solid Waste				
Solid waste sent to disposal	kg/person	200	380 (Belleville, ON)	–66
Organic waste processed on site	kg/person	80	156 (Fraser Valley, BC)	63
Organic debris processed on site	%	100	30 (Vancouver, BC)	
Transportation and accessibility				
Accessibility to transit	% within 350 m	100	90 (Toronto, ON)	ca. 80
Accessibility to services	% within 350 m	100	80 (Toronto, ON)	ca. 10-30
Extent of street dedicated to walk/cycle transit	%	60	78 (Trondheim, Norway)	40
Extent of affordable housing	%	30	70 (Langley, BC)	
Energy				
Level of domestic use of non-renewable energy	kwh/m^2	288	192 (Victoria, BC)	–56
Level of commercial use of non-renewable energy	kwh/m^2	284	258 (Richmond, BC)	–55
Locally generated renewable energy	%	5	84 (Quebec)	5
Buildings connected to district heating	%	90	100 (Scandinavia)	88
Maximum domestic peak electrical demand	% < 33W/m^2	33	15 (Vancouver, BC) (gas)	–64
Emissions				
Distance travelled annually for work and services	km	3,392	3,392 (West End, Vancouver)	–49
Total CO$_2$ emissions	kg	1,498	1,312 (GVRD)	–50
Buildings designed to minimize index pollutants	%	25	17 (Ontario)	25

	Unit	Value	Benchmark	
Water				
Potable water consumption	L/person/day	100	0 (Toronto scheme)	−66
Impervious site coverage	%	54	10 (Davis, CA)	−36
Sewage treated on-site	%	25	100 (Vancouver, BC)	
Open Space				
Bird habitats on-site	no	30	equal	
Open foreshore with habitat value	%	80	80 (Stanley Park, Vancouver, BC)	
Space with habitat value	%	60	100 (Switzerland) (new)	
Roofs with habitat value	%	25	24 (Davis, CA)	
Produce consumed grown on-site	%	12.5		
Building targets				
Dwelling units with solar orientation	%	75	100 (Boulder, CO)	
Recycled material use	%	30	50 (Vancouver, BC)	

Source: Adapted from Vancouver (1998ii)

Most of the design principles avowed thus far have explicit roots in both urban design theory and contextual analysis. The design guidelines closely followed innovations in postmodern urban design theory that proceeded apace in the 1960s and 1970s. Jane Jacobs (1961), Kevin Lynch (1960; 1971), and Christopher Alexander (1977) have all been acknowledged and their ideas of mixed uses and mixed tenure, permeable layouts, imageable neighbourhoods, active frontages and quiet backs, and defensible space have been adopted. They are clearly evident in the megaproject planning principles and the advocacy of the perimeter block, as well as in the complex of ideas that delineate neotraditional design or new urbanism.

One of these generic design principles, set up in opposition to modernist design, is respect for context. Contextual analysis and design has been an integral part of the Vancouver approach, clearly expressed in the development and refinement of character area guidelines in downtown, which sought to build on the distinctiveness of particular streets and small neighbourhoods, and in view protection policies to ensure continued enjoyment of the city's setting. The megaproject planning principles and detailed design guidelines set out to respond to adjacent morphologies and building forms, or to respond to the waterfront with different palettes of materials and colours. The apotheosis of contextualism was of course the guidelines for RS-5 zoning that invented a specific methodology whereby elevational treatment and landscaping would be derived from a study of adjacent properties. It went too far down the road of responding to the architectural detail of the locality, but the guidelines applied only to those seeking to maximize their zoning entitlement to build a large house on a lot.

A sophisticated design control system intent on contextualism is often in danger of becoming over-prescriptive in its zoning and guidelines, thus losing its ability to encourage innovation and spontaneity. The RS-5 zoning is the example that most architects would cite because, while they welcome the increase in commissions that has been created by the new zoning and guidelines, they find the contextual rules quite limiting in terms of potential design solutions. Many city planners contest this, arguing that the wide choice of contextual features gives considerable design scope. Still, most commentators accept that a less prescriptive system – such as that provided by RS-6 or RS-7 – would be preferable.

Another dimension of the debate must not be forgotten – potential racial discrimination. The zoning designation RS-5 was devised as a specific solution to protect "traditional" westside neighbourhoods from developers' interpretations of the aesthetic preferences of wealthy Asian immigrants. In practice the issues were much more complex and there is evidence to suggest that the Asian purchasers disavowed such tastes in design. But in the close regulation of the elevations of single-family housing, there is inevitably a clash of taste that seriously distracts planning from more important issues concerning livability, housing flexibility, and the future housing needs of the city.

The issuing of over-prescriptive design guidelines also arose in the megaprojects. But, there, under the cooperative planning model, private-sector architects employed by developers were often drafting the detailed design guidelines with contributions from city planners. There was a sense in which the guideline writing was part of the detailed design process. Sometimes such guidelines did not work and had to be abandoned (i.e., in Quayside Neighbourhood), and at times they constrained architects and developers from rethinking the concepts and re-examining individual sites (i.e., in Beach Neighbourhood). In general, as False Creek North progressed, the guidelines became less detailed and prescriptive, as trust increased between developer and city and the latter recognized the need for flexibility. City planners learned a great deal from this experience.

Some commentators argue that the megaprojects lack organic spontaneity and vitality, and they blame over-prescriptive guidelines and Vancouverites' desires to control everything (Blore and Sutherland 1999; Berelowitz 1997). But these criticisms seem rather premature, a verdict that makes no allowance for the area to develop a lived-in quality and to establish its own patterns of public life. There is plenty of design diversity, design innovation, and public art and landscape creativity evident in the differentiated neighbourhoods. This is because some of Vancouver's best architectural practices and landscape architects made major contributions to the guidelines, designed the buildings, and won architectural awards for their efforts (see Appendix 1). Competitions for public art have also raised the quality of the public realm and injected more complexity into the townscape. In addition, the Urban Design Panel has been a design champion, quick to support innovative or original design approaches, and a valuable force against standardized solutions and tendencies to over-prescriptive controls. Overall, Vancouver's practices exhibit a concern with a deep concept of urban design, a strong commitment to generic design principles and contextual analysis, and a desire to encourage architectural innovation.

Ensuring Due Process and Skilled Advice

Finally, in this evaluation of urban design processes, it is necessary to assess a set of criteria related to "due process" and the creation of a fair, transparent, and efficient permitting system where the public authority has adequate skills and expertise, and common consent, to exercise its design controls. In Vancouver there are clear a priori rules for design intervention that are set out in the form of official development plans (in the principal redevelopment areas), zoning bylaws, and in supporting design guidelines where these exist. Conformity to the standard zoning requirements will guarantee a permit but the pursuit of conditional uses, relaxations, or floor-space incentives – widely used to encourage neighbourly design – will trigger a much more exacting evaluation of the proposals. Zoning establishes the acceptable uses, building heights, density, form, siting, massing, privacy, parking, and relationships to the street. Design guidelines, which set out the contextual factors to be considered, vary from very general character area guidelines for downtown to quite detailed and specific guidelines embracing desired streetscape character, views, microclimate, safety, open space, landscaping, and "architectural components" in such areas as Downtown South. As has been shown, all these guidelines have been through thoroughgoing consultation with the public and the development and design industries as part of their formulation and adoption processes.

Beyond policies and guidelines, there are clear requirements for application presentation. All major applications are required to include a design rationale, to demonstrate contextual relationships within a block and relationships to windows and balconies on adjacent properties for privacy, as well as view and shadow impacts, and to include a streetscape analysis and a landscape plan. Full site plans, elevations, and sections and a model are also required. Aside from making a project easier to evaluate accurately, these preparations ensure that a significant amount of urban design thinking goes into each permit application. These ideas have been extended into single-family neighbourhoods where the guidelines may dictate specific contextual analysis. Thus, the rules for design intervention are clearly established and published, many of them with workbooks to help the applicant apply the necessary design procedures. However, numerous complaints have been raised about the complexity of some of these regulations and guidelines.

Administrative procedures of permit processing have been subject to repeated and very detailed scrutiny over the last thirty years. The design and development industries have helped shape a process that ensures that the exercise of discretion is transparent, consistent, and fully justified. The provision of publicly available written opinions, which can be challenged through appropriate appeal mechanisms, is an important component of this system. Vancouver has three such documents that summarize the complex decision-making processes: the Development Permit Staff Committee report that tests an application against all bylaws and guidelines, records consultations, and lists the conditions; the decision of the Urban Design Panel, published on the web and summarized in the staff committee's report; and the minutes of the Development Permit Board, which record a final rigorous appraisal of the proposals to which the public, development, and design industries' spokes-persons contribute and which are published on the city's website.

Since at least January 1997, the minutes of both panel and board record no serious substantive or procedural issues for applicants, save for very rare comments about disagreements between the panel and the development planner over design guidelines, and very occasional complaints about late changes in design negotiations or the inflexible application of guidelines. This is reaffirmed by the absence of refusals of applications that have gone to the board. The appeal system has been rendered almost obsolete as regards major applications, in contrast to the mid-1980s when it was repeatedly over-turning city decisions. This suggests that the administrative procedures on major applications are working well.

Much recent debate has centred on the efficiency of the permitting process and ways in which it can be made quicker, more predictable, and more constructive. There are few difficulties with single- or two-family housing applications that seek outright approval uses. These can be obtained in a few days and have the advantage of combining building and development per-mits. But those applications seeking to take advantage of increased floor areas or height, in return for more neighbourly or better design, are subjected to the full application process, likely to take between two or three months at present. There are long-standing concerns about the speed of the permitting process, a minimum of four months for proposals going to the Development Permit Board. Current reforms aim to take decisions on minor applications in ten weeks and major applications in twelve weeks, but these targets are not yet being met.

The fairness and constructive nature of the system have been constant preoccupations of the development industry and design professions who have sought and obtained changes. Development Permit Board and Urban Design Panel procedures now provide checks and balances on the exercise of discretion. The introduction of the pre-application and pre-design confer-ence allows applicants to have all the zoning requirements and guidelines interpreted and spelled out to them by development planners. A preliminary application process can be used to establish the key parameters and to seek the advice of the Urban Design Panel. The new process resolves all these issues at a conceptual design stage and introduces project facilitators to man-age the process positively.

A major factor in Vancouver's design achievement has been the high level of design skills input into the design negotiation and review process. The key here is the role of development planners, architect-trained and private-sector experi-enced so that they understand the design problems from the development side. Their design skills, contextual knowledge, process expertise, and negotiation abilities play a major role in achieving quality development. They are closely supervised by the co-director of planning, who will take them to task for any lapses in professionalism, even at the Development Permit Board hearing. The development planners' constructive, facilitating role has been enshrined at the heart of the new permitting process being implemented by the Development and Building Regulation Review. The second source of design expertise is the Urban Design Panel. The panel's membership has been broadened, its procedures made more transparent, and its advice focused to the point where it now operates perhaps principally as a peer-review system for major permit applications. Most designers seek the unanimous support of the panel as an endorsement of their own professional competence. The panel also contributes positively to guideline and policy development. These two sources of design expertise complement each other, combining rigorous scrutiny of all aspects of design against zoning and design guidelines with a peer-review system that is more conceptual and multi-disciplinary. Considering due process in the round, one can claim that Vancouver has a very carefully defined, transparently operated, skilled, constructive, and effective – if slow – process of design review.

Finally, the effectiveness of the system requires a judgment on the value-added to development by the detailed zoning and design guidelines, and the elaborate scrutiny of the permitting process. Most commentators suggest that the system delivers a consistent medium-to-high quality of development (interviews). This stance is shared in American planners' analysis of the quality of the megaprojects (Blore and Sutherland 1999), community assessments of the outputs of zoning designations RS-5 and RS-6 (Vancouver 1999w), the planning department's celebration of its urban design achievements (Vancouver 1999v), voting patterns of the Urban Design Panel (Figure 62), and architectural awards (listed in Appendix 1). The major exceptions to the generally high standards achieved have been the leaky condo phenomenon and major office buildings downtown, but the former is primarily a failure of building regulations and inspections insofar as it is a failure of regulation at all.

Overall, Vancouver's design review system – deeply embedded in its plan, policy, zoning, and permitting system – fully measures up to the challenging principles established by those who have most critically scrutinized urban planning practice in major American cities. It is a system that has evolved through a political and professional zeal for reform to establish a more participatory and corporate control process that can deliver contextually sensitive, neighbourly development. Driven by a vision of a dense, mixed, livable city set in glorious natural surroundings, where new buildings must enhance whenever possible, this system is very much battle-hardened by continued pressures from the development and design industries, from council, and from the city manager's office for speed, efficiency, transparency, and professionalism. But it is also a system in evolution, with major reforms to permit processing and development levies underway, and new challenges appearing through neighbourhood visions and regeneration programs in the city's most deprived neighbourhood.

Six Reasons for Success

Six factors help explain how it was possible for Vancouver to create and sustain such a multi-faceted, elaborate, and demanding system:

- the environmental quality of the city's site, setting, and location
- sustained economic growth and demand for quality property
- shared public and political beliefs in environmental quality, the livable city, and participatory planning
- independence and delegated powers to establish technical excellence and incentives for design
- an encapsulated planning and design community where there is substantial peer pressure to conform and perform
- gifted, committed, long-serving politicians, planners, and architects with a shared ethos.

The environmental and landscape quality of Vancouver's site and setting creates an attractive location and an economic and cultural imperative not to squander these assets. The temperate climate, lush vegetation, and extensive legacy of heavily tree-planted Craftsman neighbourhoods – many allowing wonderful views and easy access to the coast – make it easy to understand why neighbourhood conservation is so important to Vancouverites, and why they enjoy a quality of life that cannot be matched in many cities in the world. The desirability of living on the downtown peninsula is immeasurably increased by residents being able to enjoy a high-quality natural world on their doorstep, to look out across sea, islands, and mountains, and partake of "the cult of the view." Those who wish can literally sail off into the sunset. Removing heavy industry and not building freeways has ensured that two of the biggest threats to urban environmental quality were eliminated, so that central area living in Vancouver hardly has to be marketed at all.

The second reason why Vancouver has succeeded in imposing a firm design-control regime is sustained economic growth and a consequent demand for quality property. Richard Lai's overriding argument is that demanding design controls are likely to work only "if the market incentive for development is overwhelming" (Lai 1998: 349). Vancouver's population has grown steadily at about 2 percent per annum for most of the postwar era, while shrinking household size has further increased the demand for residential property. Since 1984 it has been a particular target for affluent Asian business immigrants. The demand for commercial property has been much more variable, particularly depressed through the 1990s, but the demand for residential development has maintained land values and development profits that ensure competition for appropriate sites. While property investment returns and development profits remain good, investors and developers are willing to accede to the control processes and able to pay development-cost levies and community-amenity contributions. A buoyant demand for property has helped the city impose controls on all forms of development, establish high standards of design in each project, and pay for investment in high-quality streets and neighbourhood facilities and amenities. After thirty years of these controls, standards have been set that are now market norms, so there is little or no debate over requirements for street improvements, landscape standards, underground car parking, or private and communal amenity space. A good example is provided by the market adoption of the Craftsman vernacular for single- and multi-family housing in many neighbourhoods, even for projects that are not going through the discretionary design review process.

The third reason for Vancouver's strong planning regime is a public and political consensus about the importance of the city's environment. People move to Vancouver specifically to enjoy its site, setting, temperate climate, and the qualities of its urban landscape, as well as its economic prosperity, safety, and social stability. Once there, many become active defenders of its neighbourhoods, green spaces, views, and heritage buildings, and demanding critics of the quality of development, particularly that close to their own homes. That they have come to share a set of sociopolitical beliefs in environmentalism, the livable city, and participatory planning is exemplified in the single-family zoning and design guideline innovations across the city in the 1990s. The CityPlan consultations confirmed general public preoccupations with the look of the city (see Figure 27) and the way this extends to concerns about views, waterfronts, streetscapes, landscaping, building types (especially heights), and building design. These preoccupations had become evident in the late 1960s as a younger, better educated, more cosmopolitan, and environmentally conscious generation of professional and service workers established new households, particularly in the inner city. It was this new constituency that TEAM urban reformers tapped from the late 1960s and early 1970s until the "livable city" agenda became an indispensable component of every politician's appeal to the electorate. Now the concern for design quality is deeply enshrined in conservative and liberal opinion in the city, particularly on the Westside. Although it is evident that the majority of less affluent eastside neighbourhoods do not wish to enshrine design review, they are none-theless very concerned with issues of greener, traffic-calmed, more pedestrian-friendly streets and the retention of neighbourhood character (see Figure 33).

TEAM reformers first tapped the desire of Vancouverites to be involved in planning decisions in the city, not just in their own neighbourhoods but also downtown and in the major redevelopment areas. All planning processes were subjected to increasing levels of public participation, particularly in the neighbourhood planning endeavours of the 1970s, where planners helped to build community activism and neighbourhood committees. In the megaprojects three levels of public interest – citywide, neighbourhood, and special – were defined for open inclusive processes in regular meetings and workshops. For CityPlan, the mayor insisted that the public directly define planning issues and generate solutions, and this process has continued into the neighbour-hood visions. Power was never devolved to neighbourhood committees – a criticism made by COPE councillors past and present – but intense public participation in planning decision making has been a feature of practice since 1972, and it has strongly reinforced the development of a design-conscious planning system.

These three elements of place, economy, and politics underpin Vancou-ver's planning approaches toward the pursuit of environmental and design quality. But other administrative and organizational characteristics of the sys-tem and the quality of people who operate it have helped to account for the technical excellence and persistence of the planning and urban design re-gime in the city. The Vancouver Charter gave the city very considerable inde-pendence from the provincial government and the chance to forge its own policies and administrative procedures. The city has taken full opportunity to devise its own planning system and unique responses to its development and environmental problems. It has not, as Toronto has, had a provincially con-trolled municipal board intervening in its plans or decisions or trying to safe-guard wider provincial economic goals, often at the expense of local aspirations. Planning independence has been deepened by the delegation of decision making to the planning director, and a policy since 1972 of political non-interference in major planning decisions. The small council and the lack of ward representation naturally reinforce this policy. Council still sets and ap-proves major policy directions and shapes practice. The city manager keeps a close rein on the resources devoted to planning and the efficiency of deci-sion making. But there is a striking level of independence accorded to the department to shape its own practices and develop technical excellence, and this is the fourth reason for success.

The stable organizational structure and the long service of staff in the plan-ning department are a testament to this independence, and the scope for action and job satisfaction that it provides (see Appendix 3). They also allude to the fifth important factor underpinning the Vancouver achievement – the fact that the design and development community in the city is a comparatively small and isolated world, despite globalization. Architects, planners, and developers all refer to its encapsulated nature. The American border immediately to the south and the mountains to the east cut the city off from other large centres of population. While the burgeoning reputation of Vancouver architects is now leading to prominent commissions across the continent, practices are still quite localized. Once practising in Vancouver and its adjacent municipalities, designers are not inclined to leave and, within the development field, everyone knows everyone else. Because reputations are based on local practice, developers and design professionals feel it is essential to build good working relationships with the public sector, in part because of their planning powers, and in part because they are a source of much research and guideline work. Whether the planning department has shaped or been shaped by these practices is an interesting research question, but it has certainly exploited the situation, the Urban Design Panel being the best example. Key developers and designers serve on various working committees established to explore development permitting, zoning regulations, and development levies, where they are in constant dialogue with planners. The cooperative planning model of the megaprojects is a classic demonstration of this ethic, as is the "travelling together" concept of CityPlan visions. A range of consultancy studies commissioned by the city from local practices since the 1970s have informed and structured planning and design practices. The highly localized nature of this activity, the frequency and depth of contact, and the longevity of the relationships cement this close community and develop an ongoing public/private partnership to pursue high-quality design in the city (Vancouver 1999v).

Finally, within this community, very skilled and committed individual designers, design practices, planners, and politicians have left their mark on the city's buildings and streetscapes, and on its planning policies and processes. Extremely gifted architects – Richard Henriquez, James Cheng, and Roger Hughes – have not only consistently produced buildings that would grace any city, but have helped to develop prototype solutions to the city's design problems that have been adopted by others and enshrined in planning practices. The slim and highly glazed view-articulated tower, the tower and townhouse perimeter block or terrace model, and the low-rise internal street/courtyard for ground-oriented housing were initially nurtured by these architectural practices. Other leading practices whose work is repeatedly found in individual quality buildings or in seminal design guidelines include Baker McGarva Hart, Hughes Baldwin, Bing Thom, Busby Bridger, Davidson Yuen

Simpson, Hotson Bakker, Arthur Erickson, Rick Hulbert, Paul Merrick, and John Perkins. Many architects in their practices have been active as Urban Design panellists. Landscape architects have made major contributions with Phillips Farevaag Smallenberg, Harold Neufeldt, and Don Vaughan leading the way.

City planning leadership, vision, and innovative thinking in Vancouver have come from Ray Spaxman between 1973 and 1989, and during the 1990s from Larry Beasley and Ann McAfee. The notion of co-directors of a planning department is perhaps unique, but the complementarity of interests and experience is an irresistible one for the city. Both Jacquie Forbes Robertson and Rick Scobie have also played major roles in establishing new planning practices and in managing the broader agenda in community and development services, respectively. The development planners, led by Ralph Segal, have been critical to urban design endeavours. These departmental leaders have working with them two generations of extremely able individuals with equal intelligence and commitment, and rapidly developing experience.

Politicians who have shaped policy and practices supported the planning department against its critics and often worked alongside it to develop new approaches to recurrent problems. Particularly notable are Alderman Walter Hardwick as the visionary of the livable city; Gordon Campbell, the so-called developers' mayor, who invented the method of CityPlan, reinforced the cooperative planning model, and imposed the development levies; and more recently Mayor Philip Owen who wholeheartedly took up the cause of the Downtown Eastside. Alderman and later mayor Mike Harcourt championed affordable housing, and Alderman Price promoted all manner of planning initiatives and acted as the city's environmental conscience. Less obvious, but frequently cited by planners, were the contributions of Aldermen Mae Brown, Marguerite Ford, and Carole Taylor in defending planning functions in the 1980s. What is especially interesting is the liberal ideology, social conscience, environmental awareness, and participatory ethos that these politicians share with the senior planning staff. This ethos has greatly influenced city practices. To emphasize the importance of individuals to Vancouver's achievement, it is worth quoting leading architect James Cheng: "a discretionary system is only as good as those exercising the discretion" (interview).

The Challenges for the Future

Vancouver's planning system measures up well against the best practice principles established internationally, but still has major challenges to resolve (see Figure 68). These challenges are the subject of current planning reforms, although there are insufficient staff resources to advance them all simultaneously. Interlinked, they have important design implications, even if they are rooted in planning and development issues. They are issues common to most major western cities as they seek to cope with global competition, the withdrawal of senior government welfare funding, the ensuing municipal fiscal crisis, structural economic change, social exclusion, household and lifestyle change, and ethnic diversification.

The provision of enough affordable housing is going to be an ever-increasing challenge as pressures from growth are maintained and the city's supply of land for redevelopment becomes ever more limited. Securing the 20 percent affordable component has proved a challenge in megaprojects with the federal withdrawal from social housing subsidies, but a 30 percent affordable component is now considered to be an appropriate target. Funding remains the primary problem and many observers consider that developers should be expected to supply more than sites for such housing – perhaps land deeded to the city and/or subsidized construction and/or operating costs. Such policies have not been considered in the current Financing Growth Review, which is examining ways to maintain existing levels of infrastructure, facility, and amenity provision. Any resolution of affordable housing issues has to be a broad-based initiative and has to consider not just specific subsidies for social housing but the supply of small, relatively inexpensive housing units across the city, especially for young people. It must encourage secondary suites in single-family neighbourhoods, secondary housing units in back lanes, multiplex and apartment housing intensification on arterial roads, as well as rezoning in and around the new neighbourhood centres. The rejection of even medium-rise housing (i.e., 6 to 12 storeys) in the initial neighbourhood planning visions highlights the need to gain the acceptance of C-2 zoning in single-family neighbourhoods and to improve the livability of the units that it creates. New medium-density ground-oriented housing prototypes are needed at 1.5 to 2.5 floor-space ratio, particularly to make denser neighbourhood centres livable, and to make them acceptable to existing residents.

The second issue is financing growth, and the need to raise development-cost levies from $25 to $60 per square metre, and set appropriate levels of community-amenity contributions on rezoning well above the current $30 per square metre of additional floor space allowed (Vancouver 2001j: 12). Establishing the demographic and fiscal parameters of this debate has been a considerable achievement, but the modest increases in levies introduced in 2000 and 2001 indicate that city politicians are still not prepared to place the full financial burden on the development industry. The alternative of higher property taxes, which might also be required to deliver more social housing, has not been placed on the political agenda, and successive councils have prided themselves on keeping municipal expenditure increases level with the cost of living. Political decisions need to be made about how contributions to the financing of infrastructure and amenities necessary to maintain the city's enviable quality of life will be apportioned.

The issues of affordable housing provision and the financing of growth underpin the question of whether the city will be able to deliver its strategy of the neighbourhood centre as the principal locus of residential intensification and neighbourhood service improvement. Optimism might be derived from looking at the intensification taking place south of the Oakridge Shopping Centre. In the Broadway–Commercial area, however, where accessibility has been dramatically increased by a new interchange and a SkyTrain extension, no zoning changes are planned and the opportunities for intensification are limited to the few vacant or underused sites. Will residents citywide agree to rezoning for denser forms of residential development? Experience shows that residents recognize in principle the need for such developments, but are reluctant to give majority support for rezoning of specific locations near them. There is some optimism in the closeness of the votes on these matters in the first two neighbourhood visions, suggestive of the growing awareness among residents that they themselves may need such housing in the future (Vancouver 1999c). Generally, though, the ability of neighbourhood centres to accommodate significant growth – and with it the delivery of the CityPlan vision – remains uncertain.

The rethinking of single-family zoning and design guidelines is another major housing challenge, although its complexity, political sensitivity, and resource requirements resulted in the project being put on hold in 1999. The goals of the RS Rethink program complement those of the Development and Building Regulation Review, but city planners had another, more profound agenda for zoning changes – to increase the supply of affordable housing in these neighbourhoods by facilitating further secondary suite provision, allowing home-working, and creating more opportunities for ground-oriented housing. The planners argued that "proposed changes to our processes and controls should anticipate these opportunities" (Vancouver 1999n), recognizing the political difficulties inherent in making the RS zoning less exclusionary and more adaptable. Without such changes half of the city will make no real contribution to CityPlan objectives and the accommodation of household growth; clearly this is a major concern for the next decade. The simplification and freeing up of the single-family regulations was to be an integral part of the original conception of the Development and Building Regulation Review. Implementation of the review's recommendations is beginning to deliver improvements in the speed, efficiency, and effectiveness of permitting, and to offer a better service to applicants and adjacent residents. Maintaining community and development/design industry assent to a complex and demanding control regime has not been easy to achieve. More community involvement, conflict resolution mechanisms, third party appeals, and the creation of sector and area generalists to link visions to policy and permitting are stated objectives. These pose even greater challenges to the creation of a truly state-of-the-art permitting process that can offer the neighbourhoods more constructive inputs into the process.

Related to these issues at a strategic level is the future pattern of rapid transit provision in the city, and how it will shape patterns of residential intensification and commercial development outside downtown. A persistent complaint of people living, studying in, or visiting Vancouver is the time required to move around the city using the transport system, the exception being the southeastern corridor, which is well served by the SkyTrain. The failure to develop new rapid transit lines elsewhere in the city in the last fifteen years is particularly evident, although this is not a failure of the city alone, as transit provision is under regional jurisdiction. The failure of the previous provincial government to approve a regional car levy to fund transit was a severe setback. In 1997 the city prepared a transportation plan subsequent to the completion of CityPlan and committed itself to support three new rapid transit lines. One, recently completed, is the looped extension of the existing SkyTrain route from New Westminster to Lougheed Mall and back to the Broadway–Commercial interchange, with a future extension to Coquitlam still in limbo. Detailed studies have been undertaken for transit in the Broadway corridor, possibly extending the SkyTrain from the Broadway–Commercial interchange right across the city to the University of British Columbia at an estimated cost of $710 million. An alternative is to use a rapid transit system for the route or a rapid or trolley bus system on dedicated bus lanes, at an estimated cost of $90 million. The projected sixteen rapid transit stops or twelve to thirteen SkyTrain station locations could become the focus of new commercial and residential development, and consultants' studies have noted the possibilities for improvements to the look and feel of the Broadway corridor with the transit and SkyTrain option.

As significant, but far more politically sensitive, is the transit line linking downtown Vancouver with the international airport and Richmond Centre, which would run through westside Vancouver. This would use one of three routes – the disused Arbutus rail corridor (recently protected by the city), Granville Street (the current rapid bus route), or Cambie Street, each with progressively less intrusion into the heartlands of the Westside. Again it is possible to imagine up to half a dozen new neighbourhood centres being created around the stations en route, of which the Arbutus Neighbourhood is a prototype, but with increased core densities. This transit line is at least a decade away from implementation, but the tensions between its strategic regional role and its potential local role in providing neighbourhood centres on the Westside are obvious. Will the westside neighbourhoods, and the Non-Partisan council that relies on their support, take a positive or negative stance on this opportunity for urban restructuring? Will the compromise reached reinforce the social exclusion perpetuated by the 1990s rezoning? The answers to these challenging questions are crucial for the future of Vancouver.

Sustainability dimensions of planning and design regulations have already been broached. The preparation of the Southeast False Creek official development plan has delineated the wide range of issues that need to be addressed if the city is to realize a deeper commitment to sustainable forms of development. The megaproject will become a testing ground for new regulatory policies and sustainability targets (see Figure 69), and a demonstration project for more sustainable buildings, new energy and building technologies, and new forms of neighbourhood management and economic development. Experience there will shape new building and planning regulations, facility and infrastructure requirements, and planning and environmental management processes citywide, and will impact on all aspects of development from the individual building to the neighbourhood level. It will reshape existing urban design objectives, principles, and policies, and be a major planning preoccupation for at least the next decade. None of these challenges for the future, however, should dim the achievements of Vancouver's urban renaissance in the last thirty years.

This book contends that Vancouver's planning and urban design policies, its discretionary zoning system and the plans, guidelines, consultation, and decision-making processes that implement them are international exemplars of innovative and creative planning from which other cities can learn. Can the city maintain these achievements through the next phase of neighbourhood intensification? Can Vancouver continue to afford a high level of public amenities and quality infrastructure? Can it ensure that all its citizens have access to affordable housing and pleasant, safe neighbourhoods? And finally, a crucial question that has only sporadically been addressed in all the preceding discussions – how will the city's relatively new ethnic diversity, and particularly its large and fast growing Asian community, express itself in planning and design in the future?

Postscript

As this book went to press, the 2002 municipal elections resulted in a stunning defeat of the Non-Partisan Association by the Coalition of Progressive Electors, and a sharp change in Vancouver politics. A near record turnout of electors (50 percent) inverted the 1999 results, leaving COPE with a 9-2 majority and ending sixteen years of comfortable NPA control. The new mayor, Larry Campbell, who decided to run as a COPE candidate only a few months previously, received double the vote of his nearest challenger, the NPA leader Jennifer Clarke. She had deposed Mayor Philip Owen earlier in the year, largely because of his commitment to harm reduction strategies and regeneration in Downtown Eastside, and she had attempted to chart a more business-oriented future for the city. But Larry Campbell, a former police officer and coroner, deeply committed to the Four-Pillar drug program and to the creation of safe injection sites, proved much more attractive to Vancouver voters concerned to promote a more socially compassionate city. To emphasize the self-inflicted nature of the NPA's demise, the new mayor paid tribute to the previous mayor Philip Owen's role in tackling Downtown Eastside's social problems, and stated his intention to ask him to continue his work in the area's various regeneration initiatives. Clarke's "Lady Macbeth" betrayal of Owen was a major element in the NPA's poor showing, but its campaign was further hampered by the unpopularity of provincial premier Gordon Campbell's Liberal government and its neoliberal agenda of cutting public expenditure. This had revived the fortunes of the political left in the city that were at an all-time low after the devastating defeat of the provincial New Democratic Party in 2000.

There were a number of other planning and development issues that emphasized the different political agenda of the two parties. COPE stressed its desire to restore and expand bus services (key NPA politicians were deeply implicated in the prolonged bus strike of 2001 and subsequent cuts in services including the withdrawal of night buses), favouring Rapid bus services over a very expensive subway system linking Downtown to the airport and Richmond city centre (the Cambie Street subway route had been endorsed by council in April 2002). COPE argued for a major social housing component in the stalled Woodward's redevelopment project in Downtown Eastside, and for a referendum on the bid for the 2010 Winter Olympics. It also supported more public involvement in decision making and the opening up of City Hall to delegations and citizen representations in a manner reminiscent of the Harcourt regime of the early 1980s. When COPE councillors were interviewed in 2001, they both expressed their desire for more inclusive forms of local government where diversity was more strongly represented, to revive the campaign for a ward system of government, and to develop more creative models to harness community initiative. Their models were the Office of Neighbourhood Associations in Portland, Oregon, or the Department of Neighbourhoods in Seattle. Their bible was Charles Dobson's (Vancouver Citizens Committee) *The Citizen's Handbook* (www.vcn.bc.ca), with its strong critique of the city's lack of consultation of neighbourhood associations and lack of support for community problem solving. How this would alter the current neighbourhood visioning processes is not entirely clear but COPE councillors obviously believed that public participation was controlled too much from the top in such initiatives. Both councillors stated their commitment to more profound sustainability initiatives for the city and to look more seriously at issues of environmental pollution, particularly sewage treatment, and the city's ecological footprint.

The CityPlan visions continue with the completion of the exercise in Sunset and Victoria–Fraserview/Killarney. Both communities emphasized the desire for cleaner, safer, greener, and more traffic-calmed neighbourhoods and both were more positive towards housing intensification than Dunbar had been. In Sunset residents were prepared to accept duplexes throughout single-family areas to meet housing shortfalls, but were uncertain about denser forms of housing. In Victoria–Fraserview/Killarney there was narrow acceptance of duplexes and rowhouses along transit routes and of low-rise apartments for seniors adjacent to parks, transit, and commercial areas. New visions are underway in Hastings–Sunrise and Renfrew–Collingwood.

Significant developments in transportation planning include the previous council's endorsement of a rapid transit strategy for recommendation to TransLink and federal and provincial governments, and the completion of a draft of the Downtown Transportation Plan. The former recommends a SkyTrain extension from Commercial to Broadway at Granville, and a subway from downtown to Richmond along Cambie (which the new mayor has already questioned). Also included is a possible streetcar route along the Arbutus corridor from False Creek North and a B-line express bus loop to link the Broadway route to a second crosstown route on 41st Avenue, as well as a new line on East Hastings. Transit ridership to work is projected to increase 45 percent to 2021 to absorb most of the increase in commuting (car driver trips will increase by only 18 percent). The draft Downtown Transportation Plan, approved by council in April 2002, is impressive in its ambition, comprehensiveness, and detail. It has four strategies – of pedestrians first, a downtown cycling network, a network of transit including two streetcar routes, and safe and sustainable traffic management. It identifies fifty-three "spot improvements" to the road network, two-thirds of which deliver significant benefits to pedestrians and cyclists. So major progress is being made and key strategic decisions await endorsement by the new council.

Alongside the election there were three referenda on whether the city should be allowed to borrow funds for public works, parks and recreation, and cost-shared infrastructure (the latter to ensure monies from higher levels of government). All three were comfortably approved, but they emphasize the financial constraints imposed on the city. The Financing Growth Review is now out for public debate and review, which will be completed early in 2003 when the level of development-cost levies will be resolved at somewhere between the current $25 and a maximum $75 per square metre (covering a third to virtually all additional infrastructure costs respectively). With COPE in power there is more likelihood of a full cost-recovering development levy being set and this would be a significant step forward for the city.

Time will tell whether more significant changes in planning practices will emerge but, as one commentator noted in the post-election analysis in the *Vancouver Sun*, there is unlikely to be a great deal of change because the city is run by its bureaucracy and is required by law to have a balanced budget. The broad lineaments of Vancouver's planning and design are unlikely to be disturbed even by this quite radical shift in political power, a testament to the consensus that has been established on planning matters over the last three decades, and the system's delivery of tangible environmental and social benefits.

Appendix 1
Awards for planning and design in Vancouver

Awards to the Vancouver Planning Department for Contributions to Planning

1974   Blood Alley Square and Trounce Alley: Finalist, Park and Tilford Trophy for Contributions to Community Beautification

1974   National Award of Honour for Outstanding Contributions to Heritage Conservation, Heritage Canada

1975   Award of Excellence Vancouver Planning, Canadian Institute of Planners

1984   "8 Years After": Award of Excellence, Canadian Institute of Planners

1985   Georgia Street and Robson Street Character Area Guidelines, Award of Excellence, Canadian Institute of Planners

1986   False Creek South Shore, Special Achievement Award, International Downtown Association

1987   Legacies Program, Downtown Vancouver Association Achievement Award and Special Achievement Award, International Downtown Association

1988   Vancouver Legacies and Gifts Program: National Honour Award, Canadian Institute of Planners

1989   Artist Studios in Vancouver: Award of Excellence, Canadian Institute of Planners

1991   Heritage Plaque Program: Award of Honour, Heritage BC

1991   Coal Harbour Policy Plan: Award of Merit, Planning Institute of BC

1992   Central Area Plan: Award of Merit, Planning Institute of BC

1992   False Creek North Plan: "Golden Nugget" Award, Pacific Coast Builders

1992   Coal Harbour Plan: Excellence on the Waterfront, Honour Award, Waterfront Centre Society

1993   Special Achievement Award for CityPlan Public Process, International Downtown Association

1993   Downtown South Plan/Implementation: Award for Planning Excellence, Planning Institute of BC

1994 Contributions to Local Democracy Award: CityPlan Resource Centre, Social Planning and Research Council of BC

1994 Contributions to Local Democracy Award: Victory Square Planning Program, Social Planning and Research Council of BC

1994 Georgie Silver Award: Excellence in Government Cooperation for Concord Pacific Place, Canadian Home Builders Association of BC

1995 Georgie Award: Excellence in Government Cooperation for Collingwood Village, Canadian Home Builders Association of BC

1995 CityPlan Public Process: National Honour Award for Citizen Participation, Canadian Institute of Planners

1995 Central Waterfront Port Lands Policy and Protocol: National Honour Award for Intergovernmental Cooperation, Canadian Institute of Planners

1996 Downtown Public Realm Improvements: Award of Merit, Planning Institute of BC

1996 Waterfront Planning Process and Plans, World's 100 Best Planning Practices, United Nations Centre for Human Settlements, Habitat II

1996 False Creek Policy Broadsheet and Official Development Plan: Award of Excellence, Planning Institute of BC

1997 Ridgeway Greenway Regional Award of Merit, Canadian Association of Landscape Architects

1998 Vancouver Skyline Study: Award for Planning Excellence, Planning Institute of BC

1999 Case Studies in Heritage Revitalization: Outstanding Achievement Award, Heritage Society of BC

1999 City of Vancouver Heritage Conservation Program Website: Outstanding Achievement Award, Heritage Society of BC

2000 Southeast False Creek Environmentally Sustainable Community Policy Statement: National Honour Award, Canadian Institute of Planners

2000 Community Web Pages: Spirit of Innovation Award, Municipal Information Systems Association of BC

2001 Public Process Guide: Education Award, Canadian Association of Municipal Administrators

2001 Public Practices Award, British Columbia Society of Landscape Architects

Source: This list was compiled by Ann McAfee, co-director of the City of Vancouver planning department, and staff.

Awards from Architectural Institute of British Columbia for Buildings in the City of Vancouver

Year	Building	Architect	Award
1992	Presidio	Henriquez and Partners Architects	merit
	AIBC Offices rehab/conversion	Marshall Fisher Architects	medal
	Cathedral Place	Paul Merrick Architects Ltd	merit
	False Creek Yacht Club	Bing Thom Architects, Inc.	merit
1993	No awards		
1994	No awards		
1995	Central City Lodge	Neale Staniszkis Doll Adams	medal
	Studio for Two Architects	Bourque Bruegger Architects	medal
	2211 West 4th Avenue	Hotson Bakker Architects	honourable mention
	Concord Pacific Place, 1088 Pacific	Busby Bridger Architects	honourable mention
1996	No awards		
1997	No awards		
1998	Bantleman Court Youth Housing, Strathcona	Architectura Planning Architecture Interiors, Inc.	medal
	The Residences on Georgia: 1200-1288 West Georgia Street	James K.M. Cheng Architects, Inc.	medal
	Villa Carital	Neale Staniszkis Doll Adams Architects	merit
	Palisades Residential Towers: 1200-1288 Alberni	James K.M. Cheng Architects, Inc.	medal
1999	VanCity Place for Youth	Nigel Baldwin Architects Ltd	medal
	House in West Vancouver	Peter Cardew Architect	medal
	Morris and Helen Belkin Art Gallery, UBC	Peter Cardew Architect	medal

Year	Building	Architect	Award
1999	Odlum Drive Live/Work Studios	Peter Cardew Architect	medal
	E-Comm	Architectura Planning Architecture Interiors, Inc.	merit
2000	Pacific Canada Pavilion	Bing Thom Architects	medal
	Bruce Eriksen Place	Henriquez Partners Architects	medal
	Kitsilano Community Centre	Francl Architect Inc.	merit
	Case Study 547	Baker McGarva Hart, Inc.	merit
2001	Coal Harbour Community Centre and Park	Henriquez Partners Architects	medal
	Roundhouse Community Centre	Baker McGarva Hart, Inc.	merit
	Aquarius at the Quayside Neighbourhood (Phase 1)	James K.M. Cheng Architects, Inc.	merit

Appendix 2
Chronology of key planning initiatives, policy documents, government policies, and politics in the City of Vancouver, 1965-2001

Chronology of key planning initiatives and policy documents in the City of Vancouver, 1965-2001

Year	Policy and plan	Guidance and publications	Landmark developments
65			Beach Towers (Van Norman)
68			Pacific Centre Phase 1 (Pelli/Gruen) Bentall Centre Phase 1 (Musson & Cattell)
69			Guinness Tower (Paine) MacMillan Bloedel (Erickson/Massey)
70	False Creek Concept Plan		
71			Toronto Dominion (Pelli)
72			The Blood and Trounce alleys (conservation)
73	Spaxman appointed	Urban Design Panel established	805 Broadway Centre (Plavsic & Assoc.) Maple Tree Square (rehab)
74	NIP program starts Residential zoning 0.45 = >0.6 FAR False Creek South ODP: Annual Reviews begin	Shaping the Future: Planning goal statement Heritage Commission established: first listings	
75	Downtown ODP Downtown Character Areas	Development Permit Board changes	

Year	Policy and plan	Guidance and publications	Landmark developments
76		Central Broadway – Urban Design Guidelines	Harbour Centre (WZMH)
77			False Creek South Housing Phase 1 Scotia Tower (WZMH)
78		Housing Families at High Densities guidelines	Crown Life Plaza (Rhone & Iredale) Evergreen Building (Erickson)
79	Central Waterfront ODP		Provincial Law Courts (Erickson) Robson Square (Erickson)
80			Granville Island (CMHC/Hotson)
81			Daon Building (MCM Partnership)
82	First Shaughnessy ODP Downtown Eastside ODP City forms Urban Design Section	First Shaughnessy Design Guidelines and Panel	
83			BC Place Stadium (Phillips Barratt)
84	SE Granville Slopes ODP (BC Place Phase 1)	Chilton Report on permit processing	Park Place (Musson Cattell Mackey)
85			Pacific Heights Housing Co-op (Roger Hughes Architects) Hongkong Bank (WZMH)
86	Single-Family Residential rezoning reduces house size	Heritage Policies and Guidelines Vancouver Heritage Inventory	Canada Place (Zeidler Roberts) Sinclair Centre (Henriquez)
87	Yaletown/Gastown rezoning Secondary Suites Policy		Sylvia Hotel Extension (Henriquez)
88	Single-Family Residential rezoning	False Creek North Policy Broadsheets Hardwick Report on permit processing	Tudor Manor (Merrick)

Year	Policy and plan	Guidance and publications	Landmark developments
89	Spaxman resigns Fletcher appointed Annual reviews end Downtown South rezoning Affordable housing policy	Vancouver Views Study and Protection Policy Public Involvement in False Creek North Report	Cambridge Gardens (Cheng) City Square (Merrick) Pacific Centre Phase 2 (Zeidler Roberts)
90	False Creek North ODP Residential rezoning Coal Harbour COP	View corridors amended *Clouds of Change* Report: UDI Brief on permitting	Eugenia Place (Henriquez)
91	Central Area Plan – Goals and Land Use Housing opportunities strategy	Shoreline Treatment Study Downtown South Guidelines	Presidio (Henriquez) Cathedral Place (Merrick)
92	CityPlan initiated Heritage policies consolidated	High-Density Housing Guidelines revised Urban Landscape Task Force Plaza Design Guidelines Triangle West Character	BC Hydro (MCM) Waterfront Centre (MCM)
93	CityPlan: Ideas exercise: Making Choices	South Shaughnessy Design Guidelines Downtown Character Areas revised	1000 Beach Avenue (Hulbert) 888 Beach (Cheng)
94	Private property Tree Bylaw CityPlan Futures Co-Directors of Planning appointed CityPlan: Making Choices Industrial Land Strategy	Kitsilano Guidelines Streetscape Manual (Downtown South)	
95	Vancouver Greenways Plan CityPlan adopted	Oakridge–Langara Policy	Public Library (Safdie) Capers Block (Hotson Bakker)
96	Downtown ODP revised False Creek Flats Concept Plan City Transportation Plan	Ecological Planning Framework RS-5, RS-6 Guidelines terms of reference	

Year	Policy and plan	Guidance and publications	Landmark developments
97		Downtown Skyline Study Development and Building Regulation Review starts	False Creek North Phase 1: Yaletown Edge
98	Dunbar: KCC visions completed (CityPlan) RS-5, RS-6 rezonings completed	Single-family zoning review starts Southeast False Creek Charrette	The Residences on Georgia (Cheng) False Creek North Phase 2: Roundhouse False Creek North Phase 3: Waterworks False Creek North Phase 3: Aquarius (Cheng)
99	Victoria– Fraserview; Sunset–Killarney Visions initiated	Designing Safer Urban Environments Financing Growth Review commences	
00	DCLs extended across city Arbutus Corridor ODP: protects RT line Southeast False Creek policy statement	Downtown Transportation Plan	Coal Harbour Marina Neighbourhood Portside Convention Centre abandoned
01	RS-7S Rezoning	Gastown Heritage Management Plan	Wall Centre (Busby)

Chronology of regional and provincial initiatives and politics in the City of Vancouver, 1965-2001

Year	Regional and provincial initiatives	City politics
66	Lower Mainland Regional Planning Board Plan approved	
67	Greater Vancouver Regional District established	Freeway controversy
68	GVRD takes over regional planning	ELECTION: T. Campbell Mayor: NPA (8) TEAM (2) COPE (1)
70		ELECTION: NPA (7) TEAM (2) COPE (1) IND (1)
71	Province designates Gastown/ Chinatown historic districts	Gastown riots
72		ELECTION: Phillips Mayor: TEAM (9) COPE (2); NDP defeat Social Credit provincially; DERA formed
74	Federal NIP and RRAP programs commence	ELECTION: Phillips Mayor: TEAM (6) COPE (2) NPA (3)
75	GVRD Livable Region Plan approved	
76		ELECTION: Phillips Mayor: TEAM (5) COPE (2) NPA (4)
78		ELECTION: Volrich Mayor: TEAM (4) COPE (2) NPA (5); Social Credit defeat NDP provincially
80	Livable Region Plan revised Province announces Expo, SkyTrain, and related developments	ELECTION: Harcourt Mayor: COPE (3) TEAM (2) NPA (5)
81		Municipal staff strike
83	Province makes GVRD advisory body only	
84		ELECTION: Harcourt Mayor: NPA (5) COPE (4) NDP (2)
85	SkyTrain opens	
86	Expo '86 held	ELECTION: G. Campbell Mayor: NPA (9) COPE (1)
88	North False Creek lands sold to Li Ka-shing	Regatta Condo sale controversy
89		Condo fever
90	Province approves city use of development-cost levies GVRD Planning Review	ELECTION: G. Campbell Mayor: NPA (6) COPE (5); NDP defeat Social Credit provincially; Monster houses
93	Federal government withdraws from social housing subsidies	ELECTION: Owen Mayor: NPA (10) COPE (1)

Year	Regional and provincial initiatives	City politics
94	GVRD's Livable Region Strategic Plan adopts compact development option Provincial heritage legislation	
96		ELECTION: Owen Mayor: NPA sweep all 11 seats
98	Quality of Condominium Construction Report	
99		ELECTION: Owen Mayor: NPA (9) COPE (2)
00	Provincial levy for "leaky condos"	Municipal staff industrial action Vancouver Agreement with federal and provincial governments and Health Board to tackle Downtown Eastside problems
01		NDP defeated provincially: Liberals take all but 2 seats

Appendix 3
Organization charts for the city planning function, 1975-2001

There are a number of striking features about these organizational diagrams, not least the continuity of key personnel as planners, associate directors, and then (co-)directors, over the last thirty years. The strong individual leadership of the period 1973-87 contrasts with the co-direction that began with the early departure of Spaxman's successor. This has continued through to the present. It is interesting, too, that Larry Beasley has retained control of those areas of planning activity that most interested Ray Spaxman, while Ann McAfee has taken on those areas that were not Spaxman's forte. It is important to note that Development Services has been separated from planning but remains within the overall Community Services Group. The organizational units established by the mid-1980s have persisted through to the present, largely, one suspects, because of the long-standing, clearly defined interests of those who now have the senior positions. Again, the continuity is striking.

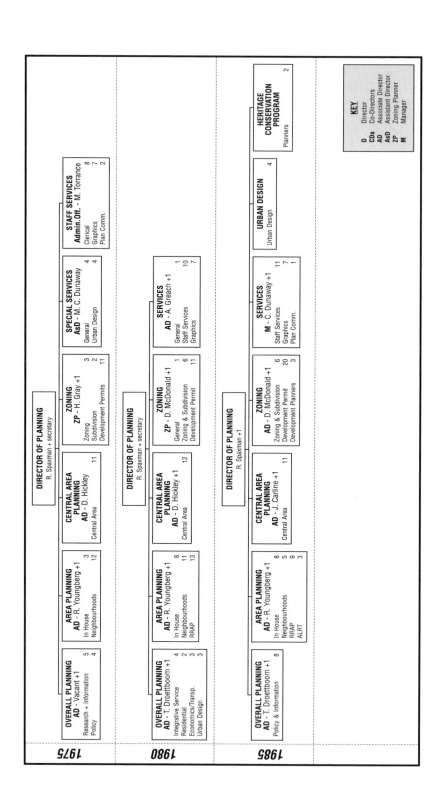

Organizational chart — Director of Planning, 1975 / 1980 / 1985

1975

DIRECTOR OF PLANNING — R. Spaxman + secretary

- OVERALL PLANNING — AD - Vacant +1
  - Research + Information 5
  - Policy 4
- AREA PLANNING — AD - R. Youngberg +1
  - In House 3
  - Neighbourhoods 12
- CENTRAL AREA PLANNING — AD - D. Hickley
  - Central Area 11
- ZONING — ZP - H. Gray +1
  - Zoning 3
  - Subdivision 2
  - Development Permits 11
- SPECIAL SERVICES — AsD - M. C. Dunaway
  - General 4
  - Urban Design 4
- STAFF SERVICES — Admin.Off. - M. Torrance
  - Clerical 8
  - Graphics 7
  - Plan Comm. 2

1980

DIRECTOR OF PLANNING — R. Spaxman + secretary

- OVERALL PLANNING — AD - T. Droettboom +1
  - Integrative Service 4
  - Residential 2
  - Economics/Transp. 3
  - Urban Design 3
- AREA PLANNING — AD - R. Youngberg +1
  - In House 8
  - Neighbourhoods 11
  - RRAP 13
- CENTRAL AREA PLANNING — AD - D. Hickley +1
  - Central Area 12
- ZONING — ZP - D. McDonald +1
  - General 1
  - Zoning & Subdivision 6
  - Development Permit 11
- SERVICES — AD - A. Greach +1
  - General 1
  - Staff Services 10
  - Graphics 7

1985

DIRECTOR OF PLANNING — R. Spaxman +1

- OVERALL PLANNING — AD - T. Droettboom +1
  - Policy & Information 8
- AREA PLANNING — AD - R. Youngberg +1
  - In House 8
  - Neighbourhoods 5
  - RRAP 9
  - ALRT 3
- CENTRAL AREA PLANNING — AD - J. Carline +1
  - Central Area 11
- ZONING — AD - D. McDonald +1
  - Zoning & Subdivision 6
  - Development Permit 20
  - Development Planners 3
- SERVICES — M - C. Dunaway +1
  - Staff Services 11
  - Graphics 7
  - Plan Comm. 1
- URBAN DESIGN
  - Urban Design 4
- HERITAGE CONSERVATION PROGRAM
  - Planners 2

KEY

D	Director
CDs	Co-Directors
AD	Associate Director
AsD	Assistant Director
ZP	Zoning Planner
M	Manager

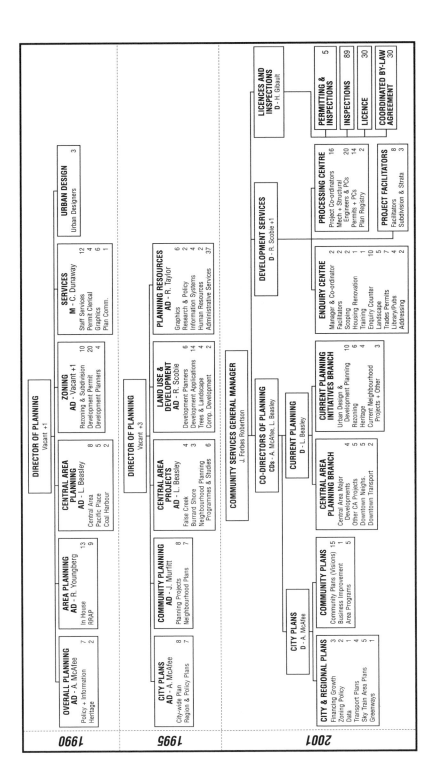

1990

DIRECTOR OF PLANNING — Vacant +1

OVERALL PLANNING — AD - A. McAfee
- Policy + Information — 7
- Heritage — 2

AREA PLANNING — AD - R. Youngberg
- In House — 13
- RRAP — 9

CENTRAL AREA PLANNING — AD - L. Beasley
- Central Area — 8
- Pacific Place — 5
- Coal Harbour — 2

ZONING — AD - Vacant +1
- Rezoning & Subdivision — 10
- Development Permit — 20
- Development Planners — 4

SERVICES — M - C. Dunaway
- Staff Services — 12
- Permit Clerical — 4
- Graphics — 6
- Plan Comm. — 1

URBAN DESIGN
- Urban Designers — 3

1995

DIRECTOR OF PLANNING — Vacant +3

CITY PLANS — AD - A. McAfee
- City-wide Plan — 8
- Region & Policy Plans — 7

COMMUNITY PLANNING — AD - J. Murfitt
- Planning Projects — 8
- Neighbourhood Plans — 7

CENTRAL AREA PROJECTS — AD - L. Beasley
- False Creek — 4
- Burrard Shore — 3
- Neighbourhood Planning Programmes & Studies — 6

LAND USE & DEVELOPMENT — AD - R. Scobie
- Development Planners — 6
- Development Applications — 14
- Trees & Landscape — 4
- Comp. Development — 2

PLANNING RESOURCES — AD - R. Taylor
- Graphics — 6
- Research & Policy — 2
- Information Systems — 4
- Human Resources — 2
- Administrative Services — 37

2001

COMMUNITY SERVICES GENERAL MANAGER — J. Forbes Robertson

CO-DIRECTORS of PLANNING — CDs - A. McAfee, L. Beasley

CITY PLANS — D - A. McAfee

CITY & REGIONAL PLANS
- Financing Growth — 3
- Zoning Policy — 2
- Data — 1
- Transport Plans — 4
- Sky Train Area Plans — 5
- Greenways — 1

COMMUNITY PLANS
- Community Plans (Visions) — 15
- Business Improvement — 1
- Area Programs — 5

CURRENT PLANNING — D - L. Beasley

CENTRAL AREA PLANNING BRANCH
- Central Area Major Developments — 4
- Other CA Projects — 5
- Downtown Neighs. — 5
- Downtown Transport — 2

CURRENT PLANNING INITIATIVES BRANCH
- Urban Design & Development Planning — 10
- Rezoning — 6
- Heritage — 4
- Current Neighbourhood Projects + Other — 3

DEVELOPMENT SERVICES — D - R. Scobie +1

ENQUIRY CENTRE
- Manager & Co-ordinator — 2
- Facilitators — 2
- Scoping — 2
- Housing Renovation — 1
- Training — 1
- Enquiry Counter — 10
- Landscape — 5
- Trades Permits — 7
- Library/Pubs — 4
- Addressing — 2

PROCESSING CENTRE
- Project Co-ordinators — 16
- Mech + Structural Engineers & PCs — 20
- Permits + PCs — 14
- Plan Registry — 2

PROJECT FACILITATORS
- Facilitators — 8
- Subdivision & Strata — 3

LICENCES AND INSPECTIONS — D - H. Gibault
- PERMITTING & INSPECTIONS — 5
- INSPECTIONS — 89
- LICENCE — 30
- COORDINATED BY-LAW AGREEMENT — 30

Glossary

amenity: amenity is a catch-all term meaning "the quality of being pleasant," widely used in planning practice to describe one of its principal objectives. So amenity is a composite of both aesthetic and environmental qualities, but it is also used to describe physical installations that deliver these qualities. These can be private (views, privacy, quiet, sitting out space, landscaped and play spaces, and other recreational facilities) or public (views from public places, pleasant streets and sidewalks, furnishings, landscaping public spaces, and public art).

back of sidewalk: a phrase used to describe development that is built hard up against the street, in contrast to much modern development that employs setbacks (originally to improve internal daylighting conditions).

Board of Variance: Vancouver independent appeal body that hears and decides upon appeals regarding refusals of rezoning, development permits, signage, tree permits, and parking matters. The province and the city each appoint two members, with a fifth, the chair, appointed by the members themselves.

C-2, C-3A, etc: a Vancouver zoning category for commercial land use (shops, offices) with residential units above, usually at least 3 storeys overall.

CD-1 comprehensive development zoning: a Vancouver zoning category used for areas being completely redeveloped, negotiated on a site-by-site or project-by-project basis (over 400 of these in the city).

Central (now Canada) Mortgage and Housing Corporation (CMHC): federal Crown corporation funding urban initiatives and housing.

Character area guidelines: category of design guidelines applied to particular streets and sub-areas of downtown, elucidating area character as a basis for new designs.

charette: a term used to describe a participative and collaborative design exercise, involving the public, design professionals, and others, set up to test out a range of design ideas and develop consensus.

CityPlan: the citywide plan approved in 1995, more accurately "a broad vision, to guide policy decisions."

community-amenity contributions: charges levied on some private rezonings since 1989; from 1999, these charges were levied on all private rezonings. The charges pay for parks, social housing, and community centres.

Confederation of Progressive Electors (COPE): Vancouver municipal party established in 1968 with affiliations to the New Democratic Party, organized labour, and community activists; returned to power in the 2002 civic election with Larry Campbell as mayor.

Crime Prevention through Environmental Design: a report produced by a mayor's task force in 1994, and a phrase used for public safety-oriented design initiatives.

Development Application and Information Centre: a Vancouver planning service, suggested in 1993, established in 1994, but superseded by the Enquiry Centre established in 1999, that handled over-the-counter inquiries and minor developments in the permitting process.

Development and Building Regulation Review: a process initiated in Vancouver in 1997 to reorganize and improve permitting processes; this is ongoing.

development-cost levies: charges on development permits introduced area by area from 1989 onward; from 2000, such levies were applied citywide on all permits for more than four housing units; largely used to fund parks, daycare, and replacement housing.

Development Permit Board: a Vancouver city board of three municipal department heads (planning, engineering, city manager) that decides major permit applications, now chaired by the non-voting director of Development Services.

Development Permit Board Advisory Panel: a Vancouver panel appointed by council in 1974 to offer advice to the Development Permit Board. It has four community, two developer, and two designer appointees.

Development Permit Process Liaison Committee: established by council in 1991 to provide advice on reforms of permit processing; now defunct.

Development Permit Staff Committee: internal committee (planning and engineering) that prepares reports on all development permits that go before the Development Permit Board.

development planners: the architect-trained Vancouver planners who manage major permit applications and minor applications with significant design implications. Each of the seven planners is also responsible for reviewing the application of a particular category of zoning.

dwelling units per hectare: an urban planning measure of the density of residential development.

facadism: the practice of retaining only the facade of older buildings, rather than retaining their shell or interiors intact.

floor plate: the footprint or floor plan of a building, usually qualified by its dimensions (slim/broad, etc.).

floor-space ratio: an urban planning/zoning measure for the amount of floor space allowed on a building site, expressed as a multiple of the site area, so a 2:1 FSR would allow a floor space of twice the area of the lot size.

gentrification: the process whereby an area becomes occupied by progressively more affluent residents, and the types of accommodation, land uses, and services that reflect their needs.

Greater Vancouver Regional District (GVRD): established by the province in 1987, a single, upper-tier municipal government embracing twenty municipalities including the City of Vancouver (see Figure 4).

greenfield development: development that takes place on rural land previously not built on.

greenway: a Vancouver innovation of 1995, these are green paths for pedestrians or cyclists, a network of landscaped routes designed to cover the city to encourage walking and cycling.

ground-oriented housing: housing generally of 4 storeys or less that has easy access to the ground (i.e., does not rely on elevator access).

Heritage Revitalization Agreements: an agreement negotiated by the city and an owner of a heritage property, allowing variance or additions to bylaws or permits in order to ensure the conservation of heritage structures. The agreement may supersede land-use regulations and vary use, density, and siting regulations.

incubator units: low-rent units that provide small businesses (retail/commercial) with cheap accommodation to help them grow.

infill: new free-standing development in a neighbourhood, usually applied to one building alongside another fronting the street, but can generally describe the addition of new buildings alongside existing structures.

live/work units: units that are built to accommodate both commercial and residential functions, commercial and business uses traditionally being excluded from residential neighbourhoods by zoning.

major project public amenity requirements (MPPARs): facilities that urban planners require developers to provide in the megaprojects.

monster houses: term given to houses that maximize their zoning allowance, but which also adopt architectural treatments that sharply diverge from traditional architecture in a neighbourhood.

Neighbourhood Integrated Service Teams (NIST): instituted by council in 1994 to provide an effective community-based city service delivery system; there are fifteen teams to cover the city's twenty-three neighbourhoods.

NIMBY: stands for not in my backyard, a syndrome to describe public opposition to growth or change, or a particular development project proposed in their neighbourhood or the city at large.

Non-Partisan Association: a political association in western Canada that dominated Vancouver city elections from 1937 to 2002.

official development plan: an area plan that has legal status under the Vancouver Charter and which regulates development in the area defined by the plan. There are eight current plans covering parts of the city; two others have been repealed.

perimeter block: development that encloses all four sides of a city block with units that directly address the street through their windows and doorways.

pilotis: columns that raise a building above the ground to allow free movement for pedestrians (and vehicles) at the ground floor level, an important modernist device in architecture.

podium: a base for a tower, covering much more of the building plot than the tower itself, and used as a device to retain the enclosure of the street and to accommodate other building uses and additional floor space.

RM-1/RM-2: multiple-family residential zoning allowing various densities.

RS-1/RS-15, etc: single-family residential zoning that regulates conversions, extensions, and new buildings. The suffix S indicates provision for one supplementary suite (a "for rent" suite within the house). Each designation RS-1, RS-3, RS-5, RS-6, and RS-7 has different regulations and design guidelines.

RT-1/RT-2, etc: two-family residential zoning.

Sea bus: ferry connecting downtown to North Vancouver, initiated in 1977.

seawall: the constructed wall that retains the sea, and underpins the coastal walk/cycleway in downtown Vancouver.

single-room occupancy: small rental housing units, usually unserviced rooms without amenities.

SkyTrain: advanced light rapid transit (ALRT) linking downtown to New Westminster, Burnaby, and Surrey since 1986, and Coquitlam since 2002; largely constructed above ground and much of it on concrete pylons.

skywalk: overground pedestrian bridges linking shops and offices.

Street-wall, street-wall apartments: buildings (usually 5 to 12 storeys) that enclose the street with a continuous wall.

The Electors Action Movement (TEAM): centrist but reform-oriented city political party established in 1968 but inactive by the late 1980s. Revived in 2002.

townhouse: a 3- or 4-storey house built back of sidewalk or with minimum setback, applied to detached dwellings of the early twentieth century. In Vancouver the term is particularly applied to terraced housing built in the downtown peninsula from the late 1980s onwards as part of high-rise redevelopment.

transfer-of-development rights: utilized to transfer zoning entitlements from sites with historic buildings, to ensure retention of the heritage structure without penalizing the owner.

Urban Design Panel: established in 1973 to replace the Architectural Advisory Panel to give impartial, professional advice to the director of planning.

Urban Development Institute: a Canadian developers' lobby group that represents the industry's views to council and higher levels of government.

Vancouver Board of Parks and Recreation (Park Board): established by council to care for and manage city parks and run by seven elected commissioners; also responsible for care of city trees.

Vancouver Charter: replaced the 1886 Vancouver Incorporation Act in 1953 and specifies powers to govern and provide services for citizens. Can be amended by application to the provincial government. Gives the city significant independence and freedom of action.

Vancouver Planning Commission: established in 1926 as the Vancouver Town Planning Commission, this council-appointed commission originally served as the city's planning department until 1951. Its role was redefined in 1977 to advise council on planning matters and keep up-to-date goals and a program of policy or a plan, but the latter responsibilities were removed in 1997.

Vancouver Port Authority: federal agency owning and managing the port of Vancouver.

zoning: a set of regulations that determine allowable land uses and the dimensions of built forms in an area, almost universally applied to built-up areas in North America.

Further details on all Vancouver institutions and organizations are available in a brochure published by the City of Vancouver Planning Department, *A to Z: Answers to Some of the Most Frequently Asked Questions About our City* (Vancouver, 1998), and in C. Davis, ed., *The Greater Vancouver Book: An Urban Encyclopedia* (Surrey, BC: Linkman Books, 1997).

References

Books, Articles, and Other Publications

Abbott, C. 1991. Urban Design in Portland, Oregon, as Policy and Process: 1960-1989. *Planning Perspectives* 6(1): 1-18.

–. 2001. *Greater Portland in Urban Life and Landscape in the Pacific North West.* Philadelphia: University of Pennsylvania Press.

Alexander, C. 1977. *A Pattern Language: Towns, Buildings, Construction.* Oxford, UK: Oxford University Press. (Unpublished draft circulated in 1971 as Cells for Subcultures).

–. 1987. *A New Theory of Urban Design.* Oxford, UK: Oxford University Press.

Anderson, K.J. 1988. Cultural Hegemony and the Race-Definition Process in Chinatown, Vancouver: 1880-1980. *Environment and Planning D: Society and Space* 6(2): 127-49.

Anderson, S. 1978. *On Streets.* Cambridge, MA: MIT Press.

Award of Excellence: Public Market Complex, Granville Island, Vancouver. 1976. *Canadian Architect Yearbook.* Np.

Bancroft-Jones, A., B. Burgess, and M. Chu. 1986. Amenity Bonuses: The Record since 1976. *Quarterly Review* 3(1): 3-4.

Barnett, J. 1974. *Urban Design as Public Policy: Practical Methods for Improving Cities.* New York: McGraw-Hill.

–. 1982. *An Introduction to Urban Design.* New York: Harper and Row.

–. 1995. *The Fractured Metropolis: Improving the New City, Restoring the Old City, Reshaping the Region.* New York: Harper Collins.

Beasley, L. 1997. Vancouver, British Columbia: New Urban Neighbourhoods in Old Urban Ways. Paper presented to the Making Cities Livable Conference in April at Sante Fe, NM.

–. 2000a. The Vancouver Waterfront Experience: The City Perspective. Paper presented to the Worldwide Waterfront '99 Conference. 6-8 October 1999. Vancouver, BC.

–. 2000b. "Living First" in Downtown Vancouver. *Zoning News,* April: 1-4.

Beers, D. 1998. Beyond Tacky-Leaky-Condos. *Vancouver Magazine,* September: 76-80.

Bentley, I., A. Alcock, S. McGlynn, P. Murrain, and G. Smith. 1985. *Responsive Environments: A Manual for Designers.* London: Architectural Press.

Berelowitz, L. 1985. Edge City Vancouver: Repository of Form and Style. *Canadian Architect* 30(10): 16-23.

–. 1988. The Liveable City: Social Housing in Vancouver. *Canadian Architect* 33(2): 34-37.

–. 1992. High-Rise Anxiety in Vancouver. *Canadian Architect* 37(1): 9-13.

–. 1993. Remaking History: Cathedral Place in Vancouver. *Canadian Architect* 38(6): 18-19.

–. 1995. Yaletown on the Edge. *Canadian Architect* 40(3): 20-21.

–. 1997. From Factor 15 to Feu d'artifice: The Nature of Public Space in Vancouver. *a/r/c: Architecture Research Criticism* 1(5): 32-37.

–. 1998. Reinventing Vancouver's Waterfront, Projects for a New Urban Mythology. *Bauwelt* 89(12): 600-5 (in German; author's original in English).

Berman, M. 1982. *All That Is Solid Melts into Air: The Experience of Modernity.* London: Verso.

Biddle, V. 1986. Downtown Office Space. *Quarterly Review* 13(1): 18-19.

Birmingham and Wood Architects. 1972. *Restoration Report: The Case for Renewed Life in the Old City.* Vancouver: Vancouver City Council.

Blaesser, B.W. 1994. The Abuse of Discretionary Power. In B.C. Scheer and W. Preiser, eds., *Design Review: Challenging Urban Aesthetic Control,* 42-55. New York: Chapman and Hall.

Blore, S. 1998. The *S* Word. *Georgia Straight,* 25 June to 2 July, 17-25.

Blore, S., and J. Sutherland. 1999. Building Smileyville. *Vancouver Magazine* 32(9): 48-58, 105.

Boddy, T. 1982. Arthur Erickson's Vancouver Art Gallery. *Section A* 2(2): 4-7.

–. 1994a. Post Terminal City: Urban Design in Vancouver. *Canadian Architect* 29(3): 16-21.

–. 1994b. Plastic Lion's Gate: A Short History of the Postmodern in Vancouver Architecture. In P. Delany, ed., *Vancouver: Representing the Postmodern City,* 25-49. Vancouver: Arsenal Pulp Press.

Boyer, C. 1994. *The City of Collective Memory.* Cambridge, MA: MIT Press.

Brine, J. 1997. Urban Design Advisory Panels. *Australian Planner* 34(2): 116-20.

British Columbia. 1997. *Development Cost Charge: Best Practices Guide.* Victoria, BC.

–. 1998. *The Renewal of Trust in Residential Construction.* Report of the Commission of Inquiry into the Quality of Condominium Architecture in British Columbia. Victoria, BC: Lieutenant-Governor.

–. 1999. *Which Legacy? Vancouver's Downtown Communities and the Expansion of the Vancouver Convention and Exhibition Centre.* Victoria, BC: Government of British Columbia. Ministry of Employment and Investment. Community Development Unit.

Brolin, B. 1980. *Architecture in Context.* New York: Van Nostrand Reinhold.

Bula, F. 1995. How Design Affects Taste. *Vancouver Sun,* 10 November.

–. 2000. It Grows on You. *Vancouver Sun,* 5 August: E11.

Calthorpe, P. 1993. *The Next American Metropolis: Ecology, Community, and the American Dream.* New York: Princeton Architectural Press.

Canada Mortgage and Housing Corporation. 1990. *Quarterly Housing Statistics.* Ottawa: CMHC.

Canada Place. 1987. *Architectural Review* 18(1080): 82-5.

Carline, J. 1986. Planning BC Place Sweeter the Second Time. *Quarterly Review* 13(1): 15.

Carter, T., and A. McAfee. 1990. The Municipal Role in Housing the Homeless and the Poor. In G. Fallis and A. McAfee, eds., *Housing the Homeless and the Poor,* 227-62. Toronto: University of Toronto Press.

Caulfield, J. 1974. *The Tiny Perfect Mayor.* Toronto: James Lorimer and Co.

–. 1994. *City Form and Everyday Life: Toronto's Gentrification and Critical Social Practice.* Toronto: University of Toronto Press.

Cepka, E. 1984. Postmodern Controversy. *Canadian Architect* 29(8): 32-33.

Chalmers, G., and F. Moorcroft. 1981. *British Columbian Houses: Guide to the Styles of Domestic Architecture in British Columbia*. Vancouver: University of British Columbia, Western Education Development Group.

Chermayeff, S., and C. Alexander. 1963. *Community and Privacy: Toward a New Architecture of Community*. New York: Doubleday.

Coates, J. 1982. Downtown South: Completing Downtown. *Quarterly Review* 9(4): 4-7.

Concord Pacific Developments. 1997. Northeast False Creek: Urban Design. Charrettes. Vancouver, BC.

–. 1998. Area 1 Beach Neighbourhood. Prepared by Pacific Place Developments Corporation. Vancouver, BC.

Condon, P., ed. 1996. *Urban Landscapes: The Surrey Charrette*. Vancouver: University of British Columbia Landscape Architecture Program.

Constantineau, B. 1995. Who Owns the Land? *Vancouver Sun,* 30 September: A1-4.

Cornejo, D. 1977. Vancouver's Neighbourhood Improvement Program. *Quarterly Review* 4(1): 10-11.

–. 1981. British Columbia Place. *Quarterly Review* 8(3) 16-19.

Costonis, J.J. 1989. *Icons and Aliens: Law, Aesthetics and Environmental Change*. Urbana, IL: University of Illinois Press.

Coupland, D. 1997. *Girlfriend in a Coma*. London: Flamingo.

Crickmore, E., and K. Holm. 1986. The Changing Face of the Downtown. *Quarterly Review* January 13(1): 12-14.

Crofton, F. 1998. *Southeast False Creek Design Charrette*. Vancouver: Orcad Consulting.

Cullen, G. 1961. *Townscape*. London: Architectural Press.

Cybriwsky, R.A., D. Ley, and J. Western. 1986. The Political and Social Construction of Rental Neighbourhoods: Society Hill, Philadelphia, and False Creek, Vancouver. In N. Smith and P. Williams, eds., *Gentrification of the City*, 92-120. Boston, MA: Allen and Unwin.

Davey, P. 1987. Outrage (article on Vancouver Library). *Architectural Review* 201(1199): 21.

Davidoff, P. 1961. Advocacy and Pluralism in Planning. *Journal of the American Institute of Planners* 31(4): 331-38.

Davis, C., ed. 1997. *The Greater Vancouver Book: An Urban Encyclopedia*. Surrey, BC: Linkman Books.

Davis, M. 1990. *City of Quartz: Excavating the Future in Los Angeles*. New York: Verso.

Delany, P., ed. 1994. *Vancouver: Representing the Postmodern City*. Vancouver: Arsenal Pulp Press.

Dennis, M. 1979. *St. Lawrence, 1974-1979*. Toronto: City Housing Department.

Duncan, J. 1994. Shaughnessy Heights: The Protection of Privilege. In S. Hasson and D. Ley, eds., *Neighbourhood Organizations and the Welfare State*, 58-82. Toronto: University of Toronto Press.

Duncan, J., and N. Duncan. 1988. (Re)reading the Landscape. *Environment and Planning D: Society and Space* 8(2): 117-26.

–. 1992. Elite Landscapes as Cultural (Re)Productions: The Case of Shaughnessy Heights. In K. Anderson and F. Gale, eds., *Inventing Places: Studies in Cultural Geography*. Melbourne: Longman Cheshire.

Ellin, N. 1996. *Postmodern Urbanism*. Oxford, UK: Blackwell.

Executive City or Citizens' City for Vancouver? 1991. *City Magazine* 12(3): 15-18.

Fitch, R. 1993. *The Assassination of New York*. London: Verso.

Frampton, K. 1985. *Modern Architecture: A Critical History*. (Revised ed.) London: Thames and Hudson.

French, T. 1977. Urban Design. *Quarterly Review* 4(3): 7-12.

–. 1980a. Downtown Core Height Study. *Quarterly Review* 7(3): 3-5.

–. 1980b. Urban Design, Four Basic Values. *Quarterly Review* 8(1): 5-7.

Fried, M. 1963. Grieving for a Lost Home. In J. Duhl, ed., *The Urban Condition,* 151-71. New York: Simon L. Schuster.

Frieden, B., and L.B. Sagalyn. 1989. *Downtown Inc: How America Rebuilds Cities.* Cambridge, MA: MIT Press.

Frisken, F. 1988. *City Policy Making in Theory and Practice: The Case of Toronto's Downtown Plan.* London, ON: University of Western Ontario, Department of Political Science. Local Government Case Studies no. 3.

Gans, H. 1962. *The Urban Villagers: Group and Class Life in the Life of Italian-Americans.* Glencoe, NY: Free Press.

–. 1968. *People and Plans: Essay on Urban Problems and Solutions.* New York: Basic.

Garreau, J. 1991. *Edge City: Life on the New Frontier.* New York: Anchor Doubleday.

Gates, R. 1980. Neighbourhood Planning. *Quarterly Review* 8(4): 2-9.

Gehl, J. 1987. *Life between Buildings: Using Public Space.* New York: Van Nostrand Reiinhold.

Gerecke, K. 1991a. Vancouver: Election Surprises. *City Magazine* 12(3): 4-5.

–. 1991b. Success in Revitalizing the Inner City: The Story of DERA [Downtown Eastside Residents Association]. *City Magazine* 12(4) 11-19.

–. 1991c. Executive City or Citizens' City for Vancouver? *City Magazine* 12(3) 15-18.

Gilliard, J., and M. Whyte. 1995. The House That Ate the Neighbourhood. *Metropolis,* 15 July-August 15-17.

Gilroy, R. 1996. *Building the Vision of a City for Everyone: Planning in the Context of Multiculturalism in Vancouver.* Newcastle: University of Newcastle upon Tyne. Centre for Research into the European Urban Environment. Working Paper no. 54.

Godley, E. 1997. Landscape Architecture. In C. Davis, ed., *The Greater Vancouver Book: An Urban Encyclopedia,* 204-5. Surrey, BC: Linkman Books.

Gourley, C. 1988. *Island in the Creek: The Granville Island Story.* Madeira Park, BC: Harbour Publishing.

Greater Vancouver Regional District (GVRD). 1975. *The Livable Region 1976/1986.* Vancouver: GVRD.

–. 1990. Creating Our Future: Steps to a More Livable Region. Vancouver, GVRD.

–. 1994. *Livable Region Strategic Plan.* Vancouver: GVRD.

Grey, C. 1984. False Creek South Shore: Ten Years After. *Quarterly Review* 11(4): 9-15.

Gruft, A. 1983. Vancouver Architecture: The Last Fifteen Years. *Vancouver: Art and Artists 1931-1983,* 318-31. Vancouver: Vancouver Art Gallery.

–. 1984. Greening Vancouver? Tradition and Typology. *Section A* 2(1): 24-25.

Gutstein, D. 1974-75. The Developers' TEAM: Vancouver's Reform Party in Power. *City Magazine* 1(2): 13-25.

–. 1975a. *Vancouver Ltd.* Toronto: James Lorimer and Co.

–. 1975b. Neighbourhood Improvement: What It Means in Calgary, Vancouver, and Toronto. *City Magazine* 1(5-6): 15-28.

–. 1983a. Vancouver. In W. Magnusson and A. Sancton, eds. *City Politics in Canada,* 189-221. Toronto: University of Toronto Press.

–. 1983b. Vancouver: Progressive Majority Impotent. *City Magazine* 6(1): 12-15.

–. 1986-87. Vancouver Voters Swing Right. *City Magazine* 9(1): 30-32.

–. 1990. *The New Landlords: Asian Investment in Canadian Real Estate.* Victoria, BC: Porcépic Books.

Habe, R. 1989. Public Design Control in American Communities. *Town Planning Review* 60(3): 195-219.

Hall, P. 1988. *Cities of Tomorrow.* Oxford, UK: Basil Blackwell.

Hardwick, W.G. 1974. *Vancouver*. Don Mills, ON: Collier Macmillan.

–. 1994. Responding to the 1960s: Designing Adaptable Communities in Vancouver. *Environment and Behaviour* 26(3): 338-62.

Harvey, D. 1989. *The Condition of Postmodernity*. Oxford, UK: Basil Blackwell.

Hasson, S., and D. Ley. 1994. *Neighbourhood Organizations and the Welfare State*. Toronto: University of Toronto Press.

Hayes, P., and P. Johnston. 1975. Housing Conversion: The Potential for Additional Suites in Single-Family Houses. *Quarterly Review* 2(2): 14-21.

Hertzberger, H. 1991. *Lessons for Students in Architecture*. Rotterdam: 010 Publishers.

Heywood, P. 1997. The Emerging Social Metropolis: Successful Planning Initiatives in Five New World Metropolitan Regions. *Progress in Planning* 47(2): 159-250.

Hickley, D. 1975. False Creek 1975. *Quarterly Review* 2(1) 14-18.

Hinshaw, M.L. 1995. *Design Review*. Planning Advisory Service Report 454. Chicago: American Planning Association.

Hlavach, J. 1985. Art, Architecture, and Heritage Conservation. *Quarterly Review* 12(4): 14-16.

Hough, M. 1985. *City Form and Natural Process*. New York: Van Nostrand Reinhold.

Howard, R. 1984. BC Place and Expo '86: An Overview. *Quarterly Review* 11(2): 3-6.

Hulchanski, D. 1984. *St. Lawrence and False Creek: A Review of the Planning and Development of Two Inner City Neighbourhoods*. Vancouver: UBC Planning Papers, Canadian Planning Issues no. 10.

–. 1990. *Planning New Urban Neighbourhoods: Lessons from Toronto's St. Lawrence Neighbourhood*. Vancouver: UBC Planning Papers, Canadian Planning Issues no. 28.

Hutton, T.A. 1994. City Profile: Vancouver. *Cities* 11(4): 219-39.

Huxtable, A.L. 1976. *Kicked a Building Lately?* New York: Quadrangle/New York Times Book Co.

Jacobs, A. 1993. *Great Streets*. Cambridge, MA: MIT Press.

Jacobs, A. 1998. Draft Policy Document: Southeast False Creek. Memorandum of 14 September to Vancouver Planning Commission.

Jacobs, J. 1961. *The Death and Life of Great American Cities*. New York: Vintage.

Jenkins, C. 1987. *The Language of Postmodern Architecture*. London: Academy Editions.

Kalman, H. 1974. *Exploring Vancouver: Ten Tours of the City and Its Buildings*. Vancouver: UBC Press.

–. 1996. *A History of Canadian Architecture*. Oxford, UK: Oxford University Press.

Kalman, H., R. Phillips, and R. Ward. 1993. *Exploring Vancouver: The Essential Architectural Guide*. Vancouver: UBC Press.

Kaplan, R.D. 1998. Travels into America's Future (Part 2). *Atlantic Monthly*, August: 37-61.

Katz, P. 1994. *The New Urbanism: Toward an Architecture of Community*. New York: McGraw-Hill.

Kelbaugh, D., ed. 1989. *The Pedestrian Pocket Book: A New Suburban Design Strategy*. New York: Princeton Architectural Press.

Kostuk, P. 1997. Designing a New Development and Building Review Process in Vancouver, B.C. Paper presented to National Conference of States on Building Codes and Standards by City of Vancouver, Community Services Group.

Krieger, A., and W. Lennertz. 1991. *Andres Duany and Elizabeth Plater-Zyberk: Towns and Town-Making Principles*. Cambridge, MA: Harvard University Graduate School of Design; New York: Rizzoli.

Krier, L. 1978. *Rational Architecture*. Brussels: Archives d'Architecture Moderne.

Kwok Consultants, Inc. 1997. Creekside Landing, Southeast False Creek. Vancouver, BC.

Ladner, P. 2000. Compromise on Wall Tower. *Business in Vancouver*, 23 May: 3.

Lai, R.T. 1988. *Law in Urban Design and Planning: The Invisible Web*. New York: Van Nostrand Reinhold.

Lang, J. 1994. *Urban Design: An American Perspective*. New York: Van Nostrand Reinhold.

Larson, M.S. 1993. *Behind the Postmodern Facade: Architectural Change in Late Twentieth Century America*. Berkeley, CA: University of California Press.

Ledger, B. 1992. A Public Affair: Vancouver Library Square Competition. *Canadian Architect* 37(7): 20-27, 39.

Lees, L. 1987. Ageographia, Heterotopia, and Vancouver's New Public Library. *Environment and Planning D: Society and Space* 15: 321-47.

–. 1998. Vancouver: A Portfolio. *Urban Geography* 19(4): 283-86.

–. 1999. Urban Renaissance and the Street: Spaces of Control and Contestation. In N. Fyfe, ed., *Images of the Streets: Representation, Experience, and Control in Public Space*, 236-53. London: Routledge.

Lees, L., and D. Demeritt. 1998. Envisioning the Livable City: The Interplay of "Sin City" and "Sim City" in Vancouver's Planning Discourse. *Urban Geography* 19(4): 332-59.

Lemon, J. 1985. *Toronto Since 1918*. Toronto: James Lorimer.

Lemon, R.G. 1997. Designated Historic Structures and Historical Sites. In C. Davis, ed., *The Greater Vancouver Book: An Urban Encyclopedia*, 224-26. Surrey, BC: Linkman Books.

Leung, H. 1982. The Georgia-Robson Corridor Urban Design Study. *Quarterly Review* 9(4): 16-17.

–. 1984. Urban Design in Vancouver. *Quarterly Review* 11(4): 3-6.

Lewinberg, F.R. 1985. Neighbourhood Planning: The Reform Years in Toronto. In *Toronto Neighbourhoods: The Next Ten Years*. Toronto: City of Toronto Planning and Development Department.

Ley, D. 1980. Liberal Ideology and the Postindustrial City. *Annals of the Association of American Geographers* 70(2): 238-58.

–. 1987. Styles of the Times: Liberal and Neo-Conservative Landscapes in Inner Vancouver, 1968-1986. *Journal of Historical Geography* 13(1): 40-56.

–. 1993a. Gentrification in Recession: Social Change in Six Canadian Inner Cities. *Urban Geography* 13(3): 230-56.

–. 1993b. Past Elites and Present Gentry: Neighbourhoods of Privilege in the Inner City. In L.S. Bourne and D.F. Ley, eds., *The Changing Social Geography of Canadian Cities*, 214-33. Montreal/Kingston: McGill-Queen's University Press.

–. 1994. Gentrification and the Politics of the New Middle Class. *Environment and Planning D: Society and Space* 12(1): 53-74.

–. 1995. Between Europe and Asia: The Case of the Missing Sequoias. *Ecumene* 2(2): 185-210.

–. 1996. *The Middle Class and the Making of the Central City*. Oxford, UK: Oxford University Press.

Ley, D., D. Hiebert, and G. Pratt. 1992. Time to Grow Up? From Urban Village to World City, 1966-91. In G. Wynn and T. Oke, eds., *Vancouver and Its Region*, 234-66. Vancouver: UBC Press.

Ley, D., and K. Olds. 1988. Landscape as Spectacle: World's Fairs and the Culture of Heroic Consumption. *Environment and Planning D: Society and Space* 6: 191-212.

Li, P.S. 1994. Unneighbourly Houses or Unwelcome Chinese? The Social Construction of Race in the Battle over Monster Homes in Vancouver, Canada. *International Journal of Comparative Race and Ethnic Studies* 1(1): 14-33.

Loukaitou-Sideris, A., and T. Banerjee. 1998. *Urban Design Downtown: Poetics and Politics of Form*. Berkeley, CA: University of California Press.

Lynch, K. 1960. *Image of the City*. Cambridge, MA: MIT Press.

–. 1971. *Site Planning*. 2nd edition. Cambridge, MA: MIT Press.

–. 1972. *What Time Is This Place?* Cambridge, MA: MIT Press.

–. 1976. *Managing the Sense of a Region*. Cambridge, MA: MIT Press.

–. 1981. *A Theory of Good City Form*. Cambridge, MA: MIT Press.

Malbert, B. 1998. Participatory Approaches to Sustainable Urban Development: Reflections on Practice in Seattle, Vancouver, and Waitakere. *Planning Practice and Research* 13(2): 183-89.

Marathon. 1974. A Visit to the North Side of False Creek. Prepared by Marathon Realty. Vancouver, BC.

–. 1989. Proposals for the North Shore of False Creek. Prepared by Marathon Realty. Vancouver, BC.

–. 1991/1993/1995. Coal Harbour: Vancouver's Downtown Waterfront, Public Information Bulletins. Prepared by Marathon Building Group. Vancouver, BC.

–. 1997. North East False Creek: Urban Design. Charrettes. Prepared by Marathon Realty. Vancouver, BC.

–. 2000. Expansion of the Vancouver Convention and Exhibition Centre Burrard Landing Design Proposal Evaluation. Prepared by Marathon Building Group for the Vancouver Convention Centre Expansion Task Force. Vancouver, BC.

McAfee, A. 1978. Housing Families at High Density. *Urban Forum* 4(3): 8-17.

–. 1983. The Renewed Inner City: Is One Out of Three Sufficient? Paper presented to the New Neighbourhood International Forum. 31 January. Toronto.

–. 1985a. Consumers Evaluate New High-Density Housing. *Quarterly Review* 12(2): 3-4.

–. 1985b. New Neighbourhoods. *Quarterly Review* 12(3): 12-15.

–. 1986a. Vancouver's Single-family Areas. *Quarterly Review* 13(3): 3-6.

–. 1986b. The Design of New Single-Family Homes. *Quarterly Review* 13(4): 17.

–. 1990. Four Decades of Geographical Impact by Canadian Social Housing Policies. In B.M. Barr, ed., *Studies in Canadian Regional Geography: Essays in Honour of J. Lewis Robinson*. BC Geographical Series no. 37, 92-108. Vancouver: Tantalus Research.

–. 1995. Vancouver's CityPlan: People Participating in Planning. *Plan Canada* 35(5): 15-16.

–. 1997a. Secondary Suites: The Issues. *Quarterly Review* 14(2): 16-18.

–. 1997b. When Theory Meets Practice: Citizen Participation in Planning. *Plan Canada* 37(5): 18-22.

–. 1997c. CityPlan. In C. Davis, ed., *The Greater Vancouver Book: An Urban Encyclopedia*, 245-46. Surrey, BC: Linkman Books.

McBeath, C. 1997. Central Business District. In C. Davis, ed., *The Greater Vancouver Book: An Urban Encyclopedia*, 82-85. Surrey, BC: Linkman Books.

McHarg, I. 1969. *Design with Nature*. New York: Natural History Press.

McMordie, M.J. 1984. Modern Architecture in Vancouver. *Canadian Architect* 29(3): 22-27.

Miller, S.E. 1994. The Grid: Living in Hollywood North. In P. Delany, ed., *Vancouver: Representing the Postmodern City*, 282-94. Vancouver: Arsenal Pulp Press.

Mills, C.A. 1986-7. Lifestyle and Landscape on the Fairview Slopes. *City Magazine* 9(1): 20-24.

–. 1988. "Life on the Upslope": The Postmodern Landscape of Gentrification. *Environment and Planning D: Society and Space* 6(2): 169-90.

Mitchell, K. 1993. Multiculturalism, or the United Colours of Capitalism? *Antipode* 25(4): 263-94.

–. 1996. Visions of Vancouver: Ideology, Democracy and the Future of Urban Development. *Urban Geography* 17(6): 478-90.

–. 1997. Fast Capital, Race, Modernity, and the Monster House. In R. George, ed., *Burning down the House: Recycling Domesticity*, 187-212. New York: Harper Collins.

Mondor, P. 1981. An Overall Development Strategy for the Core. *Quarterly Review* 8(4): 12-16.

Moudon, A.V. 1987. *Public Streets for Public Use*. New York: Van Nostrand Reinhold.

Mulgrew, I. 1998a. The Battle for Hastings. *Vancouver Sun,* 19 September: A20.

–. 1998b. A Neighbourhood on Guard. *Vancouver Sun,* 22 September: A15-21.

–. 1998c. In Search of Solutions. *Vancouver Sun,* 24 September: A17.

–. 1998d. The Door Is Open. *Vancouver Sun,* 25 September: A21.

–. 1998e. Hard Lessons Learned. *Vancouver Sun,* 23 September: A15.

Murchie, G. 1995. Looking Beyond Vancouver's Picture-Postcard Beauty. *Plan Canada* 35(5): 9-10.

Nasar, J.L., and P. Grannis. 1999. Design Review Reviewed: Administrative versus Discretionary Methods. *Journal of the American Planning Association* 65(4): 424-33.

Norberg-Schulz, C. 1979. *Genius Loci: Towards a Phenomenology of Architecture.* New York: Rizzoli.

North, R.N., and W.G. Hardwick. 1992. Vancouver since the Second World War: An Economic Geography. In G. Wynn and T. Oke, eds., *Vancouver and Its Regions*, 200-33. Vancouver: UBC Press.

Oberlander, J. 1997. History of Planning in Greater Vancouver. In C. Davis, ed., *The Greater Vancouver Book: An Urban Encyclopedia*, 247–50. Surrey, BC: Linkman Books.

Ohannesian, P. 1990. How We Saved Shaughnessy from Monsters. *Vancouver Sun,* 23 July: D10-11.

Olds, K. 1988. Globalization and Urban Change: Tales from Vancouver Via Hong Kong. *Urban Geography* 19(4): 360-86.

–. 1995. Globalization and the Production of New Urban Spaces: Pacific Rim Megaprojects in the Late 20th Century. *Environment and Planning A: International Journal of Urban and Regional Research* 27: 1713-43.

Oliver, N. 1974. Heritage Preservation in Vancouver. *Quarterly Review* 1(14): 20-23.

Pastier, J. 1989. Evaluation: Skyscraper on Its Side. *Architecture: The AIA Journal* 78(11): 64-67.

Pawley, M. 1974. *The Private Future*. London: Architectural Press.

Perez-Gomez, A. 1994. The Architecture of Richard Henriquez. In P. Delany, ed., *Vancouver: Representing the Postmodern City*, 50-59. Vancouver: Arsenal Pulp Press.

Pettit, B. 1992. Zoning, the Market, and the Single-Family Landscape: Neighbourhood Change in Vancouver, Canada. PhD thesis, Department of Geography. University of British Columbia, Vancouver.

–. 1997. *Survey of North American Cities: Single-Family Zoning Regulations*. Rev. ed. Vancouver: City of Vancouver Planning Department.

Pivo, G. 1996. Towards Sustainable Urbanization in Mainstreet Cascadia. *Cities* 13(5): 339-54.

Portoghesi, P. 1983. *Postmodern: The Architecture of Post-Industrial Society*. New York: Rizzoli.

Punter, J.V. 1999a. *Design Guidelines in American Cities: A Review of Design Policies and Guidance in Five West-Coast Cities*. Liverpool, UK: University of Liverpool Press.

–. 1999b. The Vancouver Experience. *Urban Design Quarterly* 70: 33-37.

Reid, B. 1988. Upcoming Election: Executive City, Limousine Liberals, or Affordable City? *City Magazine* 10(2): 11-12.

–. 1991. Metro Vancouver Elections Report: The Suburbs Turn Left-Ward as They Begin to Embrace a Green Agenda. *City Magazine* 12(2): 5-6.

–. 1993. Vancouver Civic Elections 1993. *City Magazine* 14(4): 7-9.

Relph, E. 1988. *The Modern Urban Landscape*. London: Croom Helm.

Riera, B., T. Fletcher, and A. McAfee. 1993. New Partnerships, New Directions: Vancouver's CityPlan. *Plan Canada* 33(11): 16-20.

Robson Square and the Law Courts: Vancouver. 1989. *Detail* 29(6): 590-94.

Rossi, A. 1982. *Architecture of the City* (English translation). Cambridge, MA: MIT Press.

Rossiter, S. 1988. Deciding the Fate of a City Landmark. *Georgia Straight,* 6-13 May: 7-9.

–. 1997. Architects and Architecture of Greater Vancouver. In C. Davis, ed., *The Greater Vancouver Book: An Urban Encyclopedia,* 198-201. Surrey, BC: Linkman Books.

Rowe, C., and F. Koetter. 1978. *Collage City.* Cambridge, MA: MIT Press.

Rudofsky, B. 1964. *Architecture without Architects: An Introduction to Non-Pedigreed Architecture.* New York: Museum of Modern Art.

Russell, F.P. 1994. *Battery Park City: An American Dream of Urbanism.* In B.C. Scheer and W. Preiser, eds., *Design Review: Challenging Urban Aesthetic Control,* 197-209. New York: Chapman and Hall.

Sandercock, L. 1998. *Towards Cosmopolis: Planning for Multicultural Cities.* New York: John Wiley.

Schack, J. 1987. Sinclair Centre, Vancouver. *Canadian Architect* 32(3): 22-32.

Scheer, B.C. 1994. Foreword. In B.C. Scheer and W. Preiser, eds., *Design Review: Challenging Urban Aesthetic Control,* vii-xvii. New York: Chapman and Hall.

Scheer, B.C., and W. Preiser, eds. 1994. *Design Review: Challenging Urban Aesthetic Control.* New York: Chapman and Hall.

Schuster, J.M.D. 1990. *Design Review: The View from the Architecture Profession.* Cambridge, MA: MIT, Design and Development Group Paper.

Scobie, R. 1986. Dealing with SkyTrain Impacts. *Quarterly Review* 13(4): 3-6.

Scully, V. 1969. *American Architecture and Urbanism.* New York: Henry Holt.

Seelig, M., and A. Artibise. 1990. Growing to Extremes. *Vancouver Sun,* 10 November: B2 (and subsequent columns, 12-15 November: B2).

Seelig, M., and J. Seelig. 1990. Recycling Vancouver's Granville Island. *Architectural Record* (9): 75-81.

–. 1997. CityPlan: Participation or Abdication? *Plan Canada* 37(5): 18-22.

Sennett, R. 1970. *The Uses of Disorder: Personal Identity and City Life.* New York: Random House.

–. 1990. *The Conscience of the Eye: The Design and Social Life of Cities.* New York: Knopf.

Sewell, J. 1993. *The Shape of the City: Toronto Struggles with Modern Planning.* Toronto: University of Toronto Press.

Shadbolt, D. 1983. Post-War Architecture in Vancouver. In *Vancouver: Art and Artists 1931-1983,* 108-19. Vancouver: Vancouver Art Gallery.

Shirvani, H. 1981. *Urban Design Review: A Guide for Planners.* Chicago: Planners Press.

–. 1992. *Beyond Public Architecture: Strategies for Design Evaluation.* New York: Van Nostrand Reinhold.

Simmons, L. 1985. *Downtown Plaza Study.* Vancouver: City Social Planning Department.

Smith, N. 1996. *New Urban Frontier: Gentrification and the Revanchist City.* London: Routledge.

Smith, N., and P. Williams, eds. 1986. *Gentrification of the City.* Boston, MA: Allen and Unwin.

Soja, E. 1996. *Thirdspace: Journeys to Los Angeles and Other Real-and-Imagined Places.* Oxford, UK: Basil Blackwell.

Sorkin, M., ed. 1992. *Variations on a Theme Park: The New American City and the End of Public Space.* New York: Hill and Wang.

Southworth, M. 1989. Theory and Practice of Contemporary Urban Design: A Review of Urban Design Plans in the United States. *Town Planning Review* 60(4): 369-402.

Southworth, M., and S. Southworth. 1973. Environmental Quality in Cities and Designs. *Town Planning Review* 44(3): 231-53.

Spaxman, R. 1979. The Development Community and the City. *Quarterly Review* 6(3): 3-5.

–. 1990. Contributing to the Quality of the City. *Plan Canada* 30(6): 10-12.

–. 1994. What's New in Urban Design. *Plan Canada* 34(5): 6-8.

Stamp, G. 1999. The Developers: A Tale of Two Waterfronts. Paper presented at Worldwide Waterfront '99 Conference. 6-8 October 1999. Vancouver, BC.

Stamps, A.E. and J.L. Nasar. 1997. Design Review and Public Preferences: Effects of geographical location, public consensus, sensation seeking and architectural styles. *Journal of Environmental Psychology* 17(1): 11-32.

Starkins, E. 1997. West End. In C. Davis, ed., *The Greater Vancouver Book: An Urban Encyclopedia*, 80-81. Surrey, BC: Linkman Books.

Steyn, D.G., M. Bovis, M. North, and O. Slaymaker. 1992. The Biophysical Environment Today. In G. Wynn and T. Oke, eds., *Vancouver and Its Region,* 267-90. Vancouver: UBC Press.

Sutherland, J. 1998. Realty Bites. *Vancouver Magazine,* September: 67-75.

Taggart, J. 1997. Lean and Green. *Urban Development and Architectural Report* (Vancouver) 3(4): 7-8.

Tennant, P., and J. West. 1998. Half of Vancouver's Municipal Voters Go without Representation. *Vancouver Sun,* 19 September: A23.

Thomsett, D. 1976. More Townhouses for Vancouver? *Quarterly Review* 3(4): 10-11.

Tomalty, R. 1998. *The Compact Metropolis: Growth Management and Intensification in Vancouver, Toronto and Montreal.* Toronto: ICURR.

Toronto City Planning Department unpublished documents: see list at end of bibliography.

Trancik, R. 1986. *Finding Lost Space: Theories of Urban Design.* New York: Van Nostrand Reinhold.

Urban Development Institute. 1997. Re. Proposed City Policy to Tax 100% of Increase in Value of Rezonings. Letter to Mayor and Council, City of Vancouver, 10 July.

–. 1998. Re. City of Vancouver Proposal: Financing Growth Discussion Paper. Letter to Mayor and Council, City of Vancouver, 24 February.

Vancouver. 1994-. *Panorama.* Public art newsletter. Vancouver: City of Vancouver, Vancouver Affairs Office.

Vancouver Art Gallery. 1983. *Vancouver: Art and Artists, 1931-1983.* Vancouver: Vancouver Art Gallery.

Vancouver City Planning Department unpublished documents: see list at end of bibliography.

Vancouver League for Studies in Architecture and Environment. 1988. *The Vancouver Special Competition.* Vancouver, BC.

Van der Ryn, S., and P. Calthorpe. 1986. *Sustainable Communities.* San Francisco, CA: Sierra Club Books.

Varrki George, R., and M.C. Campbell. 2000. Balancing Different Interests in Aesthetic Control. *Journal of Planning Education and Research* 20(2): 163-75.

Vaughan, M. 1984. Eyes on Urban Design: Vancouver's Urban Design Panel. *Quarterly Review* 11(4): 7-8.

Venturi, R. 1966. *Complexity and Contradiction in Architecture.* New York: Museum of Modern Art.

Venturi, R., and D. Scott Brown. 1977. *Learning from Las Vegas.* Cambridge, MA: MIT Press.

Vischer, J.C. 1983. Community and Privacy: Planners' Intentions and Residents' Reactions. *Plan Canada* 23(4): 112-21.

Wakeford, R. 1990. *American Development Control: Parallels and Paradoxes from an English Perspective.* London: HMSO.

Ward, R. 1993a. Column on the Electra Building. *Vancouver Sun,* 28 August (all Ward articles copied in files in Community Services Group Library).

–. 1993b. Column on the BC Hydro Building. *Vancouver Sun,* 6 November.

–. 1993c. Column on Yaletown. *Vancouver Sun,* 13 November.

–. 1993d. Column on Victory Square. *Vancouver Sun,* 4 December.

–. 1994. Column on the Homer Street Theatre. *Vancouver Sun,* 6 August.

–. 1995a. Column on New Modernism. *Vancouver Sun,* 7 January.

–. 1995b. Between a Rock and a Hard Place on the Library. *Vancouver Sun,* 18 February.

–. 1995c. A Bridge Upgrade Too Far? *Vancouver Sun,* 11 March.

–. 1995d. Column on 8 East Cordova. *Vancouver Sun,* 18 March.

–. 1995e. Column on Strathcona. *Vancouver Sun,* 8 May.

–. 1995f. Column on Shanghai Alley. *Vancouver Sun,* 13 May.

–. 1995g. Roamin' the Ruins. *Vancouver Sun,* 3 June.

–. 1995h. Column on Tudor Manor. *Vancouver Sun,* 10 June.

–. 1995i. Column on RS-5 zoning. *Vancouver Sun,* 22 July.

–. 1995j. Column on the Vancouver Public Library. *Vancouver Sun,* 5 August.

–. 1995k. Column on Chinatown. *Vancouver Sun,* 15 September.

–. 1995l. Column on Mole Hill. *Vancouver Sun,* 25 November.

–. 1996a. Column on the Alexander. *Vancouver Sun,* 27 January.

–. 1996b. Vancouver Could Use More Tall Buildings. *Vancouver Sun,* 10 February.

–. 1996c. Shrinking from the Past. *Georgia Straight,* 22-29 February: 13-20.

–. 1996d. A Building at Odds with Its Surroundings. *Vancouver Sun,* 23 March.

–. 1996e. The Spirit of Mole Hill Keeps Heritage Alive. *Vancouver Sun,* 13 April.

–. 1996f. New Gastown Project Is a Lamentable Effort. *Vancouver Sun,* 8 June.

–. 1996g. Greystone's Portside Misses the Boat on Design. *Vancouver Sun,* 27 July.

–. 1996h. Marathon's Plan: Faulty. *Vancouver Sun,* 29 July.

–. 1996i. A Dim View of Bright Lights. *Vancouver Sun,* 31 August.

–. 1996j. Civic Pride Fades with Library Plaque. *Vancouver Sun,* 18 December.

–. 1997a. City Planners Face Mountainous Debate over Skyline. *Vancouver Sun,* 12 February.

–. 1997b. Budget Cuts Threaten City's Heritage Conservation Program. *Vancouver Sun,* 19 February.

–. 1997c. Tower Design a Model of What Can Go Wrong. *Vancouver Sun,* 5 March.

–. 1997d. New Name for Granville Will Not Solve Its Problems. *Vancouver Sun,* 9 May.

–. 1997e. Mole Hill Needs to Be Preserved. *Vancouver Sun,* 18 June.

–. 1997f. Warehouse Plans Due to Fire Debate. *Vancouver Sun,* 30 July.

–. 1997g. If Council Ignores the City's History, It's Doomed to Repeat Its Mistakes. *Vancouver Sun,* 6 August.

–. 1998a. Theme Park Design No Answer to Granville Street's Problems. *Vancouver Sun,* 6 March.

–. 1998b. Architecture Centre Preserves Past the Right Way. *Vancouver Sun,* 15 April.

–. 1998c. Eriksen Project a Symbol of Dignitary. *Vancouver Sun,* 24 June.

–. 1998d. Waterfront Project Is Still Adrift. *Vancouver Sun,* 15 July.

–. 1998e. Big City Heritage. *Georgia Straight,* 1-8 October: 13, 15, 17, 19, 21.

–. 1998f. Stanley Makeover Deserves Standing Ovation. *Vancouver Sun,* 9 December.

–. 1998g. Heritage Lost and Faked while Advances Made in High Tech Design. *Vancouver Sun,* 28 December.

–. 1999a. Project in Funding Limbo a Model of Good Design. *Vancouver Sun,* 6 January.

–. 1999b. Heritage versus Development in Gastown. *Vancouver Sun,* 24 February.

–. 1999c. Controversial Sculpture Shines a Light on City's Real Industrial History. *Vancouver Sun,* 2 March.

–. 1999d. Deft Blend of the Old and New on Beatty. *Vancouver Sun,* 20 November.

Weder, A. 2001. Sky's the Limit for Bullish Vancouver Developer. *National Post Online,* 28 July <www.nationalpost.com>.

Whyte, W.H. 1980. *The Social Life of Small Urban Spaces.* Washington, DC: Conservation Foundation.

–. 1988. *City: Rediscovering the Centre.* New York: Doubleday.

Wilson, J.Q. 1966. *Urban Renewal: The Record and the Controversy.* Cambridge, MA: MIT Press.

Winner, L. 1992. Silicon Valley Mystery Home. In M. Sorkin, ed., *Variations on a Theme Park: The New American City and the End of Public Space,* 31-60. New York: Hill and Wang.

Wynn, G. 1992. The Rise of Vancouver. In G. Wynn and T. Oke, eds., *Vancouver and Its Regions,* 69-148. Vancouver: UBC Press.

Zukin, S. 1989. *Loft Living: Culture and Capital in Urban Change* (2nd ed.). New Brunswick, NJ: Rutgers University Press.

–. 1996. *The Cultures of Cities.* Cambridge, MA: Blackwell.

Municipal Documents

Note: Municipal documents are listed in alphabetical order within a year. Since 1994, the City of Vancouver Planning Department has been part of the Community Services Group. Most City of Vancouver sources can be accessed through the Community Services Group Library; many can still be purchased. See city website at <www.city.vancouver.bc.ca/planning>.

Toronto. 1974. On Building Downtown: Design Guidelines for the Core Area. Toronto: City Planning Board.

–. 1990. Living Downtown in Toronto. vol. 1 and 2. no. 21. Toronto: City Planning and Development Department.

–. 1991a. Cityplan 91: Proposals. June. Toronto: City Planning and Development Department.

–. 1991b. Guidelines for the Urbanization of Metropolitan Toronto. Prepared by Berridge, Lewinberg, and Greenberg. Toronto: City of Toronto Planning and Development Department.

–. 1991c. Living on Main Streets. Prepared by Berridge, Lewinberg, and Greenberg. Toronto: City of Toronto Planning and Development Department.

–. 1994. City of Toronto Official Plan. Toronto: City Planning and Development Department.

Vancouver. 1970. False Creek Development Concepts. Vancouver: City Planning Department.

–. 1971. False Creek Proposals: Report 3. Vancouver: City Planning Department.

–. 1973. Downtown Vancouver Part 1: Proposed Goals. Vancouver: City Planning Department.

–. 1974a. Analysis of Overall City Planning Policies. Prepared by Gerhard Sixta Associates. Vancouver: City Planning Department.

–. 1974b. Shaping the Future: The City Planning Department's Goals and Objectives for 1974. Vancouver: City Planning Department.

–. 1974c. False Creek Official and Area Development Plan. Vancouver: City Planning Department.

–. 1974d. Downtown Vancouver: Development Planning and Controls. Vancouver: City Planning Department.

–. 1974e. Shaping the Future: The City Planning Department's Goals and Objectives for 1974. Vancouver: City Planning Department.

–. 1974f. Urban Structural Form and Zoning Constraints. Vancouver: City Planning Department.

–. 1974-75 to 1988-89. Annual Reviews. Vancouver: City Planning Department.

–. 1975a. A View Analysis of Downtown Vancouver. Prepared by Genevieve Le Marchand. Vancouver: City Planning Department.

–. 1975b. Downtown Official Development Plan. Vancouver: City Planning Department.

–. 1975c. Downtown Zoning. Vancouver: City Planning Department.

–. 1975d. Gastown: Economic Study: 1966-1974. Summary Report. Vancouver: City Planning Department.

–. 1975e. The Development Control Process for the Central Area. Vancouver: City Planning Department.

–. 1975f. The Development Permit Board and Advisory Panel: Composition, Duties, Functions, Procedures and Jurisdiction. Vancouver: City Planning Department.

–. 1975g. West End Zoning. Vancouver: City Planning Department.

–. 1979a. Central Waterfront Official Development Plan. Vancouver: City Planning Department.

–. 1979b. Response to City Planning Department Report. Review of Development Permit Process. Vancouver: City Planning Department.

–. 1979c. Review of Vancouver's Development Permit Process. Vancouver: City Planning Department.

–. 1979d. Review of Vancouver's Development Permit Process: Recommendation. Report prepared by planning department manager, 14 November. Vancouver: City Planning Department.

–. 1979e. Urban Design Paper 3: Context of Change. Vancouver: City Planning Department.

–. 1980. Residential Rehabilitation: An Analysis of Current Activities: City of Vancouver; City of Victoria. Prepared by Dunhill Services. Vancouver: City Planning Department.

–. 1981a. The Vancouver Specials Study. Vancouver: City Planning Department.

–. 1981b. 8 Years After: Case Studies of Discretionary Zoning in Vancouver. Vancouver: City Planning Department.

–. 1982a. Downtown Eastside. Oppenheimer Official Development Plan. Vancouver: City Planning Department.

–. 1982b. Downtown Eastside. Oppenheimer Design Guidelines. Vancouver: City Planning Department.

–. 1982c. Downtown South Urban Design. Prepared by Cunningham du Toit. Vancouver: City Planning Department.

–. 1982d. First Shaughnessy Advisory Design Panel. Vancouver: City Planning Department.

–. 1982e. First Shaughnessy Design Guidelines. Vancouver: City Planning Department.

–. 1982f. First Shaughnessy Official Development Plan. Vancouver: City Planning Department.

–. 1982g. Greening Downtown: An Urban Design Study of the Georgia/Robson Corridor. Prepared by Baird/Sampson Associates. Vancouver: City Planning Department.

–. 1982h. North and East False Creek: Development Objectives for BC Place. Vancouver: City Planning Department.

–. 1982i. Yaletown Design Guidelines. Vancouver: City Planning Department.

–. 1983a. British Columbia Place: A Proposed City Response. Vancouver: City Planning Department.

–. 1983b. Case Studies on Residential Density. Vancouver: City Planning Department.

–. 1983c. South of Granville Island Study. Prepared by TWGG Consultants. Vancouver: City Planning Department.

–. 1983d. Vancouver Neighbourhood Improvement Program Review. Vancouver: City Planning Department.

–. 1984a. City of Vancouver Review of the Development Permit Process February 1984. Prepared by Western Management Consultants. Vancouver: City Planning Department.

–. 1984b. Downtown Plaza Study. Prepared by Buchan and Simmons. Vancouver: City Social Planning.

–. 1984c. East False Creek Policy Plan. Vancouver: City Planning Department.

–. 1984d. Southeast Granville Slopes Official Development Plan. Vancouver: City Planning Department.

–. 1984e. Vancouver Plan. Vancouver: City Planning Department.

–. 1984-5 to 1988-9. Vancouver Plan Monitor (supplement to Annual Review). Vancouver: City Planning Department.

–. 1985a. Development Permit Board Procedures. Vancouver: City Planning Department.

–. 1985b. Granville Mall and Street Chronology. Vancouver: City Planning Department.

–. 1985c. The Urbanarium Project. Vancouver: City Planning Department.

–. 1986a. East False Creek FC-1 Guidelines. Vancouver: City Planning Department.

–. 1986b. Georgia Street: Second Century. Prepared by Georgia Street Public Realm Advisory Committee. Vancouver: City Planning Department.

–. 1986c. New Neighbours: How Vancouver's Single-family Residents Feel about Higher-Density Housing. Vancouver: City Planning Department.

–. 1986d. Proposed Changes to RS-1 Single-family Regulations. Vancouver: City Planning Department.

–. 1986e. RS-1 Single-family Information Package. Report presented to City Council, August. Vancouver: City Planning Department.

–. 1986f. Review of the Amenity Bonus Program: Background Report. Vancouver: City Planning Department.

–. 1986g. Rezoning application: 1000 Beach Avenue. Report presented to City Council, 19 August. Vancouver: City Planning Department.

–. 1986h. Secondary Suites in RS-1 Single-family Neighbourhoods. Vancouver: City Planning Department.

–. 1987a. Joyce Station Area Plan in Summary. Vancouver: City Planning Department.

–. 1987b. Rezoning Procedures in Vancouver. Vancouver: City Planning Department.

–. 1987c. RS-1 Regulations Review: Critique of Proposals, with Emphasis on Housing Retentions and Renovations. Prepared by Paul B. Ohannesian, Architect. Vancouver: City Planning Department.

-. 1987d. Downtown South Design Guidelines. Vancouver: City Planning Department.

–. 1988a. Amendments to RS-1 Single-family Regulations. Report presented to City Council, 13 December. Vancouver: City Planning Department.

–. 1988b. Development Permit Review Process. Report by departmental manager, 2 August. Vancouver: City Planning Department.

–. 1988c. Downtown Vancouver: Planning Strategies for a Changing World. Vancouver: City Planning Department.

–. 1988d. Review of Charter Planning Powers. Prepared by D.N. McDonald. Vancouver: City Planning Department.

–. 1988e. Urban Amenities Advisory Committee: Report. Vancouver: City Planning Department.

–. 1988f. Withholding Development Permit Applications Pending Enactment of Changes to the RS-1/RS-15 District Schedule and RS-1/RS-15 House Site and Location. Report to City Council, 11 February. Vancouver: City Planning Department.

–. 1988g. Coal Harbour: A Future for Vancouver's Waterfront. Information Pamphlet. Vancouver: City Planning Department.

–. 1989a. Downtown South Rezoning. Vancouver: City Planning Department.

–. 1989b. Downtown South Rezoning. Report to City Council, September. Vancouver: City Planning Department.

–. 1989c. False Creek Development Projects Community Facilities Study. Vancouver: City Planning Department.

–. 1989d. False Creek Policy Broadsheets. Vancouver: City Planning Department.

–. 1989e. Granville Slopes Area Study. Prepared by Civitas Urban Design Planning Inc. Vancouver: City Planning Department.

–. 1989f. Local Area Planning in Vancouver: Citizen Participation and Priorities. Vancouver: City Planning Department.

–. 1989g. Public Involvement in Planning the North Shore of False Creek. Vancouver: City Planning Department.

–. 1989h. Review of Major Application Process. Report by departmental manager, 29 December. Vancouver: City Planning Department.

–. 1989i. Rezoning of North Park Area (International Village from BCPED and DD to CD-1). Vancouver: City Planning Department.

–. 1989j. Selected Interviews on the Future of Downtown Vancouver. Vancouver: City Planning Department.

–. 1989k. Station/La Farge Site: Rezoning of a Portion of East False Creek. Vancouver: City Planning Department.

–. 1989l. The Downtown South Urban Design Study. Prepared by Aitken Wreglesworth Associates. Vancouver: City Planning Department.

–. 1989m. Vancouver Housing Strategy. Vancouver: City Planning Department.

–. 1989n. Vancouver Views Study: Implementation. Report by departmental manager, 27 October. Vancouver: City Planning Department.

–. 1989o. Vancouver Views Study: Implementation. Report by departmental manager, 7 December. Vancouver: City Planning Department.

–. 1989p. Vancouver Views Study: Summary Report. Prepared by Busby Bridger Architects. Vancouver: City Planning Department.

–. 1989q. West End Georgia/Alberni Guidelines. Vancouver: City Planning Department.

–. 1990a. Clouds of Change: Final Report of the City of Vancouver Task Force on Atmospheric Change. Vols. 1 and 2. Vancouver, BC.

–. 1990b. Coal Harbour Adjacent Area: Impact Studies Summary Report. Vancouver: City Planning Department.

–. 1990c. Coal Harbour Official Development Plan. Vancouver: City Planning Department.

–. 1990d. Coal Harbour Policy Statement. Vancouver: City Planning Department.

–. 1990e. False Creek North Official Development Plan. Vancouver: City Planning Department.

–. 1990f. Granville Street Built-Form Study. Vancouver: City Planning Department.

–. 1990g. RS-1/RS-1S Further Amendments: Summary Report. Vancouver: City Planning Department.

–. 1990h. Station/La Farge CD-1 Bylaw and Form of Development: 101 Terminal Avenue. Vancouver: City Planning Department.

–. 1990i. Study Team Report on Heritage and Urban Design. Vancouver: City Planning Department.

–. 1990j. Trees on Single-family Lots: A Program for the Protection of Trees on Private Property. Vancouver: City Planning Department.

–. 1990k. Urban Design Group. Internal report. Vancouver: City Planning Department.
–. 1990l. Victory Square Policy. Vancouver: City Planning Department.
–. 1991a. Arbutus Neighbourhood Policy Plan. Vancouver: City Planning Department.
–. 1991b. Central Area Pedestrian Weather Protection (except Downtown South). Vancouver: City Planning Department.
–. 1991c. Central Area Plan: Goals and Land Use Policy. Vancouver: City Planning Department.
–. 1991d. Development Permit Process: Terms of Reference for a City and Development Industry Liaison Committee. Vancouver: City Planning Department.
–. 1991e. Downtown (except Downtown South) Design Guidelines. Vancouver: City Planning Department.
–. 1991f. Downtown South Streetscape Design Study. Prepared by Christopher Phillips and Associates Landscape Architects Inc. Vancouver: City Planning Department.
–. 1991g. Downtown South: A Community Plan. Report by departmental manager, 7 February. Vancouver: City Planning Department.
–. 1991h. Downtown South Workbook on New Zoning. Memorandum, 21 May. Vancouver: City Planning Department.
–. 1991i. Downtown South Zoning Bulletin. Vancouver: City Planning Department.
–. 1991j. Downtown Vancouver Pedestrian Survey. Vancouver: City Engineering Services.
–. 1991k. Granville Street (Downtown South Guidelines). Vancouver: City Planning Department.
–. 1991l. Housing Opportunities Strategy. Includes Committee Reports, 10 July 1990. Vancouver: City Planning Department.
–. 1991m. Shoreline Treatment Study. Vancouver: City Planning Department.
–. 1991n. Summary of the Report on the Findings of the Vancouver Planning Department Survey. Prepared by the Architectural Institute of British Columbia. October 1988. Vancouver: City Planning Department.
–. 1991o. Summary of the City of Vancouver Review of the Development Permit Process "The Chilton Report," February 1984. Vancouver: City Planning Department.
–. 1991p. View Protection Guidelines. Vancouver: City Planning Department.
–. 1992a. City of Vancouver Zoning Districts. Vancouver: City Planning Department.
–. 1992b. CityPlan Tool Kit. Vancouver: City Planning Department.
–. 1992c. Greenways: Public Ways. Report of the City of Vancouver Urban Landscape Task Force. Vancouver, BC.
–. 1992d. Heritage Policies and Guidelines. Vancouver: City Planning Department.
–. 1992e. High-Density Housing for Families with Children Guidelines. Vancouver: City Planning Department.
–. 1992f. Plaza Design Guidelines. Vancouver: City Planning Department.
–. 1992g. RT-2 Infill and Multiple-Dwelling Guidelines. Vancouver: City Planning Department.
–. 1992h. Triangle West: A Downtown Area. Characteristics and Planning Issues. Vancouver: City Planning Department.
–. 1992i. Triangle West Streetscape Study. Prepared by Matrix and Don Vaughan Ltd. Vancouver: City Planning Department.
–. 1993a. CD-1 (324) 800-1100 Pacific Blvd. Bylaw no. 7248. Vancouver: City Planning Department.
–. 1993b. Central Area Pedestrian Weather Protection (excluding Downtown South). Vancouver: City Planning Department.
–. 1993c. Central Broadway C-3A Urban Design Guidelines. Vancouver: City Planning Department.
–. 1993d. CityPlan: Ideas Illustrated. Vancouver: City Planning Department.
–. 1993e. CityPlan: Making Choices. Vancouver: City Planning Department.

–. 1993f. C-2 Residential Guidelines. Vancouver: City Planning Department.

–. 1993g. DD (except Downtown South) C-5, HA-1 and HA-2 Character Area Descriptions. Vancouver: City Planning Department.

–. 1993h. Library Precinct Design Guidelines Workbook. Vancouver: City Planning Department.

–. 1993i. Marina Neighbourhood (300 Cordova Street) CD-1 Guidelines for Marina Development Bylaw no. 7200. Vancouver: City Planning Department.

–. 1993j. Roundhouse Neighbourhood (1200-1300 Pacific Boulevard) CDI Bylaw. Vancouver: City Planning Department.

–. 1993k. Safer City Task Force: Final Report. Vancouver: City of Vancouver.

–. 1993l. Safer City Task Force: Final Report Recommendations: Summary. Vancouver: City Planning Department.

–. 1994a. Central Area Plan, Goals and Land Use Policy. Vancouver: City Planning Department.

–. 1994b. Central Waterfront Port Lands: Policy Statement. Vancouver: City Planning Department.

–. 1994c. Chinatown HA-1 Guidelines for Designated/Non-designated Sites. 2 vol. Vancouver: City Planning Department.

–. 1994d. CityPlan: Futures: City of Main Streets and Mixed-Residential Neighbourhoods. Vancouver: City Planning Department.

–. 1994e. CityPlan: Futures: City of Neighbourhood Centres. Vancouver: City Planning Department.

–. 1994f. CityPlan: Futures: The Central City. Vancouver: City Planning Department.

–. 1994g. CityPlan: Making Choices. Vancouver: City Planning Department.

–. 1994h. CityPlan: Making Choices Workbook. Vancouver: City Planning Department.

–. 1994i. Community Amenity Contributions. Vancouver: City Planning Department.

–. 1994j. Community Amenity Contributions: Information Bulletin #3. Vancouver: City Planning Department.

–. 1994k. Discretionary Zoning Backgrounder. Vancouver: City Planning Department.

–. 1994l. Discretionary Zoning in Low- and Medium-Density Districts. Vancouver: City Planning Department.

–. 1994m. Discretionary Zoning Review Update. Memorandum, 8 November. Vancouver: City Planning Department.

–. 1994n. Downtown South Streetscape Manual. Vancouver: City Planning Department.

–. 1994o. First Shaughnessy Design Guidelines. Vancouver: City Planning Department.

–. 1994p. Granville Slopes Policies. Vancouver: City Planning Department.

–. 1994q. Industrial Lands Strategy. Vancouver: City Planning Department.

–. 1994r. Interdepartmental Pre-application Meetings: Information Bulletin #2. Vancouver: City Planning Department.

–. 1994s. Kitsilano RT-7 and RT-8 Guidelines. Vancouver: City Planning Department.

–. 1994t. South Shaughnessy RS-5 Design Guidelines. Vancouver: City Planning Department.

–. 1994u. Tree Retention, Relocation, and Replacement Guidelines. Vancouver: City Planning Department.

–. 1994v. Triangle West Policies. Vancouver: City Planning Department.

–. 1994w. Triangle West Streetscape Concept Plan. Committee Report, 6 July. Vancouver: City Planning Department.

–. 1995a. CityPlan: Directions for Vancouver. Vancouver: City Planning Department.

–. 1995b. CityPlan Process. Vancouver: City Planning Department.

–. 1995c. Development Cost Levies: Information Bulletin #1. Vancouver: City Planning Department.

–. 1995d. False Creek South Shore: An Evaluation of the City's Social Objectives. Vancouver: City Planning Department.

–. 1995e. Heritage Policies and Guidelines. Vancouver: City Planning Department.

–. 1995f. Industrial Lands Policy. Vancouver: City Planning Department.

–. 1995g. New Trade and Convention Facilities Review Program: Preliminary Development Progress Description. Prepared by Zaha, Inc. Vancouver: City Planning Department.

–. 1995h. New Trade and Convention Facilities Review Program: Stage One: A Call for Developer Expressions of Interest. Vancouver: City Planning Department.

–. 1995i. New Trade and Convention Facilities Review Program: Stage One: Response to the Call for Developer Expressions of Interest. Vancouver: City Planning Department.

–. 1995j. Oakridge-Langara Policy Statement. Vancouver: City Planning Department.

–. 1995k. Residential Density and Built Form: Selected Case Studies. 2nd ed. Vancouver: City Planning Department.

–. 1995l. Vancouver Greenways Plan. Vancouver: City Planning Department.

–. 1996a. An Ecological Planning Framework for Sustainable Development. Prepared by Mark Holland. Vancouver: City Planning Department.

–. 1996b. Balcony Enclosure Guidelines. Vancouver: City Planning Department.

–. 1996c. Beach Neighbourhood East (500 Pacific Street) CD-1 Guidelines. Vancouver: City Planning Department.

–. 1996d. Burrard Landing (201 Burrard Street). Vancouver: City Planning Department.

–. 1996e. Central Bridgeheads Study. Terms of Reference. Vancouver: City Planning Department.

–. 1996f. Central Broadway C-3A Urban Design Guidelines. Vancouver: City Planning Department.

–. 1996g. CityPlan Community Visions: Terms of Reference. Vancouver: City Planning Department.

–. 1996h. CityPlan Community Vision: Terms of Reference [revised 1999]. Vancouver: City Planning Department.

–. 1996i. City Plan Rezoning Policy: Before and During Neighbourhood Visions. Vancouver: City Planning Department.

–. 1996j. C-2 Residential Guidelines. Vancouver: City Planning Department.

–. 1996k. DD (except Downtown South) C-5, C-6, HA-1 and HA-2 Character Area Descriptions. Vancouver: City Planning Department.

–. 1996l. Designing Safer Environments: Information Bulletin #4. Vancouver: City Planning Department.

–. 1996m. Development Permits for Major Applications. Vancouver: City Planning Department.

–. 1996n. Downtown Official Development Plan. Vancouver: City Planning Department.

–. 1996o. East False Creek FC-1 Guidelines. Vancouver: City Planning Department.

–. 1996p. False Creek Flats Preliminary Concept Plan. Vancouver: City Planning Department.

–. 1996q. First Shaughnessy Advisory Design Panel. Vancouver: City Planning Department.

–. 1996r. Harbour Green Neighbourhood (501 Bute Street) CD-1 Guidelines. Vancouver: City Planning Department.

–. 1996s. Key City Policies: Summary of Key City of Vancouver Policies. Vancouver: City Planning Department.

–. 1996t. Public Involvement Guide. Memorandum, June. Vancouver: City Planning Department.

–. 1996u. Quayside Neighbourhood CD-1 Guidelines. Vancouver: City Planning Department.

–. 1996v. RS-5 Design Workbook. Vancouver: City Planning Department.

—. 1996w. RS-6 Design Guidelines. With explanatory notes. 2 vols. Vancouver: City Planning Department.

—. 1996x. The Development Permit Process. Vancouver: City Planning Department.

—. 1996y. Urban Design Panel. Vancouver: City Planning Department.

—. 1996z. Zoning and Development Permits in Vancouver. Vancouver: City Planning Department.

—. 1997a. Bridgehead Guidelines. Vancouver: City Planning Department.

—. 1997b. Building in the Audience: A Design Handbook for Building Frontages on Granville Street. Prepared by Hotson Bakker Architects. Vancouver: City Planning Department.

—. 1997c. CD-1 Text Amendment of 12 November: 4255 Arbutus Street. Policy Report, Development and Building. Vancouver: City Planning Department.

—. 1997d. City of Vancouver Transportation Plan. Vancouver, BC.

—. 1997e. City of Vancouver Zoning Districts. With maps. Vancouver: City Planning Department.

—. 1997f. Downtown South Guidelines (excluding Granville Street). Vancouver: City Planning Department.

—. 1997g. Downtown Vancouver Skyline Study: Wall Centre Phase II. Committee Report, 6 February. Vancouver: City Planning Department.

—. 1997h. Dunbar Community Visions Program: Community Workshop Results. Vancouver: City Planning Department.

—. 1997i. Granville Street Business Revitalization Strategy. Prepared by Urbanics Consultants. Vancouver: City Planning Department.

—. 1997j. Heritage Fact Sheets. 9 papers. Vancouver: City Planning Department.

—. 1997k. How to … Zoning and Development Permits in Vancouver. no. 1-5. Vancouver: City Planning Department.

—. 1997l. Private Property Tree Bylaw no. 7347. Vancouver: City Planning Department.

—. 1997m. Residential Density and Built Form: Selected Case Studies. 3rd ed. Vancouver: City Planning Department.

—. 1997n. RS-5 and RS-5S Districts Schedule. Vancouver: City Planning Department.

—. 1997o. RS-5/RS-5S Design Guidelines. Vancouver: City Planning Department.

—. 1997p. RS-6 District Schedule. Vancouver: City Planning Department.

—. 1997q. RS-6 Explanatory Notes. Vancouver: City Planning Department.

—. 1997r. RT-4, RT-4A, RT-4N, RT-4AN, RT-5, RT-5A, RT-5N, RT-5AN, and RT-6 Design Guidelines. Vancouver: City Planning Department.

—. 1997s. Single-family Residential (RS) Zoning Information. Vancouver: City Planning Department.

—. 1997t. Summary of Municipal Planning Controls for Typical Single-family Residential Areas. Vancouver: City Planning Department.

—. 1997u. Vancouver, Canada: Summary of Municipal Planning Controls for Typical Single-family Residential Areas. Vancouver: City Planning Department.

—. 1997v. Vancouver Trends. Vancouver: City Planning Department.

—. 1997-. Minutes of Development Permit Board and Advisory Panel and of Urban Design Panel (available online at <www.city.vancouver.bc.ca/planning>). Vancouver: City Planning Department.

—. 1998a. Affordable Housing Policies. Vancouver: City Planning Department.

—. 1998b. An Introduction to the City of Vancouver Private Property Tree Bylaw no. 7347. Vancouver: City Planning Department.

—. 1998c. A Program of Strategic Actions for the Downtown Eastside. Vancouver: City Planning Department.

—. 1998d. Arbutus Neighbourhood C-7 and C-8 Guidelines. Vancouver: City Planning Department.

—. 1998e. Arbutus Neighbourhood Policy Plan. Vancouver: City Planning Department.

–. 1998f. A Review of Financing the Costs of Growth. Policy Report, Urban Structure, 2 December. Vancouver: City Planning Department.

–. 1998g. A to Z: Answers to Some of the Most Frequently Asked Questions About our City (Brochure). Vancouver: City Planning Department.

–. 1998h. Background Paper on Drug Treatment Needs in Vancouver. Vancouver, BC: City of Vancouver.

–. 1998i. Business Improvement Area: Davie Village, South Granville, Yaletown. Committee Report, 18 December. Vancouver: City Planning Department.

–. 1998j. Central Business District Policies. Vancouver: City Planning Department.

–. 1998k. Charrette Synopsis: Southeast False Creek, Vancouver BC. Prepared by Fiona Crofton and Orcad Consulting Group. Vancouver: City Planning Department.

–. 1998l. City of Vancouver Proposal: Financing Growth. Report prepared by city manager's office. Vancouver, BC.

–. 1998m. Community Visions: Dunbar: Choices Survey. Vancouver: City Planning Department.

–. 1998n. Development 1995-2004 [for Granville Island]. Vancouver: City Planning Department.

–. 1998o. Development and Building Regulation Review Pilot Project. Leaflet. Vancouver: City Planning Department.

–. 1998p. Development and Building Regulation Review: Pilot Progress Status Report. Administrative report, 30 July. Vancouver: City Planning Department.

–. 1998q. Development Cost Levies. Vancouver: City Planning Department.

–. 1998r. Downtown Eastside: Building a Common Future. Vancouver: City Planning Department.

–. 1998s. Downtown South Development Cost Levy Bylaw. Administrative report, 23 February.

–. 1998t. Dunbar Community Vision: Vision Directions and Survey Results. Vancouver: City Planning Department.

–. 1998u. Financing Growth: Background Information. Vancouver: City Planning Department.

–. 1998v. Financing Growth in City of Vancouver. Discussion Paper. Prepared by city manager for meeting, 25 March. Vancouver, BC.

–. 1998w. Granville Street (Downtown South) Guidelines. Vancouver: City Planning Department.

–. 1998x. High-Tech Industry in the Urban Context: A Discussion Paper. Vancouver: City Planning Department.

–. 1998y. Housing Plan for the Downtown Eastside, Chinatown, Gastown, Strathcona. Vancouver: Housing Department.

–. 1998z. Kensington–Cedar Cottage Community Vision: Vision Directions and Survey Results. Vancouver: City Planning Department.

–. 1998aa. New Trade and Convention Facilities Review Program: Stage Two Evaluation "Site and Community Context": Summary. Vancouver: City Planning Department.

–. 1998bb. RS Rethink Issues Paper. Vancouver: City Planning Department.

–. 1998cc. RS-1 and RS-1S Districts Schedule. Vancouver: City Planning Department.

–. 1998dd. RT-4 etc., RT-5 etc., and RT-6 Guidelines. Vancouver: City Planning Department.

–. 1998ee. Single-family Areas: Why RS Rethink. Vancouver: City Planning Department.

–. 1998ff. Single-family Areas: Why RS Rethink. Presentation slides. Vancouver: City Planning Department.

–. 1998gg. Southeast False Creek Charrette: Design Brief. Vancouver: City Planning Department.

—. 1998hh. The Development Permit Board and Advisory Panel Information Pamphlet. Vancouver: City Planning Department.

—. 1998ii. Urban Sustainable Development: Southeast False Creek. Prepared by The Sheltair Group. Summary prepared by Mark Holland. Vancouver: City Planning Department.

—. 1998jj. Vancouver Downtown Streetcar Study. Prepared by Baker McGarva Hart. Vancouver: City Planning Department.

—. 1998kk. Vancouver Heritage Register. Vancouver: City Planning Department.

—. 1998ll. Victory Square Area Concept Plan. Vancouver: City Planning Department.

—. 1998mm. Visions, Tools, and Targets: Environmentally Sustainable Development Guidelines for Southeast False Creek, Vancouver. Prepared by The Sheltair Group. Vancouver: City Planning Department.

—. 1998nn. West Georgia Street Tree and Sidewalk Design Guidelines. Vancouver: City Planning Department.

—. 1998oo. Work/Live in Vancouver. Prepared by Leshgold, Dolan, Ivison (architects). Vancouver: City Planning Department.

—. 1998pp. 1996 Census: Housing Data. Vancouver: City Housing Centre.

—. 1999a. Broadway/Commercial Station Precinct Design Charrette. Vancouver: City Rapid Transit Office.

—. 1999b. Central Area Pedestrian Weather Protection (except Downtown South). Vancouver: City Planning Department.

—. 1999c. CityPlan: Dunbar Community Vision. Vancouver: City Planning Department.

—. 1999d. City Plan: Kensington–Cedar Cottage Community Vision. Vancouver: City Planning Department.

—. 1999e. Designing Safer Urban Environments. Vancouver: City Planning Department.

—. 1999f. Downtown Eastside Community Monitoring Report. Vancouver: City Planning Department.

—. 1999g. Dunbar and Kensington–Cedar Cottage Vision Programs: Public Involvement Evaluation. Prepared by Context Research and Communications. Vancouver: City Planning Department.

—. 1999h. False Creek Flats Preliminary Concept Plan. Vancouver: City Planning Department.

—. 1999i. Financing Growth Review: Terms of Reference. Policy Report, Urban Structure, 9 February. Vancouver: City Planning Department.

—. 1999j. Granville Island: False Creek Area 9. Reference document. Vancouver: City Planning Department.

—. 1999k. Interim City-Wide Development-Cost Levy Bylaw and Interim City-Wide Community-Amenity Contributions Policy. Vancouver: City Planning Department.

—. 1999l. Monitoring RS-5/5S and RS-6 in Areas Rezoned as Part of the RS-Interim Zoning Program. Administrative report, 19 August. Vancouver: City Planning Department.

—. 1999m. Planning for a Downtown in Transition. Leaflet. Vancouver: City Planning Department.

—. 1999n. RS Rethink Program Proposal. Report to City Council, 10 June. Vancouver: City Planning Department.

—. 1999o. Social Indicators: City of Vancouver: 1996 Census. Vancouver: City Community Services.

—. 1999p. Southeast False Creek: Policy Statement. Vancouver: City Planning Department.

—. 1999q. Support for Social Housing. Vancouver, BC: City Housing Centre (available online at <www.city.vancouver.bc.ca/commsves/housing>).

—. 1999r. The Future of Rapid Transit on Broadway. Vancouver: City Planning Department.

–. 1999s. Transfer of Density Policy and Procedure. Vancouver: City Planning Department.

–. 1999t. Urban Structure: Implementation of Kensington–Cedar Cottage and Dunbar Visions. Policy report, 8 July. Vancouver: City Planning Department.

–. 1999u. Urban Structure: RS Rethink Program Proposal. Policy Report. Vancouver: City Planning Department.

–. 1999v. Vancouver's Urban Design: A Decade of Achievement. Vancouver: City Planning Department.

–. 1999w. Vancouver Trends. Vancouver: City Planning Department.

–. 1999x. Traffic Calming Tool Kit. Vancouver: City Planning Department.

–. 1999y. 1400 West Hastings and Pender Street Guidelines. Vancouver: City Planning Department.

–. 1999z. 1998 Survey of Low-Income Housing in the Downtown Core. Vancouver (online at <www.city.vancouver.bc.ca>).

–. 1999aa. Major Project Public Amenity Requirements: Information Sheet. Vancouver: City Planning Department.

–. 2000a. A Framework for Action: A Four-Pillar Approach to Drug Problems in Vancouver. Vancouver: City Drug Policy Coordinator.

–. 2000b. Commercial Station CD-1 Guidelines. Vancouver: City Planning Department.

–. 2000c. Development Cost Levies. Vancouver: City Planning Department.

–. 2000d. Downtown Eastside Community Revitalization Program. Interim report by city manager. Vancouver: City of Vancouver.

–. 2000e. Downtown Transportation Plan. Vancouver: City Engineering Services (available online at <www.city.vancouver.bc.ca/dtp>).

–. 2000f. Draft RS-7S Zoning. Interim document. Vancouver: City Planning Department.

–. 2000g. Dunbar Neighbourhood Committee Minutes. Vancouver: City Planning Department.

–. 2000h. Impermeable Materials Site Coverage in RS Zones. Vancouver: City Planning Department.

–. 2000i. New Permit Process. Memorandum to permitting staff, 7 February. Vancouver: City Planning Department.

–. 2000j. Non-Market Housing. Vancouver: Housing Centre (available online at <www.city.vancouver.bc.ca/housing>).

–. 2000k. Rezoning: Community Amenity Contributions. Vancouver: City Planning Department.

–. 2000l. The Gastown Land Use Plan. Vancouver: City Planning Department.

–. 2000l. RS-1A and RS-2 Zoning Review. Vancouver: City Planning Department.

–. 2000m. Urban Structure: Granville Island Reference Document. Policy report, 19 June. Vancouver: City Planning Department.

–. 2001a. Broadway/Commercial C-2C Guidelines. Vancouver: City Planning Department.

–. 2001b. Broadway/Commercial C-3A Guidelines. Vancouver: City Planning Department.

–. 2001c. Business Improvement Area Program. Vancouver: City Planning Department.

–. 2001d. CityPlan: Community Visions: Choices Survey: Sunset. Vancouver: City Planning Department.

–. 2001e. CityPlan: Community Visions: Choices Survey: Fraserview/Killarney. Vancouver: City Planning Department.

–. 2001f. Development and Building Review: Implementation Progress and Next Steps. Draft report to Council. Vancouver: City Planning Department.

–. 2001g. Development Services Permit Processing: Resource Requirements. Draft report to Council. Vancouver: City Planning Department.

—. 2001h. Downtown South: Update on Development-Cost Levy Revenue. Policy report, Development and Building, 19 July. Vancouver: City Planning Department.

—. 2001i. False Creek South Shore: Evaluation of Social Mix Objectives. Vancouver: City Housing Centre.

—. 2001j. Financing Growth Review. Vancouver: City Planning Department.

—. 2001k. Gastown Heritage Management Plan Interim Report: Possible Directions. Vancouver: City Planning Department.

—. 2001l. Gastown Heritage Management Plan. Vancouver: City Planning Department.

—. 2001m. Granville Island False Creek Area 9. Reference Document. Vancouver: City Planning Department.

—. 2001n. North East False Creek Urban Design Plan. Vancouver: City Planning Department.

—. 2001o. Public Realm and Streetscape Element of Broadway/Commercial Station. Administrative report, 23 March. Vancouver: City Planning Department.

—. 2001p. RS-7S Guidelines. With explanatory notes. Vancouver: City Planning Department.

—. 2001q. Street Furniture and Amenities in Vancouver. Vancouver: City Engineering Services (available online at <www.city.vancouver.bc.ca/engsvcs/streets>).

—. 2001r. Sunset Community Visions: Choices Survey. Vancouver: City Planning Department.

—. 2001s. Victoria–Fraserview/Killarney Community Visions: Choices Survey. Vancouver: City Planning Department.

Figure Credits

The author is grateful to the following for providing permission to reproduce drawings and photographs.

City of Vancouver Community Services (Current Planning):
Figures 5, 6, 7, 8, 10, 12, 13, 14, 16, 17, 18, 19, 21, 22, 24, 25, 26, 27, 28, 29, 30, 31, 32, 33, 35, 36, 37, 38, 40, 43, 45, 46, 47, 48, 53, 54, 58, 59, 60, 61, 66, 67, 69
Plates 30, 61

Canada Mortgage and Housing Corporation:
Figure 9

Canadian Architect/Richard Henriquez, Joel Schack (photographer):
Figure 15

Barbara Pettit:
Figure 20

Wendy Grandin Ltd:
Figure 23

Vancouver League for Studies in Architecture:
Figure 24

James K.M. Cheng Architects:
Figures 39, 41

The Hulbert Group International, Inc:
Figure 40, Plate 35

Marathon Development, Inc:
Figure 42, Plate 44

Hancock Bruckner Eng & Wright:
Figure 44

Buttjes Architects, Inc:
Figure 49

Downs/Archambault & Partners:
Figure 55

Paul Merrick Architects Ltd:
Figure 57

City of Vancouver Housing Department:
Figure 56

Index

Printed and bound in Canada by Friesens

Set in Myriad and Garamond by Artegraphica Design Co. Ltd.

Copy editor: Susan Quirk

Proofreader: Deborah Kerr